of Medicine?

Charles Medawar

The Wrong Kind of Medicine?

PUBLISHED BY
CONSUMERS' ASSOCIATION AND
HODDER & STOUGHTON

First published in Great Britain by Consumers' Association
14 Buckingham Street, London WC2N 6DS and
Hodder & Stoughton Ltd
47 Bedford Square, London WC1B 3DP

Designed by Trevor Vincent
Cover designed by Andrew Kay
Cover photograph by Chris Webb

Typeset by Rowland Phototypesetting Ltd,
Bury St Edmunds, Suffolk

Printed and bound in Great Britain by
Redwood Burn Ltd, Trowbridge, Wiltshire

ISBN 0 340 35247 7

Contents

SOCIAL AUDIT

Issues

Social Audit's job is to ask timely questions about the organisations whose decisions and actions shape our lives. What, in social terms, do these organisations give to and take from the community; and how do they account for – that is, explain and justify – what they do? Social Audit publishes reports which explain why these questions seem worth asking, and what the answers seem to be.

Social Audit's concern applies to all organisations and to any government, whatever its politics. Its reports have discussed issues which range from health and safety at work to accountability in the London Electricity Board; from Parliamentary Questions to the promotion of British food and drug products in the third world; from social policy in a major rubber company to official secrecy; and from industrial pollution control to the standards of care in NHS mental hospitals.

The issues differ, but the conclusions are always the same: there is not enough accountability in the major centres of power. There is too much secrecy in government, and in the other organisations that direct and manage our lives. These organisations go to great lengths to persuade us that they are good and do good – but they also suppress evidence of the harm they do. The result is abuse of power. Unless and until there is proper accountability, these organisations will operate by their standards – which may be completely unacceptable by yours.

Operation

Social Audit is a small, independent non-profit-making body which operates in its own name – as well as through campaigning organisations such as Health Action International and the 1984 Campaign for Freedom of Information. Social Audit also acts as the publishing arm of Public Interest Research Centre Ltd., a registered charity which carries out research into the use and abuse of corporate power.

Public Interest Research Centre Ltd and Social Audit Ltd are run by Christopher Zealley (Chairman), Andrew Phillips, Anthony Sampson, Oliver Thorold (Directors), and by Charles Medawar (executive).

For further information and/or for details of publications,
please send an s.a.e. to Social Audit Ltd., PO Box 111, London NW1 8XG.

ACKNOWLEDGEMENTS

Social Audit and Public Interest Research Centre were set up in 1972, with grants from the *Joseph Rowntree Social Service and Charitable Trusts*. Their work has since been supported by *Consumers' Association*, the *Social Science Research Council*, the *Ford Foundation*, the *Allen Lane Foundation* and other individuals and organisations. *Trócaire*, the Catholic Agency for World Development, *War on Want* and the *International Organisation of Consumers' Unions* have specifically supported our research into drug policy in developing countries. This book evolved from that research.

It would not have been done without this generous assistance – and could not have been done without much help and encouragement from colleagues, family and friends. Special thanks are due to Dr Andrew Herxheimer, who gave unstinting help and advice throughout the project; to Rebecca Garland, who helped with some of the research; and to Sarah Wright, for her skills and forbearance as editor.

I would like to thank everyone who helped make this project possible. My parents, my family – and especially Caroline – made it seem worthwhile.

Charles Medawar
March 1984

Comments from readers are welcome and should be addressed to the author at Social Audit at the address given opposite.

Foreword

There is always some price to pay for taking a medicine. The price ranges from mere inconvenience and expense to the risk of an unpleasant or even dangerous effect. Despite this, large numbers of medicines are prescribed that ought not to be, a situation of which many doctors have been aware for a long time. But it is not only doctors who need to appreciate the problems: the people who take the medicines also need to know something about the issues. To be able to use appropriate medicines effectively and safely, the patient needs to have enough background information to be able to talk about his or her treatment with the doctor. Then, between them, they can decide whether the likely benefits are worth the potential costs.

This book is about products that often give poor value and briefly explains their individual disadvantages. It compares each product with better alternatives, or with taking no medicine at all. No other book does this, probably because it is an unpalatable thing to do, likely to annoy prescribers, pharmacists and manufacturers. Many doctors still feel uncomfortable about discussing the merits of medicines with patients, believing in their own clinical freedom to prescribe whatever they think appropriate without discussion or interference. Consequently, they do not readily criticise their colleagues' prescriptions, even if they disagree with them. Pharmacists are even more reluctant to comment on the value of a medicine because they do not know what the doctor intends and has said to the patient, and fear that an unwitting contradiction could confuse the patient and undermine his or her relationship with the doctor. Pharmaceutical companies who, not surprisingly, want to continue to sell their products for as long as possible, tend to argue that, if doctors prescribe them, they must be good.

Why doesn't the government do something about this? Basically, because the pharmaceutical industry would not like it and has convinced the government that it is right. The industry is a major export earner, a strong supporter of free enterprise, and very well organised and vocal. Whenever its immediate or long-term interests are threatened by new proposals, it creates a major fuss; as a result, the government is cautious and even timid. What is needed is an equally well organised and vocal expression of the public's point of view; but currently the number and political influence of those sufficiently well informed to put this view are not enough to spur the government on to effective action.

This book is a major step forward because it helps to create an informed public better able to take part in this vital debate. It very clearly describes the complicated problems we face relating to the production, supply and use of medicines, and shows how each one of us, as a user of medicines, can contribute to finding solutions.

Don't misunderstand this book. It is not about good or bad doctors, just about the undesirable medicines that some doctors prescribe. It is not about saintly or wicked pharmaceutical companies, just about some of their less valuable products. Read it, and you will be able to contribute more not only to your own health but to that of the nation as a whole.

Andrew Herxheimer

Dr Herxheimer is senior lecturer in clinical pharmacology at Charing Cross Medical School; founder–editor of *Drug and Therapeutics Bulletin* (published by Consumers' Association); a member of the World Health Organisation's Expert Panel on the Selection of Essential Drugs; and also Chairman of the Health Working Group of the International Organisation of Consumers' Unions.

Introduction

You can use this book in several different ways.

One way is simply to check any medicine you are prescribed against the list of medicines starting on p. 107. The drug profiles at the end of this book could tell you:

- whether or not you have been prescribed a medicine that experts think is less effective or less safe than you would feel entitled to expect
- whether or not you might usefully have been told more about a prescribed medicine than you were in fact told
- whether or not your doctor prescribes medicines scientifically and economically, and whether or not this is what you want.

This book can also tell you something about the ingredients found in many widely used medicines. You can find these by turning to the index (p. 101) which lists different medicines by 'therapeutic category' – that is, according to the part of the body they work on and what they are meant to do. This index will direct you to the main entries in the drug list: these discuss whole classes of drugs – for example, 'antihistamines', 'vitamins' or 'iron supplements'. The entries outline what these different kinds of medicines are meant to do, and also briefly explain when and why they are likely to work or fail.

Chapter One takes the discussion further. It explains how the usefulness of any medicine depends on the ways it is made and used, and why even 'good' medicines often do not help people to get better or to stay well. The reasons why hundreds of drugs do not work well are not unlike the reasons why other consumer products fail. The reasons include use of poor materials (drug ingredients) and bad design (the formulation or mix of ingredients), and also the failure to provide or act on realistic instructions for use.

Chapter One explains that many drugs have been listed because their active ingredients have not been proved effective, or because there is too much or (more likely) too little of the ingredients to do what is required. Other medicines have an irrational mix of ingredients, or are formulated to go into the body by one route (eg by mouth) when they would be more effective going in by another (eg by injection). There are also many examples (such as antihistamines for asthma) in which medicines are recommended for conditions which they do not help.

Therapeutic value for money

Chapter One also discusses the cost of drugs and the question of 'therapeutic value for money'. It emphasises not that a drug has to be cheap to be good, but that if a cheaper drug is as effective as a more expensive one, the cheaper one is the one to use. It explains how the National Health Service (NHS) gets poor 'therapeutic value for money' in three main ways:

- The NHS spends tens of millions of pounds a year buying expensive brands of medicines instead of buying unbranded versions of the identical medicine, which are just as good.
- At least as much is spent on 'me-too' medicines. These are new drugs which more or less imitate the older and well-established ones. They have no great advantages and cost a lot more.
- The NHS also spends a great deal on prescriptions for unnecessary and ineffective medicines. The profiles in the list at the end of the book show that in some cases several million pounds could be saved by not buying that one brand or that kind of drug.

This is worrying for two reasons. First, the extra spending does not benefit the patients who are prescribed these drugs, but does hurt other people by wasting resources that could be used to help them. Secondly, such waste suggests indiscriminate and poor prescribing. If doctors prescribe ineffective drugs, or the latest 'me-toos', or the most expensive branded medicines, it is probably in response to commercial pressures, as well to patients' needs/demands.

Inevitably, both Chapter One and the drug list contain much detailed information. But you do not have to read them exhaustively to get to the nub of the thing. The underlying point is that the way in which medicines are prescribed and used is profoundly affected by lack of information and understanding.

The part the industry plays

Chapter Two is about the pharmaceutical industry. It discusses why the drug companies need to make products like the ones listed in this book, and how the companies justify doing so. Publicly, the drug industry says that all its products 'meet standards of quality, efficacy and safety that are acceptable in the state of present knowledge and experience' [ABPI, 1983]. The industry also undertakes only to make products 'which have full regard to the needs of public health' [IFPMA, 1981].

These high standards are defined in the drug industry's national (UK) and international Codes of Marketing Practice. The industry claims to observe these standards because its products fully meet the requirements of law: the products likewise are approved by doctors who would otherwise not prescribe them in the best interests of their patients.

The industry also claims that its products are worth what is paid for them. The companies say, with obvious justification, that many people benefit from the medicines they make, and that the whole country benefits because the industry's financial performance is extremely good. The companies deny making excessive profits. They point out that the government regulates drug prices, and they also emphasise that their profitability allows and encourages them to develop new medicines which we need.

Views of government and doctors

The medical profession and the government see things in much the same light. They both know that the industry exaggerates the value of its products and charges a lot for them, but they more or less accept this as they also appreciate and depend on what the drug companies provide. In any case, neither the doctors nor the government would want to advertise the waste or misuse of medicines, because it would seriously threaten their own integrity to do so.

The government would find it hard to admit that medicines are irresponsibly used because it would then be held responsible for doing something about it. But there is not a lot that government either could or would want to do about it. It would involve the loss of important income (as in the case of tobacco and alcohol

WHAT EACH OF THE THREE MAIN ACTORS CAN GIVE TO (OR TAKE FROM) THE OTHER TWO:

	Industry *can give*	**Government** *can give*	**Doctors** *can give*
Industry *needs*		*Favourable treatment and concessions; minimum control of products and interference in the business; and public expressions of confidence and support etc*	*Endorsement and use of the companies' products. Resistance to government control and restrictions on availability or use of drugs*
Government *needs*	*Adequate supplies of reasonable quality drugs; possible development of better ones. Contributions to taxes and export earnings*		*Administration of the* NHS *and regulation of use of prescription only drugs. Support in the operation of numerous health and welfare and research programmes*
Doctors *need*	*Provision of medicines and supply of new drugs which hold out hope of better treatment. Moral and material support for individual doctors and the profession. Information about drugs and how to use them*	*'Clinical freedom' – the right to choose what treatment to give individual patients – and to be judged only by professional standards in doing so. Better working conditions and contracts of work*	

revenues), and could also lead to confrontation with both the medical profession and the industry, which no government would be likely to win. See Chapter Three.

There are also limits to what the medical profession could or would want to do about extravagant or poor prescribing. It would be likely to affront some doctors and would also involve confrontation with the drug industry, whose support and services the doctors need. The drug industry, for example, provides most of the information doctors get about drugs. The industry spends some £4,000–£5,000 a year on telling a single GP about its products. There are other, independent sources of information about drugs, but far less than this is spent on promoting them. See Chapter Four.

The government, the doctors and the drug industry are in other words interdependent. Each party needs and benefits from the cooperation of the other two – and each could be sunk without it. The chart on p. 13 outlines how and why the three main actors depend on each other, and what for.

Position of consumers

The book ends by discussing the position of consumers. Chapter Five suggests that because most people have been taught virtually nothing about the medicines they use, they know very little, and therefore do not seem worth teaching. Poorly informed medicine users encourage uncritical and excessive drug use.

This Chapter argues that consumers must now define what kind of medicines they want:

> 'The present UK medicines policy is pursued in the name of consumers and at their expense, but it also reflects the view that people cannot control their own health; and may not question how it is controlled on their behalf . . . The idea that people cannot take better care of themselves and each other is destroying their confidence in their health, and is also patently untrue . . .'

What could be done?

The book is trying to answer a single question: what would happen if you tried to get a law passed which said that prescription medicines would not be allowed unless they were needed and worth having? Such a Medicines Act might say the following:

> No medicinal product shall be licensed for use in the absence of convincing evidence that it
>
> - offers significant therapeutic benefits
> - meets real medical needs

- has a satisfactory risk/benefit ratio
- provides acceptable therapeutic value for money;

all having regard to other drugs or treatments which may be used for the same condition.

If Britain had such a law – as most of the Nordic countries do – we would have perhaps one-third the number of drugs we have now. In the UK, there are an estimated 6,500 preparations available for prescribing, compared with about 1,900 preparations in Norway and about 2,500 in Sweden. Even so, the Norwegian authorities have licensed a total of 730 active ingredients, about three times as many as the World Health Organisation identifies as 'essential drugs'. In Britain, we have far more drugs than we need, and too many to use effectively.

The benefits of our huge drug list are essentially to do with trade, not health. The advantages of a restricted drug list include having fewer bad drugs and a reduction in drug-induced disease; and better information about drug use and less confusion about which drugs to use.

That is what would happen in theory. In practice, if you tried to get a law like that through, you would run into opposition from all sides:

- The industry would oppose such a measure not only because it would badly hurt its business in the UK, but because it would set an example which other countries might follow.

- The medical profession would oppose such a law because it would drastically curtail prescribers' 'clinical freedom'. This has traditionally allowed doctors the right to prescribe what they choose, without having to account for their prescribing decisions, unless they are clearly responsible for harming the patient.

Because it needs the cooperation of doctors and drug producers, the government would be very reluctant to promote new medicines laws. If it did, it would lose significant benefits. It would also be exposed to actions and pressures which could easily cause it to fail or fall. In an extreme (but not unrealistic) case, the kinds of pressure that could be applied include:

- Economic sanctions and threats of retaliation applied by governments of the major drug-producing countries (notably the US), and threats from business interests to reduce their investment in Britain.

- The threat of withdrawal of supplies and services throughout the NHS. If the companies refused to supply medicine and/or if doctors refused to use them, the government would be faced by strong public pressure to act.

- Government would also have to contend with a good deal of hostile and irrational propaganda. The government would be accused of wrecking the health services; crippling the goose which laid the golden egg and putting people in the industry out of work; depriving people of treatment they needed and drastically restricting their rights to health; and otherwise ruining the country by trying to run it on lines that might have been dictated in Moscow.

No government could expect to introduce a rational and economic drug policy without considerable public support.

I The wrong kind of medicine?

Not many people realise that medicines often do not work. There are many reasons for this, the most important being that drugs sometimes work very well. This is what happens for example when someone with a vitamin B deficiency disease (beriberi) is treated with vitamin B1 (thiamine). When the body gets exactly the drugs it needs, medicine can be superb:

> 'The disease causes the whole body to swell from an accumulation of excess water (oedema) and produces disturbances in the circulatory system which may lead to sudden death from heart failure . . . A patient with wet beriberi who is lying in bed breathless, waterlogged and apparently dying may recover in one or two hours after being given an injection of thiamine – perhaps the most dramatic cure in medicine.'
> [FAO, 1974, p.36]

No one expects all medicines to work as well as this, but nor would anyone expect to be treated with drugs that were ineffective or unsafe. Most people expect medicines to work well, if only because they ought to work well. One might reasonably assume that pharmaceutical companies compete by making good products; that the government would not allow bad drugs; and that no doctor would prescribe bad drugs.

People also expect medicines to work because they seem to work even when they do not. For example, people who take drugs for self-limiting conditions, like coughs or colds or 'travellers' diarrhoea', usually get better in spite of drug treatment rather than because of it, but are still likely to feel that medicine helped.

Medicine partly works just by concentrating the mind on cure. The drug ingredients may be inactive or of no value, but a medicine can still seem to work just because it is expected to. The power of suggestion is fundamental to all systems of medicine. It can be very strong indeed:

> 'As a young houseman in Singapore, I once treated a patient who said he was possessed with devils. I told him I could cure him with a course of injections. I said I couldn't be sure how long the treatment would last, but that he would know when the devils left his body, because he would feel them drying up his mouth and throat . . . I treated him over the next few weeks, first with injections of sterile water – and finally with a shot of atropine.* The patient

* Atropine and other derivatives of belladonna (deadly nightshade) dry up secretions in the throat and mouth. Atropine has therapeutic uses, but was used here as a dummy drug (placebo).

> *did* recover – but I've always had misgivings about deluding him that it was the medicine that cured him.'
> [Dr W: personal communication 26/7/80]

People are expected to expect medicines to work, as part of their commitment to getting well, and they naturally assume that it is the effect of chemicals on their body that helps. At the same time, people underestimate the shortcomings of medicine and are discouraged from thinking about the possible risks. Doctors tend not to discuss such things with their patients, because it would seem like inviting failure if they did so.

Potential v. actual value

No one knows how often drugs work or fail but many, possibly most, drug treatments do not benefit patients at all. Because effective drug use depends not only on what is prescribed, but on how and when drugs are used and for what and for whom, there would be no point in recommending prescription drug 'best buys' here.

It would, for example, be meaningless to describe thiamine as a good medicine because it often is not. Thiamine has great potential value: it is very effective in treating vitamin B deficiency and is also unusually safe. But its actual value depends on how it is taken and what it is used for. Most of the time it is used, thiamine probably has no effect at all. It is mainly used to treat not clear deficiency states like beriberi, but vague and commonplace symptoms such as irritability, depression or fatigue. These could be caused by a mild deficiency of vitamin B, and would be cured by thiamine if they were. But in practice these symptoms are caused by countless other things which do not respond to thiamine at all: 'there is no evidence that thiamine is of value for anything other than deficiency' [AMADE, 1980, p.832].

Nevertheless, the rationale for the use of thiamine is easily glossed over, and the myth marches on. The author of *The Vitamin Bible*, for example, recommends thiamine 'as the "morale vitamin" because of its beneficial effects on the nervous system and mental attitude' [Mindell, 1979, p.48].

Effective drug use depends on accurate diagnosis; on careful choice of treatment; on sensitive adjustment of dosage to suit individual users; and on many other criteria beyond the control of consumers. But it also depends on factors which consumers *can* control, and which they should therefore understand. Drug effectiveness does not only depend on who you are and what is wrong with you. It also depends, for example, on when a drug is taken; whether it is taken on a full or an empty stomach, or with food or alcohol or with other medicines; and on whether and even what the patient smokes [Long J. W., 1982].

The full potential of a medicine – its performance under ideal conditions of use – is often not realised. All kinds of things can and do go wrong: at one extreme there is a problem with tablets or capsules that stick in the gullet [DTB 1981, 19, 33]. At the other, it is known that 'a substantial number of patients' insert suppositories without first removing the wrapper [Open University, 1983, p.7].

Medicine's failures tend to be blamed on abnormal patient reactions of one kind or another, but this book argues that they are the products of a system in which commercial, professional and government interests dominate health care to an extent which is damaging to both individual and national health.

The wrong kind of medicine

The drug list gives several hundred examples of drugs that are identified in doctors' prescribing guides in terms such as 'obsolete', 'less suitable and safe' or 'of no value whatever'. Such drugs are nevertheless prescribed under the NHS millions of times each year.

The list also identifies brands or variants of drugs that are overvalued and/or overpriced. The NHS wastes its limited resources if it buys these drugs instead of buying generic alternatives which do the same thing at a much lower cost. The suggestion is made that little effort would be needed to save at least £100 million a year on the national drugs bill (approaching £2,000,000,000 in 1984); and that with real commitment, the NHS could save several times that amount. Savings would mean that health care could be improved in other ways.

For one reason or another, the drugs in the second part of the book may all give poor therapeutic value for money, although some are cheaper than the better alternative(s). The other reasons why drugs have been listed are briefly explained in the individual drug profiles, but they can be summarised as follows:

- A drug treatment may be unnecessary or unhelpful, even if the ingredients have the action that is claimed for them.
- One or more of the drug ingredients has no proven value.
- A drug, or one of its ingredients, may present an unacceptable risk at least to some users.
- The drug may be poorly formulated, so the active ingredients do not get into the body by the best route or work as effectively as they might.
- The product may be badly designed: the combination of ingredients may be irrational or otherwise unwarranted.

Such drugs are widely prescribed partly because doctors get the wrong kind of information. Reliable information about drugs does exist, but it is heavily obscured by propaganda. Even formal drug evaluations are often inadequate and biased. The references to learned papers which make them seem credible often only prove the triumph of the imagination over science:

> 'In the past 60 years well over 200 papers have been reported in the use of lactobacillus . . . in the treatment of diarrhea. Despite the proliferation of studies, the very few controlled studies more often show lack of effectiveness than any antidiarrheal effect.'
> [FR 40 56. 21/3/75; p.12931]
> (See: ENPAC, FLAR and UNIFLOR in the drug list)

Individual prescribers cannot possibly choose between thousands of drugs, each with reams of evidence about its benefits or costs. They are bound to take the available advice, much of which is partial and some bad. It is not surprising that many prescribers end up with an impressionistic and uncritical view of the relative merits of different drugs.

In this environment, prescribing habits die hard. Even when a drug is known to have serious limitations, and even when these are well publicised, it can take many years for the information to sink in.

Between 1964 and 1973, the Committee on Safety of Medicines received over 1,200 reports of serious reactions (over 400 fatal) to phenylbutazone [a drug used to reduce pain and inflammation in rheumatic conditions]. There have been frequent warnings since then about the hazards of phenylbutazone and doctors are now advised to prescribe it 'only when other drugs have proved ineffective' and then only for treatments of no more than one week [BNF No.6, 1983, p.296]. There were nevertheless over one-and-a-quarter million NHS prescriptions for phenylbutazone and related drugs in 1981. (See: BUTAZOLIDIN.)

Poor drugs are widely used for many other reasons discussed later, but it should be stressed that these are not all related to commercial pressure and/or professional failings. Patients can and do put doctors under intense pressure to prescribe inappropriately. And some patients are lucky enough to have doctors with the sense and sympathy to know where not to draw the line:

> 'The patient is a 47-year-old Indian with a poor grasp of English. He comes in about four times a year and we try to make contact. His family is in India and he is lonely and homesick. He always asks for another 100 tablets . . . [of a strong tranquilliser] . . . and I give them because they seem to help him. He would submit meekly if I refused but he would not understand. The smiles would become unbearably hollow.'
> [Open University, 1983, p.16]

Trust between doctor and patient, and optimism and confidence in medicine, are essential to good treatment, but they are also easily exploited and misplaced. A balance has to be struck, and it is not easy to find. On the one hand, the limitations of drugs have to be understood if they are to be effectively used. On the other hand, the confidence that a medicine will work will help to achieve a cure. Hope helps, but it is debatable how far drugs can and should be used to convey it.

Unhelpful and unnecessary drugs

Drugs are considered 'unhelpful' not because their ingredients are inactive, but because the effect they have cannot be expected to benefit the patient. Sometimes, unhelpful or ineffective treatment is due to poor prescribing (for instance if an otherwise useful antibiotic is used to treat a cold). In other cases, drugs themselves reflect misconceived ideas about treatment.

ACIDOL-PEPSIN and MURIPSIN both contain ingredients which increase the acidity of the stomach contents, and also a digestive enzyme, pepsin. They are recommended for achlorhydria (ie abnormally low stomach acid levels), but there is no convincing evidence they help the patient. Acidification of stomach contents 'serves no useful clinical or physiological purpose' [*Medical Letter* 1972, 56]; and the supplementary intake of pepsin is of no value [M 28; p.654].

Anti-diarrhoeal drugs are increasingly considered unhelpful. Some contain anti-infective agents (see: ENTEROMIDE, GUANIMYCIN). These are unlikely to help because most acute diarrhoeas are caused by viral infections, and they may even prolong illness. Other anti-diarrhoeals may comfort the patient but are best avoided because they interfere with natural defence mechanisms which (like coughing or sneezing) help the body to get rid of irritants or toxins. Drinking liquids (to replace lost salts and fluids) helps the body and speeds recovery, but drugs generally do not.

Anti-diarrhoeal drugs are especially unsuitable for young children: 'Appropriate treatment for the infant with gastro-enteritis* may be conveniently considered as the three "Ds" – drugs, dehydration and diet. Drugs are mentioned only to discard them in most circumstances' [Br.Med.J. 1981, 283, 1277]. Nevertheless, such drugs are widely used. In 1981, there were about 100,000 prescriptions for LOMOTIL liquid for children. LOMOTIL is particularly unsuitable for young children because it may be toxic at a dosage only slightly higher than the therapeutic dosage. In Australia, the authorities have withdrawn it and its use has been restricted elsewhere.

Unhelpful and/or unnecessary medicine probably includes many borderline treatments: for example, the NHS spends over £1 million a year on bath additives. It certainly includes many 'tonics', for which there are over a million prescriptions a year. LABITON, for example, is basically just alcohol (28 per cent). The most that can be said for it is that it is not recommended for use by children, unlike E R Squibb's tonic, VERDIVITON (17 per cent alcohol), which is.

Other treatments – such as iron supplements in pregnancy – may be very useful for some people, but they are unhelpful and therefore undesirable for most others (see: IRON SUPPLEMENTS). The same goes for most vitamin preparations, only more so. Many of those listed in this book contain unwanted ingredients at inappropriate dosages, inevitably at needless extra cost (see: VITAMINS).

* Inflammation of the stomach and gut. There are many possible causes (eg food poisoning, infection, food allergy). Symptoms include stomach pain, vomiting and diarrhoea.

Less effective ingredients

Many of the medicines listed later in the book contain ingredients of little or no value. Others have active ingredients rated less effective than alternatives; still others combine ingredients which are effective with ingredients which are not; and others combine ingredients which work against each other.

Expectorants are a good example of drugs of little or no proven value. Expectorants are meant to promote the coughing up of phlegm, but the assumption that they work 'is a myth' and 'there is no scientific basis' for their use [BNF No.6, 1983; p.120]. Expectorants are included in many cough medicines and in other drugs prescribed for respiratory disorders; the cost to the NHS is tens of millions of pounds a year. The NHS spends around £4 million a year on BENAFED and BENYLIN preparations alone, and over-the-counter sales account for millions more (see EXPECTORANTS AND MUCOLYTICS).

The NHS spends around £30 million a year on peripheral vasodilator drugs. These are widely prescribed for blood circulation disorders and for senile dementia, though 'the clinical literature overwhelmingly indicates that they are not useful for these indications' [Avorn J. et al., 1982]. Both the American Medical Association [AMADE p.538] and the UK Joint Formulary Committee [BNF No.6, 1983; p.89] suggest they may do more harm than good. Brands listed include: DUVADILAN, HEXOPAL, PRAXILENE; the NHS spends around £15 million on these three brands alone (see: PERIPHERAL VASODILATORS).

Several products are rated 'less than effective' because they combine useful ingredients with less useful ones. This may increase the risk of unwanted reactions and does increase cost. For example: some iron products (eg FERROGRAD; FERROMYN) contain vitamin C or succinic acid to help the body absorb more iron. Nearly all contain far less than the optimal amount (ie 7mg of ascorbic acid to 1mg of iron); but none of them is necessary or desirable. Many simple iron tablets yield the equivalent of 90mg of iron – which is plenty, even for someone who absorbs iron badly [AMADE p.1067].

Other products are listed not because they do not work, but because there are better alternatives. Sometimes, the alternative is a newer product (see: BRONCHODILATORS). In other cases (eg CARISOMA; ROBAXIN 750), a fully effective and well-established alternative is preferred.

Drug formulation

A poorly formulated drug is the high-technology counterpart of the suppository used with the wrapper on. The way a drug is formulated affects how it enters the body and how it works when it is there.

For example, BUSCOPAN (hyoscine butylbromide) is used to relieve stomach spasms, and is available as an injection or in tablet form. It is very poorly absorbed from the gut, and the evidence that it is effective by mouth is not convincing [M 28 p.302]. Some experts consider it 'only effective by injection'

[Turner P., Volans G. N., 1980; p.53]. However, BUSCOPAN is nearly always prescribed in tablet form, at a cost to the NHS of about £½ million a year.

Similarly, oral administration of vitamin B_{12} (cyanocobalamin or hydroxcobalamin) in multivitamin preparations has been described as 'futile' [BNF No.5, 1983; p.275] though such products are often prescribed (eg LIPOFLAVONOID). Other examples include local anaesthetics (eg ANETHAINE) which work well when injected, but which are poorly absorbed through skin; and pain killers applied directly to the affected area (eg AUDAX) which are less effective than when taken by mouth. Antihistamine creams (eg PHENERGAN) or suppositories containing theophylline and related drugs (eg THEOSOL) also tend to be less effective than oral preparations, and are more likely to cause irritation.

The drug list does not take into account formulation of inactive ingredients, such as things used to preserve medicines or to make them look or taste good (colouring and flavouring), though these can also affect users' health. For example, an estimated 150 medicines for children contain sucrose (sugar), and in some the amount of sucrose is 60 per cent. These medicines rot children's teeth, especially if treatment is prolonged [DTB 1981, 75]. Some medicines also contain a dye called tartrazine, which causes adverse reactions in a relatively high number of patients. In the US, manufacturers are required by law to declare such ingredients [DTB 1980, 55], but in the UK some manufacturers refuse to do so [BNF No.6, 1983; p.xiii]. Users simply have to take their chance.

Increasing numbers of drugs are taken in slow-release formulations. These preparations are designed to release drugs into the body over relatively long periods. Some kinds are made by enclosing the active ingredients in a slow-dissolving coating. In others, the ingredients are put into an insoluble and inert wax or plastic 'sponge'. Slow-release preparations are designed to help in different ways, for example:

- to get drugs to the part of the body where action is needed – perhaps to treat a duodenal ulcer (in the gut beyond the stomach) – and/or to avoid release of the drug where it might be inactivated (for instance by acidity in the stomach) or where it might irritate or do harm (such as the stomach lining)
- to maintain optimum drug levels in the body – in other words at concentrations just high enough to get the desired effect – and/or to avoid fluctuation in the amount of drug released – for example to prevent too rapid an onset of action
- to make medicines easy and convenient to take; and to make it more likely that patients remember to take them.

These advantages are sometimes well worthwhile; and sometimes not (eg DELTACORTRIL 'ENTERIC'). In any case, the claimed benefit may not always be realised (eg SLOW-TRASICOR). In practice, the ingredients may not be released evenly over time, so the concentration of drugs in the body may be too high or too low; and/or drugs may be released at the wrong site. There are significant disadvantages with two of the most widely used slow-release formulations, supplements of potassium and iron. POTASSIUM SUPPLEMENTS in wax-matrix formulations (see drug list) may cause ulcers in the gut; and slow-release IRON SUPPLEMENTS are thought to release iron too far down the intestine, where conditions for absorption are poor.

Avoiding avoidable risk

All drug use involves some risk. Sometimes, a high risk may be acceptable because the expected benefit will outweigh it. At other times, even a low risk can be unacceptable – for instance, if it is avoidable, or if the probable benefits of a drug are small. In themselves, drugs are neither 'safe' nor 'unsafe', though the more reliable and complete the information there is about a drug, the more confidently it can be used.

The products listed in this book present different degrees and kinds of risk. Virtually all drugs have unwanted effects, though there is a difference between side effects (predictable and unavoidable) and adverse reactions (unexpected and unusual). The severity and frequency of unwanted effects ranges from relatively high (eg DISTALGESIC: see below) to relatively low, and many different kinds of risk may be involved:

- Otherwise useful drugs may present risks for particular users (eg TETRACYCLINE antibiotics should not be given to children).
- Risks may be associated with long-term rather than short-term use. For instance, long-term use of BENZODIAZEPINE TRANQUILLISERS may lead to serious dependence (eg VALIUM).
- Some drugs are particularly dangerous when abused and/or are prone to abuse (eg DISTALGESIC).
- Some drugs have a low 'therapeutic margin': that is, the therapeutic and toxic dosages are not far apart (eg VERILOID).
- Risks may be created or compounded by lack of information provided by the drug company (eg OPOBYL; ALBAMYCIN T).
- Risks may be increased when drugs are formulated in certain ways (eg POTASSIUM SUPPLEMENTS).
- Risks may increase when certain ingredients are used in particular applications (eg ALOPHEN).

- Users are especially likely to become sensitised to certain ingredients – that is, they tend to react badly to them with increased use (examples include neomycin in BETNOVATE-N and other preparations, and cinchocaine in LOCAN).

In many of these and other examples, there are safer alternatives – see the individual drug profiles.

Fixed-ratio combination drugs

Products which combine several different ingredients seem to make good sense. The idea of comprehensive treatment is attractive; and it is also more convenient to take one medicine instead of several. However, many drug combinations are undesirable: it is generally accepted that their use is justified only if

- the ingredients enhance each other's performance
- the patient's willingness to take the drugs is significantly improved by only having to take a single preparation
- if the combination of ingredients reduces drug costs.

These conditions are usually not met:

> In the World Health Organisation's model list of some 250 'essential drugs', there are only 7 drug combinations. By contrast, nearly half of the branded drugs listed in the UK prescribing index, MIMS, are combination products – as are over one-third of all new drugs introduced worldwide.
> [DTB 1980, 37]

Most of the fixed-ratio combination drugs mentioned in this book are used on the grounds that they are more convenient, and that patients are more likely to take them as directed. Sometimes there is a worthwhile advantage (see BETA-BLOCKER + DIURETIC PREPARATIONS) but it is usually small. Most analgesic, respiratory and gastro-intestinal combination drugs have disadvantages which outweigh any benefits that the combination of ingredients could be expected to have.

Combination drugs have several disadvantages. They make it more likely that people will take drugs they do not need; they multiply the risk of adverse reactions; and they make it impossible to adjust the dosage of the different ingredients to suit the individual patient's needs. Proper adjustment of dosage is one of the first principles of effective drug use.

Several combination products are listed because they combine ingredients which have opposing effects. Some cough and cold remedies, for example, combine a cough suppressant with an expectorant, which is meant to stimulate the cough reflex (eg DIMOTANE WITH CODEINE). It is also irrational to combine an expectorant with an antihistamine: an expectorant is meant to liquefy and loosen bronchial secretions, but an antihistamine will tend to dry them up (eg LINCTIFED EXPECTORANT).

These and other combination drugs mostly work on the 'shotgun' (or blunderbuss) principle. They are used in the hope of making some impact on the target illness, either when the aim is shaky, or when the target is not clearly in view. The better alternative is a diagnosis which gives a clear view of the target, and a single shot, well aimed.

To this extent, many combination drugs are rather like 'Swiss Army' penknives. They are exotic and versatile, very convenient and compact: their only real disadvantage, apart from cost, is that they are very inefficient. The saw, screwdriver or scissor attachment may sometimes be useful, but never as efficient as a simple household tool. At least with one of these knives you can use the attachments one at a time: the ingredients in a fixed ratio-combination drug have to be used simultaneously.

Therapeutic value for money

Rational and economic prescribing go hand in hand. Economic prescribing does not mean buying cheap drugs. It means spending as much as is needed – but no more – to give people treatments that really benefit them. Economic prescribing means the NHS not buying drugs which are not really needed, or which do not really help users. It also means prescribers not being unduly influenced by commercial or any other pressure to prescribe in general, and/or to prescribe particular drugs.

Economic prescribing at least involves using the cheapest brands of pharmacologically identical drugs. This is already done routinely in NHS hospitals. If GPs did the same – simply by prescribing a drug by its generic rather than brand name – it could save the NHS of the order of £100 million a year. This book identifies many brands of (often useful) drugs that cost several times more than the identical drug sold under another brand or 'house' name.*

For instance, the British National Formulary (1983) lists five brands of frusemide** – a drug which is also available from a number of manufacturing chemists who sell it under the generic name as 'FRUSEMIDE BP'.*** These are all the same, and all do the same: the only difference between them is the name. However, most doctors prescribe the most heavily promoted and the most expensive brand, LASIX. If doctors prescribed the same drug by its generic (and proper) name, the NHS would save over £6 million a year.

Comparable savings could be made if doctors prescribed well-established drugs instead of 'new, improved' alternatives, which cost much more. Probably the best

* The 'house' name identifies the manufacturer; the brand name identifies the goods.

** Frusemide is a diuretic – a drug which reduces blood pressure and removes excessive fluid from body tissues by increasing the output of urine.

*** BP: ie complies with the BRITISH PHARMACOPOEIA's specifications and standards for that drug.

example of these 'pills with frills' are the BENZODIAZEPINE TRANQUILLISERS. There are far more of them than are justifiable or needed; differentiation between brands is greatly exaggerated; and they are much misused. For example, ANXON (ketazolam) has actions and uses similar to another benzodiazepine, diazepam, though the manufacturer has claimed that it causes less drowsiness in the daytime. This claim was originally based on the results of a comparison between ketazolam taken in a single dose at night, and diazepam taken three times a day. (Reversing the procedure, one would expect the opposite result.) ANXON (ketazolam) costs around ten times more than diazepam: if diazepam were prescribed instead, the NHS would save about £¾ million a year.

There are several other drugs in the list that can be very useful when well used, but which are very uneconomical when not (eg AMOXIL, TENORMIN). Such drugs have been included because the evidence suggests that they are often extravagantly prescribed. The savings that could be made by prescribing these drugs carefully would allow improved standards of health care in other areas.

Towards progress?

In 1967, about one-third of the most prescribed drug products were officially described as 'undesirable preparations'. This assessment was made by two panels of experts set up to advise an official, public enquiry into the 'Relationship of the Pharmaceutical Industry with the National Health Service' [Sainsbury, 1967, p.209]. The panels classified over 2,200 prescribed drugs as follows:

- effective drugs: 50 per cent of the total
- rational combinations: 8 per cent
- not yet classifiable ('drugs and preparations which are pharmacologically active but which are of unproven therapeutic value or safety or about which too little is known'): 7 per cent
- 'undesirable preparations' which included: 'combinations which are irrational'; 'superseded or obsolete drugs or preparations'; and 'ineffective drugs and preparations': 35 per cent.

The UK Joint Formulary Committee uses comparable criteria today to identify drugs and preparations which are 'less suitable for prescribing'. Between 22 and 24 per cent of the 2,000-plus branded drugs evaluated by the Committee are considered 'less suitable for prescribing'. (The 24 per cent includes a number of 'borderline substances', which are not dealt with here.) The remainder includes many products of 'uncertain', 'doubtful' or 'little' value [BNF No.6, 1983].

The second part of the book profiles several hundred drugs of this kind. The chapters that follow try to explain how and why such medicines are used.

2 Why are they made?

Why do the drug companies make and market hundreds of products that independent authorities say are inferior? They have to in order to survive. The companies would much prefer it if their products were well received, but there are often compelling reasons for promoting the drugs, regardless of outside opinion. For example, though experts generally disapprove of fixed-ratio combination products, they have irresistible advantages for the companies that make them:

- Being able to combine different ingredients in a single product allows companies to extend their product range and have more products to promote.
- It also means that companies can fully exploit their own inventions. When a company develops a new drug, it gets patent protection and a monopoly right to sell; that right can be extended by combining a patented drug with other ingredients, each new drug having a 'unique advantage' and its own patent.
- If products differ from each other even slightly, it reduces the likelihood of price competition (which means lower margins) and allows companies to set their own prices for their products instead.
- Experts may criticise fixed-ratio combination drugs, but prescribers and consumers may positively prefer them. Combination drugs are more convenient, and they relieve doctors of the responsibility for deciding exactly how much of each ingredient to give, or of trying each ingredient separately.
- Combination drugs may also be cheaper for the patient: each product attracts a single prescription charge, while a prescription for the two ingredients as separate products (two prescriptions) attracts two charges.
- Patients tend to be happier about taking just one tablet or applying one treatment.

There is another reason why drug companies are obliged to make 'incomparable' products. Because everyone is entitled to the best available treatment, all drugs have to be superlative, or unique, or at least first among equals, in order to survive. The companies cannot expect to meet this demand by developing 'breakthrough' drugs regularly because drug innovation is an expensive and uncertain business. Often, all they can do is to develop exactly the kind of products that are criticised here.

These products include 'new, improved' 'me-too' drugs – products which approximate or duplicate drugs already on the market but which offer no advantage over them. They also include drugs which are considered inferior or positively undesirable – the kind of products that the UK Joint Formulary Committee considers 'less suitable for prescribing'. The Table overleaf gives some idea of how different drug companies depend on these 'less suitable' products.

Self-image and reality

The drug companies deny making indifferent or bad products, and reject criticism that they promote their products for more than they are worth. The companies say that they operate to standards laid down in the industry's national (ABPI) and international (IFPMA) codes of pharmaceutical marketing practice:

> 'The pharmaceutical industry, conscious of its special position arising from its involvement in public health, and justifiably eager to fulfil its obligations in a free and fully responsible manner, undertakes:
>
> - 'to ensure that all products it makes available for prescription purposes to the public . . . have full regard to the needs of public health . . .
> - 'to base the claims for substances and formulations on valid scientific evidence . . .
> - 'to provide scientific information with objectivity and good taste (and) with scrupulous regard for truth . . .
> - 'to use complete candour in dealings with public health officials, health care professionals and the public.'
>   [IFPMA, 1981]

The drug industry has been able to reconcile this self-image with criticism of its products partly because this Code is barely operational. In the first 18 months of its existence, only three complaints were made under the Code, and none was upheld. The industry has claimed that the 'remarkably few substantiated breaches of the Code' demonstrates the commitment of individual companies to uphold it [SCRIP; 23/5/83 p.14]. Critics of the industry and its products say they have no confidence in the Code [HAI, 1982]. Social Audit, which submitted the first three complaints made under the IFPMA code, shares this view.

- One of the complaints is relevant here only because some British doctors hold shares in drug companies – this could influence how they prescribe. The ruling made in response to Social Audit's complaint under the IFPMA Code in effect upholds the right of drug companies to encourage doctors to buy their shares, and to give them advance information about share sales.

WHO OWNS WHOM IN THE PHARMACEUTICAL INDUSTRY

Companies ranked by number and proportion of their products rated 'less suitable for prescribing' in the British National Formulary 1983

Parent Company (Country of Origin)	**Subsidiaries, Divisions Affiliates** etc.	**Ranking** according to number and proportion of products rated 'less suitable for prescribing' (see important notes below)
Johnson & Johnson (USA)	*Janssen; Ortho-Cilag*	*No product rated 'less suitable for prescribing': far above average*
Schering Pharmaceuticals (D)	*Berlimed*	
Smith & Nephew (UK)		
Bristol Myers Co (USA)		
ICI (UK)	*Stuart Pharmaceuticals*	*One or two products rated 'less suitable for prescribing' and well under 10 per cent of all products listed: well above average*
Nestlé Co (CH)	*Alcon*	
DDSA (UK)		
The Boots Co (UK)	*Crookes*	
Stiefel Laboratories (USA)		
Merck Sharp & Dohme (USA)	*Thomas Morson*	
G. D. Searle (USA)	*Gold Cross*	
Akzo NV (NL)	*Organon, Ashe*	
Hoffman La Roche (CH)	*Roche; Sauter*	*Above average: 10–20 per cent of all products listed rated 'less suitable for prescribing'*
American Cyanamid (USA)	*Lederle*	
Leo Laboratories (DK)	*Burgess*	
E. R. Squibb (USA)	*FAIR Laboratories*	
Gist-Brocades NV (NL)	*Brocades*	
Revlon Inc. (USA)	*Armour; Berk*	
Reckitt & Colman (UK)		
Astra AB (S)		
Bayer AG (D)	*Dome; Miles*	
Eli Lilly (USA)	*Dista Products*	
Pfizer Inc (USA)		
The Upjohn Co (USA)		
Hoechst (D)	*Roussell; Albert; Cassenne*	
Aspro-Nicholas (Aus)	*Nicholas*	
Norgine (UK)		
Fisons Ltd (UK)	*Charnwood*	
Lipha Pharmaceuticals (UK)	*Rona*	
Schering Corp (USA)	*Kirby-Warrick; Plough*	
Beecham (UK)	*Bencard*	*Average: around 20 per cent of all products rated 'less suitable for prescribing'*
Glaxo (UK)	*Allen & Hanburys; Duncan Flockhart; Evans Medical; Farley Health*	
The Wellcome Foundation (UK)	*Calmic; Wellcome*	
American Home Products (USA)	*Ayerst, Wyeth*	
Ciba-Geigy (CH)	*Ciba; Geigy; Zyma*	
Sandoz (CH)	*Wander; Dorsey; Ex-Lax*	
Sterling Drug (USA)	*Sterling; Winthrop*	

Syntex Pharmaceuticals (Panama)	*Syntex; Bengue*	
Rhône-Poulenc (F)	*May & Baker*	
Boehringer Ingelheim (D)	*MCP Pharmaceuticals; WBP Pharmaceuticals*	
Macarthy's Laboratories (UK)	*Martindale; Dales; Farillon*	
Richardson Merrell (USA)	*Merrell Pharmaceuticals*	
Smithkline Beckman (USA)	*Smith Kline & French; Allergan*	*A bit below average: around 30 per cent of all products listed rated 'less suitable for prescribing'*
Napp Laboratories (UK)	*Priory*	
Forest Laboratories (USA)	*Pharmax*	
Abbott Laboratories (USA)		
Warner-Lambert Co (USA)	*Parke Davis; William Warner*	*Below average: around 40–50 per cent of products rated 'less suitable for prescribing'*
3M Corporation (USA)	*Riker; Carnegie*	
Sanol Schwartz (D)	*Medo Chemicals*	
Sinclair Pharmaceuticals (UK)		
Consolidated Chemicals (UK)		*Well below average: around 60 per cent of products rated 'less suitable for prescribing'*
Wallace Manufacturing (UK)	*Norma*	
W. H. Rorer Inc (USA)	*Rorer, Radiol, Wade*	
A. H. Robins (USA)		

NOTES

This list includes larger companies only, with at least 15 products listed in the BNF. The table should be interpreted very cautiously, because the designation 'less suitable for prescribing' applies equally to very different kinds of products (eg it would apply both to an innocuous multivitamin and to a potentially harmful and/or obsolete preparation). In addition, products *not* identified as 'less suitable for prescribing' may be of little or no value (see for example, PERIPHERAL VASODILATORS in drug list); or they may be dangerous if not very carefully used (see for example, BARBITURATES, BUTAZOLIDIN in the drug list).

Note that there may be considerable differences between subsidiaries of the same parent company. For example, Syntex Pharmaceuticals has 16 products listed in the BNF, none rated 'less suitable for prescribing' – but Bengue and Co. (owned by the same parent company) has 10 products listed, of which 6 are rated 'less suitable etc'.

The point of the ranking is therefore to give an idea of the commercial significance of 'less suitable' products; and to indicate roughly which companies stand where. Differences between companies in adjacent bands are not significant: differences between companies at the top and bottom of the list almost certainly are.

- Social Audit's second complaint questioned whether 20-odd anti-diarrhoeal drugs could be considered to have 'full regard to the needs of public health'. These included several products (eg GUANIMYCIN) criticised by the UK Joint Formulary Committee because they could prolong diarrhoeal illness rather than shorten it, though the complaint mainly related to the use of such drugs in developing countries where the World Health Organisation (1976) found them to be 'of no value and . . . even dangerous'. The IFPMA said that this complaint fell outside the scope of its code partly because these products were legally approved for sale, and partly because 'a substantial medical literature' supported their use.

- Social Audit's third complaint concerned the failure of the drug company, G D Searle & Co, to warn doctors in Britain not to prescribe its product LOMOTIL (diphenoxylate with atropine) to children under two. After a protracted dispute [Social Audit, 1982] G D Searle agreed to issue this warning in September 1981, but had taken no action by March 1983. The IFPMA ruled that G D Searle had acted 'positively and responsibly' throughout.

Shortly before making these complaints, Social Audit wrote to a number of companies to ask how they responded to criticism of their products in the British National Formulary. At the same time (early 1982) Social Audit notified the Association of the British Pharmaceutical Industry of this survey. The ABPI promptly advised its members not to take part. In a letter to Social Audit (3/3/82), they wrote:

> 'Thank you for your letter of 28 February informing the Association that you will shortly be sending a questionnaire to a number of member companies and for sending me a copy.
>
> 'In the first paragraph of your questionnaire you refer to pharmaceutical products identified in the British National Formulary "as being of questionable therapeutic value". I presume that you are referring to products shown in smaller type in the British National Formulary. I would remind you that on page x of the second edition of this volume such products are described in the 5th paragraph under the heading of Preparation ". . . but those considered by the Committee to be *less suitable for prescribing* are described briefly in smaller type".
>
> 'You will appreciate that the wording used here for such products has a very different meaning from the words you have chosen. Hence I would be grateful if you would justify your statement that the British National Formulary has identified the products you have listed in your letters to member companies as being "of questionable therapeutic value".
>
> 'I would also point out that the purpose and intention of the British National Formulary is described as follows on page 3 of the book under the heading "Health and Safety":
>
> > "The British National Formulary is intended for the guidance of medical practitioners, pharmacists, dentists, nurses and other workers *who have the necessary training and experience to interpret the information it provides*. It is intended as a reference book for the pocket, and should be supplemented by a study of more detailed publications when required."
>
> 'In view of this description by the authors, I would be glad to know of the mandate that Social Audit has in conducting this survey. I would also welcome more precise information on the intended use of any report you may produce.

> 'The importance of these two questions is such that we feel it is our duty to recommend member companies to withhold their replies to your circular until we have had your response.'

The main point in Social Audit's reply (5/3/82) was that the term 'of questionable therapeutic value' had been used broadly in order to identify products which the British National Formulary specifically described in the following ways:

> 'Should be avoided'; 'their use is not recommended . . .'; 'of doubtful efficacy'; 'neither has been shown to have any advantage . . .'; 'their use is to be discouraged . . .'; 'generally ineffective by mouth and cause of unacceptably high incidence of depression'; 'should not be prescribed . . . (and are) . . . to be deprecated'; '. . . of no value whatever in the treatment of bronchial asthma'; '. . . no scientific basis for prescribing these drugs . . .'; '. . . the drawbacks are not outweighed by the benefits of prescribing'; 'the increasing trend towards prescribing more than one of these drugs for the same indication is *not* recommended. It may constitute a hazard and there is no evidence that side-effects are minimised'; 'obsolete'; 'have no place in the management of depression or obesity'. And so on through 300-odd pages of text.

Six weeks later (13/4/82), the ABPI replied:

> 'It remains the responsibility of our member companies to decide individually how they respond to your organisation's request for information about their products. In these circumstances we feel that a continuation of this correspondence would appear to serve no useful purpose.'

Responsibility taken by the companies

In spite of the ABPI's intervention, several companies did reply to Social Audit's enquiries. A few went out of their way to be helpful; others saw no point in doing so:

> 'Thank you for your letters of 26 February to Dista Products Ltd and Eli Lilly & Company Ltd. As people preparing this type of report almost never take any notice of the information provided by the companies, we have found in the past that it is a complete waste of our time and effort generating responses.'

Though companies tended to argue the merits of specific products, their replies also explained how the industry as a whole reconciles criticism of its products with the high standards it claims to observe. Above all, the companies defended their products on the grounds that they were licensed for use by government authorities; or are in some way 'official'. Some companies suggested that was all there was to be said: if their products were marketed legally, the companies' responsibilities were fully discharged:

'The products identified are all the subject of a current Product Licence or Product Licence of Right and thus meet the requirements for the marketing of medicinal products in the United Kingdom, based on an independent, official view of their properties. All of them, in our opinion, are of therapeutic value to appropriate patients, when used in accordance with the Data Sheets.
[Ciba-Geigy]

'No doubt you will be aware that under the Medicines Act 1968, the Department of Health is responsible for licensing medicines for marketing in the UK. The Department of Health has to be satisfied on the quality, efficacy and safety of a product . . . Information that is provided on Boots products is confidential between the Company and the Department; therefore we do not propose to respond to the enquiries in your letters . . .'
[The Boots Company Ltd]

This puts into perspective the industry's claim to make products which 'have full regard for the needs of public health'. All this really seems to mean is that the industry undertakes not to break the law by marketing products which governments have not approved. The ABPI Code certainly implies that if a drug has a product licence, the manufacturer has a full regard for the needs of public health:

'Comprehensive legislation has been introduced to safeguard the public by ensuring that all products meet standards of quality, efficacy and safety which are acceptable in the state of present knowledge and experience.'
[Code of Practice for the Pharmaceutical Industry; 5th Edition, ABPI, 1982]

Keeping up with tradition

The companies also defended their products against criticism on the grounds that doctors like them, and in some cases have used them for many years. Some companies emphasised that they no longer actively promoted their 'less suitable' products, but there was no suggestion that doctors who prescribed them were doing less than they might for their patients:

'We do not actively promote the products mentioned in your letter to physicians, all of whom have a copy of the BNF. If they wish to prescribe such a product for a particular patient, it would seem inappropriate to fault their professional judgement since individuals respond differently to medication . . . The Company provides the above products in the knowledge that some physicians want them and find them of use in selected patients.'
[Merck Sharp & Dohme Ltd]

'These products have been retained because there is a small but persistent demand for them from the Medical Profession . . . While this demand exists we consider it our duty to meet it . . .'
[Philip Harris Medical Ltd]

'Many of them are old formulations, but they are still being prescribed by doctors in the best interests of their patients. We are satisfied that all of them play a useful part in treatment, which is evidenced not only by clinical trials but by the more testing assessment of use in everyday practice.'
[Riker Laboratories]

'FRANOL . . . was introduced in 1943. Our general view on this is that a product that has been in use for 39 years has by now probably demonstrated itself to be of some therapeutic value.'
[Sterling-Winthrop Group Ltd]

'As you will probably be aware, we do not promote either of the two products you mention; they have relied on reputation for the last twelve years. This might suggest appropriate efficacy.'
[Carter-Wallace Ltd]

Many companies have essentially the same reasons for rejecting criticism of their products in the British National Formulary. The companies' views on the BNF closely reflected those of their trade association, which concluded that: 'the value judgements made of products discriminate academically and arbitrarily against some of them and may conflict with the views of many prescribing doctors based on their personal experience in treating patients' [ABPI press statement: February 1981].

Social Audit asked companies for information to support the use of products identified as 'less suitable for prescribing', and a specific request was made for data from 'relevant, objective research reports, clinical trials etc'. The companies responded to this appeal in very different ways.

One or two simply gave sweeping but unsupported assurances: 'the mixture . . . has been found to be particularly suitable for the purposes for which it is designed'; 'thirteen thousand patients were monitored'; or 'all substantiated by Laboratory and Clinical Publications'. Other companies emphasised that the ingredients in their products were in some way accredited (this need have nothing to do with their therapeutic efficacy):

'The active ingredient [in ALEUDRIN] is Isoprenaline Sulphate, which has been official in the BP [British Pharmacopoeia] since 1953. . . . We feel this is sufficient evidence of its efficacy but should you require any further information on this product, please do not hesitate to contact us.'
[Lewis Laboratories]

'At the present time, we feel we can do no better than to enclose herewith a photocopy of an entry about MEPRATE (meprobamate) from the *United States Dispensatory* 26th Edition published in 1960. We have no doubt that much of what is written there is valid today.'
[*DDSA* Pharmaceuticals]

Evidence lacking

Several companies said that convincing documentary evidence could not be provided, in particular for older drugs and combination products. The evidence for these tends to be weak, either because there have been no clinical trials, or because (by today's standards) they were not properly done:

> 'Since the remaining three products have been on the market for a considerable time and none contained ingredients that were novel at the date of introduction, published literature is limited. A list of relevant publications is attached. You will appreciate that long-standing clinical acceptance does not attract the kind of study that appears in publications.'
> [Reckitt & Colman]

> 'It is difficult to prove in a clinical trial the advantages of some combination products, but I would suggest that the fact of their continuing widespread use in spite of academic criticism for many years is more a reflection of clinical response than of pharmaceutical promotion.'
> [Sterling-Winthrop Group]

> 'These products . . . have not been the subject of research reports or clinical trials and were put on the market many years ago when a doctor made his own choice of the formulation – the active ingredients were "Official" drugs.'
> [Philip Harris Medical]

> '. . . Information on these products is derived from clinical trials which were carried out many years ago and may not accord with modern views on methods.'
> [Smith Kline & French]

Beecham Pharmaceuticals proved this last point in sending copies of 33 papers supporting their antacid product, NULACIN. The product itself has a relatively minor disadvantage, and is far less open to criticism than the 33 reports on its use, most of which fall well short of the standards required for drug approvals today.

Evidence offered

However, a few companies did provide a detailed explanation for their products. Hoechst, for instance, defended its combination products LASIX-K and LASIKAL (diuretic plus potassium supplement) on the grounds that the combination made it more likely that patients would take the drugs. Hoechst also said that its products combined ingredients at the optimum dosage (best for most patients).

Another company, Roche Products, said there were good reasons for promoting its product LIMBITROL, a combination of an antidepressant (amitriptyline) and a tranquilliser (chlordiazepoxide).

'In the years following the introduction of LIBRIUM (chlordiazepoxide), it became increasingly obvious to us that the drug was frequently co-prescribed. . . . With the object of simplifying treatment, we introduced LIMBITROL which enabled the combined treatment to be given in either a single tablet or capsule. . . .

'We are of course aware of the argument that when two drugs are given together the dosage should be carefully titrated to suit each individual patient. In practice, however, this rarely happens and the survey undertaken before the introduction of LIMBITROL indicated that the dosages of the product were those prescribed by a large majority of doctors.'

[Roche Products]

The last word goes to the Medical Director of Smith Kline & French:

'Virtually every time we have withdrawn an old and outdated product, problems have been caused for individual patients, occasionally quite unexpectedly so, for whom we have had to continue supplies whenever we can. The whole problem of old pharmaceutical products is not as easy as it sometimes seems, and modern clinical pharmacological methods are not the whole answer (nor are they infallible or even sometimes applicable). Some of the "ex cathedra" unsupported pronouncements of the BNF have not, in my view, helped patients or doctors as much as they might have done.'

Promotional excesses

The drug companies are still open to the criticism that they contribute to bad prescribing habits. They do this partly by making undesirable products; partly by making far too many of them; and partly by the way they promote their products when they are in vogue. The scale of drug promotion is formidable, and the methods used are sometimes distinctly unfair.

In 1982, the industry in Britain spent some £150 million on drug promotion, roughly the equivalent of £4,000–£5,000 on each general practitioner. Just under half of the promotional budget was spent on medical representatives: one representative per eight doctors. Enough is spent on advertising to expose doctors to an average of over 50 drug advertisements each day, most of them sent in free magazines.

The industry also acts as benefactor and sponsor in all kinds of medical activities: it gives financial support for scientific meetings and research; funds academic and other journals; provides information and educational materials; and supplies free medicines and equipment in hospitals and surgeries. This kind of help can be indispensible. The industry also lobbies vigorously; contributes substantially to party political funds; and is tireless in organising professional and public relations campaigns.

The Code of Practice for the Pharmaceutical Industry (ABPI, 1982) has detailed guidelines on drug promotion, and requires that: 'Methods of promotion must never be such as to bring discredit upon, or reduce confidence in, the pharmaceutical industry.' It is difficult to know precisely what this Code achieves, partly because all enforcement decisions have been made and are kept in secret (although the ABPI announced that from 1983 it would publish details of any complaints upheld). However, in 1983, the outgoing President of the ABPI privately chided member companies for 'promotional excesses'. It is also pretty clear that his remarks were largely prompted by two BBC-TV *Panorama* programmes on drug promotion, shown in early 1983.

Promotion of NSAIDs

Panorama discussed the relationship between the industry and the medical profession in the context of a report on OPREN (benoxaprofen), which was marketed in Britain by Dista Products, a subsidiary of the US drug firm Eli Lilly. OPREN was introduced in 1979 into an already over-saturated but lucrative market of 'non-steroidal anti-inflammatory drugs' (NSAIDs): aspirin-like compounds used to relieve pain and inflammation in arthritis and related disorders. The history of OPREN – until the withdrawal of its product licence in 1982 – demonstrated many of the less savoury aspects of drug promotion. Extravagant hospitality is one.

The ABPI Code of Practice says that hospitality given to members of the medical profession 'should be appropriate and not out of proportion to the occasion. Its cost should not exceed that level which the recipients might normally adopt when paying for themselves' [ABPI, 1982]. Nevertheless, the industry routinely pays for influential members of the profession to attend promotional and other meetings abroad; and it entertains them well. The UK launch of OPREN was held on board a luxury cruise ship on the Rhine, and a symposium on the drug held in Paris a year later was estimated to have cost Dista/Lilly around £¼ million.

Another example from *Panorama* is of particular interest because the ABPI refused to consider it as a possible breach of the Code, unless the reporter, Tom Mangold, made it the subject of a formal complaint. Mangold declined, saying he had his job to do, and the ABPI had theirs.

In 1982, the Italian drug company, Farmitalia Carlo Erba, invited 100 senior British rheumatologists to a four-day symposium in Venice to mark the UK launch of another NSAID, called FLOSINT (indoprofen). Participants travelled on the luxury train, 'The Orient Express', and stayed in a £90-a-night hotel. On board the train, Mangold interviewed one of the rheumatologists in the middle of a five-course meal:

'Is this trip costing you anything at all?'

'It is costing me money, yes.'

'And . . . without obviously telling me how much . . .

what do you have to spend money on? . . . The travel is free?'

'The travel isn't totally free, no. I paid my own fare to the airport . . .'

'The accommodation is free?'

'The accommodation is free.'

'The food is free?'

'The food is free . . . the drink is not free.'

Hospitality at this level is reserved for opinion-formers (usually consultants), but GPs are also feted, particularly when a new product is launched. *Panorama* obtained the records of a medical representative involved in the OPREN launch: it appeared that this one member of the 70-strong sales force had spent over £800 on food and drink in 13 days, entertaining GPs 'and their wives'. For the drug companies, this kind of 'hospitality' is simply an investment, which like any other investment is made to get a good financial return:

> 'All the doctors in this sales area and presumably elsewhere have been listed and programmed into a computer by the Dista sales people. This print-out carefully notes each doctor's name, address, and . . . his drug-ordering habits. Generous prescribers of OPREN were suitably coded – as were those doctors who were to be targeted to use more of the drug.'

A meeting of top Eli Lilly executives was held in Arizona in 1979: 'At the meeting's close, a Lilly Vice-President delivered a short message about marketing opportunities. It was: "Grab it". Then to show everyone present they were sitting on a pharmaceutical goldmine, each director was told to look under the chair; there he discovered a brand new dollar bill. Each Lilly director then wrote "Grab it" on the dollar bill, and had it personally signed by the President of Eli Lilly International, as a souvenir.' [*Panorama*, BBC-TV, 17/1/83]

The industry sustains a close relationship with both opinion-formers and prescribers partly by sponsoring research. Some of this research is essential and some is clearly not, but all of it involves some risk of loss of independence for the research worker. Evidence from the *Panorama* report emphasised the risks involved when companies substantially overpaid, or when they discriminated against physicians with all their critical faculties intact.

Evidence from many other sources has shown how 'research' is contracted to GPs as an integral part of marketing strategy. Typically, doctors are paid, say, £10–£20 for each patient they treat with a new drug. Doctors may then be asked to fill in a questionnaire about the patient's response, but the real point of the exercise may be to get the patient switched to the new drug.

With NSAIDs and other drugs used for long-term treatments, the companies' initial investment may be handsomely repaid. Here is one example of a practice that is now widespread:

> In 1977, Merck Sharp & Dohme launched a new drug, CLINORIL (sulindac) – another NSAID. During that year, 8,000 GPs (one-third of the UK total) tested the drug on 30,000 patients over a period of one month. The results of this study showed that many doctors had failed even to read the test protocol, because at least 600 patients should not have been prescribed this drug at all. The drug was specifically 'contra-indicated' for these patients who were suffering from ulcers or related conditions. In this trial, payments to doctors (1977 prices) were about £120,000. Because about half of the patients who tried CLINORIL continued to use it, the return to the company was about £1 million in one year.
> [*Sunday Times* 29/1/78]

The OPREN story adds to a good deal of evidence which suggests that drugs are often promoted partly on the strength of inadequate or unattested research. In the promotion of OPREN, much was made of a completely unsupportable claim that the drug might actually arrest the progress of rheumatoid arthritis, rather than simply relieve symptoms of inflammation and pain. The study on which this claim was based was reported in a supplement to the *European Journal of Rheumatology*, whose publication and distribution was paid for by Eli Lilly. The Editor of the Journal, a consultant rheumatologist at St Bartholomew's Hospital, Dr Ted Huskisson, defended publication on the grounds that the findings were 'of considerable interest' – though he agreed with the *Panorama* reporter, Tom Mangold, that both the design and interpretation of the study were 'extremely suspect'.

> **'I remember a study involving chickens. It was a carcinogenesis study – a study to determine whether or not the drug caused cancer. The report to FDA said the test drug caused cancer no more often than placebo, or a sugar pill – and in fact that was true. What they failed to tell us was that half the chickens died of heart failure. That's putting your best foot forward.'** [Physician, formerly employed by the US Food and Drug Administration, interviewed on *Panorama*, BBC-TV, 17/1/83]

Panorama also gave evidence of suppression of information – both about the harmful effects of drugs, and about the status of one of the key figures who recommended OPREN. The programme revealed that Derek Willoughby, Professor of Experimental Pathology at St Bartholomew's Hospital, had repeatedly been introduced to doctors, the press and even Dista's own sales representatives 'as an impartial outsider at the top of his field' – though he was in fact a paid consultant to Dista's parent company, Eli Lilly. Full disclosure of a financial interest could only have strengthened Professor Willoughby's reassurance 'that his intellectual independence and integrity have never been affected by this commercial relationship with the Company'.

It is precisely because such associations may be perfectly proper that disclosure of a financial interest is desirable. Disclosure is also desirable because of the possibility of abuse. The Editor of the *Side Effects of Drugs Annual* has commented:

> 'I now find myself obliged to maintain a black-list of authors I can no longer use since they lend their names to papers compiled or re-edited within the promotional departments of pharmaceutical companies. Their activities seem to impede the early identification of adverse reactions and interactions. . . . I often invite (and value) views expressed by reputable pharmaceutical houses in their own name, but one cannot have much respect for promotion masquerading as science.'
> [Dukes M. N. G., 1979]

Going public

Shortcuts and shortcomings in the promotion of drugs to doctors must add to anxiety about the increasing trend towards promoting prescription drugs directly to consumers. In 1982, the Commissioner of the US Food and Drug Administration predicted 'an exponential increase' in direct-to-consumer drug advertising [*Scrip* No.770; 21/2/83, p.10]; the first TV commercial for a prescription drug was shown in the US in 1983. The ABPI Code of Practice specifically warns against such advertising, but the evidence suggests in vain. The trend seems unstoppable:

> 'It can take a long time to persuade a doctor to change his prescribing habits, but if patients ask for the latest beta-blocker they read about in yesterday's newspaper, results can be achieved in weeks that advertising in medical journals cannot achieve in years of promotion.'
> [The Editor of *Scrip*, Dr Philip Brown, quoted in *Marketing*, 30/9/81]

Dista Products certainly flouted the relevant part of the ABPI Code in promoting OPREN:

> '. . . in their overall marketing plans and strategy for the sale of OPREN, Dista told their salesmen that they would be initiating a fully coordinated public relations programme aimed at the consumer as well as the medical profession. Indeed, the salesmen were advised to use the resulting "patient pull" – patient demand – to their own advantage.'
> [*Panorama*, 17/1/83]

Independent experts also spoke publicly for OPREN: one was Dr Ted Huskisson of St Bartholomew's Hospital, who gave a very favourable account of the drug in an interview for Thames TV. Dr Huskisson later told *Panorama* that he had given a balanced interview, but that his remarks had been heavily edited. He concluded: 'I very much regret giving the interview and shall be most careful another time. . . . I really don't think that we ought to be seeing information about new drugs in the newspapers.'

As Editor of the *European Journal of Rheumatology*, and as the supervisor of a company-sponsored clinical trial on OPREN, Dr Huskisson was to some extent involved with Dista/Lilly. However, he had also spoken for two other NSAIDs, made by rival firms. He was Chairman of the Venice conference which launched Farmitalia Carlo Erba's product FLOSINT (indoprofen); and he spoke about Ortho's ZOMAX (zomepirac) at the 1981 Edinburgh World Congress on Pain.

After the Edinburgh Congress, Dr Huskisson was quoted in the *Daily Mirror* (7/9/81) as saying that ZOMAX might overtake aspirin because it was superior as a pain-killer and did not have such serious side effects. He was also reported as saying that ZOMAX would be safe to sell across the counter.

ZOMAX was withdrawn from all world markets, on safety grounds, early in 1983. FLOSINT was withdrawn in Britain, also on safety grounds, later that year.

Promotion, prices and profits

The drug companies advertise and promote their products not only to sell them in large quantities, but also to sell them at a good price. This means advertising and promoting products to emphasise both their benefits as medicines and their distinctiveness as brands. By emphasising differences between brands, companies can avoid competing on price:

- A drug company can take a well-established drug – say, an out-of-patent drug like aspirin – and then change it from something ordinary into something special. Aspirin has great therapeutic value but it has little commercial value because different brands are well-known to be identical as medicines, and therefore tend to compete on price. To sell a drug like aspirin at a good price, it has to be given a brand identity: it can be called something else (eg ASPRO); or it can be disguised (eg as 'the one doctors prescribe most'). It can be mixed with other ingredients; or it can be reformulated (eg into an effervescent or slow-release tablet, or even chewing-gum).

- The alternative is for companies to develop new chemical entities (NCEs). This is what all major drug firms try to do because then they get patent protection which gives them monopoly rights on their inventions for up to 20 years. Sometimes companies come up with an NCE by making a real breakthrough: they develop a thoroughly new drug, and make an important therapeutic advance. But more usually, innovation means very slightly modifying an existing drug: it becomes an NCE, though its therapeutic and pharmacological properties are hardly changed at all. Most innovation involves making 'me-too' drugs which brings commercial rather than therapeutic gain.

The 1977 Patent Act extended protection from 16 to 20 years. However, it usually takes several years to develop and test an NCE, so the patent life on a newly launched product is reduced. The industry estimates that it takes an average of eight years from the time a patent is granted to full marketing in the UK, and it complains that patent protection does not last long enough [Office of Health Economics, 1983; p.15].

Nevertheless, companies get protection which allows them to exploit their innovations long after the patent has expired. At the end of a patent life, other companies can introduce their versions of the same drug, but they usually find it very hard to compete with a brand which has dominated the market for a decade or more. Companies which compete on price alone – by producing unbranded ('generic') versions of out-of-patent drugs – make relatively little impact on the UK drugs market. In 1980, generic drugs accounted for only 5 per cent by value (16 per cent by number) of all NHS prescriptions in England [Health and Personal Social Services Statistics for England, 1982; p.83].

All the evidence suggests that innovating companies can command substantially higher prices for their products, and continue to dominate the market, well after the patent life of their drugs has expired. In the list of drugs at the end of the book, there are many examples of this. Hoffman La Roche's patent for VALIUM (diazepam), for instance, expired in 1976. By 1983, there were five other branded versions of diazepam (tablets or capsules 5mg) and many other unbranded ones. Roche nevertheless held about 75 per cent of the market for diazepam (by value); and also managed to command a 'premium' price for its brand. Eight years after the expiry of Roche's patent, the basic NHS price for diazepam (1,000 tablets 5mg) was £1.60, compared with £13.62 for VALIUM [DHSS Drug Tariff, 1984]

The promotion of such drugs contributes substantially to the industry's profitability. Though the government has some control over drug prices, it has permitted profits which the Public Accounts Committee [1983] has criticised as excessive. This Select Committee's enquiry showed that in 1978, the drug industry earned an average rate of return on capital of 21 per cent – 5 per cent more than for industry generally. By 1980, this figure had increased to over 23 per cent, while the corresponding figure for the rest of industry had declined.

Promises and threats

The pharmaceutical industry does not defend itself by answering criticism of its products or promotions. But there are exceptions: for example, in *The Future for Pharmaceuticals*, a paper prepared by the research arm of the ABPI, the Office of Health Economics (1983). The OHE acknowledges that some things are not quite right, but does not suggest that anything much can or should be done:

> '. . . There is apparent extravagance in spending by certain companies. The industry's strict Code of Practice which prohibits excessive entertainment is particularly hard to administer. Doctors are flattered by generous and unusual entertainments provided to attract their attention. . . . The recipients of lavish hospitality do not complain. The uninitiated do.'

> '. . . No one could argue that twenty or more similar compounds were all individually necessary. The problem is that any artificial limitation on multiplication of this sort may prevent a particularly useful medicine reaching the market. More seriously, it would distort the necessary competitive structure of the industry.'

> 'Apparently unnecessary duplication of medicines is, however, admittedly a market imperfection in Utopian terms. But taking a broader view, it is an economic price which is justified by the overall pattern of therapeutic achievement from the pharmaceutical industry over the past four decades.'

The industry does not admit to weakness. It emphasises its role in the health-care revolution, and its model contribution to the national economy. The industry provides secure employment for over 70,000 people; it pays a substantial amount in taxes; and by exporting its products, it contributes a net £600 million a year to the UK's balance of trade. The Office of Health Economics (1983) argues in effect that this exempts the industry from both criticism and control.

The OHE emphasises that the industry's success depends on its ability to innovate. In turn, this depends on the industry's willingness to invest, because the process of product innovation is neither certain nor cheap: 'For an organisation to expect even limited success in pharmaceutical innovation . . . it must invest . . . say a minimum of £20 million a year.' Therefore, the industry has to be protected. It cannot be expected to innovate if the climate is not right: 'An industry such as pharmaceuticals which is wholly dependent on innovation for survival must to some extent be sheltered from the unbridled forces of competition' . . . 'it is only in those countries where the government creates a favourable environment for pharmaceutical innovation that substantial numbers of new medicines are developed. A hostile environment is inimical to successful pharmaceutical research.'

The good news from the OHE is that the industry feels that it has been fairly treated by successive governments in Britain, which has allowed the country to share in the pharmaceutical industry's success. The bad news is that the industry is not very happy about the future:

> 'The problem in financing the industry's research can be set out under seven headings . . . excessive regulation, restrictions on prices and profits, erosion of patent protection, the undermining of brand names, restrictions on promotion, pressures on prescribing and consumer criticisms.'

The OHE explains how all of these things hurt the industry, and then comes to the point. 'There is no automatic right for Britain to continue to enjoy the success in pharmaceutical innovation which has contributed so substantially to the national health and the national economy over the past 30 years', but unstinting support for the industry could lead to 'a new upsurge of pharmaceutical innovation in the 1980s and beyond.' 'By the 21st century, cancer may have become a scourge from the past. . . .' On the other hand, continuing criticism of the industry could prove fatal: 'A "cheap drug" policy would seriously damage the interests of British patients. It would delay their access to the latest available medicines which could include treatments for cancer and heart disease.'

What is innovation?

The pharmaceutical industry will make important contributions to health in the future, as it has in the past. But there are limits to what can be achieved, as well as doubts about what we should be aiming for. We could treat everyone much better if we knew or thought more about the drugs we already have. We can already prevent much disease, but we fail to do so. We have a growing community of elderly people, but increasingly fail them. Above all, we tend to ignore and exploit other people's ill-health: all of the criticisms made of the drugs companies and their products apply in the third world, but infinitely more so.

In this context, it is worth mentioning briefly what innovation by the drug industry actually amounts to:

> Two doctors from the UK Department of Health and Social Security (DHSS) analysed the 204 new chemical entities (NCEs) granted product licences between 1971 and 1980. They concluded that NCEs have generally been for diseases which are 'common, largely chronic, and occur principally in the affluent Western society'. They also noted: 'more sadly only one new chemical entity, namely oxamniquine, has been introduced for the treatment of schistosomiasis which is the world's commonest disease'.
> [Griffin J. P., Diggle G. E., 1981]

Partly because of this, but perhaps mainly for other reasons, these authors also concluded that innovation is 'directed toward commercial returns rather than therapeutic need'.

> 'The pattern of introduction on to the United Kingdom market of new chemical entities over the last ten years fully justifies the criticisms levelled at the pharmaceutical industry by Franz Gross (1979) which were as follows:
>
> "Drug research within the pharmaceutical industry is in a critical phase, since it lacks innovating impulses and in many companies beats tracks. . . . Instead of limiting the number of drugs that are qualitatively and quantitatively quite similar to those already available, many drug companies are copying or

> slightly modifying successful therapeutic principles, with the result that an abundance of analogous drugs is offered, not rarely with exaggerated claims for efficacy. We now witness the flood of beta-blockers. . . . We have a plethora of closely related penicillin and cephalosporin derivatives, of topical corticosteroids, of diuretics or of minor tranquillisers . . . the temptation to look for a share of a big cake exceeds all too often rational and scientific reasoning."'

The evidence suggests that at best only about one new drug in ten offers anything that could be described as 'a substantial therapeutic gain'. The exact figure depends both on the classification used; and on which kind of new drugs are included:

- The US Food and Drug Administration rates all drugs approved for marketing as 'A' (important therapeutic gain), 'B' (modest therapeutic gain) or 'C' (little or no therapeutic gain). In the US, during the 1970s, of every 20 new drugs approved, roughly one was rated 'A', 3 were rated 'B', and 16 were found to give little or no gain.

- The ratings for NCEs alone are more encouraging. In 1982, the 28 new chemical entities approved in the US were rated as follows:

Class	*Degree of therapeutic gain*	*No. of* NECS	%
A	important	4	14
B	modest	5	18
C	little or none	19	68

[Source: *Scrip* No.763; 26/1/83; p.10]

- Similar ratings are not generally used in the UK. However, Drs Griffin and Diggle (1981) did assess the degree of innovation in 103 applications for product licences, made between 1973 and 1977, which manufacturers subsequently withdrew. They used the classification designed by Dukes and Lunde (1980):

Fully innovative	4 NCES	4%
Semi-innovative	32 NCES	31%
Non-innovative	67 NCES	65%

Drs Griffin and Diggle also compared the numbers of NCEs granted to different kinds of company. Their figures suggest that the OHE's appeals to patriotism are greatly exaggerated. Many NCEs were developed by companies with a research-base in the UK, but most were not:

Product licence holder	*Number of* NCES (1971–1981)	%
with UK research facility		
British-owned company	30	15
Foreign-owned company	58	28
with no UK research facility		
US-owned company	57	28
EEC-owned company	46	23
European-owned company (outside EEC)	13	6

It is against this background that the industry's objections to criticism must be seen.

Industry under fire

There has been increasing criticism of the drug industry, in the UK and elsewhere, for the reasons outlined in this chapter. No one disputes the real contributions to health that the industry has made, but there is serious and growing concern about the quality and numbers of drugs that are made, and about their promotion and cost. The industry answers such criticism in two main ways:

- It cannot be held responsible for putting right what is wrong, so long as governments license its products and doctors prescribe them. The industry would argue that it makes no difference if it lobbies the government and puts pressure on doctors to prescribe, because the government and doctors hold the ultimate authority.

- The industry does not deny that there are imperfections, but argues that the overall benefits of its operations far outweigh any costs. The benefits include therapeutic and economic advantages, and include therapeutic advances still to come.

Beyond this, the industry has no answers; and can only react to criticism. It does this mainly by giving an overwhelmingly good account of itself. If it fails to convince, it tends to respond first by blustering, and then by fighting back:

- One of the ways in which the industry deals with criticism is to denounce its critics, in particular by questioning their political affiliations. Critics of the industry's operations in developing countries (these notably include Oxfam, War on Want, Social Audit and the International Organisation of Consumers' Unions) have, for example, been identified as members of 'a movement which has as its real goal the redistribution of wealth worldwide and the seizure – by

political force if necessary – of economic power by those with no respect for the profit incentive and the rights of private property on which our society is based.'
[Press statement from the US Pharmaceutical Manufacturers' Association, 28/9/81]

- The industry also has something of a reputation for leaning on publishers. Martin Weitz refers to this in a postscript to his book *Health Shock* [London: Hamlyn, 1982] – which was serialised by the *Daily Mirror*: '"Many newspapers would have been intimidated by the drug industry's barrage of legal and psychological pressure designed to stop publication," admits Michael Hellicar, the *Mirror*'s special writer in charge of serialisation. "Constant phone calls at home, threatening cables and telexes sent to the *Mirror*'s chief lawyer and editor put immense pressure on the newspaper, but this just encouraged us to go ahead." In 25 years of journalism Hellicar said he had never come across an industry so defensive and bullying as the drug industry.'

To some extent, the industry's sensitivity to criticism is understandable. Serious criticism undermines its credibility with prescribers and the public, and also increases the likelihood of government regulation and control. In addition, criticism threatens the almost flawless self-image that the industry has created for itself – and this may explain why some members of the industry are reported (from within) to be utterly demoralised as a result:

> 'There are those working in the industry who are so obsessed by the attacks on it that they doubt whether it can survive into the 21st century.'
> [Office of Health Economics, 1983]

It is difficult to know how to interpret this reaction. Does this mean that people in the industry are simply frustrated – angry about being obstructed when they can see no reason for it? Is this a warning of a future in which criticism of a prosperous industry will be regarded as an economic crime? Or is it perhaps a hopeful sign – a hint that some people recognise that the industry's image of itself cannot automatically be reconciled with the health needs of the real world?

Whichever way, the industry's response to criticism is an important indicator of its willingness and ability to keep its house in order. The industry has to face facts if it is to be trusted to regulate its own affairs.

3 Why are they allowed?

Why do governments allow the wrong kind of medicine? The short answer is that they have to. All governments would prefer to see better drugs more economically prescribed, but there may be compelling reasons for allowing them, regardless of the drugs' usefulness or cost. A government cannot simply insist on having its own way. It must not exceed its legal powers; nor does it have effective power without cooperation from the medical profession and the industry.

This applies to all governments, whatever their politics. Different governments try to achieve different things, but they also share many interests and concerns. All governments have tried to reduce the NHS drug bill, and all of them have operated some form of drug price control. The similarities between governments in controlling drug quality are much greater than any differences between them.

Different governments therefore share many of the same frustrations. No government has made real headway in promoting rational or economic drug use because this could only be done by restricting what companies make and what doctors prescribe. The drug industry would reject this as an attack on free enterprise and the medical profession would see it as a threat to clinical freedom. In the face of this combined opposition, there is not much a government can do.

However, governments have become more or less reconciled to the situation as the industry has grown and contributed more to exports and the economy. Over the years, successive governments have increasingly emphasised their role as the industry's sponsor or partner. The Department of Health itself now spends rather more on promoting the industry's exports than on promoting better prescribing [DHSS, 1980]. The government therefore has a vested and somewhat conflicting interest in the industry's growth because the more the industry earns, the bigger the government's cut.

Machinery of drug control

In the early 1960s, at the time of the thalidomide disaster, 'any drug manufacturer could market any product, however inadequately tested, without having to satisfy any independent body as to its efficacy or its safety' [Kenneth Robinson, Minister of Health 1964–8, quoted by Lesser F., 1980]. The thalidomide affair had the effect of 'softening up the industry' for legislation that was to follow [Kenneth Robinson, quoted by Phillips E. M., 1982; p.18].

The Medicines Act 1968 set up the present drug licensing system, which has affected all products registered after September 1971. The licensing authority, the

(continued on page 54)

DIFFERENT DRUG AUTHORITIES MAY DISAGREE ABOUT HOW DRUGS ARE USED

	UK	USA
Action	*Tranxene is a tranquilliser exhibiting many characteristics of the benzodiazepine group of preparations. Particular features which distinguish* TRANXENE *from other members of this group are the rapid appearance in the blood of the anxiolytic [anxiety-reducing] compound nordiazepam, the maintenance of satisfactory therapeutic effect with once daily administration, and little sedation.*	*Chemically,* TRANXENE *is a benzodiazepine . . . Pharmacologically, clorazepate dipotassium has the characteristics of the benzodiazepines . . .*
Indications	*Relief of all forms of anxiety, tension and agitation in acute and chronic anxiety states.*	TRANXENE *is indicated for the management of anxiety disorders or for the short-term relief of the symptoms of anxiety. Anxiety or tension associated with the stress of everyday life usually does not require treatment with an anxiolytic . . .* *The effectiveness of* TRANXENE *in long-term management of anxiety, that is, more than 4 months, has not been assessed by systematic clinical studies . . .*
Dosage and admin-istration*	*15mg daily, usually administered at night.*	*. . . administered orally in divided doses. The usual daily dose is 26mg.* TRANXENE *. . . may also be administered in a single dose daily at bedtime; the recommended initial dose is 13mg.*
Dosage range	*No information.*	*13–52mg.*
Dosage for elderly patients	*No information.*	*Initiate treatment at a daily dose of 6.5–13mg.*
Use by the young	*Adults only, not generally recommended for children under 12 years.*	*Not recommended for use in patients less than 9 years old.*
Contra-indications	*There are no absolute contra-indications to the use of* TRANXENE.	*Contra-indicated in patients with a known hypersensitivity to the drug, and in those with acute narrow-angle glaucoma.*

* TRANXENE is supplied in the UK as potassium clorazepate. In the other three countries it is supplied as dipotassium clorazepate. Their effects are identical, but 15mg of the dipotassium salt are equivalent to 13mg of the monopotassium salt (M28 p.1518).

	CANADA	AUSTRALIA
Action	*The pharmacological actions of clorazepate are qualitatively similar to those of other benzodiazepines.*	TRANXENE *is a 1,4 benzodiazepine which at different dose levels has the anxiolytic, sedative-hypnotic, muscle relaxant and anticonvulsant properties characteristic of this group.*
Indications	*The symptomatic relief of excessive anxiety or tension in psychoneurotic patients including those with functional somatic complaints.*	*Symptomatic relief of anxiety associated with anxiety neurosis; in other psychoneuroses in which anxiety symptoms are prominent features; and as an adjunct in disease states in which anxiety is manifested.*
Dosage and administration*	*Clorazepate is administered daily in divided doses. The usual daily dose is 26mg.*	*The usual dose is between 13mg and 26mg daily.*
Dosage range	*13–52mg.*	*4.3–52mg.*
Dosage for elderly patients	*Treatment should be initiated with 3.25mg once a day, preferably at night.*	*Treatment should be initiated at 4.3mg–13mg daily.*
Use by the young	*Not recommended for use in patients less than 18 years of age.*	*There is insufficient evidence of safety or efficacy to recommend use in children.*
Contra-indications	*Myasthenia gravis. Known hypersensitivity to benzodiazepines.*	*Myasthenia gravis; known hypersensitivity to the drug; acute narrow angle glaucoma.*

(table continues overleaf)

	UK	USA
Use in pregnancy	*Although* TRANXENE *has been in wide general use for many years, there is no definite evidence of ill-consequence during human pregnancy; animal studies have shown no hazard. Medicines should not be used in pregnancy, especially the first trimester, unless the expected benefit is thought to outweigh any possible risk to the foetus.*	*An increased risk of congenital malformations associated with the minor tranquillisers . . . during the first trimester of pregnancy has been suggested in several studies.* TRANXENE *has not been studied adequately to determine whether it too may be associated with an increased risk of fetal abnormality. Because use of these drugs is rarely a matter of urgency, their use during this period should almost always be avoided.*
Use during lactation	TRANXENE *and its metabolites [breakdown products] are excreted in human milk in minimal quantities.*	TRANXENE *should not be given to nursing mothers since it has been reported that nordiazepam (a metabolite) is excreted in human breast milk.*
Main side effect**	*Drowsiness has occasionally been reported, but does not constitute a major problem.*	*The side effect most frequently reported was drowsiness.*
Other precautions, not referred to in UK Data Sheet		*See opposite.*

** The lower incidence of drowsiness reported in the UK Data Sheet presumably largely reflects the lower recommended dosage, and the administration at night.

	CANADA	AUSTRALIA
Use in pregnancy	*Safety of use in pregnancy has not been established. Therefore clorazepate is not recommended for use during pregnancy or lactation.*	*Safety in pregnancy has not yet been established.*
Use during lactation	*See above.*	*It is not known whether* TRANXENE *or its metabolites are excreted in human milk; therefore, the drug should not be given to nursing mothers.*
Main side effect	*The one adverse effect most frequently reported was drowsiness.*	*Drowsiness, ataxia and forgetfulness were most commonly reported. [Ataxia is lack of muscular coordination: clumsiness is the result.]*
Other precautions, not referred to in UK Data Sheet	*Should not be administered to individuals prone to drug abuse. Withdrawal symptoms have been observed after abrupt discontinuation of drug. Not recommended for the treatment of patients with possible suicidal tendencies. Patients on clorazepate for long periods should have periodic blood counts and liver function tests.*	

Sources:

UK Data Sheet Compendium 1983–84 [London: ABPI, 1983] p.198.
US Physicians' Desk Reference [Oradell N.J.: Medical Economics Co., 1982] p.565.
Canadian Compendium of Pharmaceuticals and Specialities [Ottawa: Canadian Pharmaceutical Association, 1981] p.609.
MIMS Annual, Incorporating the Australian Drug Compendium [Artarmon NSW: IMS Publishing, 1980] p.4.28.

Department of Health (DHSS), is advised on the suitability of drugs by an independent body, the Committee on Safety of Medicines (CSM). The licensing process is carried out in secret. The evidence on which a licence is given or refused is not made public; nor is it very clear what standards the law requires. The Medicines Act gives the authorities great discretion, so their decisions can really only be questioned by the companies concerned:

> '. . . in dealing with an application for a product licence the licensing authority shall in particular take into consideration (a) the safety of medicinal products of each description to which the application relates; (b) the efficacy of medicinal products . . .; and (c) the quality . . .' [s.19]

On the other hand, the Medicines Act very specifically says that the licensing authority must not take into account a product's comparative value. Unless it is less safe than another product used for the same condition, 'the licensing authority shall leave out of account any question whether medicinal products of another description would or might be equally or more efficacious for that purpose' [s.19(2)]. In addition, 'the licensing authority shall not refuse to grant any licence on any grounds relating to the price of any product . . .' [s.20(2)].

When the Medicines Act came into force, there were about 30,000 'finished products' (and another 25,000 'dispensing ingredients') already on the market. These products were given 'Licences of Right'. This meant that they were allowed to stay on the market, though they did later become liable to an appraisal by the Committee on Review of Medicines (CRM), after it was set up in 1975.

The review of these older medicines – which was also required under an EEC Directive – formally began in November 1976. At that time, it was officially estimated that the review would be completed in 'about eight years' [COI, 1976]. The present target date is 1990 and will be difficult to meet. At the end of 1981, the CRM had another 14,000 products to review, but was dealing with only 750 cases a year [Medicines Commission, 1982]. Most of the products criticised in this book for lack of evidence of safety or effectiveness are older products which hold Licences of Right. There are often better alternatives.

Data sheets

The terms of a product licence are not made public. However, the information for prescribers given on a product's Data Sheet must be consistent with the terms of the Licence, and product advertising 'must not be inconsistent with the Data Sheet' [DHSS, MAL 37, undated]. A product's Data Sheet 'is intended as a factual and objective statement about the product and its uses for the information of practitioners' [COI, 1976].

In practice, Data Sheets are often neither factual nor objective, and therefore not as useful as they might seem. They compete with many other sources of drug information, and the evidence suggests that doctors do not find them especially helpful. An industry report on *Sources of information for prescribing doctors in Britain* suggested that only three per cent of doctors consider Data Sheets the most important source of information about products. In this survey, more doctors said they found drug advertisements and 'mailings' more useful [OHE, 1977, p.18]. One reason for this is that Data Sheets for older products may not have been properly checked and, they largely reflect the companies' own views. Data Sheets for products with Licences of Right 'should therefore be regarded as a form of promotional material' [DTB, 1980, 15, 60].

The usefulness of Data Sheets is affected by two other factors. One is that there is often real uncertainty and disagreement about what products should be used for, and how. The other is that the value of information in Data Sheets much depends on the emphasis and tone of the language used. The significance of these two things can be shown by comparing what is said about the same product in Data Sheets (or their equivalent) used in different parts of the world. The Table on pp.50–3 compares the official prescribing information given in the US, Canada, Australia and the UK for a benzodiazepine tranquilliser, TRANXENE (dipotassium clorazepate).

The UK Data Sheet does not do well in this comparison. It appears to over-emphasise small differences between TRANXENE and other benzodiazepines, and to play down evidence of disadvantages and risks. The UK Data Sheet also seems to omit a good deal of useful and important prescribing information (though the drug has a full licence, not a Licence of Right). These shortcomings suggest weakness in the licensing system itself.

Control of drug use

No government readily admits concern about the problems caused by bad drugs, inadequate information and poor prescribing. To do so would mean simultaneously advertising the government's own weakness; alienating the medical profession and the industry; and alarming the public. However, officials from the DHSS have reported through the World Health Organisation that, in the UK: 'Drugs frequently give concern because of their doubtful therapeutic value or undesirable effects [Darby F. J., Greenberg G.; 1979].

Official policy is not to restrict poor drugs, nor to stop poor prescribing. It is 'to help doctors to be reliably informed about drugs and therapeutics and the effect of their own prescribing habits' [H. C. Deb. 19/6/80, c.635w]. This is done in a variety of ways, always with the emphasis on helping the medical profession to help itself. The government is mainly concerned with 'damage control'. It tries to avoid direct responsibility for the quality of prescribing, and to keep at arm's length from the medical profession and the industry, whenever it can:

- The DHSS itself publishes neither assessments of prescribing practice nor evaluations of drugs. Instead it commissions independent research; it also pays for doctors to be sent publications which encourage effective prescribing. These include *The British National Formulary, Prescribers' Journal* and *Drug & Therapeutics Bulletin.*

- The DHSS requires companies to keep records of adverse drug reactions, and can direct companies to report back. But most information on unexpected toxic reactions and side effects is voluntarily reported by doctors to the Committee on Safety of Medicines, under the 'yellow card' system. There is chronic under-reporting (about one report for every two GPs a year): the CSM has issued fewer than fifteen warnings of serious hazards since the yellow card scheme began in 1974.

The Department also arranges meetings 'to discuss prescribing matters' between DHSS Regional Medical Officers (RMOs) and individual prescribers. These contacts tend to be infrequent and low-key: 'choice of treatment is entirely within the general practitioner's discretion and DHSS say that it would be wrong for the RMO to question it in any way. . . . The RMO is . . . positively briefed not to instruct a general practitioner to prescribe one product rather than another' [Monopolies Commission, 1973, p.32]. An RMO would normally make a visit only if routine analysis of his/her prescriptions suggested that the doctor was for some reason conspicuously out of line. An RMO might visit a practice:

- if clearly less suitable drugs (such as barbiturate sedatives) were being prescribed in large quantities (for instance over twice the average for all other prescribers)
- if individual prescriptions otherwise seemed to be unreasonable or unwise. This might be because: 'the combinations on the prescription form appear to be dangerous, the quantities seem unjustifiably large, or the prescription is unusual in some way'
  [Darby F. J., Greenberg G., 1979]
- if certain 'controlled' drugs (drugs liable to abuse) seemed to be excessively prescribed

Lack of information makes it difficult to assess the overall impact of these measures. Information about prescribing in individual practices is not published, and prescribing rates for individual drugs are officially secret. This information is treated as 'commercial in confidence', though much the same information is collected and published (at a price) by commercial market research organisations. In 1983, following a 'Rayner Scrutiny' recommendation, the DHSS said it also was thinking in terms of selling this information.

If this proposal goes ahead, it will set a new precedent for official secrecy, since access to information has never previously been determined by means test. The proposal also seems to conflict with the government's aim of promoting effective prescribing. People cannot really be expected to take an intelligent interest in this, if they are not told what drugs are prescribed:

> 'Economical prescribing results from effective prescribing. I believe this can be achieved only when everyone – doctor and patient alike – adopts a more rational approach to the use of medicines generally.'
> [Dr Gerard Vaughan, Minister of Health: H.C. Deb. 19/6/80 c.635w]

Control of drug costs

Governments try to influence prescribing habits mainly to reduce drug costs. Again, the emphasis is on gentle persuasion, even when DHSS Regional Medical Officers are called on 'to assist GPs in the review of their prescribing':

> 'On those occasions when the RMO is asked to visit doctors with very high prescribing costs, the emphasis should be on support, advice and encouragement to future self-review.'
> [Greenfield, 1982]

Doctors' prescribing (in England) is regularly reviewed by the Prescription Pricing Authority (PPA). The PPA collects all NHS prescriptions and then analyses a sample (0.5 per cent) – enough to identify prescribing costs in individual practices and to compare them with the norm. The PPA routinely tells doctors how their prescribing costs compare with the average for the area. It also homes in on individual practices where costs are 25 per cent or more above the norm.

If the prescribing costs in a practice are much higher than average, the PPA prepares a more detailed report – for example on the individual doctors in a practice. In 80–90 per cent of cases, this is said to be all that is needed to bring a practice's prescribing costs down to within 25 per cent of the average level. In the remaining cases, the PPA may do a more detailed prescribing audit, and the RMO may be called in to help.

In addition, it is official policy to encourage doctors to prescribe drugs by generic ('approved') name. This is done in the name of 'effective prescribing', but its main purpose is to reduce costs. Examples in the list at the end of this report show that if doctors prescribed *out of patent* drugs by generic name, instead of specifying an expensive brand of the identical drug, it could substantially reduce the NHS drug bill. Estimates of possible savings have ranged from about £20 million to £200 million a year. The true figure depends on what is calculated, and on who is counting.

Government estimates of possible savings have proved entirely misleading. In February 1983, the UK Health Minister, Kenneth Clarke, told Parliament: 'If all prescriptions in England in 1981 had been written and dispensed using generic names whenever possible, the saving to the NHS would have been £23 million.' One month later, a Junior Health Minister, Geoffrey Finsberg, told Parliament that the NHS could save £30 million a year if just nine top brands of medicine were prescribed by generic name. He was replying to a question from an MP who had access to figures similar to those the DHSS itself had held since mid-1982. These show possible savings – at 1981 prices for England only – of the following kind:

Brand	*Generic name*	*Total saving (£m)*
LASIX	frusemide	6.4
ALDOMET	methyldopa	5.7
INDOCID	indomethacin	3.8
MOGADON	nitrazepam	3.4
INDERAL	propranolol	2.8
PENBRITIN	ampicillin	2.8
VALIUM	diazepam	2.7
DISTALGESIC	dextropropoxyphene/paracetamol	2.0
MAXOLON	metoclopramide	1.8

Other estimates vary partly because different things have been calculated and different assumptions made. For example:

- The government and industry usually calculate savings on the basis of 'net ingredient cost' or manufacturers' prices, but the total cost to the NHS (which includes dispensing costs) is about 25 per cent higher.
- Estimates made for savings in the UK are about 25 per cent higher than estimates for England only. Estimates also vary because calculations are made for different years: a saving of £30 million in 1981 may easily be a £40 million-plus saving in 1984.
- Substantial variations can be expected when different pricing information is used. For example, in early 1983, the anti-depressant drug imipramine was available at at least three different prices (for 500 tablets × 25mg):

Cheapest version (Evans Medical)	£1.50
Official Drug Tariff price	£2.40
Most expensive brand (TOFRANIL)	£16.25

- Higher estimates of possible savings from generic substitution usually take into account savings that could be made if there were generic equivalents for all widely prescribed out-of-patent drugs. The assumption is that a national policy of generic substitution would lead to the introduction of many cheaper brands, which do not now exist. To give one example: LOMOTIL is the only available brand of the constipating agent diphenoxylate (with atropine) though it has been out of patent for over a decade, and sales to the NHS exceed

£1 million a year. Even if doctors prescribe LOMOTIL by its generic name, the NHS has to pay the going rate for LOMOTIL itself, which is much higher than the international free-market price because there is no competing generic equivalent.

Uncertainty about possible savings from generic substitution reflects confusion over government policies. It is official policy to encourage generic prescribing, and the use of approved drug names – but it is also official policy not to. Of the two policies, the latter appears to have been the more successful. Over the years, generic prescribing has been decreasing, and for the past decade or more, savings by the NHS have been consistently low.

When the NHS started (1949), the percentage of prescriptions for branded products was 16 per cent of the total. By 1970, the proportion of prescriptions for branded products had increased to just under 80 per cent of the total – and by 1980 to just over 80 per cent of the total. The proportion of prescriptions for unbranded products fell until the mid-1970s, and since then has remained largely unchanged.

Since the mid-1950s, there has been a succession of government reports recommending prescribing by generic name. The most important of these recommended simply that 'there should be no brand names for new pharmaceutical products' and that 'all such products, whether the subject of patents or not, should be marketed only under a name approved by the [Medicines] Commission' [Sainsbury, 1967]. The most recent recommendation was made in the report of the Informal Working Group on Effective Prescribing [Greenfield, 1982]. The Greenfield Report suggested a compromise:

> 'We consider that many doctors would be quite content for their patients to receive an alternative version of the drug prescribed, but that they tend to prescribe the proprietary brand with which they are most familiar. We therefore suggest the introduction of a simple scheme which would require doctors to indicate a positive preference for the proprietary version by initialling a box provided for that purpose on the FP10 (the prescription form). In the absence of the doctor's initials, and assuming that an alternative "generic" version exists, the pharmacist would be expected to dispense the approved name preparation and would be paid according to the basic price indicated in the Drug Tariff. This could bring about a significant change in the pattern of prescribing which would result in savings to the NHS.'

The government's response to this proposal is worth considering in detail. Why did the government not seize the opportunity to make savings? Why did it dismiss the Greenfield proposal, when the national drug bill was highly inflationary and clearly contributing to the deterioration of the NHS?

By the middle of 1984 the NHS drug bill (UK total) can be expected to be close to £2,000 million a year.

HOW DRUG COSTS HAVE RISEN

	Cost of drug ingredients	*Cost per* NHS *prescription*	*No. of* NHS *prescriptions*
1978	+ 19.9	+ 16.0	+ 3.9
1979	+ 14.2	+ 15.0	− 0.8
1980	+ 20.6	+ 20.8	− 0.4
1981	+ 13.9	+ 15.5	− 1.1
1982	+ 15.1	+ 10.8	+ 3.8

(The figures indicate the percentage change on the previous year.)

Generic *v* branded drugs

Had it been left to the government alone to respond to the Greenfield report, there is no doubt that the proposal on generic substitution would have been accepted. No government passes up the opportunity to save even tens of millions of pounds a year. Therefore the government's response was not to the proposal itself, but to the reaction to the proposal by others.

The medical profession gave no indication that it welcomed the proposal on generic substitution, but at least it was prepared to consider it. However, an outright objection was never likely either: the profession accepts the need to reduce the drug bill, and the Greenfield Committee took full account of its views on how this should happen. Of the twelve members of the Committee, eleven were doctors – one of them an Under-Secretary of the British Medical Association.

The pharmaceutical industry's views were not directly represented on the Greenfield Committee, perhaps because they were already well known. It was predictable that the Association of the British Pharmaceutical Industry (ABPI) should campaign vigorously against the proposal on generic substitution. The ABPI's campaign began from the time the report was presented to the Secretary for Health, and continued well after the time the Greenfield report was finally published a year after it had been received.

During the twelve months in which the government was considering the implications of this 5,000-word report, Parliament was neither consulted nor even informed. There was some publicity and some questioning in the House because the most controversial Greenfield proposal had been leaked, and there was telling criticism of government policy (secrecy and apparent inaction), notably in *The Guardian* by Andrew Veitch, and in the House by the then SDP spokesman on Health, Mike Thomas MP. But there was no 'public response' as such.

The evidence suggests the government never intended to publish the Greenfield report. When it eventually did so, the Secretary for Social Services (Norman Fowler MP) made only a short statement. He acknowledged the need to weigh up the pros and cons of generic substitution, and announced: 'I am therefore seeking the views of interested organisations . . . I have asked for comments by 15 April' [DHSS Press Release 83/29, 4 February 1983]. This could be taken to mean that the consultation process began in February 1983, but the evidence suggests that there had already been consultation, and that the government had already decided not to accept the Greenfield recommendation, by October 1982.

The (confidential) minutes of the ABPI's half-yearly general meeting held on 14 October 1982 suggest that the industry may not have been sent a copy of the Greenfield report, but it was nevertheless invited to express its views on it:

> 'A matter of importance which had been in the background during the year concerned the report of an official working party which was rumoured to contain a recommendation that generic substitution by pharmacists should be permitted. Inevitably this would become associated with Government attempts to contain expenditure on the National Health Service.
>
> 'The industry's views had been made clear to the Secretary of State for Social Services and the Minister of State for Health. The principal concerns were the economic consequences, the net financial loss to the nation and the effects on research. A further meeting was to be held with the Minister. It was hoped that substitution would not be permitted but Ministers wanted to be able to show that costs of medicines were being constrained.'

The government's conclusions on the Greenfield proposal were effectively made known four months before the report was published, in a speech made in Malta on October 29, by Dr B A Wills, the DHSS Chief Pharmacist. Dr Wills said he was speaking in a personal capacity, but had his remarks not been authorised by the Department, he would have been liable to prosecution under the Official Secrets Acts. If there had been any risk of embarrassing Ministers, Dr Wills would not have been allowed to speak at all. The report of his speech in the pharmaceutical newsletter SCRIP [No.747, 22/11/82 p.1] began as follows:

> 'Observers believe that on the basis of the recent "personal" views expressed by the UK DHSS Chief Pharmacist . . . they now have a clear insight into the UK government's attitude to generic substitution. . . . Dr Wills . . . said that because of a variety of problems associated with generic substitution, it is not the best way of controlling NHS medicine costs.'

Dr Wills's main concern was over guaranteeing the quality of generic drug supplies. He suggested that if generics became widely used, drugs would increasingly be supplied by a variety of foreign and other firms, whose quality control arrangements could not be properly checked. The Greenfield report considered the same question. As Dr Greenfield and three other members of the working group were senior officials in the DHSS, they would have known about the obstacles that concerned Dr Wills. However, the working group came to the opposite conclusion:

> 'We are . . . aware of the commercial pressures on the doctor when a drug manufacturer draws attention to the advantages of a branded product in terms of quality and efficacy over its unbranded equivalent. We have made some enquiries about the present arrangements for checking these criteria under the provisions of the Medicines Act and we are satisfied that standards are sufficiently high for prescribers in this country not to have to take them into account.'

The pharmaceutical industry's campaign against generic substitution also emphasised the problem of product quality (see the box at the foot of the page). The ABPI acknowledged that 'monetary savings are a laudable objective, which we must support', but its main message was to warn of 'far-reaching and damaging effects on the welfare of patients, the national economy and even on the practice of medicine – effects which would be indefinite in duration and largely irreversible'. An ABPI briefing paper, widely circulated in the week before the publication of the Greenfield report, criticised the proposal for generic substitution under the following headings:

'FOR DOCTORS AND PATIENTS

a) No control of medication
b) No confidence in product quality
c) Decreased patient compliance and confidence
d) Loss of support for errors and problems
e) Loss of information and technical services
f) UK-based medical research discouraged'

It is fair to say that there are technical obstacles to the main Greenfield proposal, but there is no reason to think that they could not be overcome. Generic substitution has been established practice in UK hospitals for some time, and with appropriate safeguards would certainly be feasible in the community. The question is not can it be done, but is it worth making it happen?

Cheap is nasty?
'The Association of the British Pharmaceutical Industry (ABPI) has warned that a switch to generics would result in the market being flooded by cheap imports from Italy and Eastern Europe.'
[*The Guardian*, 5/3/83, p.3]

The industry argues that generic substitution is not worth it because in the end the economic costs would outweigh the benefits. The ABPI suggests that it would lead to 'drastic reductions of sales, exports and all activities of the UK pharmaceutical industry', and also threatens that the industry might pull out:

> 'An inevitable consequence of this situation would be loss of confidence in the UK market by industry with a gradual reduction of its investment in research and manufacturing in the UK in favour of countries where there is a more stable environment without erosion of product rights.'
> [Memorandum on the Greenfield report, submitted to the Secretary of State for Social Services by the ABPI, January 1983]

However, it must be appreciated that the ABPI is arguing not about a national policy, but about the interests of an *international* industry. The industry's real concern is not about what happens in Britain, but about Britain setting an example which other countries might follow. The industry knows perfectly well that if generic substitution were introduced only in the UK it would make little or no difference to its economic health. If Britain did adopt such a policy, the industry would hardly be affected, because its profitability is effectively guaranteed under the terms of the government's arrangements for drug price control.

Prescription price regulation

Since the early days of the NHS, successive governments have tried to control costs by negotiating drug prices with the industry. Over the same period, there have been successive enquiries into drug prices by the House of Commons Public Accounts Committee (PAC) and other independent bodies. The first PAC report on drug prices was in the Session 1950–1. Every enquiry since then has found serious weaknesses in the price control arrangements, and has concluded that drug industry profits have been excessive. A major enquiry early in 1983 found that the return on capital for the pharmaceutical companies was over 5 per cent higher than the average for industry generally, and increasing in spite of the recession.

Parliamentary and other criticism has led to the introduction of successive price control schemes. The first attempt (1951–3) proved 'largely fruitless' [Sainsbury, 1967; p.27]. This was followed by the first Voluntary Price Regulation Scheme (VPRS) which ran from 1957–64; and by a modified VPRS from 1964. The Sainsbury Committee (1967) considered that this scheme had 'serious weaknesses', and the Public Accounts Committee (1978) concluded that drug prices should be 'brought down to a satisfactory level without delay'. The second VPRS ended in 1969. At the end of that year, *The Economist* [22/11/69; p.77] reported that the return on capital earned by the pharmaceutical industry was seven per cent above the industrial average. A revised VPRS was introduced in 1969. It was revised again in 1972, and finally replaced in 1978 by the Pharmaceutical Price Regulation Scheme (PPRS). Following Parliamentary criticism of the 1978 scheme, a new PPRS was introduced in late 1983.

The DHSS considers that the 1969 VPRS represented a major departure from the earlier schemes. According to the Department, it established the principle on which negotiations between the government and the industry have been based ever since:

> 'The 1969 VPRS replaced the last of a series of earlier schemes which had attempted, with disappointing results, to regulate the prices of individual medicines by price comparisons. . . . The 1969 VPRS was operated (as is the PPRS) on the basis that – since the Health Departments are the purchasers of virtually all prescribed medicines in the UK – if a company's overall costs and profits in supplying such medicines are reasonable, the prices of individual medicines supplied by the company are not in themselves significant.'
> [DHSS private communication 25/7/80]

However, the Sainsbury Committee report suggests that negotiations in the 1960s were also usually conducted on an 'overall profitability' basis, and that the VPRS was the weaker for it. The implication is that essentially the same scheme has operated for 20 years or more, with essentially the same defects:

> 'In practice, we understand that most negotiations are on this "overall profitability" basis, because of the difficulties which the Ministry has so far found in the costing of individual products. We consider that an examination of the reasonableness of overall profits without a detailed examination of the prices of individual medicines is inadequate . . .'
> [Sainsbury, 1967, p.51]

By 1983, the Department was in fact no longer regulating either the prices of individual products or even the profitability of individual companies. Enquiries by the Comptroller and Auditor General (1983) established that the DHSS did not have the resources to check on individual companies, and aimed mainly to control the profitability of the industry as a whole. The Comptroller and Auditor General noted – among other things – 'that DHSS have inadequate evidence to establish objectively the efficiency of the industry'. It does not seem realistic to describe the arrangements between the industry and the government as a price control scheme at all.

Technical difficulties and lack of resources limit the usefulness of the Pharmaceutical Price Regulation Scheme, but its main disadvantage seems to be that it is misconceived as policy. The aims of the PPRS are not in question: the question is whether any single instrument of policy can effectively be used to achieve two entirely separate aims. One objective is to support a strong industry; the other is to control excessive profits, and to some extent they conflict.

The result is a compromise: the PPRS may help to prevent drug prices going sky-high, but only by guaranteeing that they at least get off the ground. The PPRS may stop the industry making an unacceptably high profit, but it also actually stops the drug bill from ever going down. Under the PPRS, the NHS drug bill seems bound to increase at an inflationary rate, unless there is some fundamental change in the way drugs are licensed, used or prescribed.

So long as the industry innovates and has patent protection – and can charge what the market will bear for its products – it can maintain profitability in absorbing losses on some products by charging more for others. This means, for example, that generic substitution could not seriously harm the industry, and would *not* in fact save the country between £20 and £200 million a year. The DHSS has acknowledged this:

> '. . . Pharmaceutical manufacturers do not set the price of individual products in isolation. Rather, they adopt a pricing policy for their entire range of products designed to produce a given return on capital. If sales of a particular branded product declined substantially there could well be a compensating increase in the cost of some other product for which there was no generic equivalent.'
> [DHSS private communication, 9/12/82]

For the same reason, the PPRS completely undermines all other attempts to encourage economic prescribing. For instance, the Prescription Pricing Authority and DHSS Regional Medical Officers may well succeed in reducing prescribing costs in individual practices, but this has no discernible effect on the national drug bill. The profitability of individual companies may be affected by some clamp-down, but this would not affect the profitability of the industry as a whole. Under the PPRS, the main yardstick is the profitability of the whole industry, so if some companies make less profit, it leaves other companies free to make more.

There are signs that government recognises that this position is untenable, and that the DHSS has considered ways of correcting what is wrong. For example, in mid-1982, the DHSS began to explore the possibility of ending its 'sponsorship' of the industry, and of handing over this responsibility to the Department of Trade:

> 'According to industry sources, evidence of the new "distancing policy" has come from a number of sources and events in recent weeks, particularly in the course of the informal industry meeting with the new health minister, Kenneth Clarke, which took place in early July. The industry delegation came away from the discussions "most concerned", one company senior executive told *Scrip*. One member of the DHSS team is reported to have described the PPRS as "quite a cosy arrangement" at one stage in the discussions, which, given the fact that the scheme is the cornerstone of the sponsor relationship and is to be negotiated before March 1983, was regarded as "a somewhat ominous remark".'
> [*Scrip* No.716; 4/8/82; p.1]

Eight months later, at a private lunch with senior people in the industry, Kenneth Clarke confirmed his view that the DHSS should not continue to sponsor the industry but should operate mainly as a purchasing department. The report in *Scrip* [27/4/83] said:

> 'It was explained to Mr Clarke by the company representatives that the sponsorship role of the DHSS had served both parties well. It ensured that domestic NHS drug decisions took into account the possible international consequences and had resulted not only in the development of a strong UK-based industry but also a highly favourable balance of trade that now amounted to almost 60 per cent of NHS drug costs.
>
> 'It was also made clear to Mr Clarke, *Scrip* understands, that a number of the executives present would strongly oppose any change in the sponsorship arrangements. If the DHSS as monopolistic buyer acted solely as a purchasing agency, they said, the risk was great that decisions could be taken which would seriously undermine confidence in Britain as a base for multinational pharmaceutical firms, and much of the good that had been achieved would rapidly be demolished. Mr Clarke was, reportedly, surprised by the strength of the industry feeling on the issue.'

The minister should not have been surprised, either at the industry's reaction, or by the fact that his proposed 'distancing policy' was later vetoed. British government policy is that medicines should help people *and* the national economy to get better and stay well: too bad if these objectives conflict.

4 Why are they prescribed?

Why do doctors prescribe the wrong kind of medicine? The short answer is that they are bound to. Doctors would not willingly prescribe against either their own or others' better professional judgement, but they are under irresistible pressure to do so. Part of it is self-imposed: 'clinical freedom' means that the prescriber's own judgement is best, and effectively beyond criticism, unless it is plainly very bad. The wrong kind of medicine is also a natural response to the demands on doctors to heal, to manage, to learn, and to please. It has been suggested that medicine has gone profoundly wrong because these demands so far exceed what either physicians and/or drugs can supply:

> 'A professional and physician-based health care system that has grown beyond critical bounds is sickening for three reasons: it must produce clinical damage that outweighs its potential benefits; it cannot but enhance even as it obscures the political conditions that render society unhealthy; and it tends to mystify and to expropriate the power of the individual to heal himself and to shape his or her environment. Contemporary medical systems have outgrown these tolerable bounds.'
> [Illich, 1977]

The nub of it is 'clinical freedom' – the licence that doctors have to practise medicine with strictly limited liability. Clinical freedom remains to this day the excuse for bad medicine, but is justified because it has also helped medicine to improve. If doctors had not had this almost unchallengeable power, they could not have generated the faith that made at least some of their treatments work. Without clinical freedom, medicine might not have progressed at all.

Clinical freedom has enabled doctors to believe that if a patient did not get better, it was in spite of treatment and not because of it. If doctors had not been able to operate on this basis, continued illness would somehow have been seen as the doctor's fault. This would have put doctors under crushing personal, professional, and financial pressure, and medicine would have ground to a halt.

Clinical freedom has undoubtedly helped innovation in medicine. It has allowed doctors access to the human body and has encouraged them to try new healing techniques. Clinical freedom has also meant freedom from criticism, which has ensured gratifyingly good results, often regardless of the treatment used:

> 'A Dr Raymond at the Salpêtrière in Paris found 70 per cent of patients suffering from a variety of diseases, including tabes [a wasting disease], were treated successfully by suspending them by their feet, causing the blood to flow into their heads. A collaborator of Bernheim at Nancy reversed the procedure and suspended the patient's head upwards and obtained a similar per cent success in a variety of organic and nervous diseases.'
> [Volgyesi, 1954]

The crunch came first with the development of genuinely useful drugs (mainly in the last three or four decades), and later (even now) with the discovery and growing use of testing techniques which can reliably distinguish between treatments which do and which do not work. For doctors, these developments have been a mixed blessing.

Doctors now have potentially far greater healing power than ever before, though with this power there is increased responsibility to account for their actions if their treatments fail to work. Even in general practice, clinical freedom is therefore now under some threat. Clinical freedom survives, though it has been suggested recently from within the profession that the end is nigh:

> 'Clinical freedom is dead, and no one need regret its passing', according to a leading article in the *Brit. Med. J.* (29 October 1983; 287, 1237–8). The article, by J. R. Hampton, professor of cardiology at Nottingham University Hospital, concludes that: 'Clinical freedom died accidentally, crushed between the rising cost of new forms of investigation and treatment and the financial limits inevitable in an economy that cannot expand indefinitely. Clinical freedom should, however, have been strangled long ago, for at best it was a cloak for ignorance and at worst an excuse for quackery. Clinical freedom was a myth that prevented true advance. We must welcome its demise, and seize the opportunities now laid out before us.'

The implications of this are enormous, not least because a commitment to rational and economic medicine implies a corresponding loss of faith in medicine, by patients and practitioners alike. The very recent, very rapid advance of medical science has meant erosion of the healing power which has traditionally made medicine work.

The placebo response

For 2,000 years or more, the credibility of medical practitioners depended solely on faith. Many medicines, if not most, were positively harmful, so any benefit to the patient was usually the result of the suggestion and hope that the treatment would work. If a treatment seemed successful, it was often because patients got better in spite of it. They were actually helped to get better by believing that they would get better; and/or because magic really works:

> *On Warts . . .*
> 'The strangest thing about warts is that they tend to go away. Fully grown, nothing in the body has so much the look of toughness and permanence as a wart, and yet, inexplicably and often very abruptly, they come to the end of their lives and vanish without a trace. . . .
> Not everyone believes this, but the evidence goes back a long way and is persuasive . . . I was once told by a distinguished old professor of medicine . . . that it was his practice to paint gentian violet [a brilliant violet-coloured antiseptic dye] over a wart and then assure the patient firmly that it would be gone in a week, and he never saw it fail. There have been several meticulous studies by good clinical investigators, with proper controls. In one of these, fourteen patients with seemingly intractable generalised warts on both sides of the body were hypnotised, and the suggestion was made that all the warts on one side of the body would begin to go away. Within several weeks the results were indisputably positive; in nine patients, all or nearly all of the warts on the suggested side had vanished, while the control side had just as many as ever.'
> [Thomas L.; 1979]

This is a dramatic example of the placebo effect: the tendency of anything given and/or taken as medicine to do what is expected of it. It is not clear why it works. It is clear only that it does work, and that, because of it, physicians have enjoyed a highly respected place in the community for hundreds if not thousands of years.

The classic placebo or 'dummy drug' is a pharmacologically inert substance now routinely used in clinical trials as a yardstick against which to measure the effects of something else. Such trials have established that the placebo response affects the way in which active drugs work, and that it makes chemically inactive treatments work too. The placebo effect is extremely subtle and often dramatic. It is predictable and universal too:

- 'Reactions to placebos may involve practically any organ system in the body. For example, placebos provide relief in cases of angina pectoris, rheumatoid and degenerative arthritis, pain, hay fever, headache, cough, peptic ulcer and essential hypertension. In a review of fifteen studies (including seven of his own), Beecher found that an average 35.2% ± 2.2% of 1,082 patients investigated benefited from placebo treatment . . . With placebo treatment in psychiatric patients, anxiety and tension decrease, depression is alleviated and patients with schizophrenia respond positively. Comparison of supportive psychotherapy to placebo therapy in patients, most of whose diagnoses were psychoneuroses, showed similar lessening of symptoms. In fact, supportive psychotherapy has been depicted as being quite similar to the placebo effect.'
  [Benson H., Epstein M., 1975]

- 'A class experiment for medical students was devised to demonstrate the influence of the placebo effect and non-drug factors on response to drugs. The subjects were conditioned to expect sedative or stimulant effects, but all received placebo in one or two blue or pink capsules. Predictions about the size and nature of the placebo response and influence of the non-drug factors were made before the experiment and discussed afterwards. Four of six predictions were fully confirmed. Drug-associated changes were reported by 30 per cent of the subjects and were severe in 1 or 2 individuals. Two capsules produced more noticeable changes than one, and blue capsules were associated with more sedative effects than pink capsules. Students rated the experiment highly both as a learning experience and for its relevance to their future practice of medicine.'
  [Blackwell B. et al., 1972]

In Latin, 'placebo' means 'I will please' – and doctors try to. Analysis of prescriptions in the UK suggests that perhaps one-third of all drugs are prescribed for their placebo effect [*Brit. Med. J.* 23/5/70; *Lancet* 15/7/72]. However, doctors rarely if ever prescribe inert drugs, in spite of the evidence that they work.

There are many possible reasons for this: unease about the ethics of duping patients and prescribing nothing is certainly one. But perhaps the underlying reason is lack of confidence: if a doctor feels that some vitamin or tonic is not going to work, it will not work. Placebos work only when both parties are pleased:

> 'It worries me a bit. Some of my patients come with no real symptoms – I call it "non-disease". They come in because they get some sort of reassurance sitting out there, being called over the Tannoy (loudspeaker) system, coming in here towards the throne, sitting here for a while and receiving some token for coming. If they are elderly or not very bright, to explain to them that the medicine you are giving them is not really doing anything and that they are being given it because you don't think anything is wrong with them, would destroy them. So as a matter of course, you diagnose and prescribe.'
> [Dr 'E', quoted by Comaroff, 1976]

Doctors are human too

For this reason, the placebos used in general practice tend to be active agents but with little therapeutic value. They may be prescribed for any number of reasons, most of which, ultimately, are seen as a response by doctors to patient demand.

Some patients come to doctors with insoluble personal problems, and seem to want tranquillisers or other 'obscuring' drugs to take the pain away. Others seem to expect a prescription as a ratification of a diagnosis, or just to confirm that they are ill. It has been suggested that some patients need to be ill to cope with a sense of failure – for example, after a separation or on becoming unemployed: 'to prove illness, so that one may be cared for, is then a vital necessity' [Berle B. B., 1958]. A patient may even ask for a potent drug for what is evidently not a medically serious condition, and a good doctor may still feel compelled to please:

> 'The patient was a plump and pleasant woman of 52 who asked for diuretics [used to remove excess fluid from the body]. She had bought a dress for her daughter's wedding six months earlier but the wedding had been postponed and she had put on too much weight to get into the dress comfortably any longer. I gave her two frusemide tablets – one to rehearse with and one for the big day.'
> [Harris C. quoted in Open University, 1982, p.16]

But there is more to prescribing than patient demand. Experienced doctors recognise that many other factors may encourage prescribing, even when there is no pharmacological justification for it. Commenting on his experience as a GP, Ryde [quoted in Open University, 1982, p. 15] suggests eight motives of this kind:

- to temporise, through uncertainty or insecurity – that is, play safe medically or legally
- to terminate a consultation when busy, tired or bored
- to impress or mystify patients or role-play as a proper doctor
- prescribing on instruction from one's principal
- compliance on the part of the doctor to the demands of the patient
- sheer habit
- to make the consultation 'official', so justifying it
- to persuade patients to remain on the doctor's list.

Commercial influence on prescribing has not been included here but it has been shown to be strong and tends to be strongly denied. This omission from the list suggests a contract between doctors and drug companies that in some ways parallels the relationship between doctors and their patients. In both cases, the supplier of the medicine offers power (to heal and/or please) in exchange for loyalty and a belief that the drug can work.

Doctors increasingly depend on the drug companies as the source of their healing power. The companies provide new and sometimes better drugs. They inspire in doctors the hope and confidence that their products will work, if not with hard evidence of their effectiveness, then with partial information, and by pleasing. The companies court doctors with hospitality and offer little gifts or placebos. The companies make doctors feel valued and important: they understand and reassure and please.

Nevertheless, the companies seem to defer to doctors and indulge them rather in the spirit in which doctors do the same to patients. The manual used by the Dista sales force to sell Opren suggests an ambivalence towards doctors that other drug companies probably also feel:

> 'Sales reps were instructed to keep the Opren story as simple as possible: "GPS don't understand the highly technical data on the arthritis inflammatory process," the Company told its salesmen. "Even though they talk about PSI activity" (that's an aspect of the illness) "they don't really understand it." "Remember," salesmen were told, "sell the product benefits, not the science."'
> [PANORAMA, BBC-TV, 17/1/83]

How well informed?

It would take the average layman only a few minutes to learn more about effective drug use than any doctor would have known at the turn of this century. Even 20 or 30 years ago, there was widespread misunderstanding among doctors of principles and characteristics of drug use that seem basic today. Most of the following were learned by doctors only very recently, and some are still sinking in:

- the variation in and the subtlety of the individual's response to drugs
- the need to avoid drug use in pregnancy, unless there are compelling reasons for it
- the significance of drug-induced disease, the nature of drug interactions and of unwanted effects
- the wider significance of prescribing and the importance of suggestion
- the desirability of using a drug only when one has to.

Until the middle of the 20th century, doctors could not have been properly taught why and how drugs worked. Most drugs worked in mysterious ways, and there were no generally accepted procedures for reliably measuring drug effectiveness. The results from clinical trials were – and often still are – ruined by bias and procedural errors. And until the 1960s – in the wake of the thalidomide disaster – there was no effective control of drugs at all.

Doctors were not, and still are not, taught to prescribe effectively. The emphasis in the training of doctors is still very much on diagnosis – on learning how the body works and how it responds to disease. Medical students do learn how to manage different diseases, and how to use different drugs when doing so. But they are still taught very little about the principles of drug use and drug effects and are not taught much about assessing the efficacy and safety of drugs in clinical trials.

The Greenfield report on effective prescribing recognised this, suggesting that, in future, medical students be given *basic* training both in pharmacology (the study of medicinal drugs) and in therapeutics (curing):

> 'We believe that the *pre-clinical years* should provide an introduction to the general aspects of drug action, absorption, excretion and metabolism . . . The aim would be to show the link between physiology, pharmacology, and therapeutics.'
> [Greenfield, 1982]

The Greenfield report also made recommendations for the training of post-graduates: 'We are concerned about the absence of any agreed approach to post-graduate education.' And the report noted that 'there is no agreed plan for the teaching of therapeutics' to general practitioners:

> 'We consider that prescribing should have a higher priority in vocational training. There are strong reasons to put forward to support this argument: the increasing incidence of iatrogenic disease [disease caused by doctors or medicine], particularly in elderly patients; the frequency of prescriptions given in a high proportion of GP consultations resulting in high and sometimes unnecessary cost to the NHS; the need for trainees to understand that there are alternatives to a prescription which should be considered; and its attraction as a subject for review by the individual doctor.'
> [Greenfield, 1982]

The Greenfield Committee only touched on the question of commercial influence on prescribing. The report recognised the need for alternative sources of information, but is ambiguous in explaining why: 'With constant developments in drugs and therapeutics, doctors can soon become out of touch. It is clearly important that they should be in a position to assess the data presented to them by the drug companies.' This ambiguity may be intentional: although drug companies swamp doctors with propaganda in favour of their drugs, they also provide a good deal of information that doctors want and need.

In the 1950s, the companies were 'virtually the sole source' of information and education about drugs [OHE, 1977; p.23]. There are now alternative sources, though very few that are fully independent of the industry. The following data came from a survey carried out for the Sainsbury Committee enquiry in 1967. Surveys carried out since substantially confirm these results but if anything suggest that doctors' reliance on drug company representatives has increased [OHE, 1977, p.19]:

SOURCES OF INFORMATION WHICH MOST INFLUENCE GENERAL PRACTITIONERS' PRESCRIBING HABITS

Source	*Per cent*
Drug firm representatives	29
Recommendations from consultants	27
Articles in journals	12
Drug firm literature	10
Professional contacts with other doctors	8
Advertisements in journals	1
Drug firm meetings	1
Other sources	10
Don't know	2

Less is known about the sources of information doctors use during a consultation, for example to select one of several possible drugs, or to check on how the drug should be used. The evidence there is predates the introduction in 1981 of the revised version of the *British National Formulary*, which is probably used much more than the earlier version. However, in the mid- to late 1970s, by far the most popular source of information was MIMS (*Monthly Index of Medical Specialities*). MIMS is supported entirely by drug advertising and sent free to doctors and pharmacies each month. It lists only branded medicines and gives very abbreviated prescribing information about each. MIMS has been, and almost certainly still is, excessively relied on.

A survey of information sources used by 450 doctors [Eaton G.; Parish P., 1977] found that three out of four doctors used MIMS not only to select a drug for treatment, but also to check on adverse reactions and contra-indications. The authors reported:

> 'MIMS does not in fact list adverse effects. In recent years, entries on contra-indications and special precautions have increased, but these are far from complete. It cannot be regarded as an appropriate source of such information.'

The industry regularly surveys doctors' attitudes to different information sources. It finds that doctors appreciate the information that companies give: 'There is no suggestion that doctors consider that the industry's role has been superseded by the education and information on new medicines which is now available from other sources' [OHE, 1977; p.23]. Independent assessors confirm the dependence of doctors on industry sources of information, but question how desirable it is:

> 'The medical profession has not quite succumbed to accepting drug companies as principal therapeutic advisers. The traditional safeguard of "group acceptance" is being maintained. To date, the profession is still able to act as an umbrella for individual prescribers allowing each to pursue his own idiosyncrasies. . . . The fundamental issue which these suggestions raise for the medical profession is how it can continue to retain legitimation of itself by itself.'
> [Eaton G.; Parish P., 1977]

What is prescribed?

Most doctors over-prescribe. In a few practices, the proportion of consultations ending with a prescription may be as low as 15 per cent, but the average is estimated at about five times higher [Mapes R. (Ed), 1980]. Doctors associate above-average rates of prescribing mainly with pressure to prescribe from patients. Patients expect to be pleased:

> 'I would say that I prescribe in 95 per cent of my consultations. That sounds high; it is high. Not all of these prescriptions are warranted in medical terms. You see, out here in Wales at least, when people go to the doctor they expect a prescription. Even if you gave them a bottle of aspirin on prescription it would have a high therapeutic value. You can't always call this a placebo, but I'd say that the placebo effect was about 50 per cent. It's very important that everybody gets a prescription. I very rarely prescribe a placebo though. Most of the things I give have a therapeutic effect of some kind. But for some of them it is the placebo effect rather than the therapeutic effect that is more important.'
> [Dr A: quoted by Comaroff J.; 1976]

Other doctors in the same series of interviews emphasised that placebos prescribed by GPs are anything but the disguised sugar pills given as control drugs in clinical trials. Potent and potentially dangerous drugs may be prescribed, not because they are needed, but because they are thought to please:

> 'It's not just rubbish that one gives in most cases. For example, if they complain of a sore throat, I generally give penicillin. It's unnecessary in most cases, but one could turn out to be a streptococcal infection, which could have serious consequences.'
> [Dr K]

> 'A lot of these psychological conditions are really untreatable – brought about by social circumstances that you cannot change. I mean one can't really solve social situations which have developed over years with a few hours of chat. It's pompous to think that you can. You just uncover a mess that you can't clear up. You can't change these circumstances by giving pills either, but you

> can influence people to an extent by giving them faith in an anti-depressant. I think that's a good thing. But I'm a bit sceptical about the actual effects of these sorts of drugs.'
> [Dr H]

There is much evidence that patients put doctors under pressure to prescribe – also that doctors over-estimate their patients' expectations of a prescription [Stimson, 1975]. It has also been established that up to 20 per cent of patients do not get their prescriptions dispensed [Rashid A. 1982]; and many others obtain their drugs but do not take them [Anderson R. J., 1980; Silas J. H. et al., 1980]. One explanation may be that people do want doctors to prescribe, but do not necessarily want drugs. Perhaps what people most need – if the prescription is good enough to convey it – is healing information and power.

People want prescriptions partly because they prove the diagnosis. The prescription confirms or challenges people's fears about themselves. It tells them how ill they are, and in some way explains how much better things can get. The prescription conveys the doctor's sympathy, ability and understanding. It defines specifically what can be done, and what cannot be helped. Patients may be reassured by a prescription: it suggests that they have some control over the doctor, and some over their own health.

Doctors may over-estimate the demand for drugs, partly to maintain their own integrity and morale. Doctors need to keep their patients pleased, and may give drugs as a surrogate for the care they would want to but cannot provide. Doctors need to feel power, because not being able to help is often harrowing – and doctors also need to be pleased. Some find pleasure in working with nature; others are pleased to be recognised as forces of nature themselves:

> 'A prevalent cause of irritation in the surgery was the attempt by patients to dictate what they should be prescribed: "If they ask you to prescribe something that they've read about in the *News of the World*, you can't really prescribe it . . . If they select a drug for you to prescribe, you feel that they've short-circuited the approach . . . They've taken communion without going to the altar, as it were. After all, that's what they've come to me for."'
> [Dr L; quoted by Comaroff J.; 1976]

Finally, doctors may over-estimate the demand for prescriptions by way of denying that drugs are over-supplied. The medical profession does not accept that prescribing is over-influenced by pressure from the industry. It would be unethical if it were.

The tables have turned

Commercial influence on doctors' prescribing habits was suddenly forced on the medical profession. It is now very strong, and there is every reason to think it will get even stronger still.

The relationship between doctors and the drug industry began in all-out war. Today's drug industry has been established for no more than 30 years, and 30 years before that the medical profession was trying to strangle the embryonic industry at birth. The medical profession reacted so violently because the new patent medicine companies were ostentatiously competing, luring doctors' patients away. The new companies advertised everywhere, and their products cured everything. All the patient had to do was to pay up, and then take the medicine until the treatment was completed. The companies had learned from the medical profession that the treatment never was completed until the patient was cured.

The British Medical Association responded partly by publishing two reports: *Secret Remedies* (1909), and *More Secret Remedies* (1912). These classic reports led to the first serious attempt to control medicine advertising. They exposed vile medicines and gross fraud.

Patients' rights and the quality of care have since been transformed. Everything has changed, except perhaps the extent of secrecy in medicine, and the identity of those in the know. *Secret Remedies* begins with a few lofty remarks about this:

> 'To begin with, there is for the average man or woman a certain fascination in secrecy. The quack takes advantage of this common foible of human nature to impress his customers. But secrecy has other uses in his trade; it enables him to make use of cheap new or old-fashioned drugs, and to proclaim that his product possesses virtues beyond the ken of the mere doctor; his herbs have been culled in some remote prairie in America or among the mountains of Central Africa, the secret of their virtues having been confided to him by some venerable chief; or again he would have us believe that his drug has been discovered by chemical research of alchemical profundity and is produced by processes so costly and elaborate that it can only be sold at a very high price.' [BMA 1909; p.v]

It took the pharmaceutical industry no more than a few decades to persuade the medical profession of the value of its products, and today the fictional 'average' doctor (and receptionist) prescribes the equivalent of about 5 drugs an hour eight hours a day, and for 365 days a year. Of course many of these prescriptions are for genuinely useful drugs – though many, if not most, do not really help the patient at all.

In the meantime, the relationship between doctors and the drug industry is still evolving, and the evidence suggests that the companies will increasingly erode the doctor's power. The trend is clearly towards by-passing doctors (middle-men) and to forging a direct relationship between consumer and drug. The companies emphasise that they are working towards cancer cures and other drugs which will strengthen the doctor's hand, but this is far from the commercial ideal. The ideal product for a drug company is not a prescription-only cancer-cure: it is a drug that is safe enough to be sold in supermarkets and effective enough to prevent or treat everyday ills. The commercial ideal is a drug for everyone, for somehow coping better every day.

There is evidence of the by-passing of doctors in the direct advertising of prescription drugs to consumers, and in the increasing tendency to re-classify prescription drugs as medicines for general sale (see for example: *The Economist*, 3/9/83). But most striking is the increase in 'repeat prescribing'. Perhaps one-quarter of all prescriptions are now collected from the doctor's receptionist by patients who see the doctor maybe once or twice each year (see below).

As many doctors now recognise, the medical profession has tended to lose control of both the supply and the demand for medicine. This shows in the amount and in the quality of what is prescribed.

Quality of prescribing

The average general practitioner prescribes mainly from a list of 200–300 drugs, but has some 6,500 preparations to choose from. To use any one of these products successfully, the prescriber has to size up the patient, and then take stock of a great deal of information about a drug's known and claimed benefits, as well as all the known and possible side effects and drug interactions that may occur.

Evidence on the quality of prescribing is unsatisfactory. Desk analysis is of limited value, because prescription forms give little indication either of the patient's needs or of the doctor's therapeutic intent. However, prescription surveys give some idea of the extent of inappropriate drug use. For example:

- Of the 25 most frequently prescribed drugs in the US in 1976, eight were authoritatively considered to be pharmacologically or therapeutically questionable. [Knapp D. E., 1978; cited in Smith M. C., 1980]
- In a study of prescriptions for children, in a random sample of 72 GPs in Wessex, it was reported: 'only about 1 per cent (80/6,331) of prescriptions could legitimately be called into question on the basis of current modern specialist teaching, although 42 per cent of the doctors used drugs that have recently been considered to be hazardous or undesirable.' [Catford J.; 1980]
- An analysis of over 50,000 *teaching hospital* prescriptions in the US indicated a higher than 1 in 8 level of over-medication (excessive quantities of drugs and/or frequency of dosage). There was also a significant number of inappropriate combinations of drugs (risk of reduced therapeutic effect and/or harmful drug interaction). [Maronde et al., 1971]

Studies of prescribing habits have been limited partly by lack of basic statistics. Detailed information about how much of what is prescribed is inaccessible: the government keeps it secret ('commercial in confidence') and the price charged by market research firms is prohibitively high. There is also limited research into prescribing because doctors 'are not very willing to talk about their prescribing habits' and the drug industry 'is uncooperative in giving information' [Hemminki E.; 1976]. Nevertheless: 'The list of studies showing inadequate practice is extensive and they are not limited to office [surgery] practice. Hendeles [1976], for example, cited two hospital studies which discovered inappropriate use of antibiotics in over 60 per cent of cases' [Smith M. C.; 1980]. A later study of prescribing in Scottish hospitals supports these findings:

> 'In two-thirds of such patients, there was no good bacteriological evidence that an antibiotic was required. Since 11 per cent of all antibiotic exposures were associated with undesirable side effects, it was concluded that the risks of therapy were greater than the benefit to be expected, at least in a substantial proportion of the patients studied.'
> [Moir D., et al., 1979]

The prescribing of fixed-ratio combination drugs has been criticised mainly because the dosages of the active ingredients cannot be independently adjusted to suit the patient. But doctors have also been criticised because they are not always even able to identify the ingredients in the combination products they prescribe:

> 'The best-known of 23 combinations was correctly identified by only two-thirds of its prescribers; for 7 of the 23 combinations, not a single physician answered correctly. Hospital pharmacists did slightly better.'
> [Report on a pilot survey among 60 Montreal physicians in DTB 1980; 18, 38]

'Repeat' prescriptions – which patients usually get from the receptionist, rather than from the doctor – have also been singled out for criticism. Refills written by receptionists or ancillary staff account for an estimated 25–33 per cent of all prescriptions [Dajda R.; 1980]. A survey of repeat prescriptions by a team of GPs led by a psychiatrist [Balint M. et al.; 1970] concluded that over half the prescriptions examined were inappropriate for the diagnosis.

Current medical opinion

The doctrine of clinical freedom makes it very hard to assess prescribing habits against any hard and fast standards, or even 'best practice', so enquiries into the quality of prescribing tend only to measure what appears to be conspicuously wrong. But there is also uncertainty about 'right' and 'wrong', because 'current medical opinion' about the validity of different treatments changes fairly rapidly over time, and may dramatically change across national borders as well. For example, not all doctors consider that high blood pressure reduces life expectancy:

PRESCRIPTIONS WRITTEN FOR HYPOTENSION (IE TO RAISE BLOOD PRESSURE) IN 1974,
PER ONE MILLION POPULATION

UK	200	Spain	39,000
Holland	4,100	Italy	102,200
Belgium	9,300	Japan	104,400
France	20,900	Germany	154,000

[Source: OHE, 1977; p.10]

The Sainsbury Committee report [1967] gives some idea of the rate at which current national medical opinion changes. A survey carried out for the Committee asked over 400 doctors how they would be likely to prescribe for (profiled) patients suffering from five different conditions. The results of the survey show that the standard treatments in the 1960s for two of these conditions would be considered unacceptable today:

- Over one-quarter of the prescriptions for painful osteo-arthritis were for Butazolidin (phenylbutazone) and related drugs, which are now considered too dangerous for routine use. About 20 per cent of the prescriptions were for drugs now recognised as less effective for arthritic diseases: ie pain-killers with no anti-inflammatory effect (eg codeine, paracetamol).
- Prescribing recommendations for the treatment of acute adult diarrhoea have also changed. In the Sainsbury study, about 40 per cent of prescriptions were for treatments that are now discredited, and one or two were for potentially dangerous drugs (clioquinol; chloramphenicol). The authoritative view is that anti-infective drugs should not be used to treat diarrhoeas. What is essentially a non-drug treatment – oral rehydration – is now considered to be the patient's first (and often only) need.

The authoritative independent view and 'current medical practice' are inevitably years apart: the limitations and dangers of drug treatment tend to be recognised long before 'current medical practice' catches up. Several studies confirm the view that 'despite the most frequent and widespread of warnings a drug may still be used' [Mapes R., 1977]. For example, the heart drug, practolol (ICI's Eraldin), was found to be widely prescribed right up to the fairly foreseeable day on which ICI withdrew it from general use, in July 1975. 'Despite repeated warnings, 290,000 prescriptions for practolol were dispensed during 1975, or nearly 28 million tablets in England and Wales' [Melville A.; Mapes R.: 1980].

Current medical practice inevitably involves the widespread use of drugs before their effects are properly understood. In the interim, these drugs are effective and safe 'by today's standards' – a compromise between what is and ought to be known. Experienced doctors bear in mind that, by tomorrow's standards, today's are often wrong:

> 'My colleagues think I'm crazy, but I'm very hesitant about claiming any specific effects for new miracle drugs. When I was a houseman doing therapeutics, I got involved with the Medical Research Council Trial on anti-coagulants [drugs which prevent the blood clotting]. At the time, anti-coagulants were the be-all and end-all for coronary thrombosis. They were for a long time. There was a consultant at this hospital who thought this was a load of nonsense and prescribed nothing but vitamin C [for this indication, a placebo]. We thought that he was crazy, a back-to-the-leeches-era man. But, in retrospect, he was right . . .' [unidentified doctor, quoted by Comaroff, 1976]

On the receiving end

Good prescribing does not only mean choosing the right drugs: it involves providing information which ensures that medicines are effectively used. In this respect, the quality of prescribing is very poor. Doctors may fail even to provide basic information on the prescription form:

> 'We looked for missing directions, vague or unhelpful instructions, and dosage and frequency information missing. We found that 25.1 per cent of doctors' scripts were vague or had missing information. The corresponding figure for receptionist-written scripts was 56.1 per cent, thus more than half of the receptionists' written scripts contained mistakes. There was a correlation of 0.41 between the percentage of mistakes a general practitioner makes and the percentage of mistakes his receptionist makes. Hence doctors who are making mistakes are letting their receptionists write even more inadequate scripts.' [Dajda, 1980]

Equally, it has been suggested that 'members of the medical profession are notoriously bad at informing the patient population, in particular at discussing therapy with them; instead doctors appear to issue orders which they consider should be obeyed . . . research into the consultation process has indicated that more often than not the doctor assumes that it is enough simply to tell the patient to "take one, three times a day" . . .' [Eaton G., 1980].

It has been clearly shown that patients who are told about the treatment they get take medicines more sensibly and safely; are less anxious; and are more rapidly cured [see for example: Rachman S. J., Phillips C., 1978]. It is also clear that patients want more information than they are given [see for example NPHT, 1980]; and that many try alternative (but often unreliable) sources to obtain it:

> 'Other respondents said they would like to have more information about the content of prescribed medication, and some were in the habit of asking their chemist. The unusual view expressed by one man – "I don't think you're allowed to know what you are taking" – was repeated by another male respondent who said: "You aren't allowed to ask the chemist what it is."' [DHSS, 1979]

The Health Education Council has reportedly 'shown little interest in educating the public about the use of drugs'. The Council apparently only provides leaflets 'adjuring the public to take their medicines as instructed and explaining how to store them' [Eaton G., 1980]. Nevertheless, there have been many other proposals for informing patients about drugs – for example using information leaflets or checklists [Ad-Hoc Working Group, 1977; Herxheimer A., Davies C. 1982; FR 44 131 6/7/79; pp.40016–41]. The medical profession has traditionally resisted all initiatives of this kind.

They have given various reasons for this. One is lack of confidence in patients' ability to understand; another is that there is no real need; and 'many doctors [will] object that they do not have time' [Herxheimer A., Davies C., 1982]. In the US, the American Medical Association resisted a major proposal to provide 'patient package inserts' (PPIS) with widely used prescription medicines, mainly on the grounds that it 'would interfere with the physician–patient relationship' [Harvey M. W., 1978]. (The AMA has since produced its own such leaflets for doctors to give to patients, but the response to these has been disappointing.)

The medical profession's resistance to such proposals is clearly related to 'clinical freedom' – the guarantee of unchallengeable power. There is also specific concern about the liability of doctors, if and when a treatment fails, which in turn may largely explain the notorious under-reporting of the untoward effects of drugs:

> As has been said, the Committee on Safety of Medicines receives, on average, one report of an adverse drug reaction per two doctors, per year. The true incidence of untoward effects is not known. However, one of the most reliable surveys undertaken (11,526 hospital in-patients) reported that about 12 per cent of drug exposures resulted in unsatisfactory therapeutic response, and 6 per cent in adverse effects; 28 per cent of all patients experienced adverse drug reactions, 10 per cent of which were considered major [Miller R. R. on the Boston Collaborative Drug Surveillance Program in *Am. J. Hosp. Pharm.* 1973, 30, 584–92]

It is against this background of non-information that the problem of 'patient non-compliance' has to be seen. Estimates of compliance vary a lot, but perhaps half of all patients do not take medicine as directed. The orthodox view is that the patient is deviant, and the doctor not to blame:

> 'The logic behind drug company and pharmacy involvement in non-compliance appears to be based upon the premise that it is a problem of bad memory, inconvenience and lack of understanding of the doctor's instructions. One advertisement which specifically refers to non-compliance asks, "Can this patient be trusted?"'
> [Eaton G.; 1980]

The drug companies would tend to promote such views, not only because it pleases doctors, but because it suits the industry too. Patient non-compliance is the main selling-point for fixed-ratio combination products, and is the main justification for their licensing and use. The way these products are promoted and used suggests that patients are hopeless, and probably incapable of being much else. The prophecy fulfils itself.

An alternative, less popular, view sees 'non-compliance' as a rational if primitive response by the person taking the medicine. If doctors do not impress on patients the value and importance of treatment, they are less likely to comply.

The truth, as always, lies somewhere in between. Some people fail to comprehend and cannot cope; and some doctors fail to communicate and care. There is dazzling evidence of both – easily enough to convince each party of the other's breach of faith. As the conviction hardens, medicine becomes less and less effective, because it gets more and more carelessly used.

Why do we use them?

Why do we consume the wrong kind of medicine? The short answer is that we have had little or no choice but to do so. Nobody wants poor medicine if there are better alternatives, and no one willingly contributes to the waste of national health. But lack of confidence, of information and of expertise make it seem inevitable that we take medicine imprudently and on trust. All things considered, Alice in Wonderland did rather well:

> It was all very well to say 'Drink me', but the wise little Alice was not going to do *that* in a hurry. 'No, I'll look first,' she said, 'and see whether it's marked "poison" or not'; for she had read several nice little histories about children who had got burned, and eaten up by wild beasts, all because they *would* not remember the simple rules their friends had taught them: such as, that a red-hot poker will burn you if you hold it too long; and that, if you cut your finger *very* deeply with a knife, it usually bleeds; and she had never forgotten that, if you drink much from a bottle marked 'poison', it is almost certain to disagree with you sooner or later. . . .
>
> 'However, this bottle was not marked poison, so Alice ventured to taste it, and finding it very nice (it had, in fact, a sort of mixed flavour of cherry tart, custard, pineapple, roast turkey, toffee and hot buttered toast), she very soon finished it off.'
> [Carroll L., 1865]

Like many medicine-users, Alice had no idea what was in the bottle, nor why she should take it, nor what would happen to her if she did. On the other hand she did read and double-check all the instructions on the label, and then did exactly what they said – which many grown-ups do not.

> '. . . Recent studies have shown that at least two out of five patients never take their prescribed drugs as directed by their doctors and collections of unused prescribed drugs from householders [see box] indicate that a large proportion are never taken.'
> [Parish, 1982; p.10]

Not taking medicines as directed, or not taking them at all, may be harmful: for example, if a barbiturate or some other drugs are abruptly discontinued, serious risks may be involved. But whatever the outcome, non-compliance is considered wrong. The consumer cannot be right, because the prescriber would not have recommended drug treatment unless it was necessary. By tradition,* the man on the Clapham Omnibus – 'The Reasonable Man' – is expected to take medicines exactly as prescribed:

> He is one who invariably looks where he is going and is careful to examine the immediate foreground before he executes a leap or bound; who neither star-gazes nor is lost in meditation when approaching trap doors or the margin of a dock . . . who never mounts a moving omnibus and does not alight from any car while the train is still in motion; who investigates exhaustively the *bona fides* of every mendicant before giving alms, and will inform himself of the history and habits of a dog before administering a caress; who believes no gossip, nor repeats it, without firm basis for believing it to be true . . . who in the way of business looks only for that narrow margin of profit which twelve men such as himself would reckon to be 'fair', and contemplates his fellow merchants, their agents and their goods, with that degree of suspicion and distrust which the law deems admirable. . . .
> [Herbert A. P., 1924]

> Over 200,000 tablets were collected by chemists during a three-week medicine 'amnesty' in Dudley, Hereford & Worcester, in 1976, and when the exercise was repeated three years later, over 300,000 tablets were turned in. These amnesties do not appear to have curbed over-prescribing, nor to have persuaded consumers not to hoard old drugs – because an astonishing 740,000 tablets were collected during the amnesty in 1982.
> [Inglis B. in *The Health Services* 24/12/82]

It follows that consumers who do not take their medicine as prescribed – for whatever reason – in some way cannot cope. What some people call 'non-compliance', at worst, may be what others call 'functional incompetence':

> 'Four out of ten people cannot read railway time-tables, and one in four adults cannot work out the change they should receive from a £5 note after purchasing a single article. Nearly a third cannot handle multiplication, division, or percentages.'
> [From a news item on 'Numeracy Week' (*The Guardian*; 6/9/83)]

There is indeed evidence to suggest that this problem is great, and some supports the orthodox view that it is also permanent, if not intractable. For example, very

* Drug evaluation and drug approvals are based on the results of trials in which everything is administered exactly according to plan. If non-compliance is as extensive as it seems, we must be over-estimating drug benefits. What we assume drugs do, and what they actually do, may be two quite different things.

elderly people are less likely to be able to cope with medicines because they are more likely to be intimidated and confused – and the population of old people is increasing (by 1990, the EEC's population of over-80-year-olds is expected to increase by 40 per cent, to a total of 8 million).

Doctors see further evidence every day of the helplessness of consumers. The estimates vary, but about one-quarter of all consultations are thought to be 'trivial, inappropriate or unnecessary' – colds, cuts and dandruff being mainly to blame [DHSS, 1979; p.53]. There is startling evidence of over-dependence on doctors: the Royal College of General Practitioners (1977) has estimated that in an average year, the GP typically sees 600 people with coughs and colds; 325 with skin disorders; 300 suffering from depression and anxiety; 100 with chronic rheumatism; 50 with high blood pressure; 8 with heart attacks and five each with acute appendicitis, cancers and strokes.

On the other hand

The good news is that bad drug use is probably neither mainly consumers' 'fault' nor an intractable problem – for there is abundant evidence to suggest that if consumers grope, it is because they have been kept in the dark. Patients – 'poor things' – have traditionally been denied knowledge about medicine, because they had to believe in it if it was to work. Little seems to have been achieved in getting people to understand even the basics – and incompetence is naturally the result. There is much to be done:

> Patients 'need to grasp a few very basic concepts relating to medicines. They will understand the physician, the pharmacist and the PPI* much better if they understand the notion of a benefit/risk relationship, and that this is influenced by the nature and seriousness of illness; that the body gets rid of drugs, and that the speed with which this happens affects the frequency of doses; that a drug can have effects on the body that are not intended; and that medicines do not keep for ever. We have to find ways of teaching patients these and other elementary ideas, but have hardly begun to do so. It should not be difficult to devise posters, leaflets, tape slide programmes and so on for waiting rooms in surgeries, clinics and pharmacies. We should also aim at school teachers and children. Future citizens should learn all these things as children; they will then be able to teach their parents as well.'
> [Herxheimer A., Davies C., 1982]

And, on the other hand, if medicine is used without care, it may be the doctor rather than the patient who fails to comply. The true deviant is not the helpless consumer, but the hopeless prescriber – and in particular the doctor who goes so

* Patient package insert: a leaflet provided with some medicines giving the user information about the medicine and full instructions for use.

far as to claim that if he cannot do anything, nothing can be done. Patients with the will and the sense to reject this view have been able to re-invent the wheel.

Three related cases of professional non-compliance were reported in letters from readers to *Prevention* magazine*, published in January, May and July 1981. Rejection by orthodox medicine led to the simultaneous discovery of three new and different treatments for shingles, an unpleasant and very painful skin condition.

'Several months ago I broke out with shingles for the first time in my life and was quite miserable . . . My doctor said there's not much they could do for shingles but to give injections and strong pain-killing pills. Finally, I read that four 400-unit vitamin E capsules daily plus vitamin C rubbed on the blisters had helped it in some cases. I tried it. Within 24-hours the pain was gone and the blisters stopped itching . . .'

'. . . A skin specialist at the local hospital . . . took one look and said: "This is a first for me. A ten-year-old girl with shingles . . . It's too bad there is no cure for it . . ."' Later, at home, the child's grandmother becomes involved: 'So I said, "Since *nothing* can be done, let's try *something*". I use a lot of vitamin C, and so I brought it out. I told them to give her 500mg of vitamin C every hour, and to forget the aspirin. Less than four hours later the girl was resting without any pain . . . Two weeks after the original onslaught . . . the shingles were completely gone and there was not one single pock-mark or scab.'

'I had a very painful attack of shingles . . . My doctor said he could do nothing for me except give me a prescription for the pain. He also said the pain could last from six months to two years and could recur. I came home from his surgery determined to find a cure.
. . . "Letters to the Editor" in *Prevention* told of good results with vitamin E, alfalfa tablets and desiccated liver. I added these to my other vitamins and increased my intake of vitamin E from 400 to 1,600 international units daily. In six weeks, I was entirely free of any symptoms of shingles, and have since not had any recurrence.'

The moral has nothing to do with vitamins since each of the three claimed to have cured the condition with *different* vitamins. It is simply that most real healing power belongs to the body; and that no treatment helps unless given with great care.

Obfuscation rules, OK?

These three – among many others – learned the hard way. They learned that they could do more for themselves only when frustrated by doctors, and even then they

* *Prevention* magazine is owned and operated by a major supplier of vitamins (Rodale). The editorial emphasis is on vitamin use.

underestimated what they achieved. Like many other people, these three attributed their cures to vitamins and the like, rather than to the body's response to simple self-help and/or mutual aid.

It should not indeed be difficult to devise drug education programmes to teach this, but it could prove very difficult to make them work. There are two main problems:

- There is a gulf between the theory and practice of self-help and mutual aid. The notion of human frailty is powerfully reinforced in life and convincingly underlined by death. It is a prejudice as fundamental as any, and it would take commitment of enormous resources to generate an alternative faith.
- Though they have the resources, both government and the medical profession are at present pretty well disqualified from doing what needs to be done. Any attempt to preach self-reliance would readily be misinterpreted as a withdrawal of help (we're not going to help, so you'd better look after yourself).

And, in the meantime, any educational programme with real impact would inevitably threaten commercial, government and/or professional interests, and would therefore always be at political risk. The US 'Patient Package Insert' programme is a case in point: the Carter administration gave the scheme priority, but it was stopped as soon as the Reagan administration came in [*New Scientist* 23/4/81; p.206].

There may be something of a credibility gap, but the flow of partial information, and the image that the three main actors give of themselves, is designed to gain consumers' full confidence in drugs. If people were to be given information that might reduce their confidence in medicine, action would be promptly taken to stop it. Business, government and the medical profession go to really extraordinary lengths to protect their (own and each others') reputation and power. Here is one example of this:

> In 1978, the government introduced a requirement that all spermicidal contraceptives carry a safety warning for consumers. The warning to be put on all advertisements, leaflets and labels had to say: 'A higher degree of protection against pregnancy will be afforded by using another method of contraception in addition to a spermicidal contraceptive'
> [DHSS Press Release No.78/21; 27/1/78]
> The reason for this stunning failure to communicate is not official incompetence. The point is that government officials (in 'consultation' with the industry) decided that this wording represented a fair compromise between the consumers' need to know, and the manufacturers' need to sell. Consumers may need information to stop unwanted pregnancies, but the last thing the manufacturer wants is a clear warning on his product that says it is not effective enough on its own.

It would be very easy to 'copy test' official messages to the public to see what people made of them, but this is not done. There has been no evaluation of the effectiveness of official health information campaigns – not even of those which encourage the public to consume fewer drugs [Greenfield, 1982; p.14].

> One of the last major campaigns to get people to use fewer drugs was run in 1978. It was sponsored by the Department of Health and the British Medical Association, and administered by the Health Education Council. The campaign posters said:
>
> BE PREPARED
> TO LEAVE THIS SURGERY
> EMPTY-HANDED
> The doctor may not give you a prescription.
> His advice may be all you need!
> You can be sure that if you really
> need one – you'll get one.

Though the poster clearly implies that consumers are to blame for over-prescribing, the campaign was discontinued after five months after pressure from the medical profession. Doctors reportedly objected to any reference to a prescribing problem; and also resented any implication that they contributed to it by passively responding to patient demand [Phillips E. M., 1982; p.27]. The campaign may not in any case have had much effect. The ticking off seems to heighten the challenge to consumers to get themselves a prescription to prove their need.

This extreme sensitivity to reputation explains why there tends to be a strong flow of information about the benefits of drugs, and a much restricted flow about their risks and costs. Secrecy about drug defects, prices and costs, professional negligence, drug licensing and control, and government action or inaction all tend to encourage uncritical drug use. If the discriminating consumer were provided with better information, it is difficult to see how he or she could not be perceived as a nuisance, being bound to use fewer drugs less often; less likely to support governments' policies on drug use; and far less likely than the Reasonable Man to take prescribing decisions wholly on trust.

An American book *Pills that Don't Work* (an important resource for this book) strongly recommends (lay) readers to challenge doctors' prescribing decisions:

> *Question:* Is it all right for patients to challenge doctors who prescribe drugs listed in this book?
> *Answer:* Certainly. You will be doing yourself and your doctor a favor. By refusing to take such a drug, you will protect yourself from the needless risk of a bad reaction from a drug found not to be effective. You may also help the doctor because he or she too wants to avoid any bad reactions.
> [Health Research Group, 1981]

A doctor in Britain might think it anything but a favour to be challenged about a prescription. Better, tell your doctor at the outset that you would always prefer to avoid drug treatment, unless it was very important for you to have it. It could improve your health – and your relationship with the doctor as well. If everyone said it, it could really change the world.

Control of health

Individuals can help themselves by knowing something about the principles of drug use, and by getting information about drugs they are prescribed. But collective action is clearly called for too.

The present UK medicines policy is pursued in the name of consumers and at their expense, but it also reflects the view that people cannot control their own health and may not question how it is controlled.

Because of this, people are not taught about medicine; information about drug use tends to be distorted and/or withheld; and basic rights, including consumers' rights of redress, are strictly curtailed. At the same time, medicines policy has been over-influenced by the need to stimulate trade. As a result, rational and economic prescribing have been discouraged: there is poor drug use and prices have been unfairly high.

These policies have survived partly because people have been repressed and partly because they have been pleased. Many have good reason to be: some drugs are excellent, and many doctors care well. Nevertheless, our medicines policies have undermined individual and national health, almost to the point where we cannot go on. The idea that people cannot take better care of themselves and each other is destroying their confidence in their health, and is also patently untrue:

> 'The trouble is, we are being taken in by the propaganda, and it is bad not only for the spirit of society: it will make any health care system, no matter how large and efficient, unworkable. If people are educated to believe they are fundamentally fragile, always on the verge of mortal disease, perpetually in need of support by health-care professionals at every side, always dependent on an imagined discipline of "preventive" medicine, there can be no limit to the numbers of doctors' offices [surgeries], clinics and hospitals required to meet the demand. In the end, we would all become doctors, spending our days screening each other for disease.
>
> 'We are in real life a reasonably healthy people. Far from being ineptly put together, we are amazingly tough, durable organisms, full of health, ready for most contingencies. The new danger to our well-being, if we continue to listen to all the talk, is in becoming a nation of healthy hypochondriacs, living gingerly, worrying ourselves half to death.'
> [Thomas L., 1979, p.39]

People must be encouraged to take much more responsibility for their own and each others' health. If they do not, they will get sicker and the NHS will become completely unworkable too. People can take this responsibility – but only if given the power to control their health. The medical profession and the pharmaceutical companies have largely usurped this power, and the government has permitted its abuse.

Postscript

By the end of 1983, the government and the pharmaceutical industry had negotiated a new price regulation scheme. This reduced the amount that the drug companies could spend on promoting their products (from 10 per cent to 9 per cent of sales turnover, from April 1985), and also restricted the industry's profit margins. The government estimated that these measures would save upwards of £65 million a year on the NHS drug bill [DHSS press release 83/276, December 1983].

The industry's public reaction to these measures was sour, but it would be wrong to infer that the government has at last got drug prices under firm control. This seems extremely unlikely:

- The 1983 price regulation scheme operates on the same basis as earlier schemes, so there is no particular reason for thinking that this one will succeed where the others have all failed. The 1983 scheme is the tenth to have been introduced since the 1950s.
- The DHSS allows itself complete discretion in setting profit levels. The target rate of profit, agreed in secret between the DHSS and the companies, takes account of 'the circumstances of the individual company, the contribution which it makes or is likely to make to the economy, including foreign earnings, investment, employment or research' [DHSS press release 83/276, December 1983].
- The Department of Health cannot properly monitor companies' performances with the resources it has, and has acknowledged as much in evidence to the Public Accounts Committee in 1983.

Nothing much will change so long as the DHSS attempts both to sponsor the industry and to keep drug prices down. It is a ridiculous policy. It indicates bad management because it involves the pursuit of sometimes radically conflicting objectives. It conflicts deeply with the most basic principles of health care – namely that drugs should be used to improve the health of human beings rather than economies. And this policy cripples the NHS as well.

It cannot be right that the NHS is obliged to pay more than a fair price for drugs – and to permit their indiscriminate use – simply to stimulate the drug industry and to promote the export trade. Regardless of the benefits to the national economy, there can be no justification for the NHS subsidising the industry, at such cost to national health. It is arguably also in breach of EEC competition policy that this is done.

The Minister of Health at the time of writing (Kenneth Clarke) recognised the need to end the Department's sponsorship of the industry. He tried to end the arrangement but failed: there was reportedly opposition from both the Prime Minister and the Department of Trade and Industry. Their intervention underlines the basic conflict there is between economic imperatives and national health. The fact that the decision was neither announced nor publicly debated also says something about the limitations of Parliament in controlling executive power.

Because the DHSS does sponsor the industry, there is some logic in its policy towards the medical profession – and there have been some positive results from it. The DHSS has, in effect, abdicated responsibility for ensuring rational and economic prescribing: instead of taking initiatives itself, it has funded professional bodies to do the job. The Department's main contribution has been to fund publication and distribution of the new *British National Formulary*, an excellent source of information about drugs, which is sent free to doctors twice a year.

However, this is not nearly enough. However much the BNF and other government-supported, independent publications help to control indiscriminate drug use, they do not get to the root of the problem. This is self-evident: the BNF lists hundreds of drugs which are, to put it mildly, 'less suitable for prescribing' – and yet these drugs are licensed by the government, strongly promoted by the industry, and therefore widely prescribed. Against the background of 'clinical freedom', it is safe to assume that self-regulation by doctors will not work.

Nothing much is likely to work, unless and until the government adopts policies which recognise that the only good medicines – for individuals and nations alike – are medicines for which there is clear and real need. We do not need and cannot afford most of the medicines we now use, and should therefore be urgently thinking in terms of a national medicines policy based on the World Health Organisation's concept of essential drugs. These are drugs which are 'restricted to those proven to be therapeutically effective, to have acceptable safety and to satisfy the health needs of the population' [WHO, 1977; p.9]. Why should we settle for anything less?

The WHO identifies some 250 essential drugs, but there is no reason why our national drug list should not be extended to include other potentially useful drugs as well.

Most of the Nordic countries already apply such policies. Norway, for instance, has operated such a scheme since 1928 – and now has a national list of around 1,900 preparations, fewer than one-third of the number in the UK.

> 'Besides drug safety and efficacy considerations, special features in Norwegian legislation have been "the clause of need" (medical justification) and "the

5-years rule" of reconsideration. The first clause makes it possible to reject new drug products of appropriate quality if the medical needs are already covered, qualitatively and quantitatively, by those products already on the market. The second clause implies that the justification for every drug product is formally reconsidered by the drug registration authorities at 5-year intervals.'
[Lunde P. K. M., 1982]

But we have a long way to go before getting an essential drug policy in Britain. The Greenfield Committee on Effective Prescribing said it did consider the question of a limited drug list, though the Committee's report gives very little evidence of this. The Committee's full recommendations to the Secretary of State for Health were as follows:

'There are in the region of 6,500 preparations available for prescribing at NHS expense and the new BNF lists some 4,500 of these. In comparison, the average prescriber is said to use a range of 200–300 drugs. A number of schemes for the introduction of a National Limited List of drugs has been proposed at various times by different people. We have considered these, but it is our view that a limitation on prescribing at NHS expense would be interpreted by some doctors as an attempt to curtail their clinical freedom. Since we have not seen any convincing evidence suggesting that financial benefits would outweigh the administrative problems in drawing up and maintaining the list, we have concluded that such a move would not be justified and we do not recommend any measures to introduce nationwide a Limited List.'

This one-paragraph recommendation says a lot about the relationship between the government and consumers. The fact that this recommendation was nodded through raises doubts not only your right to be well treated by doctors (and to be protected and compensated if you are not) – but about your right even to have it represented in government that you deserve such rights. The Greenfield report's conclusion on essential drugs, and the fact that it was accepted without question, permits the following tentative conclusions to this dissertation. They are concerned with who takes decisions; with the quality and value of decision-making; and with the processes by which decisions are taken in your name.

First, since there is a good deal of ineffective prescribing – and because doctors are the main source if not the main cause of it – it does not seem proper that 11 of the 12 members of the committee should have been doctors. Apart from the conflict of interest involved, the notion that doctors alone can represent consumers' interests is not acceptable – because they clearly cannot.

Secondly, the Committee had no reason to conclude simply that an essential drug list would be rejected by some doctors, who would see it as a threat to their clinical freedom. The Committee should have answered several more important questions, but did not in fact even raise them. The Committee does not suggest what proportion of doctors would agree or disagree with a proposal for a limited list but, more to the point, it appears to take completely for granted that their objections are realistic, and should, in the public interest, be sustained.

Thirdly, the Committee's recommendation implies that there was no competent examination of the costs and benefits of an essential drugs policy. The Committee makes no reference to the successful and widespread use of drug formularies (limited lists) in NHS hospitals; no reference to the World Health Organisation's initiatives; and none to successful experiences in other countries, including Norway at one side of the globe and New Zealand at the other.

Fourthly, the Committee said it saw no convincing evidence that the *financial* benefits of a limited list would outweigh the costs even of producing it. This conclusion is not credible for several reasons: (a) it is not adequately substantiated; (b) it implies that NHS hospital formularies and the *British National Formulary* are not worth producing; (c) it appears to ignore evidence (not least from the WHO) of administrative savings from reducing the numbers of drugs to be bought, inventoried, stored, analysed, transported and distributed; and (d) the Committee concerns itself with the question of financial rather than therapeutic gain from a limited drug list. It appears to overlook benefits which the WHO and other authorities say include improved drug utilisation, management, information, compliance, and monitoring. If doctors have a small but complete list of drugs, they are bound to have more information and experience about those drugs' limitations and uses.

If the Committee's recommendation is inadequate, it is partly because of weakness in the process of government itself. The underlying weakness is that the government in Britain is secretive and closed; and alienation from human values is a result. The Committee's conclusions (though partly leaked), were not made public by the government for one year, and were probably never meant to be published at all. The fact that the Committee was convened and met in secret, did not invite evidence from outside bodies, and did not publish or cite the evidence on which its conclusions were based, underlines the primitive and precarious state our democracy is in. It will surely remain in this state until government is made open, and required to account properly for the decisions it takes in the public's name and at public expense. Closed government is bad government: in the words of the Royal Commission on the Press [1977] it leads to 'much injustice, some corruption and many mistakes'. In human terms, this means many victims, some exploitation and maltreatment, and much avoidable suffering and expense.

BIBLIOGRAPHY

ABPI: Association of the British Pharmaceutical Industry: *Code of Practice for the Pharmaceutical Industry* Revised 5th Edition: April 1982. Also: ABPI Data Sheet Compendium 1983/4. Details of availability from ABPI, 12 Whitehall, London SW1A 2DY. Tel: 01-839 3961.

Ad-Hoc Working Group (of mainly clinical pharmacologists and physicians from 16 countries): 'Minimum information for sensible use of self-prescribed medicines' in *The Lancet* 12 November 1977, pp.1017–9.

AMADE: *AMA Drug Evaluations* 5th Edition [Chicago, American Medical Association, 1983].

Anderson R.J.: *Epidemiol. Comm. Hlth* 1980; 34: 299–304.

Avorn J., Chen M., Hartley R.: 'Scientific versus Commercial Sources of Influence on the Prescribing Behavior of Physicians' in *The American Journal of Medicine*, Vol. 73; July 1982, 4–8.

Balint M., Hunt J., Joyce D., Marinker M., and Woodcock J.: *Treatment or Diagnosis* [London: Tavistock, 1970].

Benson H., Epstein M.D.: 'The Placebo Effect' in *JAMA* 1975, 232, 12, 1225–7.

Berle B.B.: *Eighty Puerto Rican Families in New York City* (New York: Columbia University Press, 1958) p.256 [quoted in Smith M.C., 1980].

Blackwell B., Bloomfield S. S., Buncher C. R.: 'Demonstration to Medical Students of Placebo Responses and Non-drug factors' in *The Lancet*, 10 June 1972, 1279–82.

BMA: British Medical Association: *Secret Remedies* (What they cost and what they contain) [1909]; and *More Secret Remedies* [1912].

BNF: *The British National Formulary* published twice a year by the British Medical Association and the Pharmaceutical Society of Great Britain.

Carroll L.: *Alice's Adventures in Wonderland* (first published in 1865) [London: Macmillan, 1973] pp.8–10.

Catford J.: 'Quality of prescribing for children in general practice' in *Br. Med. J.* 14 June 1980, 1435–7.

COI: Central Office of Information (Reference Division): *Control of medicines in Britain* Leaflet, Ref. No. SN 5944, April 1976.

Comaroff J.: 'A bitter pill to swallow: placebo therapy in general practice' in *Sociol. Rev.* 1976 24, 1, 79–96.

Crossman R. H. S.: *The Diaries of a Cabinet Minister* Vol.3 [London: Hamish Hamilton and Jonathan Cape, 1977].

Dajda R.: 'Who prescribes: the illusion of power-sharing in the surgery' in Mapes R. (Ed.) 1980.

Darby F. J., Greenberg G.: 'Data Collection in England' in *Studies in Drug Utilisation* [Copenhagen: World Health Organisation Regional Office for Europe, 1979] pp.83–91.

Data Sheet Compendium: see ABPI.

DHSS: Department of Health and Social Security: *DHSS activities in support of health-care exports*; report by a Rayner scrutiny team of 20 June 1980 [London: DHSS, 1980].

DHSS: *Doctor/Patient Relationship: A study in General Practice* by Fitton F. and Acheson H. W. K. [London: HMSO, 1979].

DHSS, Medicines Division: *The promotion of sales of medicinal products* [Undated pamphlet, Ref. MAL 37].

DHSS and Welsh Office: *Drug Tariff 1983* (available from DHSS Information Division, Block 4, Canons Park, Government Buildings, Honeypot Lane, Stanmore, Middlesex HA7 1AR).

DTB: *Drug and Therapeutics Bulletin* published fortnightly by Consumers' Association, 14 Buckingham Street, London WC2N 6DS. Subscription enquiries to: Consumers' Association (DTB), Castlemead, Gascoyne Way, Hertford SG14 1LH.

Dukes M. N. G.: 'Identifying the Medical Consultants of Pharmaceutical Companies' in *The Lancet* 29 September 1979, p.696 [quoted in Greenhalgh, 1982].

Dukes M. N. G. and Lunde I.: 'On regulating regulation' in *Eur. J. Clin. Pharmac.* 1981, 19, 1–2.

Eaton G.: 'Non-compliance' in Mapes R. (Ed.) 1980, pp.201–13.

Eaton G., Parish P.: 'Sources of drug information used by general practitioners' in *Prescribing in General Practice, J.Royal Coll. of General Practitioners* Supp. No.1, 1977 Vol.26, 58–68.

FAO: Food and Agriculture Organisation of the United Nations: *Handbook on Human Nutritional Requirements* [Rome: FAO, 1974] pp.36–7.

FR: US *Federal Register*. Citations in this book are to notices from the US Department of Health, Education & Welfare, Food and Drug Administration (FDA) and include:
'Proposal to Establish Monographs for Over-the-Counter Laxative, Antidiarreal, Emetic and Anti-emetic Products' [FR Vol.40. No.56, 21 March 1975, pp.12902–44].
'Establishment of a Monograph for Over-the-Counter Cold, Cough, Allergy, Bronchodilator and Antiasthmatic Products' [FR Vol.41, No.176; 9 September 1976 pp.38312–418].
'Establishment of a Monograph for Over-the-Counter Internal Analgesic, Antipyretic and Antirheumatic Products' [FR Vol.42, No.131; 8 July 1977, pp.35346–494].
'External Analgesic Drug Products for Over-the-Counter Human Use; Establishment of a Monograph and Notice of Proposed Rulemaking' [FR Vol.44, No.234; 4 December 1979; pp.69768–866].
'Ano-rectal Drug Products for Over-the-Counter Human Use: Establishment of a Monograph' [FR Vol.45, No.103; 27 May 1980, pp.35576–606].
'Prescription Drugs: Patient Package Inserts Requirements and Draft Guideline' [FR 45 179 12/9/80; Part V].
'Weight Control Drug Products for Over-the-Counter Human Use; Establishment of a Monograph' [FR Vol.47, No.39; 26 February 1982, pp.8466–84].
'Digestive Aid Drug Products for Over-the-Counter Human Use; Establishment of a Monograph [FR Vol.47, No.2; 5 January 1982; pp.454–87].

Greenfield P. R. (Chairman): *Report to the Secretary of State for Social Services of an Informal Working Group on Effective Prescribing* [London: DHSS, 1983].

Greenhalgh, T.: 'No such thing as a free lunch' – a critical look at the pharmaceuticals industry [unpublished manuscript, November 1982].

Griffin J. P. and Diggle G. E.: 'A Survey of Products Licensed in the United Kingdom from 1971–1981' in *Br. J. Clin. Pharmac.* 1981, 12, 453–63.

HAI – see Health Action International.

Harvey M. W.: 'Patient Package Inserts: Instructions or Intrusions' in *Legal Aspects of Medical Practice*, August 1978, pp.47–51.

H. C. Deb.: Hansard (House of Commons).

Health Action International: *An International Code of Pharmaceutical Marketing Practice* [discussion document produced for the World Health Assembly, Geneva, May 1982]. Details of this and other HAI papers from Social Audit Ltd, Box 111, London NW1 8XG; or from IOCU, Box 1045, Penang, Malaysia.

Health Research Group: see Wolfe S. M.

Hemminki E.: 'Factors influencing drug prescribing – inquiry into research strategy' in *Drug Intelligence and Clinical Pharmacy*, 1976, 10, 321.

Hemminki E., Starfield B.: 'Routine administration of iron and vitamins during pregnancy: review of controlled clinical trials' in *Br. J. Obstet. & Gynaec.* 1978, 85, 6, 404–10.

Hendeles L.: 'Need for "counter-detailing" antibiotics' in *American Journal of Hospital Pharmacy* 1976, 33, 913–24 [cited in Smith M.C., 1980].

Herbert A. P.: 'Misleading Cases: The Reasonable Man' in *Punch*, 9 July 1924, pp.38–9.

Herxheimer A., Davies C.: 'Drug information for patients: bringing together the messages from prescriber, pharmacist and manufacturer' in *J. Royal Coll. of General Practitioners* 1982, 32, 93–7.

Illich I.: *Limits to Medicine* – Medical Nemesis: the Expropriation of Health [Harmondsworth: Pelican, 1977].

IOCU: International Organisation of Consumers' Unions: *The availability and marketing of anabolic steroids* [report of an international survey by Foo G. S., Lachkovics E., Yee L. W.], published September 1983. Available from IOCU, Box 1045, Penang, Malaysia.

Knapp D. E.: 'Can Pharmacists Influence Drug Prescribing?' in *American Journal of Hospital Pharmacy* 1978, 35, 593 [quoted by Smith M. in Mapes R. (Ed.) 1980].

Lesser F.: 'How we keep unsafe drugs off the market' in *New Scientist*, 4 December 1980 pp.634–5.

Long J. W.: *The Essential Guide to Prescription Drugs* [New York: Harper & Row, 1982]. Information in drug profiles notes possible interactions between marijuana and prescribed medicines.

Lunde P. K. M.: 'Restricted Drug Formularies in Nordic and Developing Countries', paper presented at Management Centre Europe Conference No.5470–66, PHARMA 82, 28–30 June 1982, Geneva. Requests for reprints to: Professor P. K. M. Lunde, Chairman, Institute of Pharmacotherapeutics, University of Oslo, P.O.B. 1065, Blindern, Oslo 3, Norway.

Mapes R. (Ed.) *Prescribing Practice and Usage* [London: Croom Helm, 1980].

Mapes R.: 'Physicians' Drug Innovation and Relinquishment' in *Soc. Sci. & Med.* 1977, 11, 619–24.

Maronde R. F., Lee P. V., McCarron M. M. and Siebert S.: 'A study of Prescribing Patterns' in *Medical Care* 1971, 9, 5, 383 [quoted by Segal H. J. in Mapes R. (Ed.) 1980].

Martindale: The Extra Pharmacopoeia: 27th and 28th Editions [London: The Pharmaceutical Press, 1977 and 1982].

McMahon F. G., Ryan J. R., Akdamar K., and Ertan A.: 'Upper gastro-intestinal lesions after potassium chloride supplements: a controlled clinical trial' [*Lancet* 1982 II, 1059–60].

The Medical Letter (on drugs and therapeutics) published fortnightly by The Medical Letter Inc., 56 Harrison Street, New Rochelle, New York 10801, USA.

Medicines Commission: Annual Reports for 1981, 1982.

Melville A., Mapes R.: 'Anatomy of a Disaster: the Case of Practolol' in Mapes R. (Ed.) 1980.

MIMS: Monthly Index of Medical Specialities. Available from Medical Publications Ltd, 76 Dean Street, London W1A 1BU.

Mindell E.: *The Vitamin Bible* [New York: Warner, 1981].

Moir D. C., Christopher L. J. and Lawson D. H.: 'Data Collection in Scottish Hospitals' in *Studies in Drug Utilisation* [Copenhagen: World Health Organisation Regional Office for Europe, 1979, pp.93–102].

Moertell C. G., Taylor W. F., Roth A., Tyce F. A. J.: 'Who responds to sugar pills?' in *Mayo Clin. Proc.* Feb. 1976, 51, 96–100.

Monopolies Commission: *A Report on the Supply of Chlordiazepoxide and Diazepam* [London: HMSO, 1973].

Newman G. F. 'Is Medicine Sick?' in *The Sunday Times* [Magazine Section] 11 September 1983 pp.20–3. Excerpt from *The Nation's Health* [London: Granada, 1983].

NPHT: Nuffield Provincial Hospital Trust: 'Talking with Patients' [1980]. For-sale publication available from 3 Prince Albert Road, London NW1 7SP.

OHE: Office of Health Economics: *The Future for Pharmaceuticals*: The Potential, the Pattern and the Problems [1983]; and *Sources of Information for Prescribing Doctors in Britain* [1977]. OHE's parent body – same address – is the ABPI (see above).

Open University: *Topics in Drug Therapy* (produced by the Open University for the Council for Postgraduate Medical Education in England and Wales) [Milton Keynes: OU, 1982].

OTC-PDW. *Over-the Counter Pills that don't Work*. See Wolfe S. M., 1983.

Parish P.: *Medicines: A Guide for Everybody*, 4th Edition [Harmondsworth: Penguin, 1982].

Phillips E. M.: *British Political Action and Inaction*: National Health Service Drug Expenditures and the Advocacy for Non-Prescription Medicines [unpublished manuscript dated 14 April 1982].

PDR: *Physicians' Desk Reference*, 37th Edition [Oradell NJ: Medical Economics Co, 1983].

PDW: *Pills that don't Work*. See Wolfe S. M., 1981.

Public Accounts Committee: *Dispensing of Drugs in the NHS* [London: HMSO, 1983]. See also: *Appropriation Accounts* [Vol.8: classes XI and XII, 1981–2 [London: HMSO, 1983].

Rachman S. J., Philips C.: *Psychology and Medicine* [Harmondsworth: Penguin, 1978].

Rashid A.: *Br. Med J.* 1982; 284: 24–6.

Royal College of General Practitioners: *Trends in General Practice*, 1977 [cited in DHSS, 1979].

Rubinstein M. K.: *A Doctor's Guide to Non-Prescription Drugs* [New York: Signet, 1977].

Sainsbury, Lord (Chairman): *Report of the Committee of Enquiry into the Relationship of the Pharmaceutical Industry with the National Health Service*; Cmnd 3410 [London: HMSO, 1967].

SCRIP World Pharmaceutical News: published bi-weekly by PJB Publications Ltd. Subscription details from 18/20 Hill Rise, Richmond, Surrey, TW10 6UA (or from Suite 420, 500 5th Avenue, New York, NY 10110, USA).

Segal H. J.: 'The Social Risks and Benefits of Prescription-Writing' in Mapes R. (Ed.) 1980.

Shapiro A. K.: 'A contribution of a history of the placebo effect' in *Behavioral Science* April 1960, 5. 109–35.

Shapiro A. K., Morro L. in *Handbook of Psychotherapy and Behaviour Change* (Garfield and Bergin: Eds.); Wiley, 2nd Edn, 1978 [cited in Weitz M., 1981].

Silas J. H., Tucker G. T., Smith A. J.: *Br. J. Clin. Pharmacol.* 1980; 9: 427–30.

Smith M.C.: 'The Relationship between Pharmacy and Medicine' in Mapes R. (Ed.) 1980.

Social Audit: *Drug Diplomacy*: decoding the conduct of a multinational pharmaceutical company and the failure of a Western remedy for the third world; by Medawar C., Freese B. [London: Social Audit, 1982].

Stimson G.: 'General practitioners' estimates of patients' expectations and other aspects of their work' Occasional paper No.3 [1975] from Medical Sociology Research Centre, University College of Swansea.

Thomas L.: *The Medusa and the Snail: more notes of a biology watcher* [New York: Bantam, 1979] p.38.

Turner P., Volans G. N.: *The Drugs Handbook* 3rd Edition [London: Macmillan, 1983].

USNIGMS: US Institute of General Medical Sciences: *Medicines and You* by Pines M. [Washington DC: US National Institutes of Health, April 1981].

Volgyesi F. A.: 'School for patients' hypnosis-therapy and psychoprophylaxis' in *Brit. J. Med. Hypnotism*, 1954, 5, 8 [quoted in Shapiro, 1960].

Weitz M.: *Health Shock* [Feltham: Hamlyn, 1982].

Which? published monthly by Consumers' Association, 14 Buckingham Street, London WC2N 6DS. Subscription enquiries to: Consumers' Association, Castlemead, Gascoyne Way, Hertford SG14 1LH.

Wolfe S. M., Coley C. M. and the Health Research Group: *Pills that don't work* [1981]; and, with Kaufman J. et al.: *Over-the-Counter pills that don't work* [1983]. Both available from Health Research Group, 2000 P Street NW, Washington DC 20036, USA.

WHO: World Health Organisation: *The Selection of Essential Drugs* Report of a WHO Expert Committee; technical report series No.615 [Geneva: WHO, 1977]. (There have been further WHO Technical Reports on Essential Drugs in 1979 and 1983.)

Wingate P.: *The Penguin Medical Encyclopedia* [Harmondsworth, Penguin, 1972].

The drugs list

USING THE DRUG LIST

The drug profiles in this section explain briefly why a particular product may be less suitable for prescribing than another drug or brand or treatment. Most drugs have been listed for one or more of the following reasons:

- treatment is unnecessary, undesirable or misconceived
- alternative treatments are likely to be safer or more effective
- the product includes ingredients of little or no proven value
- the product combines ingredients which, if needed, should be separately prescribed
- the product is poorly formulated
- the product offers relatively poor value for money
- there is strong evidence of inappropriate use.

"Inappropriate use" accounts for the listing of a number of drugs that are excellent when well used. Such drugs have been included in a list of otherwise mainly inferior products on the grounds that uneconomic prescribing has the same effect as NHS spending cuts: reduced standards of health care.

Drugs are listed alphabetically by brand name, but are cross-referenced in the index which classifies them according to what they do and where they act (p.101–106). The manufacturer's name is identified directly below the brand name (see list of principal companies and subsidiaries on pp.30–31).

Each entry lists the product's ingredients by the approved (generic) name, and the effect or intended effect of the ingredients is briefly explained. The available dosage forms are shown (but *not* the recommended dose) except for injectable formulations. The abbreviation [POM] under the brand name means a prescription-only medicine; [CD] indicates a controlled drug. Several drugs which have been discontinued, withdrawn or suspended during the preparation of the book are marked 'WITHDRAWN'.

References are shown in brackets: there is a full list of sources on pp. 95–98. The six main sources used are abbreviated as follows:

AMADE	*AMA Drug Evaluations* (Chicago: American Medical Association; 5th Edition [1983]).
BNF	*British National Formulary* (London: British Medical Association and the Pharmaceutical Society of Great Britain; twice yearly from 1981).
DTB	*Drug & Therapeutics Bulletin* (London: Consumers' Association, fortnightly).
FR	a citation to the US *Federal Register*, and to the findings of one of a number of expert panels set up by the US Food and Drug Administration.
M28	*Martindale: The Extra Pharmacopoeia* (London: The Pharmaceutical Press, 28th Edition, 1982).
PDR	*Physicians' Desk Reference*, 37th Edition [Oradell, New Jersey: Medical Economics Co, 1983].

Entries include estimates of NHS expenditure on a product, when this exceeds £100,000 a year. These estimates are based on 1981 data, and are intended only as a rough guide.

For reasons made clear in the text, information about individual products or classes of drugs is *not* intended as a guide to treatment.

INDEX OF LISTED BRANDS
classified according to therapeutic category
(ie according to the part of the body they work on
and what they are supposed to do)

The digestive (alimentary) system

ANTACIDS
Drugs which neutralise excess stomach acid: used to relieve symptoms of heartburn, indigestion, stomach ulcers, and related digestive disorders.
ACTONORM (gel); ALTACITE; ALTACITE PLUS; ANDURSIL; ANTASIL; ASILONE; BISLUMINA; BISMA-REX; BISODOL; CALCIUM CARBONATE COMPOUND; CHALK MIXTURE PAEDIATRIC; DILORAN; DIMETHICONE (see ASILONE); DIOVOL; GASTROCOTE; GAVISCON; MAALOX PLUS; MAGNESIUM CARBONATE COMPOUND; MUCAINE; NULACIN; PHAZYME; POLYALK; POLYCROL; POLYCROL FORTE; ROTER; SILOXYL; SIMETHICONE (see ASILONE); SODIUM BICARBONATE; SYLOPAL; TITRALAC; TOPAL.

ANTISPASMODICS AND ANTISPASMODIC + SEDATIVE COMBINATIONS
Drugs which reduce spasm and motility in the gut (some of which also reduce intestinal secretions): used to relieve pain and discomfort caused by stomach ulcers and other disorders of the stomach and intestine. Ulcer-healing drugs are also included.*
ACTONORM (tablets, powder); ACTONORM-SED; ALKA-DONNA; ALKA-DONNA-P; ALUDROX SA; ALUHYDE; ALUMINIUM HYDROXIDE AND BELLADONNA MIXTURE, PAEDIATRIC; APP STOMACH POWDER; APP STOMACH TABLETS; BELLERGAL; BELLERGAL RETARD; BELLOCARB; BUSCOPAN; CANTIL; CANTIL WITH PHENOBARBITONE; CARBELLON; CAVED-S*; KOLANTICON; KOLANTYL; LIBRAXIN; MAGNESIUM TRISILICATE AND BELLADONNA MIXTURE; MAXOLON; NEUTRADONNA; PRO-BANTHINE WITH DARTALAN; RABRO*; ROBINUL; STELABID.

ANTIDIARRHOEALS
Includes drugs to control symptoms of acute diarrhoea (ie chemical plugs), and anti-infective and other agents intended to treat the cause.
DIARREST; ENPAC; ENTEROMIDE; FLAR; GUANIMYCIN; LOMOTIL LIQUID; NEO-SULPHAZON; STREPTOTRIAD; SULPHAMAGNA; UNIFLOR.

LAXATIVES
Includes bulk-forming agents (eg bran), stimulant laxatives (eg cascara), faecal softeners and lubricants (eg liquid paraffin) and other agents used to treat constipation.
AGAROL; ALOPHEN; CALSALETTES; CASCARA EVACUANT; EX-LAX; KEST; LIQUID PARAFFIN AND PHENOLPHTHALEIN MIXTURE; OPOBYL; PETROLAGAR No. 2; PHENOLPHTHALEIN; VERACOLATE.

ANO-RECTAL PREPARATIONS
Agents for internal and external use, used to treat itching, soreness and discomfort in the ano-rectal region, eg caused by haemorrhoids.
ANUGESIC-HC; ANUSOL-HC; BISMUTH SUBGALLATE COMPOUND; NESTOSYL; PROCTOSEDYL; UNIROID.

DIGESTIVE AIDS
Including agents used to acidify stomach contents, and enzymes intended to improve digestion.
ACIDOL-PEPSIN; COMBIZYM; COMBIZYM COMPOSITUM; COTAZYM B; ENZYPAN; MURIPSIN.

The heart and blood circulation system

DIURETICS
These drugs remove excessive fluid from body tissues (oedema) by increasing the output of urine, and help to reduce high blood pressure. Products listed here include diuretic + potassium supplements (see POTASSIUM SUPPLEMENTS in drug list).
AQUAMOX; BAYCARON; BRINALDIX K; BURINEX-K; CENTYL K; DIUMIDE-K CONTINUS; DIUREXAN; ESIDREX-K; HYGROTON; HYGROTON-K; LASIKAL; LASIX; LASIX + K; NATRILIX; NAVIDREX-K; NEO-NACLEX-K.

BETA-BLOCKERS

These drugs are widely used to treat high blood pressure, angina (heart pain) and other heart disorders. Those listed include beta-blocker + diuretic combination products (see BETA-BLOCKER + DIURETIC COMBINATIONS in drug list).

BETALOC; BETALOC SA; CO-BETALOC; CORGARETIC 40; CORGARETIC 80; INDERAL; INDERAL LA; INDERETIC; INDEREX; LOPRESOR; LOPRESOR SR; LOPRESORETIC; MODUCREN; PRESTIM; SECADREX; SECTRAL; SLOW-TRASICOR; SOTAZIDE; TENORET 50; TENORETIC; TENORMIN; TENORMIN LS; TOLERZIDE; TRASICOR; TRASIDREX; VISKALDIX.

ANTIHYPERTENSIVES

Drugs used to reduce high blood pressure, other than beta-blockers and diuretics (see above). Most of these contain RESERPINE *(see entry in list) or related drugs.*

ABICOL; ALDOMET; DECASERPYL; DECASERPYL PLUS; ENDURONYL; HARMONYL; HYPERCAL; HYPERCAL-B; RAUDIXIN; RAUTRAX; RAUWILOID; RAUWILOID + VERILOID; RAUXIDIN; RESERPINE; SEOMINAL; SERPASIL; SERPASIL-ESIDREX; SERPASIL-ESIDREX-K; THIAVER; VERILOID.

VASODILATORS

These include (a) coronary vasodilators, drugs which open the coronary arteries in the heart, used in the treatment of angina (heart pain); and (b) peripheral vasodilators and related drugs, used to treat blood circulation disorders in the legs and other limbs. (See PERIPHERAL VASODILATORS *in drug list). Also included is* PERSANTIN, *which is used as a coronary vasodilator in the treatment of angina – though strictly classified as a drug which inhibits blood clotting (anti-platelet drug).*

CARDIACAP; CYCLOBRAL; CYCLOSPASMOL; DEFENCIN CP; DUVADILAN; DUVADILAN RETARD; HEXOPAL; HYDERGINE; MYCARDOL; NATIROSE; OPILON; PAROVEN; PENTOXYLON; PERITRATE; PERITRATE SA; PERNIVIT; PERSANTIN; PRAXILENE; PRISCOL; RONICOL; RONICOL TIMESPAN.

DRUGS USED TO REDUCE BLOOD FAT LEVELS

Deposits of fats (eg cholesterol) on the walls of arteries make the arteries thicken ('harden') which reduces blood flow. Usually, the best way to prevent/treat this condition (atherosclerosis) is to change the diet, stop smoking and/or take more exercise. When these measures fail, drugs may be used – but some have harmful side effects and none is of proven value.

ATROMID-S; BEZALIP; CHOLOXIN; COLESTID; LURSELLE; QUESTRAN.

The lungs and respiration

BRONCHODILATORS

These are drugs which relax and open up the air tubes in the lungs, used to relieve breathing difficulties in asthma, bronchitis and other respiratory disorders (see BRONCHODILATORS in drug list).

ADRENALINE; ADRENALINE AND ATROPINE; ALEUDRIN; ALUPENT; AMESEC; AMINOPHYLLINE SUPPOSITORIES; ASMAPAX; ASMA-VYDRIN; BRICANYL COMPOUND; BRICANYL EXPECTORANT; BRONCHILATOR; BRONCHOTONE; BRONTINA; BRONTISOL; BROVON; BROVON PRESSURISED; CAM; DUO-AUTOHALER; DUOVENT; EPHEDRINE; ETOPHYLATE; EXPANSYL; FRANOL; FRANOL PLUS; FRANOL EXPECTORANT; ISO-AUTOHALER; ISO-BROVON PRESSURISED (PIB); ISO-BROVON PLUS PRESSURISED (PIB PLUS); LABOPHYLLINE; MEDIHALER-DUO; MEDIHALER-EPI; MEDIHALER-ISO; MEDIHALER-ISO FORTE; MILLOPHYLINE; NETHAPRIN DOSPAN; ORTHOXINE HYDROCHLORIDE; PHYLDROX; RYBARVIN INHALANT; SILBE INHALANT; SILBEPHYLLINE; TAUMASTHMAN; TEDRAL; TEDRAL SA; THEAN; THEOSOL.

COUGH REMEDIES

Products listed include cough suppressants; and inhalations, expectorants and mucolytics, which help removal of phlegm, through coughing (see EXPECTORANTS AND MUCOLYTICS).

ACTIFED COMPOUND LINCTUS; ACTIFED EXPECTORANT; AIRBRON; ALEVAIRE; ALUPENT EXPECTORANT; AMMONIA AND IPECACUANHA MIXTURE; AMMONIUM CHLORIDE AND MORPHINE MIXTURE; AMMONIUM CHLORIDE MIXTURE; BENAFED; BENYLIN EXPECTORANT; BENYLIN PAEDIATRIC; BENYLIN WITH CODEINE; BISOLVON; COPHOLCO; COPHOLCOIDS; DAVENOL; DIMOTANE EXPECTORANT; DIMOTANE EXPECTORANT DC; DIMOTANE WITH CODEINE; DIMOTANE WITH CODEINE PAEDIATRIC; EXPULIN; EXTIL COMPOUND;

EXYPHEN; FABROL; FALCODYL; FLAVELIX; GEE'S LINCTUS/PASTILLES; GUANOR EXPECTORANT; GUANOR PAEDIATRIC; HISTALIX; IPECACUANHA & MORPHINE MIXTURE; KARVOL; LINCTIFED EXPECTORANT; LINCTIFED EXPECTORANT PAEDIATRIC; LOTUSSIN; MENTHOL INHALATIONS; MUCODYNE; MUCOLEX; NETHAPRIN EXPECTORANT; NORADRAN; OPIATE SQUILL LINCTUS, PAEDIATRIC; ORGANIDIN; ORTHOXICOL; PAVACOL-D; PHENERGAN COMPOUND EXPECTORANT; PHENSEDYL; PHOLCOLIX; PHOLCOMED; PHOLCOMED DIABETIC; PHOLCOMED EXPECTORANT; PHOLCOMED FORTE; PHOLCOMED FORTE DIABETIC; PHOLTEX; RINUREL (linctus); ROBITUSSIN; ROBITUSSIN AC; RUBELIX; SANCOS CO; SUDAFED EXPECTORANT; SYRTUSSAR; TANCOLIN; TEDRAL EXPECTORANT; TERCODA; TERPALIN; TERPOIN; TIXYLIX; TRIOCOS; TRIOTUSSIC; TUSSIFANS; VALLEDRINE; VALLEX; VISCLAIR.

DECONGESTANTS

This list includes nasal and bronchial decongestants for systemic use (tablets, syrups etc). Decongestants meant for local application (drops, sprays etc) are listed with other products for ear, nose and throat.

ACTIFED; BENYLIN DECONGESTANT; CAM DECONGESTANT (re-named NEZCAAM); CONGESTEZE; DIMOTAPP; DIMOTAPP LA; DIMOTAPP P; ESKORNADE; FLAVELIX; HAYMINE; NEZCAAM; PARAGESIC; RINUREL; RINUREL SA; SUDAFED; SUDAFED-CO; TOTOLIN; TRIOGESIC; TRIOMINIC; UNIFLU PLUS GREGOVITE C

PREVENTION OF ASTHMA

This should not be used to treat asthma attacks: it should be taken to prevent attacks from happening.

INTAL COMPOUND.

Allergic disorders

ANTIHISTAMINES

These drugs are mainly used to relieve symptoms of allergy, but have many other applications (see ANTIHISTAMINES in drug list). *No one antihistamine is superior to any other, but their prices vary considerably.*

DANERAL SA; FABAHISTIN; HISTRYL; OPTIMINE; PRIMALAN; PRO-ACTIDIL; TINSET.

Antihistamines are included in many of the bronchodilators, cough remedies and decongestants listed above. Antihistamine creams are listed under skin preparations.

Central nervous system

ANTI-ANXIETY DRUGS AND DRUGS FOR INSOMNIA

The products listed here are mainly tranquillisers which belong to the same family as diazepam (VALIUM) *and barbiturate sedatives/hypnotics.* See BENZODIAZEPINE TRANQUILLISERS and BARBITURATES in drug list.

ALMAZINE; ALUPRAM; ANXON; ATARAX; ATENSINE; ATIVAN; CENTRAX; DALMANE; DORIDEN; EQUANIL; EUHYPNOS; EUHYPNOS FORTE; EVACALM; EVIDORM; FRISIUM; HALCION; LEXOTAN; LIBRIUM; LUMINAL; MEDOMIN; MEPRATE; MEPROBAMATE; MILONORM; MILTOWN; MOGADON; NEMBUTAL; NITRADOS; NOBRIUM; NOCTAMID; NOLUDAR; NORMISON; PARABAL; PHANODORM; PHENOBARBITONE SPANSULE; REMNOS; ROHYPNOL; SECONAL SODIUM; SERENID-D; SERENID FORTE; SODIUM AMYTAL; SOLIS; SOMNITE; SONERYL; SUREM; TACITIN; TENAVOID; TENSIUM; TRANCOPAL; TRANXENE; TROPIUM; TUINAL; UNISOMNIA; VALIUM; VALRELEASE; XANAX.

ANTI-DEPRESSANTS AND DRUGS USED TO TREAT PSYCHOSES

This list may appear sparse, since the clinical benefit of many other preparations is very questionable. However, the value of those unlisted preparations depends very much on how and when they are used. The preparations listed below are included because the drug itself, or the combination of ingredients, and/or the price makes satisfactory use less likely.

ELAMOL; LIMBITROL 5; LIMBITROL 10; MARPLAN; MOTIPRESS; MOTIVAL; PARNATE; PARSTELIN; SPARINE; TOFRANIL; TRIPTAFEN; TRIPTAFEN-M; TRYPTIZOL.

APPETITE SUPPRESSANTS AND STIMULANT DRUGS

CELEVAC; CELLUCON; DUROPHET; NILSTIM; PREFIL; REACTIVAN; RONYL; VILLESCON; VOLITAL.

ANTI-EMETICS (FOR NAUSEA, VOMITING ETC); DRUGS FOR MIGRAINE; AND ANTI-CONVULSANTS FOR EPILEPSY

See ANTIHISTAMINES. *These drugs are also widely used to control nausea, vomiting, vertigo, motion sickness etc.*
EPANUTIN WITH PHENOBARBITONE; GAROIN; MIDRID; MIGRALEVE; MIGRAVESS; MIGRAVESS FORTE; MIGRIL; OSPOLOT; PARABAL; PARADIONE; PARAMAX; SERC; TRIDIONE.

ANALGESICS

This list includes simple, mainly non-prescription drugs, mostly used for relief of mild to moderate pain. It includes drugs which lower high temperature (antipyretics); and products which contain sedative, skeletal muscle relaxant and related components. Some of these analgesics, like aspirin, also reduce inflammation (eg in rheumatic conditions), but see also anti-inflammatory drugs listed in the section below for treatment of pain and stiffness in joints and muscles. All these products are for systemic use, rather than for local application.
ANTOIN; ASPIRIN AND CODEINE; ASPIRIN, PARACETAMOL AND CODEINE; CAFADOL; CALPOL; CALPOL SIX PLUS; CARISOMA CO; CODEINE AND PARACETAMOL; CODIS; COSALGESIC; DELIMON; DEXTROGESIC; DIHYDROCODEINE AND PARACETAMOL; DISTALGESIC; DISTALGESIC SOLUBLE; DOLASAN; DOLOXENE COMPOUND; EQUAGESIC; FEMERITAL; FORTAGESIC; HYPON; LOBAK; MEDISED; MEDOCODENE; MYOLGIN; NAPSALGESIC; NEURODYNE; NORGESIC; ONADOX-118; PAEDO-SED; PANADEINE CO; PANADOL; PANASORB; PARACODOL; PARADEINE; PARAHYPON; PARAKE; PARALGIN; PARAMOL; PARA-SELTZER; PARAZOLIDIN; PARDALE; PAXIDAL; PHARMIDONE; PROPAIN; ROBAXISAL FORTE; SAFAPRYN; SAFAPRYN-CO; SALZONE; SOLPADEINE; SYNDOL; TANDALGESIC; TRANCOPRIN; UNIGESIC; VEGANIN; ZACTIPAR; ZACTIRIN.

Anti-infective drugs

ANTI-BACTERIAL, ANTI-FUNGAL AND OTHER ANTI-INFECTIVE DRUGS

All drugs listed are for systemic use: anti-infectives for local application are listed in the last three sections below. The value of antibiotics depends a lot on how and when they are used: the entries for AMOXIL *and* CEPHALOSPORIN ANTIBIOTICS *illustrate disadvantages of unselective drug use which apply to virtually all anti-infective drugs.*
ACHROMYCIN V; ALBAMYCIN-T; AMOXIL; AMBAXIN; BISOLVOMYCIN; BROXIL; CALTHOR; CEDURAN; CEPHALOSPORIN ANTIBIOTICS; CEPORIN; CHEMOCYCLINE; CHYMOCYCLAR; DETECLO; DISTACLOR; ENTEROMIDE; FLAGYL; FURADANTIN; G 500; HAVAPEN; HIPREX; KEFADOL; KEFLIN; LEDERMYCIN; LINCOCIN; MANDELAMINE; MYSTECLIN; MYSTECLIN SYRUP; OXYTETRACYCLINE MIXTURE; PENBRITIN; PONDOCILLIN; RONDOMYCIN; STREPTOTRIAD; SULPHATRIAD; SUSTAMYCIN; TALPEN; TERRA-BRON; TETRABID; TETRACHEL; TETRACYCLINE MIXTURE; TETRALYSAL; TETREX; UROMIDE; VIBRAMYCIN.

Drugs which act on the endocrine (hormone-producing) system

ORAL CONTRACEPTIVES

ANOVLAR; CONOVA 30; EUGYNON 30; EUGYNON 50; GYNOVLAR 21; LOESTRIN 20; MARVELON; MICROGYNON 30; MINYLIN; NORLESTRIN; OVRAN; OVRAN 30; OVRANETTE; OVULEN 50. See ORAL CONTRACEPTIVES in drug list.

OTHER PREPARATIONS

(Cortico)steroid drugs, used to suppress inflammation, are listed only when found in combination drug products (eg BETNESOL-N*). One exception:* DELTACORTRIL 'ENTERIC'. Also listed: ANAPOLON; DIABINESE; GESTONE; PLEX-HORMONE; STROMBA.

Nutrition

IRON SUPPLEMENTS

Drugs used to prevent or treat iron deficiency (anaemia). See IRON SUPPLEMENTS in drug list.
ANORVIT; BC 500 WITH IRON; FEAC; FE-CAP C; FEFOL; FEFOL-VIT; FEOSPAN; FERAVOL; FERAVOL-F; FERAVOL-G; FERFOLIC; FERFOLIC SV; FERGLUVITE; FERRAPLEX B; FERRLECIT 100; FERROCAP; FERROCAP-F 350; FERROCONTIN FOLIC CONTINUS; FERROGRAD C; FERROGRAD FOLIC; FERRO-GRADUMET; FERROMYN B; FERROMYN S; FERROMYN S FOLIC; FESOVIT; FOLICIN; FOLVRON;

FORCEVAL; GALFER-VIT; GASTROVITE; GEVRAL; GIVITOL; IBERET 500; IBEROL; IROFOL C; IRONORM capsules; PREGNAVITE FORTE; PREGNAVITE FORTE F; SIDROS; SLOW-FE; SLOW-FE FOLIC.

POTASSIUM AND OTHER MINERAL SUPPLEMENTS

Potassium supplements are mainly prescribed with diuretic drugs (see the second section above) but often unnecessarily. See POTASSIUM SUPPLEMENTS in the drug list.
K-CONTIN CONTINUS; LEO-K; NU-K; OSSOPAN; SLOW-K.

'TONICS'

ANEURONE; EFFICO; GLYKOLA; GLYKOLA INFANS; IRONORM tonic with iron; LABITON; METATONE; NEURO PHOSPHATES; TONIVITAN A & D; VERDIVITON; VIRVINA.

VITAMIN PREPARATIONS

See VITAMINS in drug list.
ABIDEC; ALLBEE WITH C; ALUZYME; BC 500; BRAVIT; CALAVITE; CALCIMAX; CE-COBALIN; CONCAVIT; CYTACON; DALIVIT; EPHYNAL; HEMOPLEX; HEPACON-B FORTE; HEPACON LIVER EXTRACT; HEPACON-PLEX; JUVEL; LANCE B + C; LEDERPLEX; LIPOFLAVONOID; LIPOTRIAD; MINAMINO; MULTIVITAMINS; MULTIVITE; OROVITE; OROVITE 7; POLYVITE; POTABA; POTABA + 6; SURBEX T; TONIVITAN; TONIVITAN B; VI-DAYLIN; VIGRANON B; VITA-E; VITAVEL; WALLACHOL.

Treatments for pain and stiffness in joints and muscles

DRUGS FOR RHEUMATIC DISEASES AND GOUT

See NSAIDs in drug list. NSAIDs *are Non-Steroidal Anti-Inflammatory Drugs – ie they are like aspirin rather than (cortico)steroid drugs, which reduce inflammation in an entirely different way.*
ARTRACIN; BUTACOTE; BUTAZOLIDIN; BUTAZOLIDIN ALKA; BUTAZONE; FLOSINT; IMBRILON; INDOCID; INDOFLEX; INDOLAR; MERALEN; MOBILAN; PONSTAN; SURGAM 200/300; TANDACOTE; TANDERIL; ZYLORIC.

MUSCLE RELAXANTS

CARISOMA; NORFLEX; ROBAXIN; TIGLYSSIN; VALIUM.

RELIEF OF SOFT-TISSUE INFLAMMATION

ANANASE FORTE; CHYMAR; CHYMORAL; DEANASE; DEANASE DC; HYALASE; TRYPURE; VARIDASE.

COUNTER-IRRITANTS: RELIEF FOR PAINS AND SPRAINS

ALGESAL; ALGIPAN; ARADOLENE; ASPELLIN; BALMOSA; BAYOLIN; BENGUE'S BALSAM; BENGUE'S BALSAM SG; CREMALGEX; CREMALGIN; CREMATHURM; DIFFLAM; DUBAM; FINALGON; INTRALGIN; MOVELAT; P R SPRAY; SKEFRON; TRANSVASIN.

Treatments for eye and ear disorders

EYE/EAR INFECTIONS AND INFLAMMATION

Most of these preparations combine an anti-infective agent with a corticosteroid drug, to reduce inflammation. The entries for BETNOSOL-N *and* SOFRAMYCIN, *in particular, explain why these combinations are undesirable.*
AUDICORT; BETNESOL-N; CHLORAMPHENICOL EAR DROPS; CHLOROMYCETIN EAR DROPS; CHLOROMYCETIN-HYDROCORTISONE; CORTUCID; EUMOVATE-N; FRAMYCORT; MAXITROL; NEO-CORTEF; OTOPRED; OTOSEPTIL; OTOSPORIN; OTOTRIPS; PREDSOL-N; SOFRADEX; SULPHAPRED; TANDERIL-CHLORAMIPHENICOL; TERRA-CORTRIL; TRI-ADCORTYL OTIC.

OTHER PREPARATIONS FOR THE EAR

Preparations for ear-ache; removal of ear wax.
AUDAX; AUDINORM; AURALGICIN; AURALTONE; CERUMOL; DIOCTYL; EXTEROL; MOLCER; NORGOTIN; SEDONAN; SOLIWAX; WAXSOL; XERUMENEX.

Treatments for nose and threat

NASAL INFECTIONS AND INFLAMMATION

ARGOTONE; BETNESOL-N; BIO-MYDRIN; DEXA-RHINASPRAY; LOCABIOTAL; RHINAMID; SOFRAMYCIN; VIBROCIL.

NASAL DECONGESTANT DROPS/SPRAYS

ANTISTIN-PRIVINE; HAYPHRYN; OTRIVINE-ANTISTIN.

ANTISEPTIC LOZENGES/SPRAYS/GARGLES ETC

For sore throat, minor infections etc.
AAA SPRAY; BETADINE; BRADOSOL; ELUDRIL; HIBITANE; MEDILAVE; MEROCAINE; MEROCET; MEROCETS; ORALCER; PYOREX; STREPSILS; TYROSOLVEN; TYROZETS.

Skin preparations

LOCAL RELIEF OF PAIN AND ITCHING ETC

Creams etc containing antihistamines and/or local anaesthetics – neither of which are particularly effective.
ANETHAINE; ANTHISAN; ANTHICAL; CALADRYL; DERMOGESIC; LOCAN; NUPERCAINAL; NESTOSYL; PHENERGAN; RBC; SOLARCAINE; XYLOCAINE.

CORTICOSTEROID + ANTI-INFECTIVE SKIN PREPARATIONS

Preparations which combine an anti-infective agent with a corticosteroid (to reduce inflammation) are of questionable value. See entry in drug list: CORTICOSTEROID + ANTI-INFECTIVE SKIN PREPARATIONS.
ADCORTYL WITH GRANEODIN; AUREOCORT; BARQUINOL HC; BETNOVATE C; BETNOVATE N; COBADEX-NYSTATIN; DAKTACORT; DERMOVATE NN; FRAMYCORT; FUCIDIN H; GENTICIN HC; GREGODERM; HAELAN-C; HALCICOMB; HYDROCORTISONE AND NEOMYCIN CREAM; HYDRODERM; LOCOID C; NEO-CORTEF; NEO-MEDRONE; NYSTADERMAL; NYSTAFORM-HC; PROPADERM-A; PROPADERM-C; REMIDERM; SILDERM; STEROXIN-HYDROCORTISONE; SYNALAR-C; SYNALAR-N; TERRA-CORTRIL; TERRA-CORTRIL NYSTATIN; TIMODINE; TRI-ADCORTYL; TRIMOVATE; ULTRALANUM; VIOFORM-HYDROCORTISONE.

ACNE PREPARATIONS

ACNIL; ACTINAC; DOME ACNE; ESKAMEL; MEDRONE; NEO-MEDRONE; QUINODERM WITH HYDROCORTISONE; RESORCINOL AND SULPHUR PASTE; SALICYLIC ACID AND SULPHUR OINTMENT; SULPHUR OINTMENT.

OTHER PREPARATIONS

eg for minor infections; circulation disorders.
AKROTHERM; CONOTRANE; HEWLETT'S ANTISEPTIC CREAM; HIRUDOID; ILONIUM; LASONIL; MONPHYTOL; PERNOMOL; PHORTINEA; PHYTEX; ROTERSEPT; SECADERM; SEPTEX No. 2.

LIST OF DRUGS A–Z

AAA

Armour
Metered aerosol (per dose)

Cetalkonium chloride 4.13 micrograms
Oral antimicrobial: used for minor throat infections.
Benzocaine 1.5mg
Local anaesthetic, intended to relieve sore throat.

Cetalkonium chloride has not been rated effective and safe by the US Food and Drug Administration [OTC-PDW p.189]. Local anaesthetics are best avoided in this kind of preparation which is considered by the UK Joint Formulary Committee as 'less suitable for prescribing'.
The NHS spends over £100,000 a year on this product, and about £1½ million on products like it.

ABICOL

Boots
[POM] Tablets

Reserpine 150 micrograms
Antihypertensive: helps control high blood pressure.
Bendrofluazide 2.5mg
Diuretic: augments the antihypertensive effect; removes excessive fluid from body tissues by increasing the output of urine.

The possibility of serious side effects (mainly depression) limits the usefulness of RESERPINE (see entry). The fixed-ratio combination is acceptable only for users who have previously taken the two ingredients separately and found that these doses suit them.

ABIDEC

Parke Davis/Warner-Lambert Health Care
Multivitamin capsules and drops

Capsules
Vitamin A 4000 units
B-vitamins: thiamine hydrochloride 1mg; **riboflavine** 1mg; **nicotinamide** 10mg; **pyridoxine hydrochloride** 500 micrograms
Vitamin C: ascorbic acid 25mg
Vitamin D: ergocalciferol 400 units.

Drops *(per 0.6ml)*
Vitamin A 4000 units; **Vitamin B: thiamine hydrochloride** 1mg; **riboflavine** 400 micrograms; **nicotinamide** 5mg; **pyridoxine hydrochloric** 500 micrograms; **ascorbic acid** 50mg; **Vitamin D: ergocalciferol** 400 units.

This preparation provides around 100%–200% of daily vitamin requirements, ie roughly the same as a normal diet should provide. It is intended as a dietary supplement, and is not suitable for therapeutic use. See VITAMINS. Like many multivitamin preparations it is relatively expensive: about twice the cost of Vitamins Capsules BPC.

ACHROMYCIN V

Lederle
[POM] Capsules; syrup (per 10ml)

Tetracycline *equivalent to* **tetracycline hydrochloride** 250mg
Antibiotic: used in the treatment of bronchitis and many other infections.

ACHROMYCIN V capsules are 'buffered' with sodium metaphosphate. The manufacturer makes no claim for this formulation, but it is intended to improve absorption of tetracycline from the stomach. There is no convincing evidence of any significant advantage to this formulation, which costs about eight times more than conventional versions of tetracycline. See also TETREX.
ACHROMYCIN V syrup is recommended for children. See TETRACYCLINE MIXTURE.
NHS expenditure on this product is about £¼ million a year.

ACIDOL PEPSIN

Sterling Research
Tablets

Betaine 388mg
Acidifying agent: intended to help digestion by increasing the acidity of stomach contents to 'normal' levels.
Pepsin 97mg
Digestive enzyme: intended as a supplement when pepsin levels in the stomach are abnormally low. (Pepsin helps to break down protein in food so it can be utilised in the body; the stomach usually makes all the pepsin the body needs.)

This treatment is considered obsolete. Acidification of stomach contents serves 'no useful clinical or physiological purpose . . .' [Medical Letter 1972, 14, 56]. The supplementary intake of pepsin is not considered of value [M28 p.654].

ACNIL

Fisons
Acne cream

Resorcinol 0.5%
Precipitated sulphur 3%
Keratolytic
Cetrimide 0.5%
Antiseptic

Resorcinol is best avoided, and the value of sulphur is uncertain. Compare dose with ESKAMEL. See also RESORCINOL AND SULPHUR PASTE.

ACTIFED

Wellcome
Tablets; syrup (per 10ml)

Triprolidine hydrochloride 2.5mg
Antihistamine
Pseudoephedrine hydrochloride 60mg
Decongestant

Antihistamines have no place in treating common cold symptoms. It is doubtful whether sympathomimetics (used here to reduce nasal congestion and inflammation) add to the effectiveness of antihistamines in the treatment of allergy. The combination is considered less suitable for prescribing.
NHS expenditure on this product is about £2 million per year.

ACTIFED COMPOUND LINCTUS

Wellcome
Syrup (per 5ml)

Codeine phosphate 10mg
Cough suppressant.
Pseudoephedrine hydrochloride 30mg
Nasal, bronchial decongestant.
Triprolidine hydrochloride 1.25mg
Antihistamine: used to suppress symptoms of allergy, eg to dry up nasal secretions in hay fever.

The UK Joint Formulary Committee considers that 'there is no scientific basis' for prescribing mixtures of this kind [BNF No.6, 1983, p.120]. Codeine alone is a good treatment for a dry or distressing cough. Nasal decongestant sprays tend to be more effective than oral preparations. Antihistamines have no proven value in the treatment of common cold symptoms; for treatment of allergy, antihistamines are best on their own.
NHS expenditure on this product is about £4 million a year.

ACTIFED EXPECTORANT

Wellcome
Elixir (per 5ml)

Guaiphenesin 100mg
Pseudoephedrine hydrochloride 30mg
Triprolidine hydrochloride 1.25mg

Irrational combination. See ACTIFED COMPOUND LINCTUS. The value of guaiphenesin is doubtful. See EXPECTORANTS AND MUCOLYTICS.

ACTINAC

Roussel
Acne lotion

Precipitated sulphur 10.94%
Keratolytic: promotes sloughing or peeling of scaly, callused skin; antiseptic.
Chloramphenicol 1.25%
Antibacterial antibiotic.
Hydrocortisone acetate 1.25%
Corticosteroid: used to reduce inflammation.
Allantoin 0.75%
Claimed to speed wound-healing.
Butoxyethyl nicotinate 0.75%
Topical vasodilator: intended to increase blood circulation; applied directly to the area.

Topical corticosteroids should be avoided if possible, especially for treatment on the face: they may complicate treatment and cause unpleasant side effects, and may alter the appearance of skin, making it thin and shiny. The UK Joint Formulary Committee says: 'Topical corticosteroids should not be used in acne' [BNF No.6 1983, p.348]. Topical antibiotic treatment is of questionable value; also see notes on CORTICOSTEROID + ANTI-INFECTIVE COMBINATIONS. Both allantoin and butoxyethyl nicotinate lack evidence of effectiveness. The value of sulphur is uncertain. See RESORCINOL AND SULPHUR PASTE.

ACTONORM

Wallace
[POM] Tablets; powder

Tablets
Atropine sulphate 500 micrograms
Antispasmodic: intended to relieve abdominal spasms and pain by reducing contractions of the stomach and intenstine.
Papaverine hydrochloride 200 micrograms
Intended to relax muscle in gut wall.
Dried aluminium hydroxide 25mg
Calcium carbonate 109mg

Magnesium carbonate 225mg
Magnesium trisilicate 50mg
Antacids: neutralise excess stomach acid.
Diastase 5mg
Pancreatin 5mg
Enzymes: intended as digestive aids.
Light kaolin 75mg
Adsorbent
Thiamine hydrochloride 500 micrograms
Vitamin B_1

Powder *(per gram)*
Atropine sulphate 100 micrograms
Papaverine hydrochloride 400 micrograms
Dried aluminium hydroxide 50mg
Calcium carbonate 145mg
Magnesium carbonate 300mg
Magnesium trisilicate 50mg
Diastase 10mg
Pancreatin 10mg
Light kaolin 50mg
Thiamine hydrochloride 1mg

An irrational, undesirable combination product. See ALKA-DONNA P. There is little evidence to justify the use of papaverine [M28 p.1059], and there is no good reason for the vitamin and digestive aids.

ACTONORM
Wallace
Antacid gel

See comparable product: ASILONE.

ACTONORM-SED
Wallace
[POM] Gel (per 5ml)

Belladonna alkaloids 45 micrograms
Dried aluminium hydroxide 220mg
Magnesium hydroxide 100mg
Dimethicone 25mg

See notes on antispasmodic/antacid combination products in entry for ALKA-DONNA P. See also remarks about dimethicone in entry for ASILONE.

ADCORTYL WITH GRANEODIN
Squibb
[POM] Cream and ointment

Triamcinolone acetonide 0.1%
Corticosteroid to reduce inflammation.
Gramicidin 0.025%
Neomycin sulphate 0.25%
Anti-infective agents.

Only likely to be of value where an area of eczema or dermatitis is infected. See CORTICOSTEROID + ANTI-INFECTIVE SKIN PREPARATIONS.

ADRENALINE BP
Solution for spray

Adrenaline 1mg/ml as **adrenaline acid tartrate** 1.8mg/ml
Bronchodilator: relieves breathing difficulties in asthma, bronchitis etc.

Adrenaline acts unselectively: it improves airflow, but may also overstimulate the heart and central nervous system. Common adverse effects include palpitations and anxiety. There are generally better and more modern alternatives.

ADRENALINE & ATROPINE BP
Spray compound

Adrenaline acid tartrate 0.8%
Bronchodilator: relieves breathing difficulties in asthma, bronchitis etc.
Atropine methonitrate 0.1%
Antispasmodic: intended to control coughing spasms. Anticholinergic: dries up bronchial secretions.
Papaverine hydrochloride 0.8%
Muscle relaxant: intended to act on muscles in walls of airways.

Both adrenaline and atropine are considered less effective than other bronchodilators, because they are relatively unselective in their actions. Both can ease breathing difficulties but, at the same time, adrenaline tends to overstimulate the body, and atropine may complicate breathing by drying up secretions in the airways. See BRONCHODILATORS. The value of papaverine is very doubtful: there is little evidence to justify its use [M28 p.1059; AMADE p.678; PDW p.28].

AGAROL
Warner
Mixture (per 5ml)

Phenolphthalein 66mg
Laxative.
Liquid paraffin 1.6ml
Laxative; lubricant.
Agar 10mg

PHENOLPHTHALEIN is considered less satisfactory than many other laxatives. Prolonged use of liquid paraffin may be harmful and should be avoided [M28 p.1063].
NHS expenditure on this product is over £100,000 a year.

AIRBRON
Duncan Flockhart
[POM] Solution for use as a spray or by direct instillation

Acetylcysteine 200mg/ml
Mucolytic: reduces viscosity of phlegm, to help coughing up.

There is no convincing evidence of the value of acetylcysteine, and it 'does not seem worth using' [DTB, 1975, 13, 12]. See EXPECTORANTS AND MUCOLYTICS.

AKROTHERM
Napp
Ointment for chilblains

Acetylcholine chloride 0.2%
Vasodilator: intended to improve blood circulation in limbs.
Histamine 0.1%
Counter-irritant: produces local inflammation which is meant to improve blood circulation in skin.
Oxycholesterol 1%
Emulsifying agent.

Of no real value: chilblains generally do not respond to drug treatment. Warmth and body movement are more likely to prevent and cure them.

ALBAMYCIN T
Upjohn
[POM] Capsules and syrup

Capsules
Novobiocin 125mg
As sodium salt.
Tetracycline 125mg
As hydrochloride.

Syrup *(per 5ml)*
Novobiocin 62.5mg
As calcium salt.
Tetracycline 62.5mg

Bacteria readily acquire resistance to novobiocin, and side effects are frequent. 'There appears to be little reason for the continued use of novobiocin, as alternative therapy for susceptible infections is usually safer . . . Combinations of novobiocin with tetracycline . . . have been condemned by some authorities.' Novobiocin should not be given to children under 6 months of age [M28 p.1194]. The Data Sheet Compendium [1983/4] suggests dosages for children up to 6 months (and is otherwise notably uninformative).

ALDOMET
MSD
[POM] Tablets and suspension

Tablets
Methyldopa 125mg, 250mg, 500mg

Suspension
Methyldopa 250mg/5ml
Centrally acting antihypertensive: used to treat moderate to severe cases of high blood pressure, usually prescribed with a diuretic (which removes excessive fluid from the body tissues by increasing the output of urine.

This is an effective and widely prescribed drug, strongly promoted by brand name.
If the identical medicine were prescribed under its generic name, methyldopa, the NHS could save at least £5½ million a year.

ALEUDRIN
Lewis
[POM] Sublingual tablets; solution for inhalation

Sublingual tablets
Isoprenaline sulphate 20mg

Solution
Isoprenaline sulphate 1%
Bronchodilator: relieves breathing difficulties in asthma, bronchitis etc.

There are generally better (more selective) alternatives to isoprenaline. See BRONCHODILATORS. Isoprenaline tablets dissolved under the tongue are not absorbed reliably and have 'little place in the treatment of asthma' [AMADE p.480]; and there is some evidence that they damage teeth [M28 15].

ALEVAIRE
Winthrop
Spray

Tyloxapol 0.125%
Mucolytic: reduces viscosity of phlegm to help coughing up.

There is no convincing evidence of the value of tyloxapol; the US Food and Drug Administration has withdrawn approval for it. See EXPECTORANTS AND MUCOLYTICS.

ALGESAL
Duphar
Counter-irritant cream

Diethylamine salicylate 10%
Triethanolamine 3%

Considered less suitable for prescribing. See ALGIPAN.

ALGIPAN
Wyeth
Cream

Methyl nicotinate 1%
Capsicum oleoresin 0.1%
Glycol salicylate 10%
Histamine hydrochloride 0.1%
Counter-irritants: intended to relieve pain in muscles, joints etc, when rubbed into skin.

There is no convincing evidence that aspirin preparations such as glycol salicylate are effective when applied externally to relieve deep-seated pain [BNF no.6, p.311]. The other three ingredients are considered effective and safe at the recommended dosages [OTC-PDW pp.177–225]. The UK Joint Formulary Committee considers this product less suitable for prescribing. The Committee recommends as alternatives Methyl Salicylate Ointment BP or Methyl Salicylate Liniment BP.
NHS expenditure on this product is estimated at £100,000 a year.

ALKA-DONNA
Carlton
Tablets and suspension

Belladonna alkaloids
Dried aluminium hydroxide
Magnesium trisilicate

See ALKA-DONNA P.

ALKA-DONNA P
Carlton
[POM] Tablets and mixture

Tablets
Dried aluminium hydroxide 250mg
Magnesium trisilicate 500mg
Antacids: neutralise excess stomach acid.
Belladonna dry extract 8mg
Antispasmodic: intended to relieve abdominal spasms and pain by reducing stomach acid secretion.
Phenobarbitone 8mg
Barbiturate sedative.

Mixture *(per 5ml)*
Aluminium hydroxide mixture 2.15ml
Magnesium trisilicate 342.5ml
Belladonna tincture 0.2ml
Phenobarbitone 8mg

The best dosage of atropine-like antispasmodic drugs varies greatly for different people, and dosage should be individualised. With this fixed-ratio combination product, the dosage of the individual ingredients cannot be independently adjusted. Antispasmodic drugs like atropine have not been shown to better the results of antacids given alone, and can produce unpleasant side effects, such as dry mouth, blurred vision and retention of urine [DTB 1980, 18, 19].

Sedatives are rarely indicated in ulcer therapy but, if needed, should be prescribed on their own. Barbiturates should be avoided: they may cause addiction and have unpleasant side effects. See BARBITURATES.

ALLBEE WITH C
Robins
Tablets; elixir (per 12.5ml)

B-vitamins: thiamine mononitrate 15mg; **riboflavine** 10mg; **nicotinamide** 50mg; **pyridoxine hydrochloride** 5mg; **calcium pantothenate** 10mg
Vitamin C: ascorbic acid 300mg

Less suitable for prescribing. See entry for similar product: BC 500; VITAMINS.
Good alternatives could save the NHS about £100,000 a year

ALMAZINE
Steinhard
[POM] Tablets. See ATIVAN.

ALOPHEN
Warner-Lambert Health Care
Pills

Phenolphthalein 30mg
Laxative.
Ipecacuanha 4mg
Gastric irritant, possibly intended to cause vomiting if too much laxative is taken.
Belladonna dry extract 5mg
Antispasmodic: probably meant to counteract any griping caused by aloin (see below).
Aloin 15mg
Purgative: gut irritant.

A US expert panel has concluded that the use of either ipecacuanha or belladonna in a laxative combination is 'irrational and unsafe therapy'

[FR 40 56 21/3/75 p.12915]. Aloin tends to cause griping and 'has been superseded by less toxic purgatives' [M28.1362]. PHENOLPHTHALEIN is considered less satisfactory than other laxatives. NHS expenditure on this product is over £100,000 a year.

ALTACITE
Roussel
Antacid tablets; suspension (per 5ml)

Hydrotalcite 500mg
Antacid: neutralises excess stomach acid.

There is no convincing evidence that this preparation is significantly more effective than other, simple antacid preparations, but it is much more expensive.
If a simple and effective antacid (eg aluminium hydroxide, magnesium trisilicate) were prescribed instead of this product, the NHS would save about £½ million each year.

ALTACITE PLUS
Roussel
Antacid tablets, suspension (per 5ml)

Hydrotalcite 500mg
Dimethicone (tablets: 250mg; suspension: 125mg)

The value of dimethicone is uncertain. See ASILONE. This product costs several times more than equivalent preparations without dimethicone, such as aluminium hydroxide or magnesium trisilicate tablets or mixture.
If these were prescribed instead, the NHS would save about £1 million a year.

ALUDROX SA
Wyeth
[POM] Suspension (per 5ml)

Ambutonium bromide 2.5mg
Antispasmodic: intended to relieve abdominal spasms and ulcer-like pain by reducing contractions of the stomach and intestine.
Aluminium hydroxide mixture 4.75ml
Magnesium hydroxide 100mg
Antacids: neutralise excess stomach acid.

Atropine-like antispasmodic drugs have not been shown to better the results of antacids given alone; and can produce unpleasant side effects, such as dry mouth, blurred vision, and retention of urine [DTB 1980, 18, 19].
NHS expenditure on this product is about £¼ million a year.
Similar preparations include: ALUMINIUM HYDROXIDE AND BELLADONNA MIXTURE (BPC); MAGNESIUM TRISILICATE AND BELLADONNA MIXTURE (BPC); ALUHYDE tablets (Sinclair); BELLOCARB tablets (Sinclair); CARBELLON tablets (Medo); NEUTRADONNA (tablets and powder) (Nicholas).

ALUHYDE
Sinclair
[POM] Tablets

See comparable product ALUDROX SA.

ALUMINIUM HYDROXIDE AND BELLADONNA MIXTURE BPC

See comparable product ALUDROX SA.

ALUPENT
Boehringer Ingelheim
[POM] Various formulations

All formulations contain
Orciprenaline sulphate
Bronchodilator: relieves breathing difficulties in asthma, bronchitis etc.

Tablets 20mg

Syrup *(per 5ml)* 10mg

Aerosol *(per dose)* 750 micrograms

Inhalant solution (withdrawn 1983)

Orciprenaline acts less selectively than some other bronchodilators: it does improve airflow, but also tends to over-stimulate the heart and central nervous system, causing adverse effects such as palpitations and tremor. Alternative products are generally preferred. See BRONCHODILATORS.
NHS expenditure on these preparations is about £1 million a year.

ALUPENT EXPECTORANT
Boehringer-Ingelheim
[POM] Tablets; mixture (per 10ml)

Orciprenaline sulphate 20mg
Bronchodilator.
Bromhexine hydrochloride 8mg
Mucolytic.

Undesirable combination of rather unsatisfactory ingredients. See ALUPENT, BISOLVON. See also BRONCHODILATORS, EXPECTORANTS AND MUCOLYTICS.
NHS expenditure on this product is about £1½ million a year.

ALUPRAM
Steinhard
[POM] Tablets

See VALIUM.

ALUZYME
Phillips Yeast
Tablets

Folic acid 14 micrograms
Thiamine hydrochloride 160 micrograms
Riboflavine 210 micrograms
Nicotinic acid 2.5mg
Dried yeast 297mg
Other B vitamins.

Marmite is half the price. See VITAMINS.

AMBAXIN
Upjohn

See similar product: AMOXIL.

AMESEC
Lilly
[POM] Capsules

Aminophylline 130mg
Ephedrine hydrochloride 25mg
Bronchodilators: relieve breathing difficulties in asthma, bronchitis etc.

The fixed-ratio combination is undesirable because it makes it impossible to adjust the dosage of each ingredient independently to suit the needs of individual users. The dosage of aminophylline (and related compounds) needs sensitive adjustment because of unusual variation in the dose-response; some people need up to eight times more aminophylline than others in order to maintain a therapeutic level of the drug in their blood [FR 41 176 9/9/76 p.38373]. It is also known that smokers excrete aminophylline faster than non-smokers and may need about twice the dosage to get the same therapeutic effect. The dosage of aminophylline and related drugs in this and other combined preparations (eg FRANOL) tends to be too low to be effective. See also *The Lancet* 1983, II, pp.607–613.
Careful adjustment of the dosage of EPHEDRINE is also necessary in order to get the best results and to avoid unwanted effects. (The US version of this drug includes a barbiturate component, partly to suppress these effects.) There are generally safer and more effective products.
NHS expenditure on this product is about £¼ million a year.

AMINOPHYLLINE
Suppositories

Aminophylline 50mg; 100mg; 150mg; 180mg; 360mg
Bronchodilator: relieves breathing difficulties in asthma, bronchitis etc.

Rectal absorption of aminophylline (and other theophylline-related drugs) tends to be erratic, and suppositories may irritate as well. Most reported cases of theophylline and aminophylline toxicity in children have been associated with the use of aminophylline suppositories [FR 41 176 9/9/76 p.38373]. Newer sustained-release oral preparations are generally preferred [AMADE p.591].

AMMONIA AND IPECACUANHA MIXTURE BP
Main ingredients in mixture (per 10ml)

Ammonium bicarbonate 200mg
Ipecacuanha tincture 0.3ml

Ineffective. See EXPECTORANTS AND MUCOLYTICS.

AMMONIUM CHLORIDE AND MORPHINE MIXTURE BP
Main ingredients in mixture (per 10ml)

Ammonium chloride 300mg
Ammonium bicarbonate 200mg
Chloroform and morphine tincture 0.3ml

Irrational combination: includes ingredients intended both to stimulate the cough reflex (ammonium salts); and to suppress it (chloroform and morphine). The value of ammonium salts is doubtful. See EXPECTORANTS AND MUCOLYTICS.

AMMONIUM CHLORIDE MIXTURE BP
Main ingredients in mixture (per 10ml)

Ammonium chloride 1g
Aromatic ammonia solution 0.5ml

Ineffective. See EXPECTORANTS AND MUCOLYTICS.

AMOXIL
Bencard
[POM] Powder for injection and other formulations

Amoxycillin 250mg, 500mg and 1g
Also, **amoxycillin** in capsules (250mg, 500mg); dispersible tablets (500mg); mixture and strong mixture, per 5ml (125mg, 250mg); suspension

for children, per 1.25ml (125mg); sachets (per unit) 3g

Amoxycillin

Broad spectrum penicillin (ie active against a wide variety of organisms) used to treat chronic bronchitis; ear, urinary tract, and other infections.

Amoxycillin (and related drugs listed below) have actions and uses similar to ampicillin, but they are better absorbed than ampicillin when taken with food, and are less likely to cause side effects (mainly diarrhoea).

The fact that amoxycillin is sometimes better absorbed than ampicillin is not necessarily an advantage because, when the dosage of each drug is adjusted to give the same blood (plasma) concentrations, both drugs have the same effect. The lower frequency of side effects with amoxycillin could significantly benefit perhaps one user in ten. Though ampicillin is generally well tolerated, around 12% of users can be expected to suffer from diarrhoea – against about 2% who get diarrhoea from amoxycillin and related drugs. In both cases the reactions are usually mild [DTB 1981, 80].

In short, ampicillin is an effective drug, whereas amoxycillin is probably more effective for one person in ten. The question is, does this justify the routine use of amoxycillin and related drugs instead of ampicillin, when it will make no difference to the large majority of users which drug they have? The question arises because prescriptions for amoxycillin and related drugs outnumber prescriptions for ampicillin by over 3:1; also because amoxycillin and similar drugs cost much more than ampicillin. (Drugs related to ampicillin include bacampicillin [AMBAXIN]; ciclacillin [CALTHOR]; pivampicillin [PONDOCILLIN]; talampicillin [TALPEN].)

If ampicillin were prescribed instead of AMOXIL and these other brands, the NHS would save around £4–£5 million a year.

ANANASE FORTE

Rorer

Enteric-coated tablets (ones designed to dissolve in the small intestine rather than in the stomach)

Bromelains 100,000 Rorer units

Concentrate of enzymes derived from pineapple plant, claimed to relive inflammation, bruising, swelling etc in damaged soft tissues.

The US Food and Drug Administration has rated this product ineffective ('lacking substantial evidence of effectiveness') for its recommended uses. Treatment is expensive: the UK Joint Formulary Committee considers it of doubtful value [BNF 1983, No.6 p.309].

ANAPOLON

Syntex

[POM] Tablets

Oxymetholone 5mg

Anabolic steroid: stimulates growth of body tissues.

Until 1982, this product was recommended for treatment of delayed growth and development in children but this use is not justified. The evidence suggests that the possible benefits of treatment are slight and that there is a serious risk of irreversible disturbances of growth and sexual development, particularly in younger children. Other uses for which there is inadequate evidence of effectiveness include treatment of severe debility and/or in convalescence [DTB, 1979, 17, 54].

ANDURSIL

Geigy

Antacid tablets; mixture

See similar product ASILONE.

ANETHAINE

Farley

Local anaesthetic cream

Amethocaine hydrochloride 1%

Use of local anaesthetic creams is best avoided because they may cause sensitisation. Amethocaine seems more likely to cause irritation than other local anaesthetics [BNF No.6, 1983, pp.58, 336; also M28, p.899). Oral analgesics will relieve pain, but there is no fully effective treatment for itching. There is insufficient evidence of the effectiveness of amethocaine for the treatment of ano-rectal pain and itching (pruritus ani) [FR 45 103 27/5/80 p.35619].

ANEURONE

Philip Harris

[POM] Tonic

Broadly similar to EFFICO; NEURO PHOSPHATES.

ANORVIT
Cox-Continental
Tablets

WITHDRAWN

Dried ferrous sulphate 200mg (equivalent to 60mg iron)
Ascorbic acid 10mg
Vitamin C.
Acetomenaphthone 2mg
Synthetic vitamin K.

VITAMINS are not needed with iron, and the rationale for including vitamin K is not clear. This product costs about twice as much as effective alternatives.

ANOVLAR 21
Schering
[POM] Oral contraceptive

Norethisterone acetate 4mg
Ethinyloestradiol 50 micrograms
Hormones.

A lower-strength pill may be safer. See ORAL CONTRACEPTIVES.

ANTASIL
Stuart
Antacid tablets; mixture

See similar product ASILONE.

ANTHICAL
May & Baker
Antihistamine cream

Mepyramine maleate 1.5%
Zinc oxide 15% in vanishing cream basis.

See ANTHISAN.

ANTHISAN
May & Baker
Cream

Mepyramine maleate 2%
Antihistamine: intended to relieve allergic and itchy skin conditions.

Antihistamine creams applied to the skin are relatively ineffective, and may cause skin reactions; antihistamines are more effective when taken by mouth. This product is specifically recommended for insect stings and bites but 'may cause sensitisation' [M28 p.1315] and these are 'best treated with calamine preparations . . .' [BNF No.6 1983 p.336].

ANTIHISTAMINES

Histamine is a chemical that the body produces in response to various allergy-causing agents, and is also one of the poisons present in insect stings and nettles. Antihistamine drugs oppose the effects of histamine, and are often effective in relieving symptoms of allergy, eg in hay fever or urticaria (nettle rash). Some antihistamines are also used as anti-emetics (ie to prevent or control nausea, vomiting and related disorders). Others (eg diphenhydramine) are used for their sedative effect, and to suppress cough.

Different antihistamines vary in their duration of action and in the frequency of side effects but 'there is no evidence that any one antihistamine is superior to another' [BNF No.6, 1983, p.110]. There is considerable variation between effective dosages of individual antihistamines, so careful adjustment of dosage is required. Slow-release formulations are increasingly used, but drug action may be neither uniform nor reliable.

Antihistamines are currently included in many preparations when there is little or no justification for their use. Antihistamines generally have no place in the treatment of the common cold, chronic bronchitis, nasal congestion or inflammation caused by an infection, and are of no value whatever in the treatment of asthma [BNF 1983, No.6, p.106].

Antihistamines should be taken by mouth: they are of limited value when topically applied, eg in creams or in nasal decongestant sprays.

The most common side effect of antihistamines is sedation. Astemizole (Hismanal) and terfenadine (Triludan) are exceptions, but most antihistamines cause anything from mild drowsiness to deep sleep, depending largely on the drug and the dosage. Sedative and related effects – dizziness and lack of concentration and coordination – are known to contribute to traffic and other accidents. Alcohol should be avoided: it increases these effects. Other fairly common side effects include dryness of nose, mouth and throat, and stomach upsets.

ANTISTIN-PRIVINE
Ciba
Nose drops; spray

Naphazoline nitrate 0.025%
Sympathomimetic: nasal decongestant.
Antazoline sulphate 0.5%
Antihistamine: suppresses symptoms of allergy.

Antihistamines are ineffective when locally applied; sympathomimetics (nasal decongestants) are not suitable for treatment of allergic conditions. See HAYPHRYN; ANTIHISTAMINES.

ANTOIN
Cox-Continental
Dispersible tablets

Aspirin 400mg
Codeine phosphate 5mg
Caffeine citrate 15mg

The dosage of codeine may be less than effective, and the caffeine has no significant effect. This product is much more expensive – but unlikely to be more effective – than aspirin 400mg alone. See ASPIRIN AND CODEINE.

ANUGESIC-HC
Warner
[POM] Cream for internal/external use

Zinc oxide 12.33%
Protectant with mild astringent action for the treatment of haemorrhoids and related ano-rectal disorders.
Bismuth oxide 0.87%
Protectant.
Hydrocortisone acetate 0.5%
Corticosteroid: to reduce local swelling and inflammation.
Peru balsam 1.8%
Intended as wound-healing agent.
Pramoxine hydrochloride 1%
Local anaesthetic.
Benzyl benzoate 1.2%
Antipruritic: relieves itching.
Resorcinol 0.87%
Skin preparation with antiseptic, itch-relieving and other actions.

A US expert panel has concluded that resorcinol is neither effective nor safe and 'has no legitimate internal use' [FR 45 103 27/5/80 p.35668]. It is rapidly absorbed into the body through mucous membranes and can interfere with the functioning of the thyroid gland. There is insufficient evidence of the effectiveness of either bismuth oxide or Peru balsam; the safety and effectiveness of local anaesthetics used internally is doubtful [FR 45 103 27/5/80 pp.35607, 35638, 35649]. NHS expenditure on this product is estimated at £¼ million a year.

ANUSOL-HC
Warner
[POM] Ointment; suppositories for treatment of haemorrhoids and other ano-rectal disorders (**zinc oxide; hydrocortisone acetate; bismuth subgallate; bismuth oxide; Peru balsam; benzyl benzoate; resorcinol**).

See entry for similar product ANUGESIC-HC. NHS expenditure on this product is estimated at over £¼ million a year.

ANXON
Beecham
[POM] Capsules

Ketazolam 15mg, 30mg

Ketazolam has actions and uses similar to diazepam and other BENZODIAZEPINE TRANQUILLISERS (see entry). In the body, ketazolam is rapidly converted to nordiazepam, the main active break-down product of diazepam; therefore the similarities between these drugs are much more striking than any differences, though the manufacturer has claimed that ketazolam causes less daytime drowsiness. This claim is not justified by the evidence: it was originally based on the results of a comparison between ketazolam taken once nightly, and diazepam taken three times a day. (In a comparison between diazepam taken at night, and ketazolam taken by day, the opposite result could be expected [DTB 1980, 18, 95].) Any advantage of ketazolam over diazepam is probably small, since ketazolam is usually taken as a sedative in a single dose at night. Ketazolam (ANXON) is one of the most expensive benzodiazepines, at least ten times more expensive than diazepam. It is unlikely to have advantages that are often worth this extra cost. If diazepam 10mg were prescribed instead of 30mg ketazolam (ANXON), the NHS could save about £¾ million a year.

APP STOMACH TABLETS
Consolidated
[POM] Tablets

Homatropine methyl bromide 1.5mg
Antispasmodic: intended to relieve abdominal spasms and ulcer-like pain by reducing contractions of the stomach and intestine.
Papaverine hydrochloride 3mg
Intended to relax muscle in gut wall.
Aluminium hydroxide mixture 15mg
Bismuth carbonate 12.5mg
Calcium carbonate 180mg
Magnesium trisilicate 92.5mg
Magnesium carbonate 180mg
Antacids: neutralise excess stomach acid.

APP Stomach Powder *(per gram)*
Homatropine methylbromide 1mg
Papaverine hydrochloride 1mg
Aluminium hydroxide mixture 30mg
Bismuth carbonate 20mg

Calcium carbonate 378mg
Magnesium carbonate 375mg
Magnesium trisilicate 195mg

An irrational and undesirable combination of ingredients. See ALKA-DONNA P. The value of papaverine is doubtful [M28 p.1059]. Bismuth salts have been largely superseded by more effective antacids. Their use has been restricted in some countries (eg France, Switzerland, Australia) because they may cause serious toxic effects if overused. If used for long periods, calcium salts are more likely to upset body chemistry than magnesium and/or aluminium salts. See CALCIUM CARBONATE.

AQUAMOX

WITHDRAWN

Lederle
[POM] Tablets

Quinethazone 50mg
Diuretic: helps to control high blood pressure; removes excessive fluid from body tissues by increasing the output of urine.

This drug has actions and uses similar to those of other 'thiazide' type diuretics, but costs up to ten times more.

ARADOLENE

Rorer
Counter-irritant cream

Diethylamine salicylate 5%
'Capsicum water soluble' 0.4%
Menthol 2.5%
Rectified camphor oil 1.4% in lanolin base.

Considered less suitable for prescribing. See ALGIPAN.

ARGOTONE

Lipha
Nose drops; spray

Ephedrine hydrochloride 0.9%
Sympathomimetic: reduces nasal congestion and inflammation.
Mild silver protein 1%
Anti-bacterial.

Significant infections would normally be treated systemically (ie affecting the whole body); this preparation is outmoded and unlikely to be of real value. For routine decongestion – though only for short-term use – ephedrine nasal drops are appropriate, and cost much less.

ARTRACIN

DDSA
[POM] Capsules

Indomethacin 25mg, 50mg

See INDOCID.

ASILONE

Berk
Antacid tablets

Dried aluminium hydroxide 500mg
Antacid: neutralises excess stomach acid.
Dimethicone 270mg
Anti-foaming agent: intended to relieve flatulence.
ASILONE gel and suspension (per 5ml)
Dried aluminium hydroxide 420mg
Light magnesium oxide 70mg
Dimethicone 135mg

ASILONE FOR INFANTS suspension (per 5ml)
Dried aluminium hydroxide 84mg
Light magnesium oxide 14mg
Dimethicone 27mg

This is an effective but very expensive range of products, strongly promoted by brand name, and very widely prescribed. The only significant difference between ASILONE and other simple antacids is the presence of an 'anti-flatulent', an anti-foaming agent, dimethicone. Dimethicone (simethicone) is a silicone, found in many other brands of antacid. The effectiveness of dimethicone is uncertain. There is even uncertainty about what it is effective for: thus, US expert panels have decided that dimethicone does have an anti-flatulent effect, but have found no convincing evidence that it is effective in relieving classic symptoms of stomach discomfort. The American Medical Association has reported that the efficacy of dimethicone is 'doubtful, and the rationale for its method of action is dubious' [AMADE p.1274]. The implication seems to be that the benefits of dimethicone, as a standard antacid ingredient, are at best marginal. It seems very unlikely that any benefits are worth the substantial extra costs. ASILONE products cost several times more than equivalent preparations without dimethicone, such as aluminium hydroxide or magnesium trisilicate tablets or mixture. If either of these were prescribed instead of ASILONE products, the NHS could save an estimated £4 million each year.
Similar products: ACTONORM (Wallace); ANDURSIL (Geigy); ANTASIL (Stuart); DILORAN (Lipha); DIOVOL (Pharmax); MAALOX PLUS

(Rorer); POLYALK (Galen); POLYCROL and POLYCROL FORTE (Nicholas); SILOXYL (Martindale); SYLOPAL (Norton). Possible saving on these brands is estimated at about £½ million a year.

ASMAPAX

Nicholas
[POM] Sustained-release tablets

Theophylline 65mg
Ephedrine hydrochloride 50mg

There are generally safer and more effective alternatives. See similar product AMESEC.

ASMA-VYDRIN

Lewis
Solution for spray

Adrenaline 0.55%
Atropine methonitrate 0.14%
Papaverine hydrochloride 0.88%
Chlorbutol 0.5%

There are generally better alternatives. See ADRENALINE AND ATROPINE.

ASPELLIN

Radiol
Counter-irritant liniment and spray

Ammonium salicylate 1%
Camphor 0.6%
Menthol 1.4%
Ethyl and methyl salicylate 0.54%

Considered less suitable for prescribing. See ALGIPAN.

ASPIRIN AND CODEINE BP

Tablets; and dispersible tablets (in effervescent formulation)

Aspirin 400mg
Relieves mild to moderate pain, reduces inflammation and lowers high temperature.
Codeine phosphate 8mg
Narcotic analgesic: relieves mild to moderate pain; also acts as cough suppressant, and constipating agent.

A dose of 10mg or under of codeine phosphate has no discernible analgesic (pain-relieving) effect; the effective analgesic dose of codeine is usually between 30–60mg, though a 15mg dose of codeine 'might have some analgesic effect' [FR 42 131 8/7/77 p.35423]. At the recommended dose (1–2 tablets every 4–6 hours), this combination could not be expected to be much more effective than 400mg of aspirin alone.
The combination of aspirin and codeine as pain relievers is probably unnecessary, but it is rational: although codeine and aspirin have the same general effect, they work in different ways and at different sites in the body. In theory, the combination of aspirin and codeine is slightly more effective than equivalent doses of either drug alone, but only when ingredients are supplied at an effective dosage. This combination could complicate treatment of overdose, because each ingredient produces different symptoms of poisoning.

ASPIRIN, PARACETAMOL AND CODEINE

Tablets

Aspirin 250mg
Paracetamol 250mg
Codeine phosphate 6.8mg
Analgesics: relieve mild to moderate pain.

The combination is rational, though probably unnecessary. The dose of codeine is less than effective: see ASPIRIN AND CODEINE. The combination of aspirin (250mg) plus paracetamol (250mg) could be expected to be as effective in relieving pain as either paracetamol (500mg) or aspirin (500mg). The combination would be less effective for rheumatic diseases because paracetamol has no anti-inflammatory action, but symptoms of intolerance (stomach irritation) to aspirin might be less.

ATARAX

Pfizer
[POM] Tablets; syrup (per 5ml)

Hydroxyzine hydrochloride 10mg
(25mg: *tablets only)*
Central nervous system depressant with anti-emetic and antihistaminic actions: used to treat anxiety, also stress-related skin disorders (eg urticaria).

ATARAX is promoted mainly for the treatment of anxiety and tension, though it is reported to be 'a less potent anti-anxiety agent than the benzodiazepines' [AMADE p.207]. See BENZODIAZEPINE TRANQUILLISERS. Hydroxyzine (ATARAX) costs around ten times more than the usual first choice among benzodiazepines, diazepam.
NHS expenditure on this product is about £¼ million a year.

ATENSINE
Berk
[POM] Tablets

Diazepam 2mg, 5mg, 10mg

See VALIUM.

ATIVAN
Wyeth
[POM] Tablets

Lorazepam 1mg, 2.5mg

Lorazepam has actions and uses similar to diazepam and other BENZODIAZEPINE TRANQUILLISERS, but is more rapidly excreted from the body. It could therefore be expected to sedate less when used to treat anxiety, and to cause less hangover when taken to induce sleep. However, this potential advantage appears neither great nor marked: 'studies comparing lorazepam with established benzodiazepines in the treatment of anxiety suggest that it is of equivalent efficacy but in no way better' [DTB 1973, 11, 28]. Lorazepam (ATIVAN) costs about three times as much as diazepam, and it seems doubtful if its potential advantages are often worth this extra cost. If diazepam were prescribed instead, the NHS could save around £3 million a year.

ATROMID-S
ICI
[POM] Capsules

Clofibrate 500mg
Used to lower blood levels of lipids (fatty substances, like cholesterol).

Carefully selected, high-risk users may be helped by clofibrate, but drug-induced reduction of blood lipid levels has not clearly been shown to reduce diseases of the arteries to the heart. Two large trials on this drug suggest that clofibrate is most likely to help people with no previous history of heart attacks or heart pain (angina). These users seem less likely to suffer from non-fatal heart attacks (ie myocardial infarction: death of part of the heart muscle resulting from poor blood supply). However, clofibrate has not been shown to affect the frequency of fatal heart attacks. The same studies indicated that clofibrate users risk a small but significant increase in fatal illness from diseases other than heart failure. This drug should therefore be used very cautiously, and only if alternative measures fail: restrictions on diet, alcohol intake and smoking should normally be tried first.
There were about ¼ million prescriptions for this drug in 1981.

AUDAX
Napp
Ear drops

Choline salicylate 20%
Local analgesic (pain-killer) for ear ache.
Macrogol 1.25%
Solvent and penetrating agent.

Choline salicylate is relatively ineffective when applied to the affected area. Any analgesic effect from such an application of salicylates results from absorption of the drug into the blood stream, when it would work in the same way as it would if it had been taken by mouth [FR 44 234 4/12/79 p.69847]. Ear ache should be treated with a simple analgesic (eg aspirin, paracetamol) taken by mouth, provided there is no infection in the ear.

AUDICORT
Lederle
[POM] Ear drops

Neomycin 0.35%
Anti-bacterial agent.
Undecenoic acid 0.7%
Anti-fungal.
Triamcinolone acetonide 0.1%
Corticosteroid.
Benzocaine 5%
Local anaesthetic.

Benzocaine is not usually effective in relieving ear pain (see AURALGICIN). See also CORTICOSTEROID + ANTI-INFECTIVE SKIN PREPARATIONS.
Less suitable for prescribing.
NHS expenditure on this product is about £¾ million a year.

AUDINORM
Carlton
Ear drops

Dioctyl sodium sulphosuccinate (**docusate sodium**) 5%
Glycerol 10%
Used to soften ear wax before it is removed.

This product is not needed. There are many simple, effective and cheaper alternatives such as sodium bicarbonate ear drops, baby oil, arachis oil, almond oil etc.

AURALGICIN
Fisons
Ear drops

Phenazone 5.5%
Local analgesic (pain-killer) for ear ache.
Benzocaine 1.4%
Local anaesthetic.
Ephedrine hydrochloride 1%
Vasoconstrictor: to reduce inflammation.
Chlorbutol 1%
Anti-bacterial and anti-fungal agent.
Potassium hydroxyquinolone sulphate 0.1% *in glycerol*
Anti-bacterial, anti-fungal agent.

Benzocaine and related local anaesthetics are inadequately absorbed from the skin (or tympanic membrane in the ear) and their effectiveness is unpredictable. They may also cause hypersensitivity reactions [AMADE p.546]. (In other applications, a 5%–20% concentration of benzocaine is required for an effective local anaesthetic action.) Phenazone 'is liable to give rise to skin eruptions and in susceptible individuals even small doses may have this effect' [M 28 p.272]. Local analgesics tend to be ineffective (see AUDAX).

AURALTONE
Rorer
Ear drops

Benzocaine 1%
Phenazone 5% *in glycerol.*

Effectiveness very doubtful. See AUDAX, AURALGICIN.

AUREOCORT
Lederle
[POM] Cream and ointment

Triamcinolone acetonide 0.1%
Corticosteroid to reduce inflammation.
Chlortetracycline hydrochloride 3%
Anti-infective agent.

[POM] Pressurised aerosol spray
(60 gram container)

Triamcinolone acetonide 0.025%
Chlortetracycline hydrochloride 1%

Only likely to be of value where an area of eczema or dermatitis is infected. See CORTICOSTEROID + ANTI-INFECTIVE SKIN PREPARATIONS. NHS expenditure on this product is about £200,000 a year.

BALMOSA
Pharmax
Counter-irritant cream

Camphor 4%
Menthol 2%
Capsicum oleoresin 0.035%
Methyl salicylate 4%
Sodium iodide 1.2%

Considered less suitable for prescribing: see ALGIPAN.

BARBITURATES

Barbiturate drugs can be effective in controlling convulsions, and in anaesthesia, but their use as sedatives or hynoptics has been largely superseded by BENZODIAZEPINE TRANQUILLISERS which, in spite of their limitations, are thought to be much safer [BNF 1983, No.6, p.131].

The disadvantages of barbiturates include addiction and liability to abuse; serious withdrawal symptoms (dangerous, if withdrawal is abrupt); and the tendency to interfere with the actions of many other drugs. Barbiturates are also dangerous in overdose. They caused one-quarter of the 2,900 deaths from poisoning in the UK in 1978, and one-third of these cases were caused by a single product, TUINAL.

The Committee on Safety of Medicines (CSM) announced in 1980 that it intended to withdraw product licences for all products which combined barbiturates with other ingredients, but this process, which gives manufacturers a right of appeal, has taken time. Several such products (eg FRANOL) were still on the market in late 1983, and still heavily prescribed.

The CSM proposed that single-ingredient barbiturates still be allowed. But it was stressed that these should be used only as a last resort, for 'severe intractable insomnia', and not as sedatives or anti-anxiety agents. However, in the 1983/4 Data Sheets, several products were still being recommended for such uses. In 1981, an estimated 1½ million NHS prescriptions were written for barbiturate hypnotics or sedatives.

Barbiturate drugs listed include: amylobarbitone: SODIUM AMYTAL (Lilly); TUINAL (Lilly); butobarbitone: SONERYL (May & Baker); cyclobarbitone: PHANODORM (Winthrop); heptabarbitone: MEDOMIN (Geigy); phenobarbitone: LUMINAL (Winthrop); PARABAL (Sinclair); PHENOBARBITONE SPANSULE (SKF); quinalbarbitone: SECONAL SODIUM (Lilly). Barbiturate-like drugs include glutethimide: DORIDEN (Ciba); and methprylone: NOLUDAR (Roche).

BARQUINOL HC

Fisons
[POM] Cream

Hydrocortisone 0.5%
Cortiocosteroid to reduce inflammation.
Clioquinol 3%
Anti-infective agent

Only likely to be of value where an area of excema or dermatitis is infected. See: CORTICOSTERIOD + ANTI-INFECTIVE SKIN PREPARATIONS.

BAYCARON

Bayer
[POM] Tablets

Mefruside 25mg
Diuretic: helps to control high blood pressure; removes excessive fluid from body tissues by increasing output of urine.

Mefruside has actions and uses similar to those of the thiazide diuretics. It has no special advantage over other diuretics but is much more expensive.
If bendrofluazide (5mg) were prescribed instead of this drug (25mg), the NHS could save about £200,000 a year.

BAYOLIN

Bayer
Cream

Benzyl nicotinate 2.5%
Heparinoid 500 units/gram
Glycol salicylate 10%
Counter-irritant intended to relieve pain in muscles, joints etc, when rubbed into skin.

There is no convincing evidence that glycol salicylate is effective when applied externally to relieve deep-seated pain [FR 44 234 4/12/79 p.69845]. Methyl Salicylate Ointment BP or Methyl Salicylate Liniment BP are much cheaper alternatives.
NHS expenditure on this product is estimated at £100,000 a year.

BC 500

Ayerst
Tablets

Thiamine mononitrate 25mg
Riboflavine 12.5mg
Nicotinamide 100mg
Pyridoxine hydrochloride 10mg
Cyanocobalamin 5 micrograms
Calcium pantothenate 20mg
B vitamins.
Ascorbic acid 500mg
Vitamin C.

Clear vitamin deficiency is normally treated by injection of much greater amounts of vitamins B and C. For routine prevention of deficiency states, this product is less suitable for prescribing because it provides much higher doses of vitamins than the body either needs or can utilise. (Vitamins B and C are rapidly excreted, rather than stored in the body.) It costs at least 2–3 times more than unbranded vitamin preparations which supply daily needs in full. If appropriate amounts of Compound Vitamin B Tablets (Strong) and Ascorbic Acid Tablets BP were prescribed instead, the NHS could save around £¼ million a year.

BC 500 WITH IRON

Ayerst
Iron supplement tablets with vitamins

Ferrous fumarate 200mg (65mg iron)
B-vitamins:
As for BC 500, less cyanocobalamin.

Independent authorities say there is 'no justification' for adding vitamins to iron supplements, and consider that the use of such combinations should be 'strongly discouraged'. See VITAMINS. This product costs the NHS about fifteen times more than completely adequate iron preparations. NHS expenditure on this product is about £¼ million a year.

BELLADONNA MIXTURE, PAEDIATRIC BPC

See comparable product
ALUDROX SA.

BELLERGAL

Sandoz
[POM] Tablets

WITHDRAWN

Belladonna alkaloids 200 micrograms
Antispasmodic: intended to relieve abdominal spasms and ulcer-like pain by reducing contractions of the stomach and intestine.
Ergotamine tartrate 300 micrograms
Vasoconstrictor: intended to relieve symptoms of migraine headache.
Phenobarbitone 20mg
Barbiturate sedative.

This product has been recommended for a rag-bag of symptoms, ranging from gynaecological disorders to a variety of skin conditions. It is not well suited to the treatment of any – if only because the dosage of the ingredients cannot be independently adjusted. The dosage of ergotamine is too low to be effective. Sedatives are rarely indicated in ulcer therapy but, if needed, should be prescribed on their own. BARBITURATES should be avoided: they may cause addiction and have unpleasant side effects.

BELLERGAL RETARD WITHDRAWN
Sandoz
[POM] slow-release tablets

See the previous entry, and see remarks about slow-release preparations in Chapter One.

BELLOCARB
Sinclair
Tablets

See comparable product ALUDROX SA.

BENAFED
Parke Davis
Linctus (per 5ml)

Ammonium chloride 125mg
Expectorant: intended to help removal of phlegm from airways.
Sodium citrate 57mg
Expectorant and buffering agent.
Dextromethorphan hydrobromide 15mg
Cough suppressant.
Diphenhydramine hydrochloride 12.5mg
Antihistamine: used to control symptoms of allergy; to suppress cough; and to sedate.
Menthol 1mg
Aromatic oil.
Pseudoephedrine hydrochloride 30mg
Nasal, bronchial decongestant.

It is irrational to combine an antihistamine (which dries secretions in the airways) with an expectorant (intended to liquefy and loosen secretions); and to combine ingredients which otherwise both stimulate and suppress the cough reflex. The value of EXPECTORANTS is doubtful: see entry. Diphenhydramine has a marked sedative effect: driving skills etc may be impaired. Nasal decongestant sprays are more effective than oral preparations. The UK Joint Formulary Committee says 'there is no scientific basis' for prescribing mixtures of this kind, and deprecates their use [BNF No.6, 1983, p.120].
NHS expenditure on this product is about £1/4 million a year.

BENGUE'S BALSAM
Bengue
Counter-irritant ointment

Menthol 20%
Methyl salicylate 20% in a lanolin base. (BENGUE'S BALSAM SG has a vanishing cream base.)

Considered less suitable for prescribing: Methyl Salicylate Ointment or Liniment BP are cheaper alternatives.

BENYLIN DECONGESTANT
Parke Davis
Syrup (per 5ml)

Diphenhydramine hydrochloride 14mg
Pseudoephedrine 10mg
Menthol 1.1mg
Sodium citrate 57mg

Undesirable combination. See BENAFED.
NHS expenditure on this product is over £1/4 million a year.

BENYLIN EXPECTORANT
Parke Davis
Syrup (per 5ml)

Ammonium chloride 135mg
Diphenhydramine hydrochloride 14mg
Menthol 1.1mg
Sodium citrate 57mg

Irrational combination. See BENAFED. See also entry for EXPECTORANTS AND MUCOLYTICS.
NHS expenditure on this product is about £2 1/2 million a year.

BENYLIN FORTIFIED LINCTUS
Warner-Lambert Health Care
Syrup (per 5ml)

Diphenhydramine hydrochloride 14mg
Dextromethorphan hydrobromide 6.5mg
Sodium citrate 57mg
Menthol 1.1mg

Similar to BENYLIN WITH CODEINE. See also BENAFED.

BENYLIN PAEDIATRIC
Parke Davis
Syrup (per 5ml)

Diphenhydramine hydrochloride 7mg
Menthol 550 micrograms
Sodium citrate 28.5mg

Undesirable combination. See BENAFED; GUANOR PAEDIATRIC. Antihistamines produce

an unpredictable response in young children, and may stimulate rather than sedate: they should be used only under medical supervision.
NHS expenditure on this product is about £1/4 million a year.

BENYLIN WITH CODEINE

Parke Davis
Syrup (per 5ml)

Codeine phosphate 5.7mg
Diphenhydramine hydrochloride 14mg
Menthol 1.1mg
Sodium citrate 57mg

Undesirable combination: codeine phosphate (10–20mg, 4–6 hourly) is likely to be as effective or more effective in suppressing a dry cough. See BENAFED.
NHS expenditure on this product is about £1 1/4 million a year.

BENZODIAZEPINE TRANQUILLISERS

Benzodiazepine tranquillisers are mainly used as sedatives (to reduce arousal) and as hypnotics (to promote sleep). Different benzodiazepines tend to be promoted either as sedatives (for the control of anxiety) or for insomnia, depending on the dosage. At lower dosages, all benzodiazepines sedate, and at higher dosages they all promote sleep. Benzodiazepines are also used as skeletal muscle relaxants and to control convulsions and other disorders.

The benzodiazepines have largely replaced the BARBITURATES (see entry) as sedatives and hypnotics: they are not as dangerous in overdose and serious side effects are less common. Dependence and withdrawal problems are also less serious with benzodiazepines, though they are increasingly recognised as a major problem, especially if these drugs are taken for more than a few weeks. Each year, there are around 30 million (often repeat) prescriptions for benzodiazepine tranquillisers, which suggests epidemic misuse.

The differences between the various kinds of benzodiazepine tranquillisers are far less marked than the similarities between them, though a distinction can be made between the shorter- and longer-acting compounds. Shorter-acting compounds (which have less cumulative effect because they are more rapidly eliminated from the body) tend to cause less hangover and daytime sedation, but all benzodiazepines have these unwanted effects. There can be no such thing as a non-sedating sedative – an anti-anxiety agent which does not in some way impair alertness.

For commercial reasons, the differences between the various kinds of benzodiazepine tranquillisers tend to be much exaggerated. However, the advantages of the shorter-acting compounds are sometimes worthwhile, though often not: it all depends on how and for how long the drug is to be used. See for example the entries for ANXON and HALCION; and the table on TRANXENE on pp.52–5.

What is quite clear, though, is that the market for benzodiazepines is already over-saturated, and that the addition of 'new' compounds is likely to hinder rather than help effective drug use. Existing benzodiazepines include the archetype, diazepam (ALUPRAM, ATENSINE, DIALAR, EVACALM, SOLIS, TENSIUM, VALIUM, and VALRELEASE) and bromazepam (LEXOTAN); chlordiazepoxide (LIBRAXIN, LIBRIUM, TROPIUM); clobazam (FRISIUM); clorazepate (TRANXENE); flunitrazepam (ROHYPNOL); flurazepam (DALMANE); ketazolam (ANXON); lorazepam (ALMAZINE, ATIVAN); lormetazepam (NOCTAMID); medazepam (NOBRIUM); nitrazepam (MOGADON, NITRADOS, NOCTASED, REMNOS, SOMNITE, SUREM and UNISOMNIA); oxazepam (SERENID-D, SERENID FORTE); prazepam (CENTRAX); temazepam (EUHYPNOS, EUHYPNOS FORTE, NORMISON); and triazolam (HALCION).

BETA-BLOCKER + DIURETIC PREPARATIONS

Mild to moderately high blood pressure usually responds to treatment with either a beta-blocker, which controls over-stimulation of the heart, or a diuretic, but the two may be prescribed together if either treatment fails on its own. Ideally, the ingredients should be prescribed separately in the appropriate dosage – but this would be more expensive for the patient (two prescription charges) though much cheaper for the NHS.
A combined preparation is convenient and may suit a patient who dislikes taking several tablets, but should never be used as a first treatment. Choice depends on the available dosage ratios and on the type of beta-blocker required; there are no important differences between the different diuretics used. None of the preparations listed differs much in efficacy or toxicity [DTB 1981, 19, 59]. Choice also depends on cost. The more expensive preparations (eg SECADREX, SOTAZIDE, TRASIDREX, VISKALDIX) cost around three times more than the cheapest ones (eg INDERETIC, PRESTIM).

BETADINE

Napp
Antiseptic gargle

Povidone-iodine 1%
Mouthwash.

Of minor importance and probably no more effective than a weak (1.5%) salt solution, though much more expensive.

BETALOC

Astra
[POM] Tablets

Metoprolol tartrate 50mg, 100mg
Beta-blocker: controls over-stimulation of the heart and regularises the heartbeat. Used mainly to treat high blood pressure, angina and heart disorders.

This is an effective and widely prescribed drug, strongly promoted by brand name. Selected users (eg with a history of wheezing) would benefit from metoprolol, which is more selective for the heart than the close equivalent, propranolol. But as a general rule 'propranolol remains the drug of choice since it is cheap and its long-term risks are clearly understood' [DTB 1980, 18, 64].
If propranolol were prescribed instead of this product, the NHS would save an estimated £3/4 million a year.

BETALOC SA

Astra
[POM] Sustained-release tablets (durules)

Metoprolol tartrate 200mg

See BETALOC.
If metoprolol (100mg × 2) were prescribed instead of BETALOC SA, the NHS could save an estimated £1/2 million a year.

BETNESOL-N

Glaxo
[POM] Drops for eye (ear and nose)

Betamethasone sodium phosphate 0.1%
Corticosteroid: used to reduce inflammation.
Neomycin sulphate 0.5%
Antibacterial antibiotic.

Corticosteroid + antibiotic combinations are widely prescribed but should normally be avoided. They are not suitable for routine treatment of eye disorders and should be used only under close specialist supervision. Corticosteroids may seriously aggravate some eye infections which are difficult to diagnose, and may cause serious side effects (steroid glaucoma) in susceptible individuals. Corticosteroids also reduce the body's resistance to infection, and may worsen the patient's condition if the antibiotic does not work (eg the dosage of the antibiotic may be too low, or the infection may be caused by organisms not susceptible to antibiotics, including fungi and viruses). In addition, if the patient is hypersensitive to the antibiotic, the corticosteroid may make things worse by masking the allergic response. Neomycin and (the very similar) framycetin readily produce sensitisation, and both are widely used in products of this kind. About one million NHS prescriptions are written each year for corticosteroid + antibiotic combinations for eye disorders alone.
NHS expenditure on this product is estimated at over £1/4 million a year.

BETNOVATE C

Glaxo
[POM] Cream and ointment

Betamethasone (as valerate) 0.1%
Corticosteroid to reduce inflammation.
Clioquinol 3%
Anti-infective agent.

Only likely to be of value where an area of eczema or dermatitis is infected. See CORTICOSTEROID + ANTI-INFECTIVE SKIN PREPARATIONS.
NHS expenditure on this product is over £1/4 million a year.

BETNOVATE-N

Glaxo
[POM] Cream, ointment and lotion

Betamethasone (as valerate) 0.1%
Corticosteroid to reduce inflammation.
Neomycin sulphate 0.5%
Antibacterial antibiotic.

Only likely to be of value where an area of eczema or dermatitis is infected. See CORTICOSTEROID + ANTI-INFECTIVE SKIN PREPARATIONS.
NHS expenditure on this product is about £400,000 a year.

BEZALIP

MCP
[POM] Tablets

Bezafibrate 200mg
Used to lower blood levels of lipids (fatty substances, like cholesterol).

This drug has been claimed to be more effective than clofibrate (see ATROMID-S); but this claim seems to be based on several small comparative trials in which differences were minor and inconsistent [DTB, 1983, 21, 75–76]. All of these trials were reported in the published proceedings of a manufacturer-sponsored symposium: as a rule, these are not vetted as scrupulously as articles published in learned journals [DTB, 1983, 21, 24]. There seems to be no reason to choose bezafibrate over clofibrate: it has no clear advantage but costs twice as much. Drugs of this kind may help certain high-risk patients, if dietary and other restrictions fail, but they should be used with caution. There is a theoretical basis for thinking that such drugs may help but 'there is currently no clinical evidence to demonstrate that BEZALIP is effective in the prevention of heart disease' [Data Sheet 1983/4].

BIOMYDRIN WITHDRAWN

Warner
[POM] Nasal spray

Neomycin sulphate 0.1%
Gramicidin 0.005%
Antibacterial antibiotics.
Phenylephrine hydrochloride 0.25%
Sympathomimetic: reduces nasal congestion and inflammation.
Thonzylamine hydrochloride 1%
Antihistamine: used to control symptoms of allergy, eg in hay fever.

Significant infections are best treated systemically: local antibiotic treatment is unlikely to be as effective, and may do harm. Antihistamines applied to the specific area are ineffective and may cause sensitisation. The combination of ingredients is undesirable because the dosage of the anti-infectives would tend to be governed by the user's perceived need for a decongestant – just as the need for anti-infective treatment could lead to excessive use of the decongestant. Sympathomimetic decongestant sprays are suitable only for short-term use: if used for more than a few days, they may cause 'rebound congestion', involving recurrence or deterioration of the original condition.

BISLUMINA WITHDRAWN

MCP
Antacid mixture (per 5ml)

Bismuth aluminate 750mg

Bismuth salts are considered obsolete. See ROTER.

BISMA-REX ANTACID

Riker
Antacid powder and tablets

Powder
Sodium bicarbonate 65%
Calcium carbonate 15%
Heavy magnesium carbonate 5%
Bismuth carbonate 1%
Light magnesium carbonate 10%
Antacids: neutralise excess stomach acid.
Peppermint oil 0.125%
Carminative: intended to relieve flatulence and spasmodic stomach pain.
Light kaolin 4%

Tablets
Bismuth carbonate 13mg
Magnesium trisilicate 90mg
Calcium carbonate 460mg
Magnesium carbonate 160mg
Peppermint oil 2mg

Bismuth salts are considered obsolete. See ROTER. CALCIUM CARBONATE and SODIUM BICARBONATE (see entries) also have disadvantages as antacids. A US panel of experts has found no convincing evidence of the effectiveness of peppermint oil in treating symptoms of indigestion [FR 47 5/1/82 p.458].

BISMUTH SUBGALLATE, COMPOUND

Suppositories

Bismuth subgallate 200mg
Protectant: intended to relieve discomfort of haemorrhoids and related ano-rectal disorders.
Castor oil 60mg
Protectant; lubricant.
Resorcinol 60mg
Skin preparation with antiseptic, itch-relieving and other actions.
Zinc oxide 120mg *in theobroma oil or other base*
Protectant; mild astringent.

A US expert panel has concluded that resorcinol is neither effective nor safe and 'has no legitimate internal use' [FR 45 103 27/5/80 p.35668]. It is rapidly absorbed into the body through mucous membranes and can interfere with the functioning of the thyroid gland. There is inadequate evidence of the effectiveness of bismuth subgallate [FR 45 103 27/5/80 p.35639].

BISODOL
International Chemical
Antacid tablets

Calcium carbonate 518mg
Light magnesium carbonate 66.7mg
Sodium bicarbonate 63.3mg
Antacids: neutralise excess stomach acid.
Diastase 9.2mg
Enzyme: digestive aid.

If used for long periods, calcium salts are more likely to upset body chemistry than magnesium and/or aluminium salts. See CALCIUM CARBONATE. SODIUM BICARBONATE (see entry) should not be taken regularly, and some people should not take it at all. A US panel of experts has found no convincing evidence of either the safety or effectiveness of diastase in treating symptoms of indigestion [FR 47 2 5/1/82 p.458].

BISOLVOMYCIN
Boehringer-Ingelheim
[POM] Tablets

Oxytetracycline hydrochloride 250mg
Bacteriostatic antibiotic: used for the treatment of bronchitis and other infections.
Bromhexine hydrochloride 8mg
Mucolytic: reduces viscosity of phlegm.

Undesirable combination recommended for respiratory tract infections. The value of bromhexine is questionable. See BISOLVON.
NHS expenditure on this product is over £100,000 a year.

BISOLVON
Boehringer-Ingelheim
Tablets/elixir (per 10ml)

Bromhexine hydrochloride 8mg
Mucolytic: reduces viscosity of phlegm, to help expectoration.

Bromhexine may help some patients but in general 'does not seem worth using' [DTB, 1975, 13, 12]. See EXPECTORANTS AND MUCOLYTICS.
NHS expenditure on this product is about £1 million a year.

BRADOSOL
Ciba
Lozenges

Domiphen bromide 500 micrograms
Antimicrobial: for minor throat infections.

There is no good evidence that this preparation is of any real value. The NHS spends about £1½ million a year on products of this kind.

BRAVIT
Galen
Vitamin capsules and tablets

Both capsules and tablets are similar to ALLBEE WITH C.

BRICANYL COMPOUND
Astra
[POM] Tablets

Terbutaline sulphate 2.5mg
Bronchodilator: relieves breathing difficulties in asthma, bronchitis etc.
Guaiphenesin 100mg
Expectorant: intended to help removal of phlegm from the airways.

Terbutaline is an effective drug, but there is no good evidence that EXPECTORANTS (see entry) are effective or useful in the treatment of asthma [AMADE p.595].

BRICANYL EXPECTORANT
Astra
[POM] Elixir (per 5ml)

Terbutaline sulphate 1.5mg
Guaiphenesin 66.5mg

See BRICANYL COMPOUND.
NHS expenditure on this product is estimated at £200,000 a year.

BRINALDIX K
Sandoz
[POM] Effervescent tablets

Clopamide 20mg
Diuretic: helps to control high blood pressure; removes excessive fluid from body tissues by increasing output of urine.
Potassium 12mmol
Supplement intended to replace potassium which the body loses through diuresis.

Many people do not need a potassium supplement with a diuretic. If a supplement is needed it is best taken separately: the required dosage may be higher than the amount in this preparation. See POTASSIUM SUPPLEMENTS.
Clopamide has no clear advantage over thiazide diuretics, such as bendrofluazide [M28 p.592]. Bendrofluazide + potassium costs 4–5 times less than this clopamide + potassium combination.

BRONCHILATOR

Sterling Research
[POM] Metered aerosol (per dose)

Isoetharine mesylate 350 micrograms
Bronchodilator.
Phenylephrine hydrochloride 70 micrograms
Decongestant.

Isoetharine (similar to isoprenaline) is not a drug of first choice: see BRONCHODILATORS.

BRONCHODILATORS

Bronchodilators relax and open up the bronchi, the air tubes in the lungs. They are mainly used to control spasms which cause wheezing and shortness of breath in asthma. They are also used to relieve breathing difficulties in chronic bronchitis and other disorders but may be less effective for this.

Muscles in the bronchi are controlled in two different ways. The sympathetic nerves relax muscles and so dilate the bronchi, while the parasympathetic nerves make the bronchi constrict. Accordingly, there are two main kinds of bronchodilator: the most important are the 'sympathomimetic' drugs which enhance or imitate sympathetic nervous action, and which relax the bronchi. The other kind blocks the parasympathetic nerves, which prevents constriction of muscles in the airways.

Sympathomimetic drugs tend to be more or less selective in their action. Less selective agents (and notably adrenaline and ephedrine) do relax the bronchi, but they act on sympathetic nerves in other parts of the body too. They may overstimulate the heart and central nervous system, and often cause unpleasant side effects, including restlessness, anxiety and insomnia.

Other sympathomimetics (eg salbutamol, terbutaline) are more selective in their action: they act more specifically on the nerves that control breathing. These are usually considered the drugs of first choice – though aminophylline and other theophylline derivatives can also be effective as bronchodilators, and are also widely used. The theophylline derivatives have a different mechanism of action from the classic sympathomimetic drugs, but they also stimulate breathing and relieve spasm by relaxing muscles in the bronchi.

Antispasmodic drugs – eg atropine and other derivatives of belladonna – work by blocking the action of parasympathetic nerves (ie preventing constriction of the bronchi). These drugs can be effective but their usefulness is limited by unwanted effects. Their main disadvantage is that they tend to dry up secretions in the bronchi, and this may block the smaller airways because it makes it harder to cough up phlegm.

The simultaneous use of different bronchodilators may be helpful, but very careful adjustment of dosage is needed to get the best effect. See: fixed-ratio combination drugs (Chapter One, p.25).

BRONCHOTONE

Rorer
[POM] Liquid (per 5ml)

Ephedrine hydrochloride 22.89mg
Bronchodilator: relieves breathing difficulties in asthma, bronchitis etc.
Belladonna tincture 0.52ml
Antispasmodic: intended to control coughing spasms.
Sodium salicylate 91.85mg
Analgesic: relieves mild to moderate pain.
Sodium iodide 57.04mg
Expectorant: intended to help removal of phlegm from the airways.
Caffeine 86.5mg
Mild stimulant.

EXPECTORANTS (see entry) have no proven value in the treatment of asthma [AMADE p.595]. The combination of belladonna (which dries bronchial secretions) and an expectorant (meant to promote bronchial secretions) is irrational. Unwanted effects limit the usefulness of both EPHEDRINE (see entry) and belladonna: there are generally more effective alternatives to both. Sodium salicylate is outmoded, and the dosage here is very low. Caffeine is of little significance: a cup of coffee provides more.

BRONTINA

Brocades
[POM] Tablets

Deptropine citrate 1mg
Antihistamine: suppresses symptoms of allergy; anticholinergic: controls coughing spasms, used to ease breathing difficulties in asthma, etc.

Deptropine is considered less effective than other agents used to control breathing difficulties. See BRONCHODILATORS. Its usefulness is limited by unwanted effects: eg the tendency to dry up secretions may add to breathing problems by increasing the viscosity of phlegm in the airways.

BRONTISOL

Brocades
[POM] Metered aerosol (per inhalation)

Isoprenaline sulphate 150 micrograms
Deptropine citrate 100 micrograms

There are generally better (more selective) bronchodilators than isoprenaline. See BRONCHODILATORS; see also BRONTINA.

BROVON

Napp
Inhalant spray

Adrenaline 0.5%
Atropine methonitrate 0.14%
Papaverine hydrochloride 0.88%
Chlorbutol 0.5%

PRESSURISED BROVON

Napp
[POM] Metered aerosol (per inhalation)

Adrenaline 250 micrograms
Atropine methonitrate 500 micrograms

PRESSURISED ISO-BROVON

Napp
[POM] Metered aerosol (per inhalation)

Isoprenaline 180 micrograms
Atropine methonitrate 50 micrograms

PRESSURISED ISO-BROVON PLUS

Napp
[POM] Metered aerosol (per inhalation)

Isoprenaline 500 micrograms
Atropine methonitrate 50 micrograms

There are better bronchodilators than these compound preparations, all regarded as less suitable for prescribing. See ADRENALINE & ATROPINE SPRAY; see also BRONCHODILATORS.

BROXIL

Beecham
[POM] Tablets, capsules, syrup (per 10ml)

Phenethicillin 250mg
Antibacterial antibiotic: for penicillin-sensitive infections.

No more effective than phenoxymethylpenicillin (Penicillin V), but costs about three times more. If Penicillin V were prescribed instead of this product, the NHS could save over £100,000 a year.

BURINEX K

Leo
[POM] Tablets (slow-release potassium in wax core)

Bumetanide 500 micrograms
Diuretic: helps to control high blood pressure; removes excessive fluid from body tissues by increasing output of urine.
Potassium 7.7mmol
Supplement intended to replace potassium which the body loses through diuresis.

Many people do not need a potassium supplement with a diuretic. If a supplement is needed it is best taken separately, and preferably in solution not tablet form. The required dosage may be higher than the amount in this preparation. See POTASSIUM SUPPLEMENTS.
Bumetanide has actions and uses similar to those of another diuretic, frusemide [M28 p.586]. If frusemide + potassium were prescribed instead of this product, the NHS could save an estimated £1 million a year.

BUSCOPAN

Boehringer Ingelheim
[POM] Tablets

Hyoscine butylbromide 10mg
Antispasmodic: intended to relieve abdominal spasms and ulcer-like pain by reducing contractions of stomach and intestine.

This drug is very poorly absorbed from the gut and the evidence that it is effective by mouth is not convincing. Some authorities consider it 'only effective by injection' [Turner P., Volans G., p.54].
NHS expenditure on this product is about £½ million a year.

BUTACOTE

Geigy
[POM] Enteric-coated tablets (designed to dissolve in the small intestine rather than in the stomach)

Hazardous. See BUTAZOLIDIN.

BUTAZOLIDIN

Geigy
[POM] Tablets and suppositories

Phenylbutazone (tablets) 100mg, 200mg; (suppositories) 250mg

A non-steroidal anti-inflammatory drug (NSAID) used to treat pain and inflammation in rheumatic and related conditions.

Serious and not uncommon side effects drastically limit the usefulness of this otherwise effective drug. It can aggravate high blood pressure and give rise to leg swelling by causing salt and water retention. It can irritate and severely ulcerate the stomach, and may cause serious and sometimes fatal abnormalities of the blood cells. In the UK alone, at least 440 people are known to have died from using this and related drugs.
Phenylbutazone and related drugs should therefore only be used if alternative treatments have failed; and treatment should normally be limited to short courses (not exceeding one week). In the US, though not in the UK, this drug is contraindicated for children under 14 ('since controlled clinical trials in patients of this age group have not been conducted'). Use by people over 60 is especially inadvisable 'because of the exceedingly high risk of severe fatal toxic reactions in this age group' [PDR, 1983, p.960].
This product and identical or closely related agents (BUTACOTE, BUTAZOLIDIN ALKA, BUTAZONE, TANDALGESIC, TANDERIL, and TANDACOTE) are nevertheless still widely prescribed: around 1¼ million prescriptions in 1981. Prescribing these products by brand name costs the NHS over £1 million a year.
There are at least 20 alternative NSAIDS: it should rarely if ever be necessary to prescribe this product at all.

BUTAZOLIDIN ALKA
Geigy
[POM] Tablets

Phenylbutazone 100mg
Dried aluminium hydroxide gel 100mg
Magnesium trisilicate 150mg
NSAID.

Hazardous. See BUTAZOLIDIN.

BUTAZONE
DDSA
[POM] Tablets

Hazardous. See BUTAZOLIDIN.

CAFADOL
Typharm
Tablets

Paracetamol 500mg
Caffeine 30mg

There is more caffeine in half a cup of tea; paracetamol on its own relieves pain just as well, and is much cheaper.

CALADRYL
Warner-Lambert Health Care
Cream and lotion

Diphenhydramine hydrochloride 1%
Antihistamine: to relieve allergic and itchy skin conditions.
Calamine 8%
Mild astringent; allays itching.
Camphor 0.1%
Counter-irritant.

Antihistamine creams are relatively ineffective and may cause skin reactions. Antihistamines are more effective by mouth.

CALAVITE
Carlton
Multivitamin tablets

Broadly similar to though cheaper than ABIDEC. See VITAMINS.

CALCIMAX
Wallace Mfg
Syrup (per 5ml)

Calcium glycine hydrochloride 500mg
Provides calcium 76mg.
Thiamine hydrochloride 500 micrograms
Riboflavine 125 micrograms
Nicotinamide 2mg
Pyridoxine 125 micrograms
Cyanocobalamin 0.125 micrograms
Calcium pantothenate 125 micrograms
B vitamins.
Ascorbic acid 5mg
Vitamin C.
Ergocalciferol 100 units
Vitamin D.

Vitamins are not needed for treatment of calcium deficiency; and calcium is not needed in multivitamin preparations. Cyanocobalamin is less effective by mouth, and calcium pantothenate not of recognised value. See VITAMINS.

CALCIUM CARBONATE, COMPOUND
BPC 1973
Antacid powder (per gram)

Calcium carbonate 375mg
Heavy magnesium carbonate 125mg
Sodium bicarbonate 375mg
Antacids: neutralise excess stomach acid.
Light kaolin 125mg

Calcium salts may produce an 'acid rebound' effect: after the neutralisation has worn off, the amount of acid produced in the stomach may increase and symptoms of discomfort may recur or worsen. If used for long periods, calcium salts are more likely to upset body chemistry than magnesium and/or aluminium salts. Long-term use may also raise blood-calcium levels too high, producing side effects which include headache, weakness, nausea, vomiting, constipation and stomach pains. These symptoms are more likely if antacids containing calcium salts are taken regularly with calcium-rich foods, eg milk or cream [M28, p.76]. SODIUM BICARBONATE (see entry) should not be taken regularly, and some people should not take it at all. Simple antacid preparations, such as aluminium hydroxide or magnesium trisilicate (tablets or mixture), are preferable.

CALPOL
Wellcome
Paediatric suspension (per 5ml)

Paracetamol 120mg

An effective drug, strongly promoted by brand name.
If the identical medicine were prescribed by generic name (paracetamol paediatric elixir), the NHS would save over £½ million a year.

CALPOL SIX PLUS
Wellcome
Paediatric suspension (per 5ml)

Paracetamol 250mg

See CALPOL.

CALSALETTES
Torbet Laboratories
Tablets

Aloin 38mg
Laxative.

Aloin tends to cause griping and 'has been superseded by less toxic purgatives' [M28 p.1362].

CALTHOR
Ayerst

See similar product AMOXIL.

CAM
Rybar
Syrup (per 5ml)

Ephedrine hydrochloride 4mg
Bronchodilator: relieves breathing difficulties in asthma, bronchitis etc.
Butethamate citrate 4mg
Bronchodilator, also said to have antispasmodic effects.

Unwanted effects limit the usefulness of EPHEDRINE (see entry); and compound preparations should be avoided.
See BRONCHODILATORS.

CAM DECONGESTANT
Rybar
Syrup (per 5ml)

Phenylpropanolamine hydrochloride 7.5mg
Nasal decongestant.
Guaiphenesin 30mg
Expectorant.

This product is now called NEZCAAM. The combination of ingredients is undesirable, and the value of guaiphenesin doubtful (see EXPECTORANTS). This product is intended for children aged 2 and over. Some authorities consider this acceptable [FR 41 176;9/9/76, p.38401]; others say that phenylpropanolamine is 'not recommended for children under 8 years' [AMADE, 1983 p.556].

CANTIL
MCP
[POM] Tablets; elixir (per 5ml)

Mepenzolate bromide (tablets: 25mg; elixir: 12.5mg/5ml)
Antispasmodic: intended to relieve abdominal spasms and ulcer-like pain by reducing contractions of the stomach and intestine.

This product has no clear advantage over many other atropine-like antispasmodic drugs, but costs much more than most. US prescribing information states: 'Since there is no adequate experience in children who have received this drug, safety and efficacy in children have not been established' [PDR 1983, p.1348]. In the UK this product is recommended for children aged 6 years or over.

CANTIL WITH PHENOBARBITONE
MCP
[POM] Tablets

Mepenzolate bromide 25mg
Phenobarbitone 15mg
Barbiturate sedative.

The combination of ingredients is undesirable. The optimum dosage of atropine-like antispasmodic drugs varies greatly for different people; and dosages have to be individualised if these drugs are to be effective. Sedatives are rarely necessary in ulcer therapy but, if needed, should be prescribed on their own. BARBITURATES should be avoided: they may cause addiction and have unpleasant side effects. See entry.

CARBELLON
Medo

Charcoal tablets are an outmoded treatment for indigestion etc., otherwise similar to ALUDROX SA.

CARDIACAP
Consolidated
Slow-release capsules

Pentaerythritol tetranitrate 30mg
Coronary vasodilator: intended to improve circulation by relaxing and opening blood vessels around the heart. Used for the prevention of angina (heart pains caused by lack of oxygen in heart muscle).

The value of long-acting nitrates is uncertain: variation in dose response is wide but poorly understood and the therapy should be individualised for each patient [M28, p.1621; Am. J. Med. 1978, 64, 183]. The US Food and Drug Administration has classified pentaerythritol tetranitrate only as 'possibly effective', though acknowledges that it 'is widely regarded as useful' in preventing attacks of angina [PDR 1983, p.1533].

CARISOMA
Pharmax
[POM] Tablets

Carisoprodol 125mg, 350mg
Skeletal muscle relaxant.

Diazepam is considered the drug of first choice in treating painful muscle spasm, and is cheaper. The clinical efficacy of carisoprodol is 'not well established' [BNF no.6 1983, p.308].

CARISOMA CO
Pharmax
[POM] Tablets

Paracetamol 350mg
Carisoprodol 175mg
Caffeine 32mg

Carisoprodol is not a drug of choice. See CARISOMA. The caffeine adds only to cost: half a cup of tea would provide as much. The fixed-ratio combination is undesirable: the ingredients should be prescribed separately.

CASCARA EVACUANT
Parke Davis
Elixir (per 5ml)

WITHDRAWN

Cascara extract 2g
Laxative.

Cascara is considered less satisfactory than other preparations because its laxative action is unpredictable and sometimes violent; it may also irritate the gut.

CAVED-S
Tillots
Tablets

Deglycyrrhizinised liquorice 380mg
Ulcer-healing agent.
Aluminium hydroxide mixture 100mg
Light magnesium carbonate 200mg
Sodium bicarbonate 100mg
Bismuth subnitrate 100mg
Antacids: neutralise excess stomach acid.
Frangula bark 30mg
Laxative.

Deglycyrrhizinised liquorice 'is of doubtful efficacy' [BNF No.6; 1983; p.45). SODIUM BICARBONATE (see entry) should not be taken regularly, and some people should not take it at all. Frangula is best avoided. See ROTER.

CE-COBALIN
Paines & Byrne
Syrup (per 5ml)

Cyanocobalamin 30 micrograms
Ascorbic acid 10mg

Of very doubtful value. See similar (cheaper) product CYTACON.

CEDURAN
Tillots
[POM] Tablets

Nitrofurantoin 100mg
Antiseptic: used to treat urinary tract infections.
Deglycyrrhizinised liquorice 250mg
Intended to allay nausea, vomiting and stomach upsets that may be caused by nitrofurantoin.

The value of deglycyrrhizinised liquorice in suppressing side effects caused by nitrofurantoin is not well established. The incidence of side effects from nitrofurantoin can be reduced by taking the drug with milk or food or by lowering the dose or by taking nitrofurantoin macrocrystals (Macrodantin). See also FURADANTIN.

CELEVAC

WBP
Tablets

Methylcellulose '450' 500mg
Laxative: bulk-forming agent, intended to help users eat less by making the stomach feel full.

A daily dosage of at least 20 tablets might significantly help to reduce food intake, but there is little evidence to suggest that this product would be effective at the recommended dosage (three tablets before meals or when hungry). Only about one person in eight in a Consumers' Association survey found bulk-forming agents at all helpful in suppressing appetite: an apple eaten before meals was recommended as more effective [*Which?* April 1983].

CELLUCON

Medo
Tablets

Methylcellulose '2500' 500mg
Recommended dosage: 1–4 tablets before meals or when hungry.

Appetite suppressant found less effective than some others. See similar product CELEVAC.

CENTRAX

Warner
[POM] Tablets

Prazepam 10mg

Prazepam has actions and uses similar to diazepam and other BENZODIAZEPINE TRANQUILLISERS. In the body, prazepam is converted to desmethyldiazepam, the main break-down product of diazepam. It has no significant advantages over diazepam [DTB, 1982, 20, 68], though costs the NHS about twice as much. See BENZODIAZEPINE TRANQUILLISERS.

CENTYL K

Burgess
[POM] Tablets (slow-release potassium in wax core)

Bendrofluazide 2.5mg
Diuretic: helps to control high blood pressure; removes excessive fluid from body tissues by increasing output of urine.
Potassium 7.7mmol
Supplement intended to replace potassium which the body loses through diuresis.

Many people do not need a potassium supplement with a diuretic. If a supplement is needed it is best taken separately, and preferably in solution not tablet form. The required dose may be higher than the amount in this preparation. See POTASSIUM SUPPLEMENTS. The ingredients cost less if separately prescribed.

CEPHALOSPORIN ANTIBIOTICS

The cephalosporins (and cephamycins) are related to the penicillins. They are broad-spectrum antibiotics, active against a wide variety of organisms, including some which are resistant to penicillin and ampicillin. The cephalosporins are also relatively safe. However, there are few absolute indications for their use; most infections which will respond to these drugs can be treated at least as effectively with penicillin, tetracycline or other antibiotics – and at a fraction of the cost.

The American Medical Association has concluded that 'their very active promotion and wide therapeutic usage is out of all proportion to their importance in anti-infective therapy' [AMADE, 1980, p.1230]. The same is true in the UK: The cephalosporins 'are not omnicides: their use does not remove the need for careful choice . . .' [DTB, 1982, 20, 88]. In 1981, there were 2½ million prescriptions for cephalosporins in the UK.

There are about a dozen different cephalosporins and cephamycins available in about forty different formulations. These are the so-called first, second and third generations of these drugs; another generation is in the pipeline [DTB, 1982, 20, 86]. In spite of their similarities, many of these drugs are specifically active against certain organisms (which to some extent may just mean they are *documented* as having some specific activity) and this complicates comparison between them.

However, KEFADOL (cefamandole) is considered less suitable than alternatives: it 'has no advantage over cefuroxime', has some disadvantages and costs more [DTB, 1982, 20, 86]. DISTACLOR (cefaclor) 'offers no clear advantage over cephalexin or cephradine' [DTB, 1979, 17, 70] but costs more. If cephalexin were prescribed instead of DISTACLOR, the NHS would save around £½ million a year. In addition, the first cephalosporins – CEPORIN (cephaloridine) and KEFLIN (cephalothin) – are now considered 'redundant' [DTB, 1982, 20, 88]. Some of the newer cephalosporins are likely to be more effective and/or safer than these.

CEPORIN
Glaxo
[POM] Powder for injection

Cephaloridine 250mg, 500mg, 1g

More effective alternatives available. See CEPHALOSPORIN ANTIBIOTICS.

CERUMOL
LAB
Ear drops

Turpentine oil 10%
Organic solvent for the removal of ear wax.
Chlorbutol 5%
Antibacterial and antifungal; preservative.
Paradichlorbenzene 2%
Pharmaceutical additive.

Turpentine oil may cause sensitivity reactions. Agents which soften ear wax (eg glycerol, sodium bicarbonate ear drops, warm baby oil) are effective, cheap and less likely to irritate.

CHALK MIXTURE, PAEDIATRIC BP
Antacid mixture (per 5ml)

Chalk (calcium carbonate) 100mg
Antacid: neutralises excess stomach acid. Constipating agent.
Tragacanth, in powder 10mg
Thickening/suspending agent.
Cinnamon water (concentrated) 0.02ml
Carminative: intended to relieve flatulence and colic (painful spasm of intestine or bowel).
Chloroform water, double strength 2.5ml
Syrup 0.5ml

A US panel of experts has found no convincing evidence of the effectiveness of cinnamon in treating symptoms of indigestion [FR 47 2 5/1/82 p.458]. See also CALCIUM CARBONATE.

CHEMOCYCLINE
Consolidated
[POM] Paediatric syrup (per 5ml)

Oxytetracycline hydrochloride 125mg

Tetracyclines are not for children under 12 [BNF No.6, 1983, p.192]. See TETRACYCLINE MIXTURE.

CHLORAMPHENICOL EAR DROPS
[POM]

Chloramphenicol in propylene glycol 5%; 10%
Antibiotic.

There is a high incidence (10%) of hypersensitivity reactions; these drops should be avoided.

CHLOROMYCETIN
Parke Davis
[POM] Ear drops

Chloramphenicol in propylene glycol 10%

To be avoided. See identical product CHLORAMPHENICOL EAR DROPS.

CHLOROMYCETIN-HYDROCORTISONE
Parke Davis
[POM] Eye ointment

Hydrocortisone acetate 0.5%
Corticosteroid: used to reduce inflammation.
Chloramphenicol 1%
Antibacterial antibiotic.

Combinations of corticosteroids + antibiotics have serious limitations, and should normally be avoided. See BETNESOL-N. Chloramphenicol may cause less sensitisation than other antibiotics used to treat eye infections (though it may produce serious disorders in prolonged use).

CHOLOXIN
Travenol
[POM] Tablets

Dextrothyroxine sodium 2mg
Used to lower blood levels of lipids (fat-like substances such as cholesterol.

Dextrothyroxine works, but 'is no longer recommended as a lipid-lowering drug' (BNF no.6, 1983, p.97) because it may also cause rapid heart beat (tachycardia) or heart pain (angina). US prescribing information for the equivalent product states: 'It has not been clearly established whether the drug-induced lowering of [blood] serum cholesterol or lipid levels has a detrimental, beneficial or no effect on the morbidity or mortality due to atherosclerosis* or coronary heart disease' [PDR, 1983, p.953]. [*Atherosclerosis = 'hardening of the arteries' ie the thickening of artery walls due to deposits of fat-like substances. This can seriously impair blood flow.]

CHYMAR
Armour
[POM] Injection

Alpha-chymotrypsin 5000 Armour Units.

See CHYMORAL.

CHYMOCYCLAR
Armour
[POM] Capsules

Tetracycline hydrochloride 250mg
Bacteriostatic antibiotic.
Pancreatic enzymes (trypsin, chymotrypsin) 50,000 Armour Units
Intended to liquefy bronchial secretions to facilitate expectoration.

Undesirable combination. The value of these enzymes is doubtful. See CHYMORAL.

CHYMORAL
Armour
Enteric-coated tablets; tablets forte (double-strength)

Trypsin, alpha-chymotrypsin 50,000 and 100,000 Armour Units
Enzyme intended to relieve inflammation, bruising, swelling etc. in damaged soft tissues.

The US Food and Drug Administration has rated similar products ineffective; and the UK Joint Formulary Committee considers this one of doubtful value.

COBADEX-NYSTATIN
Cox-Continental
[POM] Ointment

Hydrocortisone 1%
Corticosteroid to reduce inflammation.
Nystatin 100,000 units/gram
Antifungal agent.
Dimethicone '350' 20%
Water repellant.
Benzalkonium chloride 0.2%
Disinfectant.

Similar to TIMODINE. Only likely to be of value where an area of eczema or dermatitis is infected. See CORTICOSTEROID + ANTI-INFECTIVE SKIN PREPARATIONS. Now called NYBADEX.

CO-BETALOC
Astra
[POM] Tablets

Metoprolol tartrate 100mg
Beta-blocker.
Hydrochlorothiazide 12.5mg
Diuretic.

See BETA-BLOCKER + DIURETIC PREPARATIONS. See also notes on relative advantages of metoprolol and propranolol under BETALOC. If propranolol and bendrofluazide were prescribed instead of this product, the NHS would save about £½ million a year.

CODEINE AND PARACETAMOL
Tablets

Codeine phosphate 8mg
Paracetamol 500mg
To relieve mild to moderate pain.

The combination is rational but probably unnecessary. The dose of codeine may be less than effective (see ASPIRIN AND CODEINE), and this combination could not be expected to be much more effective than 500mg of paracetamol alone.

CODIS
R & C
Dispersible tablets

Aspirin 500mg
Codeine phosphate 8mg

The dose of codeine may be less than effective. This combination is more expensive – but not much more effective – than aspirin 500mg alone. See ASPIRIN AND CODEINE.
If aspirin were prescribed instead of this product, the NHS could save at least £¼ million a year.

COLESTID
Upjohn
[POM] Granules (per sachet)

Colestipol hydrochloride 5g
Used to lower blood levels of lipids (fatty substances, like cholesterol).

This drug is used to prevent/treat atherosclerosis ('hardening of the arteries'; ie the thickening of artery walls due to deposits of fat-like substances, which can seriously impair blood flow to the heart). It has not been clearly established that drug-induced lowering of blood fat levels has benefits in the treatment of atherosclerosis or coronary heart disease [PDR 1983; p.2036]. However, this drug may help carefully selected users, if alternative measures fail: restrictions on diet, alcohol intake and smoking should normally be tried first.

COMBIZYM
Luitpold-Werk
Tablets

Pancreatin 220mg (in inner layer)
Amylase; cellulase, hemicellulase and proteases (outer layer) 120mg

Digestive enzymes intended to improve digestion and to relieve symptoms of indigestion.

There is no convincing evidence to suggest that any of these ingredients are effective either in improving digestion or in relieving the symptoms of indigestion [FR 47 2 5/1/82 pp.454–487]. If supplements are needed because of pancreatic insufficiency, they are generally taken in higher dosages, and in the form of powder sprinkled on food, because acid in the stomach destroys the activity of pancreatin [BNF No.6, 1983, p.64].

COMBIZYM COMPOSITUM

Luitpold Werke
Tablets

Ox bile extract 60mg
Digestive aid, laxative.
Digestive enzymes (pancreatin; amylase; cellulase; hemicellulase and protease) 400mg

There is no convincing evidence of effectiveness. See COMBIZYM.

CONCAVIT

Wallace Mfg
Multivitamin capsules, drops and syrup

Broadly similar to ABIDEC. See VITAMINS.

CONGESTEZE

Kirby-Warrick
[POM] Tablets and syrup

Tablets
Pseudoephedrine sulphate 60mg in outer layer plus 60mg in slow-release inner layer
Decongestant.
Azatadine maleate 1mg
Antihistamine.

Syrup (per 5ml)
Pseudoephedrine 30mg
Azatadine maleate 1mg

It is doubtful whether sympathomimetics add to the effectiveness of antihistamines in the treatment of allergy [DTB 1982, 20, 40].

CONOTRANE

WBP
Cream

Hydrargaphen 0.05%
Mercurial antibacterial and antifungal agent.
Dimethicone '350' 20%
Silicone: water repellant.

Minor skin infections generally need no treatment. Mercurial disinfectants are outmoded [M28 p.939], and should be avoided [BNF no.6, 1983, p.358]. This preparation is relatively very expensive.

CONOVA 30

Gold Cross
[POM] Oral contraceptive

Ethynodiol diacetate 2mg
Ethinyloestradiol 30 micrograms
Hormones.

A lower-strength pill may be safer. See ORAL CONTRACEPTIVES.

COPHOLCO

Rorer
Linctus (per 5ml)

Pholcodine 5.63mg
Cough suppressant.
Terpin hydrate 8.82mg
Expectorant: intended help removal of phlegm from airways.
Menthol 1.41mg
Cineole 0.0026ml
Aromatic oils.

It is irrational to combine ingredients which both stimulate and suppress the cough reflex. Terpin hydrate is of doubtful value. See entry on EXPECTORANTS AND MUCOLYTICS.

COPHOLCOIDS

Rorer
Pastilles

Pholcodine 4mg
Terpin hydrate 16mg
Menthol 2mg
Cineole 0.004ml
Chloroform 0.012ml

An irrational mixture. See COPHOLCO.

CORGARETIC 40

Squibb
[POM] Tablets

Nadolol 40mg
Beta-blocker.
Bendrofluazide 5mg
Diuretic.

Used to control high blood pressure. See BETA-BLOCKER + DIURETIC PREPARATIONS

CORGARETIC 80
Squibb
[POM] Tablets

Nadolol 80mg
Beta-blocker.
Bendrofluazide 5mg
Diuretic.

Used to control high blood pressure. See BETA-BLOCKER + DIURETIC PREPARATIONS.

CORTICOSTEROID + ANTI-INFECTIVE SKIN PREPARATIONS

There are about 60 prescription-only skin preparations (35 brands) which combine an anti-infective agent with a corticosteroid drug (eg hydrocortisone) to reduce inflammation. There is much controversy about their value, no doubt because they can be successfully used but often are not.

These products are criticised for two main reasons. First, there are doubts about the value of topical (applied directly to the area) anti-infective treatment – which is typically given when an infection is suspected and/or before the infective agent has been identified. Most experts think that significant infections are best treated with the appropriate antibiotic taken by mouth or injected, once the cause of the infection has been found. Secondly, there is a risk of sometimes serious complications. Corticosteroids may reduce the body's resistance to infection, and can make some infective skin conditions (eg athlete's foot, impetigo) much worse. Among other unwanted effects, corticosteroids may also mask an allergic response, if the user is or becomes allergic to the anti-infective agent. Reactions to anti-infective agents such as neomycin (and framycetin) are relatively common [AMADE p.1341].

Preparations of this kind that are also available in the US (eg VIOFORM-HYDROCORTISONE) are rated less than effective ('possibly effective') by the US Food and Drug Administration. The UK Joint Formulary Committee originally classified corticosteroid + anti-infective skin preparations as 'less suitable for prescribing' [BNF No.1, 1981, pp.290–3]. The Committee no longer rates them as such, but is not enthusiastic about them: 'There is little evidence that the inclusion of an anti-infective agent with a corticosteroid has any therapeutic benefit in most cases and it may sometimes complicate subsequent treatment. It may however be of value in eczema that has become secondarily infected, and in seborrhoeic dermatitis' [BNF No.6, 1983, p.342].

In 1981, there were about 3 million prescriptions (costing about £7 million) for corticosteroid + anti-infective skin preparations. Much of this use is probably inappropriate or unjustified.

CORTUCID
Nicholas
[POM] Eye ointment

Hydrocortisone acetate 0.5%
Corticosteroid, to reduce inflammation.
Sulphacetamide sodium 10%
Sulphonamide antibacterial antibiotic.

Combinations of corticosteroids and anti-infective agents have serious limitations. See BETNESOL-N.

COSALGESIC
Cox-Continental
[POM] Tablets

Dextropropoxyphene hydrochloride 32.5mg
Paracetamol 325mg

Potentially dangerous combination. See DISTALGESIC.
NHS expenditure on this product is estimated at £400,000 a year.

COTAZYM B
Organon
Tablets

Ox bile extract (equivalent to cholic acid 30mg)
Intended as digestive aid, laxative.
Pancreas powder (lipase 5400 BP units), cellulase
Digestive enzymes.

No convincing evidence of effectiveness. See COMBIZYM.

CREMALGEX
Norton
Counter-irritant cream

Almost identical to ALGIPAN. Less suitable for prescribing.

CREMALGIN
Berk
Counter-irritant cream

Almost identical to ALGIPAN. Less suitable for prescribing.

CREMATHURM
Sinclair
Counter-irritant cream

Capsicum oleoresin 0.1%
Methyl salicylate 10%
Ethyl nicotinate 1%
Histamine acid phosphate 0.1%

Less suitable for prescribing: Methyl Salicylate Ointment or Liniment BP are effective and cheaper alternatives. See ALGIPAN.

CYCLOBRAL
Norgine
Capsules

Cyclandelate 400mg

Lacks evidence of effectiveness. See CYCLOSPASMOL.

CYCLOSPASMOL
Brocades
Capsules; tablets; suspension (per 5ml)

Cyclandelate 400mg
Peripheral vasodilator: used to treat blood circulation disorders; also promoted to improve mental function, particularly in the elderly.

Cyclandelate lacks evidence of effectiveness: its benefits, if any, appear marginal. A US expert panel has classified this drug as 'possibly effective' for its stated indications [PDR 1982, p.985]; and the American Medical Association concurs. See entry for PERIPHERAL VASODILATORS. NHS expenditure on this product is estimated at £2¼ million a year.

CYTACON
Duncan Flockhart
Tablets and syrup

Tablets
Cyanocobalamin 50 micrograms

Syrup *(per 5ml)*
Cyanocobalamin 35 micrograms

Cyanocobalamin is less well absorbed than hydroxocobalamin (another form of vitamin B_{12}) but neither is very effective by mouth. Vitamin B_{12} deficiency (pernicious anaemia) is treated by injection, as it is more reliable [M28 p.1645; AMADE p.802].

DAKTACORT
Janssen
[POM] Cream

Hydrocortisone 1%
Corticosteroid to reduce inflammation.
Miconazole nitrate 2%
Anti-fungal agent.

Only likely to be of value where an area of eczema or dermatitis is infected. See CORTICOSTEROID + ANTI-INFECTIVE SKIN PREPARATIONS. NHS expenditure on this product is over £1 million a year.

DALIVIT
Paines & Byrne
Multivitamin capsules, drops and syrup

Broadly similar to ABIDEC. See VITAMINS.

DALMANE
Roche
[POM] Capsules

Flurazepam 15mg, 30mg

See entry for BENZODIAZEPINE TRANQUILLISERS.

DANERAL SA
Hoechst
Slow-release tablets

Pheniramine maleate 75mg
Antihistamine: used to treat symptoms of allergy eg in hay fever or urticaria (nettle rash).

The action of slow-release antihistamines may be uneven and unpredictable; and they are also more expensive than standard formulations. This product appears to have no significant advantage over other antihistamines, but is much dearer. If slow-release chlorpheniramine 12mg (as Piriton spandets) were prescribed instead of this product, the NHS could save at least £¼ million a year.

DAVENOL
Wyeth
Linctus (per 5ml)

Pholcodine 4mg
Cough suppressant.
Ephedrine hydrochloride 7mg
Bronchodilator, decongestant.
Carbinoxamine maleate 2mg
Antihistamine: used to control symptoms of allergy.

An undesirable combination, inexplicably recommended for 'treatment of all types of cough' [Data Sheet 1983/4]. It is less suitable for the treatment of productive cough: the cough suppressant and the antihistamine (which tends to dry and thicken bronchial secretions) could add to congestion of the airways. Dry or painful cough is better treated with a cough suppressant on its own. See also ACTIFED COMPOUND LINCTUS.
NHS expenditure on this product is estimated at £200,000 a year.

DEANASE
Consolidated
[POM] Powder for preparation of injections or solutions

Deoxyribonuclease 250,000 units; 1 mega unit

Intended to reduce inflammation by removing dead tissues from injured parts, but considered of doubtful value [BNF No.6, 1983, p.309].

DEANASE DC
Consolidated
Enteric-coated tablets (intended to dissolve in the small intestine rather than in the stomach)

Delta-chymotrypsin 10mg

Intended for the relief of soft tissue inflammation, but of doubtful value. Similar to VARIDASE.

DECASERPYL
Roussel
[POM] Tablets

Methoserpidine 5mg, 10mg
Antihypertensive: used to control high blood pressure.

The possibility of serious side effects limits the usefulness of this drug: 'Of 119 patients treated with methoserpidine, 22 developed mental depression, usually after 3–6 months' treatment' [W. R. Layland et al. (letter) Br. Med. J. 1962, 1, 639: quoted in M28 p.151]. See also RESERPINE. This product is about ten times more expensive than reserpine, which has similar uses and effects.
NHS prescriptions for this brand are estimated at over £100,000 a year.

DECASERPYL PLUS
Roussel
[POM] Tablets

Methoserpidine 10mg
Benzthiazide 20mg
Diuretic: removes excessive fluid from body tissues by increasing the output of urine; augments the antihypertensive effect.

See DECASERPYL. See also: RESERPINE. The use of a fixed-ratio combination is undesirable, except for patients who have originally taken the two ingredients separately and found these doses suit them.
NHS prescriptions for this brand are estimated at over £200,000 a year.

DEFENCIN CP
Bristol-Myers
Slow-release capsules
Isoxsuprine hydrochloride 40mg
Peripheral vasodilator.

Lacks evidence of effectiveness. See PERIPHERAL VASODILATORS. See also DUVADILAN.
NHS expenditure on this product is estimated at £¼ million a year.

DELIMON
Consolidated
[POM] Tablets

Paracetamol 50mg
Analgesic; antipyretic: used to lower temperature.
Morazone hydrochloride 150mg
Analgesic/anti-inflammatory agent.

There is no advantage to this combination, which costs 2–3 times more than an equivalent amount of paracetamol or aspirin alone. Morazone is not well established as a pain reliever. [M28 p.277].

DELTACORTRIL 'ENTERIC'
Pfizer
[POM] Tablets

Prednisolone 2.5mg, 5mg
Corticosteroid: anti-inflammatory agent.

The manufacturers claim that the enteric coating allows the drug to be transported intact into the small intestine (jejunum) for immediate disintegration and release of the drug, reducing the risk either of stomach ulceration or inactivation of the drug. The evidence suggests that enteric-coating does not affect the amount of prednisolone absorbed, and there is no evidence that such tablets cause less ulceration than plain ones [DTB, 1977, 15, 84].

DERMOGESIC

MSD
Ointment WITHDRAWN

Benzocaine 3%
Local anaesthetic: intended to give local relief from pain, itching etc.
Calamine 8%
Mild astringent, for relief of pruritus (itching).
Hexylated m-cresol 0.5%
Antimicrobial: checks the growth of bacteria.

A concentration of between 5% and 20% of benzocaine is required for effective local anaesthesic action. See also ANETHAINE.

DERMOVATE NN

Glaxo
[POM] Cream and ointment

Clobetasol propionate 0.5%
Corticosteroid to reduce inflammation.
Neomycin sulphate 0.5%
Nystatin 100,000 units/gram
Anti-infective agents.

Only likely to be of value where an area of eczema or dermatitis is infected. See CORTICOSTEROID + ANTI-INFECTIVE SKIN PREPARATIONS. NHS expenditure on this product is about £100,000 a year.

DETECLO

Lederle
[POM] Tablets; syrup (per 20ml)

Tetracycline hydrochloride 115.4mg
Chlortetracycline hydrochloride 115.4mg
Demeclocycline hydrochloride 69.2mg
Bacteriostatic antibiotics: used in the treatment of bronchitis and many other infections.

This combination of ingredients allows therapeutic levels to be maintained in the blood with longer intervals between doses. Doses are taken every 12 hours, rather than every 6 hours, which may be more convenient for users; it is claimed also to reduce the incidence of stomach upsets. (Gastro-intestinal disturbances occur in about 10% of patients taking 2g per day or more of tetracycline or its equivalent [AMADE p.1673].) For selected patients, this combination of ingredients could therefore be an advantage. But for most, the advantage would not seem worth the extra cost: DETECLO is 3–4 times more expensive than tetracycline.
If tetracycline (2 tablets × 250mg) were prescribed instead of this product (1 tablet), the NHS could save about £1 million a year.

DEXA-RHINASPRAY

Boehringer Ingelheim
[POM] Metered aerosol (per inhalation)

Neomycin sulphate 100 micrograms
Antibacterial antibiotic: for treatment of nasal infections.
Dexamethasone 21-isonicotinate 20 micrograms
Corticosteroid: to reduce inflammation.
Tramazoline hydrochloride 120 micrograms
Sympathomimetic: reduces nasal congestion and inflammation.

Undesirable combination. The combination of corticosteroid + antibiotic has serious limitations. See BETNESOL-N.

DEXTROGESIC

Unimed
[POM] Tablets

Dextropropoxyphene hydrochloride 32.5mg
Paracetamol 325mg

A potentially dangerous combination. See DISTALGESIC.

DIABINESE

Pfizer
[POM] Tablets

Chlorpropamide 100mg, 250mg
Anti-diabetic.

An effective drug, strongly promoted by brand name. If the identical medicine were prescribed by generic name (chlorpropamide) the NHS could save about £½ million a year.

DIARREST

Galen
[POM] Liquid (per 5ml)

Codeine phosphate 5mg
Antidiarrhoeal: constipating agent.
Dicyclomine hydrochloride 2.5mg
Antispasmodic: intended to relieve stomach pain and reduce gastric motility.
Potassium chloride 40mg
Sodium chloride 50mg
Sodium citrate 50mg
Electrolytes: taken with water to replace salts and fluid lost through diarrhoea.

Drug treatment for acute diarrhoea is best avoided [BNF No.6 1983 pp.47–49]. Diarrhoea is a natural defence mechanism (like coughing or sneezing) which helps the body get rid of irritants or toxins. Drinking fluids aids this process and speeds recovery, but chemical plugs do not. An antispasmodic drug is rarely needed: when it is, it should be prescribed separately and the dosage properly adjusted. The amount of dicyclomine in this preparation is probably too low to have any significant effect (but a higher dosage could cause unpleasant side effects for some users).

DIFFLAM
Carnegie
Cream

Benzydamine hydrochloride 3%
Intended to relieve pain in muscles, joints etc when rubbed into skin.

Considered less suitable for prescribing: Methyl Salicylate Ointment or Liniment BP are effective and much cheaper alternatives. If either of these were prescribed instead of this product the NHS could save at least £¼ million a year.

DIHYDROCODEINE AND PARACETAMOL
[POM] Tablets

Dihydrocodeine tartrate 10mg
Narcotic analgesic: similar to but a more potent pain-killer than codeine.
Paracetamol 500mg
Analgesic; antipyretic: used to lower temperature.

The combination is rational but is unlikely to offer any real gain. The amount of dihydrocodeine in this preparation is about one-third the usual adult dose and may not be effective. Compound analgesic preparations tend to be more expensive than simple preparations, and may complicate treatment of overdosage so are rated 'less suitable for prescribing' [BNF No.6, 1983, p.159]. See ASPIRIN AND CODEINE.

DILORAN WITHDRAWN
Lipha
Antacid mixture

See similar product ASILONE.

DIMETHICONE (SIMETHICONE)

Antiflatulent, antacid ingredient. See ASILONE.

DIMOTANE EXPECTORANT
Robins
Linctus (per 5ml)

Guaiphenesin 100mg
Brompheniramine maleate 2mg
Phenylephrine hydrochloride 5mg
Phenylpropanolamine hydrochloride 5mg

Irrational combination. See DIMOTANE WITH CODEINE.
NHS expenditure on this product is estimated at £200,000 a year.

DIMOTANE EXPECTORANT DC
Robins
[CD] Elixir (per 5ml)

Hydrocodone acid tartrate 1.8mg
Cough suppressant.
Guaiphenesin 100mg
Brompheniramine maleate 2mg
Phenylephrine hydrochloride 5mg
Phenylpropanolamine hydrochloride 5mg

Irrational combination. See DIMOTANE WITH CODEINE.

DIMOTANE WITH CODEINE
Robins
Elixir (per 5ml)

Codeine phosphate 10mg
Cough suppressant.
Guaiphenesin 100mg
Expectorant: intended to help removal of phlegm from the airways.
Brompheniramine maleate 2mg
Antihistamine: used to control symptoms of allergy, eg to dry up nasal secretions in hay fever.
Phenylephrine hydrochloride 5mg
Phenylpropanolamine hydrochloride 5mg
Nasal decongestants.

The UK Joint Formulary Committee deprecates the use of compound preparations in the treatment of respiratory disorders [BNF No.6, 1983, p.120]. It is irrational both to combine an expectorant and an antihistamine, and a cough suppressant and an expectorant.
The effectiveness of guaiphenesin is doubtful. See the entry for EXPECTORANTS AND MUCOLYTICS. The dosage of the two decongestants is probably too low to have any significant effect. Phenylephrine is seldom effective by mouth [AMADE p.556]; nasal decongestant sprays are more effective, though are suitable only for short-term use.
NHS expenditure on this product is about £½ million a year.

DIMOTANE WITH CODEINE PAEDIATRIC

Robins
Elixir (per 5ml)

Codeine phosphate 3mg
Guaiphenesin 50mg
Brompheniramine maleate 1mg
Phenylephrine hydrochloride 2.5mg
Phenylpropanolamine hydrochloride 2.5mg

Irrational combination. See DIMOTANE WITH CODEINE.
NHS expenditure on this product is about £¼ million a year.

DIMOTAPP

Robins
Elixir and paediatric elixir

Elixir (per 5ml)
Brompheniramine maleate 4mg
Antihistamine: used to suppress symptoms of allergy.
Phenylephrine hydrochloride 5mg
Phenylpropanolamine hydrochloride 5mg
Decongestants.

Paediatric elixir (per 5ml)
Brompheniramine maleate 1mg
Phenylephrine hydrochloride 2.5mg
Phenylpropanolamine hydrochloride 2.5mg

Undesirable combination. Antihistamines have no place in treating common cold symptoms. It is doubtful whether decongestants add to the effectiveness of antihistamines in the treatment of allergy. The dosages of phenylephrine and phenylpropanolamine in this preparation are almost certainly too low to be effective. Nasal decongestant sprays tend to be more effective than oral preparations for short-term use.
NHS expenditure on this product is around £½ million a year.

DIMOTAPP LA

Robins
Slow-release tablets

Brompheniramine maleate 12mg
Phenylephrine hydrochloride 15mg
Phenylpropanolamine hydrochloride 15mg

Undesirable combination. The action of slow-release antihistamines can be uneven and unpredictable. See DIMOTAPP.
NHS expenditure on this product is estimated at £1¼ million a year.

DIMOTAPP P

Robins
Tablets

Brompheniramine maleate 2mg
Phenylephrine hydrochloride 5mg
Phenylpropanolamine hydrochloride 5mg
Paracetamol 325mg
Analgesic; antipyretic: intended to reduce fever.

Undesirable combination. See DIMOTAPP.
NHS expenditure on this product is estimated at £100,000 a year.

DIOCTYL

Medo
Ear drops

Dioctyl sodium sulphosuccinate (docusate sodium)
Used to soften ear wax before it is removed.

This product is unnecessary. There are many simple, effective and cheaper alternatives – eg sodium bicarbonate ear drops, baby oil, arachis oil, almond oil etc.

DIOVOL

Pharmax
Antacid tablets; mixture

See similar product ASILONE.

DISTACLOR

Dista
[POM] Capsules, suspension

Cefaclor 250 mg (capsules), 125 mg and 250 mg (suspension, per 5 ml)

Cheaper and equally good alternatives available. See CEPHALOSPORIN ANTIBIOTICS.

DISTALGESIC

Dista
[POM] Tablets

Dextropropoxyphene hydrochloride 32.5mg
Narcotic analgesic: relieves mild to moderate pain.
Paracetamol 325mg
Analgesic/antipyretic: relieves mild to moderate pain, and reduces fever/high temperature.

There are more prescriptions for dextropropoxyphene + paracetamol combinations than for any other kind of pain-killer: over 6 million prescriptions a year are written for DISTALGESIC alone. This suggests that many doctors and patients consider the combination of dextropropoxy-

phene (DP) + paracetamol to be more effective than paracetamol alone, though there is not much objective data to support this. Evidence from properly conducted clinical trials suggests that sometimes paracetamol alone gave more effective relief, while in other trials, the combination of paracetamol + DP was preferred. There is an alarming lack of evidence about the effects of long-term use of paracetamol + DP, and about its effects on middle-aged or elderly users. In exceptional circumstances, a DP + paracetamol combination would be worth prescribing but generally any benefits are outweighed by serious risks. The main risk is unusual toxicity: the fatal dose of DP + paracetamol is relatively low, irreversible damage to the body is almost immediate, and effective treatment of overdose very difficult. DISTALGESIC causes more accidental deaths and suicides than any other prescribed drug. There is also some risk of drug dependence. The evidence on this is also inadequate: serious addiction appears to be rare, but mild to moderate dependence could be a greater problem than is now recognised.
DISTALGESIC is relatively expensive, and strongly promoted by brand name. If cheaper brands of the identical combination were prescribed instead, the NHS could save an estimated £2½ million each year. If paracetamol were prescribed instead of DISTALGESIC, the saving would be over £6 million a year. Identical and/or closely related brands include: COSALGESIC, DEXTROGESIC, DISTALGESIC SOLUBLE, DOLASAN, DOLOXENE COMPOUND and NAPSALGESIC. Over £1 million a year is spent on these.

DISTALGESIC SOLUBLE
Dista
[POM] Dispersible tablets

Dextropropoxyphene napsylate 50mg
Paracetamol 325mg

See DISTALGESIC.

DIUMIDE-K CONTINUS
Napp
[POM] Tablets (slow-release mechanism not specified in Data Sheet 1983/84)

Frusemide 40mg
Diuretic: helps to control high blood pressure; removes excessive fluid from body tissues by increasing output of urine.
Potassium 8mmol
Supplement intended to replace potassium which the body loses through diuresis.

Many people do not need a potassium supplement with a diuretic. If a supplement is needed it is best taken separately, and preferably in solution not tablet form. The required dose may be higher than the amount in this preparation. See POTASSIUM SUPPLEMENTS.
This product is strongly promoted by brand name. If prescriptions were written for frusemide + potassium instead, the NHS could save around £1 million a year.

DIUREXAN
E Merck
[POM] Tablets

Xipamide 20mg
Diuretic: helps to control high blood pressure; removes excessive fluid from body tissues by increasing output of urine.

Xipamide has no clear advantage over other diuretics and costs much more. Xipamide appears to cause rather more loss of potassium than other diuretics and this is a needless hazard (see POTASSIUM SUPPLEMENTS). In treating oedema (the swelling caused by excessive fluid in body tissues) its effect is comparable to another diuretic, frusemide, though its action is more gradual and prolonged. Sometimes, this could be an advantage, but it would not often seem worth the increased cost [DTB 1979 17, 74–75].
If frusemide were prescribed instead of xipamide, the NHS would save over £¾ million a year.

DOLASAN
Lilly
[POM] Tablets

Dextropropoxyphene napsylate 100mg
Aspirin 325mg

A potentially dangerous combination. See DISTALGESIC.

DOLOXENE COMPOUND
Lilly
[POM] Capsules

Dextropropoxyphene napsylate 100mg
Aspirin 375mg
Caffeine 30mg

A potentially dangerous combination. See DISTALGESIC.

DOME ACNE
Miles
Acne cream, lotion

Resorcinol monoacetate 3%
Sulphur 4%

Resorcinol should be avoided and the value of sulphur is uncertain. See RESORCINOL AND SULPHUR PASTE.

DORIDEN WITHDRAWN
Ciba
[POM] Tablets

Glutethimide 250mg

This drug is related to the BARBITURATES (see entry) and has some comparable unwanted effects. As a hypnotic/sedative, it has no advantage over BENZODIAZEPINE TRANQUILLISERS (see entry), but is less safe. Glutethimide is said to lose its effectiveness by the second week of continued use [AMADE p.206]; and in the US is labelled 'effective as a hypnotic for 3–7 days' [PDR 1983 p.2018]. The UK Data Sheet (1983/4) does not mention this. In the US, glutethimide is '*not* recommended for children'; in the UK, it is recommended for children over 1 year old.
NHS expenditure on this product is estimated at £100,000 a year.

DUBAM
Norma
Counter-irritant aerosol spray

Glycol salicylate 5%
Methyl salicylate 5%
Methyl nicotinate 1.6%

There is no convincing evidence of the effectiveness of glycol salicylate [FR 44 234 4/12/79 p.69845]. This product is considered less suitable for prescribing: Methyl Salicylate Ointment BP or Methyl Salicylate Liniment BP are effective and cheaper alternatives.

DUO-AUTOHALER
Riker
[POM] Breath-actuated metered aerosol (per inhalation)

Isoprenaline sulphate 160 micrograms
Bronchodilator: relieves breathing difficulties in asthma, bronchitis etc.
Phenylephrine bitartrate 240 micrograms
Nasal decongestant.

Isoprenaline is considered less effective than other treatments for asthma. See BRONCHODILATORS. A decongestant may be temporarily useful if asthma is complicated by a cold, but routine use is undesirable [AMADE pp.595–596].

DUOVENT
WPB
[POM] Metered aerosol (per inhalation)

Fenoterol hydrobromide 90 micrograms
Bronchodilator: relieves breathing difficulties in asthma, bronchitis etc.
Ipratropium bromide 36 micrograms
Bronchodilator.

First introduced in 1983 and immediately (and euphemistically) classified as 'less suitable for prescribing'. The ingredients individually are effective, but the UK Joint Formulary Committee, among other authorities, considers that 'compound bronchodilator preparations have no place in the management of patients with airways obstruction.' [BNF No.6, 1983, p.107].

DUROPHET
Riker
[CD] Slow-release capsules

Dexamphetamine/amphetamine combinations: 3.75mg, or 6.25mg, or 10mg in resin complexes

The use of amphetamines in controlling obesity is unjustified [BNF No.6, 1983, p.151]. Their effectiveness is limited; unwanted effects (overstimulation of heart and central nervous system; nervousness, excitability, insomnia etc) are characteristic, and their potential for abuse and dependence is high.

DUVADILAN
Duphar
Tablets

Isoxsuprine hydrochloride 20mg
Peripheral vasodilator: used to treat blood circulation disorders, also promoted to improve mental function, particularly in the elderly.

Isoxsuprine lacks evidence of effectiveness: its benefits, if any, appear marginal. A US expert panel has classified this drug as 'less than effective' for its stated indications [PDR 1983, p.1241]; and the American Medical Association concurs. See PERIPHERAL VASODILATORS.
NHS expenditure on this product is estimated at £100,000 a year.

DUVADILAN RETARD
Duphar
Slow-release capsules

Isoxsuprine hydrochloride 40mg

Lacks evidence of effectiveness. See DUVADILAN.
NHS expenditure on this product is about £2 million a year.

EFFICO
Pharmax
Elixir (per 5ml)

Thiamine hydrochloride 180 micrograms
Nicotinamide 2.1mg
B vitamins.
Caffeine 20.2mg
'Bitters' 0.31ml
Compound gentian infusion.

There are more B vitamins in a small helping of the average vitamin-fortified cereal, and more caffeine in half a cup of tea. Bitters increase production of saliva and stomach acid – a traditional 'remedy' for loss of appetite.
Over one million NHS prescriptions a year are written for tonics of this kind: about one-quarter are for this product.

ELAMOL
Brocades
[POM] Capsules

Tofenacin hydrochloride 80mg

This drug offers no advantages over other antidepressants, and the evidence for its efficacy is relatively weak. Though recommended for older patients, it may cause unwanted effects (such as blurring of vision, drying of the mouth and throat, tremor, constipation and difficulty in urination) which are especially troublesome in this age group.

ELUDRIL
Concept
Aerosol spray

Chlorhexidine gluconate 0.05%
Antimicrobial
Amethocaine hydrochloride 0.015%
Local anaesthetic for sore throat.

There is no good evidence that this preparation is of any real value. See AAA spray.

ENDURONYL
Abbott
[POM] Tablets (also tablets forte)

Deserpidine 250 micrograms (tablets forte: 500 micrograms)
Antihypertensive: reserpine-related rauwolfia derivative, used to control high blood pressure.
Methyclothiazide 5mg (tablets forte: 5mg)
Diuretic: augments the antihypertensive effect of deserpidine.

The possibility of serious side effects limits the usefulness of deserpidine. See RESERPINE. The use of a fixed-ratio combination is undesirable, except for patients who have originally taken the two ingredients separately and found that these doses suit them.

ENPAC
Aplin & Barrett
[POM] Powder

Lactobacillus acidophilus
Harmless bacteria intended to inhibit the growth of disease-causing bacteria, by making the contents of the gut more acid.

There is little evidence that such preparations are effective [M28; p.786]. A US expert panel has reported: 'In the past 60 years well over 200 papers have reported on the use of lactobacillus . . . in the treatment of diarrhea. Despite the proliferation of studies the very few controlled studies more often show lack of effectiveness than any antidiarrheal effect' [FR 40 56 21/3/75 p.12931].

ENTEROMIDE
Consolidated
[POM] Tablets

Calcium sulphaloxate 500mg
Sulphonamide antibacterial: recommended for prevention and treatment of non-specific diarrhoeas.

Most non-specific ('travellers'') diarrhoeas are probably not caused by bacteria, but even if they are, treatment with an antibacterial agent is undesirable. Antibacterials may prolong diarrhoeal states, and there is no convincing evidence they prevent them [BNF No.6, 1983, p.49].

ENZYPAN
Norgine
Tablets

Pancreatin 180mg
Digestive enzyme: intended to improve digestion and to relieve symptoms of indigestion.
Dried ox bile 60mg (in enteric-coated inner layer)
Digestive aid, laxative.
Pepsin 12mg (outer layer)
Digestive enzyme.

There is no convincing evidence to suggest that any of these ingredients is effective either in improving digestion or in relieving the symptoms of indigestion [FR 47 2 5/1/82 pp.454–487]. If supplements are needed because of pancreatic insufficiency, they are generally taken in higher doses and as powder sprinkled on to food, because acid in the stomach destroys the activity of pancreatin.

EPANUTIN WITH PHENOBARBITONE

Warner-Lambert Health Care
[POM] Tablets

Phenytoin sodium 100mg
Phenobarbitone sodium 50mg
Anticonvulsants.

The use of fixed-ratio combination products in the treatment of epilepsy is not recommended unless and until the dose of each ingredient has been established, taking into account both clinical response and drug concentrations in the blood.
NHS expenditure on this product is over £100,000 a year.

EPHEDRINE

[POM] Tablets and elixir

Tablets
Ephedrine hydrochloride 15mg, 30mg, 60mg

Elixir (per 5ml)
Ephedrine hydrochloride 15mg
Bronchodilator and decongestant: relieves breathing difficulties in asthma, bronchitis etc.

Ephedrine acts rather unselectively: it improves airflow, but may also over-stimulate the heart and central nervous system. Common adverse effects include anxiety, restlessness and insomnia. Ephedrine can be effective, but is difficult to use well: there are generally better alternatives. See BRONCHODILATORS.

EPHYNAL

Roche
Tablets

Alpha tocopheryl acetate 3mg, 10mg, 50mg, 200mg (1mg equals approximately 1 unit)
Vitamin E.

Vitamin E has been described as the vitamin in search of a disease: it is available in so many foods (eg wheat germ, maize, green leaves), it would be hard to design a diet that did not supply plenty. Deficiency states are very rare and, in adults, are usually the result of disease which prevents effective absorption. Many extravagant claims have been made for vitamin E (not this product) – eg for the treatment of impotence, sterility, heart disease, peptic ulcer, burns, skin conditions, habitual abortion etc. There is no convincing evidence of its value for anything other than deficiency.
NHS expenditure on all vitamin E preparations is estimated at over £100,000 a year.

EQUAGESIC

Wyeth
[POM] Tablets

Ethoheptazine citrate 75mg
Narcotic analgesic: relieves mild to moderate pain.
Aspirin 250mg
Analgesic/antipyretic/anti-inflammatory.
Meprobamate 150mg
Tranquilliser: for treatment of anxiety, muscle spasm.

MEPROBAMATE (see entry) is relatively ineffective: there are newer and better alternatives. Ethoheptazine lacks evidence of effectiveness. See ZACTIPAR. The combination of analgesics is not likely to offer a real advantage (see ASPIRIN AND CODEINE), and the fixed-ratio combination is undesirable.
NHS expenditure on this product is about £1½ million a year.

EQUANIL

Wyeth
[POM] Tablets

Meprobamate 200mg; 400mg
Tranquilliser.

There are safer, more effective alternatives. See MEPROBAMATE.
NHS expenditure on this product is over £100,000 a year.

ESIDREX-K

Ciba
[POM] Tablets (in slow-release wax core)

Hydrochlorothiazide 12.5mg
Diuretic: helps to control high blood pressure; removes excessive fluid from body tissues by increasing output of urine.
Potassium 8.1mmol
Supplement intended to replace potassium which the body loses through diuresis.

Many people do not need a potassium supplement with a diuretic. If a supplement is needed it is best taken separately, and preferably in solution not tablet form. The required dose may be higher than the amount in this preparation. See POTASSIUM SUPPLEMENTS.

ESKAMEL
SK & F
Acne cream

Resorcinol 2%
Keratolytic: promotes sloughing or peeling of scaly, callused skin.
Sulphur 8%
Mild antiseptic.

Resorcinol should be avoided and the value of sulphur is uncertain. Compare dosage with: ACNIL. See also RESORCINOL AND SULPHUR PASTE.

ESKORNADE
SK & F
Slow-release capsules and syrup

Capsules
Diphenylpyraline hydrochloride 5mg
Antihistamine: used to suppress symptoms of allergy.
Phenylpropanolamine hydrochloride 50mg
Nasal decongestant.
Isopropamide 2.5mg
Anticholinergic: dries secretions; used as a decongestant to relieve symptoms of allergy and common cold.

Syrup *(per 5ml)*
Diphenylpyraline hydrochloride 1.5mg
Isopropamide 750 micrograms
Phenylpropanolamine hydrochloride 15mg

Undesirable combination. Antihistamines have no place in treating common cold symptoms. It is doubtful whether sympathomimetics/anticholinergics (used to treat nasal congestion) add to the effectiveness of antihistamines in the treatment of allergy. The action of slow-release antihistamines can be uneven and unpredictable, and they tend to cost more than standard formulations.
NHS expenditure on this product is about £¼ million a year.

ETOPHYLATE
Delandale
Suppositories for children

Acepifylline 100mg; and other formulations

See BRONCHODILATORS. Acepifylline is related to theophylline and although better tolerated is 'of doubtful efficacy'. Less suitable for prescribing than newer, oral, slow-release preparations [BNF No.6, 1983, p.104]. Rectal absorption of theophylline and related drugs tends to be erratic. Oral preparations are usually preferred [AMADE p.591; DTB, 1979, 17, 92].

EUGYNON 30
Schering
[POM] Oral contraceptive

Levonorgestrel 250 micrograms
Ethinyloestradiol 30 micrograms
Hormones.

A lower-strength pill may be safer. See ORAL CONTRACEPTIVES.

EUGYNON 50
Schering
[POM] Oral contraceptive

Norgestrel 500 micrograms
Ethinyloestradiol 50 micrograms
Hormones.

A lower-strength pill may be safer. See ORAL CONTRACEPTIVES.

EUHYPNOS, EUHYPNOS FORTE
Farmitalia Carlo Erba

See entry for BENZODIAZEPINE TRANQUILLISERS.

EUMOVATE-N
Glaxo
[POM] Eye drops

Clobetasone butyrate 0.1%
Corticosteroid: used to reduce inflammation.
Neomycin sulphate 0.5%
Antibiotic.

Combinations of corticosteroids and antibiotics have serious limitations. See BETNESOL-N.

EVACALM
Unimed

See VALIUM.

EVIDORM WITHDRAWN
Winthrop
[POM] Tablets

Cyclobarbitone calcium 100mg
Hexobarbitone 250mg
For severe, intractable insomnia.

BARBITURATES (see entry) are best avoided. This combination product is also very expensive.

EX-LAX
Ex-Lax
Pills, tablets, junior tablets

Pills
Phenolphthalein 98mg

Tablets
Phenolphthalein 95mg

Junior tablets
Phenolphthalein 48mg

PHENOLPHTHALEIN (see entry) is considered less satisfactory than other laxatives.

EXPANSYL
SK & F
[POM] Slow-release capsules

Ephedrine sulphate 50mg
Bronchodilator: relieves breathing difficulties in asthma, bronchitis etc.
Diphenylpyraline hydrochloride 5mg
Antihistamine: used to suppress symptoms of allergy.
Trifluoperazine hydrochloride 2mg
Tranquilliser.

Tranquillisers are of no direct benefit in treating asthmatic conditions. If needed for the treatment of anxiety, they should be separately prescribed. Antihistamines are generally ineffective in the treatment of asthma, and their drying action may be positively undesirable. A US expert panel has reported that: 'Many physicians consider this effect to be disadvantageous in patients with bronchial asthma and some maintain that the antihistaminic drugs are contraindicated in patients with this disease' [FR 41 176: 9/9/76 p.38380].
NHS expenditure on this product is estimated at over £100,000 per year.

EXPECTORANTS AND MUCOLYTICS

These drugs are intended to ease and/or promote the removal of phlegm (sputum) from the airways, through coughing. Mucolytics work by altering the structure of phlegm, making it less sticky and tenacious. Expectorants are meant to promote secretion of mucus in the airways – to increase the volume and runniness of phlegm.

Mucolytics do reduce the viscosity of phlegm, but there is not much evidence to suggest that they have any substantial clinical benefit. The evidence suggests the mucolytics that are inhaled are no more effective than an inhalation of steam or a water aerosol. The NHS spends an estimated £3½ million on one product alone (ie MUCODYNE).

Most expectorants are in fact stomach irritants: one of the most widely used, ipecacuanha, is used at a higher dosage to induce vomiting in emergency drug poisoning cases. Because retching and vomiting are known to produce (by reflex) an increase in bronchial secretions, expectorants are added in sub-emetic dosages to many cough medicines. However, there is no good evidence that irritating the stomach a little will increase bronchial secretions enough to promote expectoration. An expectorant might cause stomach pain and/or vomiting before it had much effect on secretion of mucus in the airways.

The UK Joint Formulary Committee considers that sub-emetic doses of expectorants are ineffective and says 'there is no scientific basis for prescribing them'. The Committee suggests that certain expectorants may have some role as placebos and says their use is at least 'preferable to the indiscriminate prescribing of antibiotics' for coughs and colds [BNF No.6, 1983 p.120]. Expectorants are included in many compound preparations but the use of such mixtures should be avoided.

EXPULIN
Galen
Linctus (per 5ml)

Pholcodine 5mg
Cough suppressant.
Chlorpheniramine maleate 2mg
Antihistamine.
Ephedrine hydrochloride 8mg
Bronchial, nasal decongestant.

Undesirable combination. See ACTIFED COMPOUND LINCTUS.

EXTEROL
Dermal
Ear drops

Urea-hydrogen peroxide complex 5% in glycerol
Used to soften ear wax before it is removed.

This product is not needed. There are many simple, effective and cheaper alternatives – eg sodium bicarbonate ear drops, baby oil, arachis oil, almond oil etc.

EXTIL

Duncan Flockhart
[POM] Compound linctus (per 10ml)

Noscapine 25mg
Cough suppressant.
Carbinoxamine maleate 6mg
Antihistamine.
Pseudoephedrine hydrochloride 49.2mg
Bronchial, nasal decongestant.

Undesirable combination. See ACTIFED COMPOUND LINCTUS.

EXYPHEN

Norton
Elixir (per 5ml)

Guaiphenesin 80mg
Brompheniramine maleate 2mg
Phenylephrine hydrochloride 4.75mg
Phenylpropanolamine hydrochloride 5mg

Irrational combination. See DIMOTANE WITH CODEINE.

FABAHISTIN

Bayer
Tablets or mixture (per 5ml)

Mebhydrolin 50mg
Antihistamine: used to treat symptoms of allergy eg in hay fever or urticaria (nettle rash).

This is an effective drug but it appears to have no significant advantage over other, well-established and cheaper antihistamines.
If chlorpheniramine were prescribed instead of this product, the NHS could save about £¼ million a year.

FABROL

Ciba
Granules

Acetylcysteine 200mg per sachet
Mucolytic: reduces viscosity of phlegm, to help expectoration.

Some patients may be helped by this drug, but there is no convincing evidence of long-term benefits. See EXPECTORANTS AND MUCOLYTICS.

FALCODYL

Norton
Linctus (per 5ml)

Pholcodine 4mg
Cough suppressant.
Ephedrine hydrochloride 4mg (see EPHEDRINE).

Undesirable combination.

FEAC

Robins
Slow-release tablets

Dried ferrous sulphate 150mg (45mg **iron**)
B vitamins: thiamine mononitrate 7.5mg; **riboflavine** 5mg; **nicotinamide** 25mg; **pyridoxine hydrochloride** 2.5mg
Vitamin C: ascorbic acid 150mg

See IRON SUPPLEMENTS. VITAMINS (see entry) should not be added to iron preparations: they add to cost rather than therapeutic benefit. This product costs the NHS about ten times more than standard iron preparations.

FE-CAP C

MCP
Capsules

Ferrous glycine sulphate 565mg (100mg **iron**)
Ascorbic acid 300mg
Vitamin C.

Vitamin C increases absorption of iron, but this gives no therapeutic advantage. See entry for IRON SUPPLEMENTS. This product costs at least three times more than completely adequate alternatives.

FEFOL

SK & F
[POM] Slow-release capsules

Dried ferrous sulphate 150mg (45mg **iron**)
Folic acid 500 micrograms

See IRON SUPPLEMENTS. Slow-release preparations of iron may be less effective than standard formulations, but cost more. Iron and folic acid tablets (ferrous fumarate 304mg [100mg iron]; folic acid 0.35mg) cost about half as much as this product: if they were prescribed instead, the NHS could save about £¼ million a year.

FEFOL-VIT

SK & F
[POM] As FEFOL, plus **B-vitamins: thiamine mononitrate** 2mg; **riboflavine** 2mg; **nicotinamide** 10mg; **pyridoxine hydrochloride** 1mg; **calcium pantothenate** 2.17mg
Ascorbic acid:
Vitamin C 50mg

VITAMINS (see entry) should not be added to iron preparations. This product costs around three times more than good alternatives. If used instead, these could save the NHS over £100,000 a year.

FEMERITAL
MCP
Tablets

Paracetamol 250mg
Analgesic; antipyretic: reduces fever.
Ambucetamide 100mg
Antispasmodic: smooth muscle relaxant.

The combination is prescribed for pre-menstrual cramps and pains. Ambucetamide is not well established as a muscle relaxant; and the amount of paracetamol may be less than effective at the recommended dosage (1–2 tablets, three times a day). The ingredients, if needed, should be separately prescribed: if the muscle relaxant were effective, presumably less analgesic would be needed, but if muscle spasms continued to cause pain, the dose of paracetamol would need to be increased.

FEOSPAN
SK & F
Slow-release capsules

Dried ferrous sulphate 150mg (45mg **iron**)

See IRON SUPPLEMENTS. Slow-release preparations of iron may be less effective than standard formulations, but cost more. Ferrous sulphate tablets 200mg (60mg iron) are about one-tenth the price: if prescribed instead of this product, the NHS could save about £½ million a year.

FERAVOL F
Carlton
[POM] Tablets

Ferrous gluconate 300mg (35mg **iron**)
Folic acid 3mg

For the prevention of iron and folic acid deficiencies in pregnancy, a much lower dosage of folic acid (100–500 micrograms per day) is normally given – often with a higher dosage of iron. For treatment of most folic acid deficiency states, a dosage of 500 micrograms – 1mg/day is adequate. 'Daily doses greater than 1mg do not enhance the haematologic* effect, and most of the excess is excreted unchanged in the urine' [AMADE p.806].
[*Folic acid is needed for the formation of new blood and body cells.]

FERAVOL G
Carlton
Tablets
Ferrous gluconate 300mg (35mg **iron**)
B vitamins: thiamine hydrochloride 400 micrograms; **riboflavine** 1mg
Ascorbic acid 9mg
Vitamin C with a trace of copper.

Syrup (per 5ml)
Ferrous gluconate 300mg (35mg **iron**)
Thiamine hydrochloride 1mg

VITAMINS (see entry) should not be added to iron preparations. See also IRON SUPPLEMENTS.

FERFOLIC
Sinclair
[POM] Tablets

Ferrous gluconate 250mg (30mg **iron**)
Folic acid 5mg
B vitamins: thiamine hydrochloride 3mg; **riboflavine** 1mg; **nicotinamide** 10mg
Vitamin C: ascorbic acid 10mg

VITAMINS (see entry) should not be added to iron preparations: they add to cost rather than therapeutic benefit. See IRON SUPPLEMENTS. This product costs 3–4 times more than iron and folic acid alone.

FERFOLIC SV
Sinclair
[POM] Tablets

As FERFOLIC, but without B vitamins. Ascorbic acid improves absorption of iron only at much higher dosages (7mg ascorbic acid: 1mg iron).

FERGLUVITE
Sinclair
Tablets

As FERFOLIC but without folic acid.

FERRAPLEX B
Bencard
Tablets

Dried ferrous sulphate 167mg (50mg **iron**)
B vitamins: thiamine hydrochloride 500 micrograms; **riboflavine** 1mg; **nicotinamide** 5mg; **dried brewer's yeast** 292mg
Vitamin C: ascorbic acid 8mg
Mineral supplement: copper carbonate 400 micrograms

See IRON SUPPLEMENTS. VITAMINS (see entry) should not be added to iron preparations: they add to cost rather than therapeutic benefit. This product costs 3–4 times more than entirely adequate alternatives.

FERRLECIT 100
Wade
Tablets

Dried ferrous sulphate 165mg (50mg **iron**)
Sodium ferric citrate 150mg (50mg **iron**)
Vitamin C: ascorbic acid 50mg

Ferric salts are less well absorbed than ferrous salts. Ascorbic acid improves absorption of iron only at much higher dosages (7mg ascorbic acid: 1mg iron). See IRON SUPPLEMENTS. Good alternatives are cheaper.

FERROCAP
Consolidated
Slow-release capsules

Ferrous fumarate 330mg (110mg **iron**)
Thiamine hydrochloride 5mg
Vitamin B_1

Slow-release preparations and vitamins add to cost rather than to effectiveness. See IRON SUPPLEMENTS. This product costs about three times more than entirely adequate alternatives.

FERROCAP-F 350
Consolidated
[POM] Slow-release capsules

Ferrous fumarate 330mg
Folic acid 350 micrograms

See FERROCAP.

FERROCONTIN FOLIC CONTINUS
Napp
[POM] Slow-release tablets

Ferrous glycine sulphate 562.5mg (100mg **iron**)
Folic acid 500 micrograms

See IRON SUPPLEMENTS. Slow-release preparations of iron may be less effective than standard formulations, but cost more.

FERROGRAD C
Abbott
Slow-release tablets

Dried ferrous sulphate 325mg (105mg **iron**)
Ascorbic acid 500mg
Vitamin C, as sodium salt.

Slow-release preparations may be less effective than standard formulations [BNF No.6 1983 p.267], but cost more. See IRON SUPPLEMENTS. Vitamin C improves absorption of iron, but is not needed. See VITAMINS. Ferrous sulphate tablets 300mg (90mg iron) would be an excellent alternative: they could save the NHS about £½ million a year.

FERROGRAD FOLIC
Abbott
[POM] Slow-release tablets

Dried ferrous sulphate 325mg (105mg **iron**)
Folic acid 350 micrograms

See IRON SUPPLEMENTS. Conventional formulations of iron and folic acid may be more effective, and could save the NHS over £100,000 a year.

FERRO-GRADUMET
Abbott
Slow-release tablets

Dried ferrous sulphate 325mg (105mg **iron**)

See IRON SUPPLEMENTS. This product costs about three times more than alternatives which may be more effective.
If ferrous sulphate tablets 300mg (90mg iron) were prescribed instead of this product, the NHS could save over £¼ million a year.

FERROMYN B
Calmic
Tablets; elixir (per 5ml)

Ferrous succinate 106mg (37mg **iron**)
B vitamins: thiamine hydrochloride 1mg; **riboflavine** 1mg; **nicotinamide** 10mg

VITAMINS (see entry) should not be added to iron preparations: they add to cost rather than benefit. See IRON SUPPLEMENTS. This product costs over five times more than simple, equally effective alternatives.

FERROMYN S
Calmic
Tablets

Ferrous succinate 106mg (37mg **iron**)
Succinic acid 110mg

Ferrous sulphate 200mg (60mg iron) is fully effective and around ten times cheaper. Succinic acid is added to increase absorption of iron in the gut, but is not needed. See IRON SUPPLEMENTS. NHS expenditure on this product is about £100,000 a year.

FERROMYN S FOLIC
Calmic
[POM] Tablets

As FERROMYN S, plus folic acid 100 micrograms.

FESOVIT

SK & F
Slow-release capsules

Dried ferrous sulphate 150mg (45mg **iron**)
B vitamins: thiamine mononitrate 2mg; **riboflavine** 2mg; **nicotinamide** 10mg; **pyridoxine hydrochloride** 1mg; **calcium pantothenate** 2.17mg
Ascorbic acid 50mg
Vitamin C.

Slow-release formulations and VITAMINS (see entry) add to cost rather than effectiveness. See IRON SUPPLEMENTS. This product costs about five times more than simple, equally effective formulations of iron.
If ferrous sulphate tablets 200mg (60mg iron) were prescribed instead of this product, the NHS could save around £½ million a year.

FINALGON

Boehringer Ingelheim
Counter-irritant ointment

Butoxyethyl nicotinate 2.5%
Vanillylnonamide 0.4%
Intended to relieve pain in muscles, joints etc when rubbed into skin.

The US Food and Drug Administration has found butoxyethyl nicotinate lacks evidence of effectiveness. Methyl Salicylate Ointment BP or Methyl Salicylate Liniment BP are effective and cheaper alternatives.

FLAGYL

May & Baker
[POM] Tablets, suppositories

Metronidazole (tablets) 200mg, 400mg; (suppositories) 500mg, 1g
Antimicrobial: effective against trichomonas (a common cause of vaginal infection), amoebic and other organisms.

An effective drug, strongly promoted by brand name. Substantial savings could be made if this drug were prescribed by its generic name, metronidazole.

FLAR

Consolidated
Capsules

Lactic acid bacilli
Harmless bacteria intended to inhibit the growth of disease-causing bacteria, by making the contents of the gut more acid.

There is no good evidence that such preparations are effective [M28; p.786]. A US expert panel has reported: 'In the past 60 years well over 200 papers have been reported on the use of lactobacillus . . . in the treatment of diarrhea. Despite the proliferation of studies the very few controlled studies more often show lack of effectiveness than any antidiarrheal effect' [FR 40 56 21/3/75 p.12931].

FLAVELIX

Pharmax
Elixir (per 5ml)

Mepyramine maleate 12.5mg
Antihistamine.
Ammonium chloride 90mg
Sodium citrate 40mg
Ephedrine hydrochloride 10mg

Irrational combination. See similar product BENAFED.

FLOSINT

Farmitalia Carlo Erba
[POM] Tablets

SUSPENDED

Indoprofen 200mg
Non-steroidal anti-inflammatory drug (NSAID) *used mainly to treat pain and inflammation in rheumatic and related disorders.*

This product was introduced in 1983 into an already saturated market, but 'resembles most other NSAIDs in its efficacy and adverse effects . . . has no special virtues and is more expensive' [DTB, 1983, 21, 88]. Some of the evidence which supported its introduction seems very skimpy. For example, it is recommended for use in ankylosing spondylitis (a rheumatic condition in the spine) on the strength of an unpublished, uncontrolled study of 13 patients assessed for one year. In addition, the manufacturer's recommendation to take tablets twice daily (an advantage over a 3 or 4 times a day regimen) is based on a trial involving 20 patients with rheumatoid arthritis – of whom 8 preferred 400mg twice daily, and 9 preferred 200mg 4 times a day.
The launch symposium for this product is referred to in Chapter Two. FLOSINT costs at least 50% (and up to 10 times) more than well-established alternatives. See NSAIDS.

FOLICIN

Paines & Byrne
[POM] Tablets

Dried ferrous sulphate 200mg (60mg **iron**)
Folic acid 2.5mg

Copper sulphate 2.5mg
Manganese sulphate 2.5mg

The dosage of folic acid is higher than likely to be needed. See similar product FERAVOL F. There is no justification for the addition of mineral supplements: manganese deficiency is unknown and copper deficiency is rare, and neither mineral improves the therapeutic effect of the iron.

FOLVRON WITHDRAWN

Lederle
[POM] Tablets

Dried ferrous sulphate 194mg (57mg **iron**)
Folic acid 1.7mg

The dosage of folic acid is higher than likely to be needed. See similar product FERAVOL F.

FORCEVAL

Unigreg
Vitamin and mineral capsules

Similar product at a similar price: GEVRAL.

FORTAGESIC

Winthrop
[POM] Tablets

Pentazocine hydrochloride 15mg
Narcotic analgesic: used for relief of moderate pain.
Paracetamol 500mg
Analgesic; antipyretic: reduces fever.

Pentazocine taken by mouth is not very effective, and occasionally causes hallucinations. The mixture of ingredients is not irrational – but it is expensive.

FRAMYCORT

Fisons
[POM] Ointment

Hydrocortisone 0.5%
Corticosteroid to reduce inflammation.
Framycetin sulphate 0.5%
Anti-infective agent.

Only likely to be of value where an area of eczema or dermatitis is infected. See CORTICOSTEROID + ANTI-INFECTIVE SKIN PREPARATIONS.

FRANOL

Winthrop
[POM] Tablets

Theophylline 120mg
Ephedrine hydrochloride 11mg
Bronchodilators: relieve breathing difficulties in asthma, bronchitis etc.
Phenobarbitone 8mg
Barbiturate sedative.

Barbiturates should be avoided because they tend to depress the breathing impulse, which may endanger patients with bronchitis or asthma [DTB 1980, 18, 10]. BARBITURATES are also addictive: see entry. Phenobarbitone is used in this preparation partly to try to counteract the unwanted effects of EPHEDRINE (see entry) which tends to over-stimulate the body. It would be better to use a single ingredient bronchodilator at an optimal dosage: the fixed-ratio combination of theophylline and ephedrine is undesirable. See AMESEC.
NHS expenditure on this product is estimated at about £1 million per year.

FRANOL EXPECTORANT

Winthrop
[POM] Elixir (per 5ml)

Theophylline 60mg
Ephedrine hydrochloride 4.75mg
Phenobarbitone 4mg
Guaiphenesin 25mg

Guaiphenesin is of no proven value. See EXPECTORANTS AND MUCOLYTICS. See also FRANOL.
NHS expenditure on this product is estimated at about £¼ million a year.

FRANOL PLUS

Winthrop
[POM] Tablets

Theophylline 120mg
Ephedrine sulphate 15mg
Phenobarbitone 8mg
Thenyldiamine hydrochloride 10mg

Antihistamines (eg thenyldiamine) are generally ineffective in the treatment of asthma, and their drying action may be positively undesirable. A US expert panel has reported that: 'Many physicians consider this effect to be disadvantageous in patients with bronchial asthma and some maintain that the antihistaminic drugs are contraindicated in patients with this disease.' The same panel has reported lack of hard evidence of the effectiveness of oral thenyldiamine, but suggests that the optimum dose is at least 50 per cent higher than the amount in this preparation [FR 41 176; 9/9/76 pp.38380, 38394].
NHS expenditure on this product is estimated at about £¼ million a year.

FRISIUM

Albert
[POM] Capsules

Clobazam 10mg

Clobazam has actions and uses similar to diazepam and other BENZODIAZEPINE TRANQUILLISERS (see entry), but it is said to have a more selective anti-anxiety action. Nevertheless, in a review of 15 studies comparing clobazam with diazepam for anxiety, 'there was an equal incidence of drowsiness in 2, more drowsiness with clobazam in 5, and more drowsiness with diazepam in 8' [Koeppen D.: *Br. J. Clin. Pharmac.*, 1979, 7, Suppl. 1, 139S; cited in M28 p.1517]. Clobazam (FRISIUM) is about ten times more expensive than diazepam; it seems doubtful if its advantages are often worth this extra cost.
If diazepam were prescribed instead of FRISIUM, the NHS would save about £1½ million a year.

FUCIDIN H

Leo
[POM] Gel

Hydrocortisone acetate 1%
Corticosteroid to reduce inflammation.
Fusidic acid 2%
Anti-infective agent.

[POM] Ointment
Hydrocortisone acetate 1%
Sodium fusidate 2%

Only likely to be of value where an area of ecze ma or dermatitis is infected. See CORTICOSTEROID + ANTI-INFECTIVE SKIN PREPARATIONS.
NHS expenditure on this product is over £300,000 a year.

FURADANTIN

Norwich-Eaton
[POM] Tablets, suspension

Tablets and suspension (per 10ml)
Nitrofurantoin 50mg
(Also tablets 100mg)
Antiseptic: used to treat urinary tract infections.

An effective drug, strongly promoted by brand name. If the identical medicine were prescribed by generic name (nitrofurantoin), the NHS could save about £¼ million a year.
See also CEDURAN.

G 500

Cox-Continental
Enteric-coated tablets (ones designed to dissolve in the small intestine rather than the stomach)

Hexamine mandelate 250mg
Antiseptic used to prevent or suppress urinary tract infections.
Methionine 250mg
Amino acid.

Outmoded; considered less suitable for prescribing as it frequently causes side effects. See HIPREX.

GALFER-VIT

Galen
Capsules

Ferrous fumarate 305mg (100mg **iron**)
B vitamins: thiamine mononitrate 2mg; **riboflavine** 2mg; **nicotinamide** 10mg; **pyridoxine hydrochloride** 4mg
Vitamin C: sodium ascorbate 56mg

VITAMINS (see entry) should not be added to iron preparations. See also IRON SUPPLEMENTS.

GAROIN

May & Baker
[POM] Tablets

WITHDRAWN

Phenytoin sodium 100mg
Phenobarbitone sodium 50mg
Anti-convulsants.

Fixed-ratio combination products are not recommended for the treatment of epilepsy, unless and until the dose of each ingredient has been established, taking into account both clinical response and drug concentrations in the blood.

GASTROCOTE

MCP
Antacid tablets

See similar product GAVISCON.

GASTROVITE

MCP
Tablets

Ferrous glycine sulphate 225mg (40mg **iron**)
Ergocalciferol 200 units
Vitamin D.
Calcium gluconate 100mg
Ascorbic acid 15mg
Vitamin C.

Unnecessary, undesirable combination of ingredients. VITAMINS (see entry) should not be added to iron preparations. See IRON SUPPLEMENTS. A simple, effective iron preparation would cost five times less.

GAVISCON

Reckitt & Colman
Antacid tablets and other formulations

Aluminium hydroxide 100mg
Sodium bicarbonate 170mg
Magnesium trisilicate 25mg
Antacids: neutralise excess stomach acid.
Alginic acid 500mg
Intended to suppress regurgitation (oesophageal reflux).
Sucrose, mannitol
Flavouring.

Granules *(per 5g sachet)*
Sodium bicarbonate 177mg
Dried aluminium hydroxide 208mg
Magnesium trisilicate 52mg
Alginic acid 481mg
Sodium alginate 521mg
Sucrose.

Liquid *(per 10ml)*
Sodium bicarbonate 267mg
Sodium alginate 500mg
Saccharin.

Powder for infants *(per 2g sachet)*
Sodium bicarbonate 340mg
Magnesium trisilicate 50mg
Dried aluminium hydroxide 200mg
Colloidal silica and mannitol

This is an effective but very expensive range of products, strongly promoted by brand name and very widely prescribed. The main difference between GAVISCON preparations and other simple antacids is the presence of alginic acid/sodium alginate, intended to help suppress regurgitation of stomach contents. Other products with the same ingredient include GASTROCOTE and TOPAL.
The value of alginates is uncertain: in the US, the makers of GAVISCON describe sodium alginate as an 'inactive ingredient', but some authorities (eg the UK Joint Formulary Committee) consider it useful. The American Medical Association has said: 'There is no evidence to prove that the effects of GAVISCON are more beneficial than those of conventional antacids, although some studies demonstrate that GAVISCON is at least as effective as other antacids in relieving heartburn. Alginic acid has no demonstrable effect on reflux oesophagitis produced by acid peptic or bile reflux' [AMADE p.1274]. In the US, GAVISCON is promoted for heartburn and acid indigestion, but not for treating oesophageal reflux.
GAVISCON products cost several times more than equivalent preparations without alginates, such as aluminium hydroxide or magnesium trisilicate tablets or mixture, but it seems doubtful that they are much more effective than these.
If simple antacids were prescribed instead of GAVISCON products, the NHS could save about £4 million each year.

GEE'S LINCTUS/PASTILLES BP

See OPIATE SQUILL LINCTUS AND PASTILLES.

GENTICIN HC

Nicholas
[POM] Cream and ointment

Hydrocortisone acetate 1%
Corticosteroid to reduce inflammation.
Gentamicin *(as sulphate)* 0.3%
Anti-infective agent.

Only likely to be of value where an area of eczema or dermatitis is infected. See CORTICOSTEROID + ANTI-INFECTIVE SKIN PREPARATIONS.

GESTONE ORAL

Paines & Byrne
[POM] Tablets

Ethisterone 10mg, 25mg
Hormone used to control excessive menstrual bleeding.

Androgenic (virilising) side effects limit its usefulness.

GEVRAL

Lederle
Capsules

Ferrous fumarate 30.8mg (10mg **iron**)
Vitamin A 5000 units
B vitamins: thiamine mononitrate 5mg; **riboflavine** 5mg; **nicotinamide** 15mg; **pyridoxine hydrochloride** 500 micrograms; **cyanocobalamin** 1 microgram; **calcium pantothenate** 5mg
Vitamin C: ascorbic acid 50mg
Vitamin D 500 units
D-alpha-tocopherol acetate 10 units
Choline bitartrate 50mg
Copper 1mg (as oxide)

Iodine 100 micrograms *(as potassium iodide)*
Inositol 50mg
Lysine hydrochloride 25mg
Magnesium 1mg *(as oxide)*
Manganese 1mg *(as dioxide)*
Calcium 145mg *and* **phosphorus** 110mg *(as dibasic calcium phosphate)*
Potassium 5mg *(as sulphate)*
Zinc 500 micrograms *(as oxide)*.

This expensive product is recommended for routine use for the prevention of vitamin and mineral deficiencies, ie as a dietary supplement, rather than as a medicine. It would be much more appropriate to improve diet: anyone likely to get real benefit from even half of these ingredients might well be protein-calorie malnourished as well. This product is not suitable for the treatment of known or suspected deficiencies, which are best treated with higher doses of specific agents.
Several ingredients in this preparation are of little or no established value: d-alpha-tocopheral acetate (see EPHYNAL); cyanocobalamin (relatively ineffective by mouth); calcium pantothenate; choline; inositol and lysine.
NHS expenditure on this product is estimated at over £100,000 a year.

GIVITOL

Galen
[POM] Capsules

Ferrous fumarate 305mg (100mg **iron**)
Folic acid 500 micrograms
B vitamins: thiamine mononitrate 2mg; **riboflavine** 2mg; **nicotinamide** 10mg; **pyridoxine hydrochloride** 4mg
Vitamin C: sodium ascorbate 56mg

VITAMINS (see entry) should not be added to iron preparations. See IRON SUPPLEMENTS. This combination costs about four times more than iron and folic acid alone.

GLYKOLA

Sinclair
Elixir (per 5ml)

Ferric chloride solution 0.01ml (500 micrograms **iron**)
Caffeine 20mg
Kola liquid extract 0.12ml
Calcium glycerophosphate 30mg
Chloroform spirit 0.12ml
Alcohol (90%) 0.5ml

The main ingredient is alcohol. At these doses, the other ingredients would have about the same effect on the body as half a cup of tea. There is a junior version without alcohol GLYKOLA INFANS.

GREGODERM

Unigreg
[POM] Ointment

Hydrocortisone 1%
Corticosteroid to reduce inflammation.
Neomycin sulphate 0.4%
Nystatin 100,000 units/gram
Polymyxin B sulphate 7250 units/gram
Anti-infective agents.

Only likely to be of value where an area of eczema or dermatitis is infected. See CORTICOSTEROID + ANTI-INFECTIVE SKIN PREPARATIONS.

GUANIMYCIN

A & H
[POM] Suspension forte (per 15ml) to treat diarrhoea

Dihydrostreptomycin sulphate 250mg
Antibacterial antibiotic.
Sulphaguanidine 1.985g
Sulphonamide antibacterial.
Light kaolin 4.25g

Drug treatment for acute diarrhoea is best avoided. Diarrhoea is a natural defence mechanism (like coughing or sneezing) which helps the body get rid of irritants or toxins. Drinking fluids aids this process and speeds recovery – but anti-infective drugs do not, and there is evidence that they may even prolong illness. The US Food and Drug Administration has found that kaolin lacks evidence of effectiveness as an antidiarrhoeal ingredient [FR 40 76 21/3/75 p.12928].

GUANOR EXPECTORANT

RP Drugs
Syrup (per 5ml)

Ammonium chloride 135mg
Diphenhydramine hydrochloride 14mg
Menthol 1.1mg
Sodium citrate 57mg

Irrational combination. See BENAFED.

GUANOR PAEDIATRIC

RP Drugs
Syrup (per 5ml)

Diphenhydramine hydrochloride 7mg
Menthol 550 micrograms
Sodium citrate 28.5mg

Undesirable preparation, same as BENYLIN PAEDIATRIC. See BENAFED.

GYNOVLAR 21
Schering
[POM] Oral contraceptive

Norethisterone acetate 3mg
Ethinyloestradiol 50 micrograms
Hormones.

A lower-strength pill may be safer. See ORAL CONTRACEPTIVES.

HAELAN-C
Dista
[POM] Cream and ointment

Flurandrenolone 0.0125%
Corticosteroid to reduce inflammation.
Clioquinol 3%
Anti-infective agent.

Only likely to be of value where an area of eczema or dermatitis is infected. See CORTICOSTEROID + ANTI-INFECTIVE SKIN PREPARATIONS.

HALCICOMB WITHDRAWN
FAIR
[POM] Cream

Halcinonide 0.1%
Corticosteroid to reduce inflammation.
Neomycin sulphate 0.25%
Nystatin 100,000 units/gram
Anti-infective agents.

Only likely to be of value where an area of eczema or dermatitis is infected. See CORTICOSTEROID + ANTI-INFECTIVE SKIN PREPARATIONS.

HALCION
Upjohn
[POM] Tablets

Triazolam 125 micrograms, 250 micrograms
Benzodiazepine tranquilliser: for treatment of insomnia.

Reports of suspected adverse reactions – intolerable mental effects – led to the suspension of this drug by the Dutch drug registration authority in 1979. There were no such reports in the UK, other than in a short documentary on 'Newsnight' [BBC-TV, 6/1/83]. The reports from Holland may have been related to the higher doses used there: 500 micrograms and 1mg tablets were available [DTB, 1979, 17, 76]. The daily dose should not exceed 250 micrograms – especially not for users over 60 [M28, p.818]. See BENZODIAZEPINE TRANQUILLISERS.

HARMONYL
Abbott
[POM] Tablets

Deserpidine 250 micrograms
Antihypertensive: reserpine-related rauwolfia derivative, used to control high blood pressure.

The possibility of serious side effects (mainly depression) makes this drug less suitable for prescribing. See RESERPINE.

HAVAPEN
Wyeth
[POM] Tablets

Penamecillin 350mg
Antibacterial antibiotic.

Essentially similar to – and no more effective than – phenoxymethylpenicillin (Penicillin V), but HAVAPEN costs 2–3 times more.

HAYMINE
Pharmax
Slow-release tablets

Chlorpheniramine maleate 10mg
Antihistamine.
Ephedrine hydrochloride 60mg
Decongestant.

There is no good evidence that sympathomimetics (used to treat nasal congestion) add to the effectiveness of antihistamines in the treatment of symptoms of allergy [DTB 1982, 20, 40]. The action of slow-release antihistamines can be uneven and unpredictable, and they tend to cost more than standard formulations. This combination of ingredients is of doubtful value.
NHS expenditure on this product is about £¼ million a year.

HAYPHRYN
Winthrop
Nasal spray

Phenylephrine hydrochloride 0.5%
Sympathomimetic: reduces nasal congestion and inflammation.
Thenyldiamine hydrochloride 0.1%
Antihistamine: to control symptoms of allergy, eg in hay fever.

There is little evidence that a sympathomimetic + antihistamine combination is more effective than an antihistamine alone in treating allergic conditions like hay fever [DTB, 1982, 20, 40]. Oral antihistamines and those applied locally, eg via nasal sprays, are ineffective in treating common cold symptoms. Hay fever and other allergic conditions may last four weeks or more – but if sympathomimetic nasal decongestants are used for more than a few days, they tend to cause rebound congestion (aggravating and prolonging the original condition) and may permanently damage the sensitive lining of the nose.

HEMOPLEX
Paines & Byrne
[POM] Injection (per ml)

Crude liver extract, with B vitamins: thiamine hydrochloride 10mg; **riboflavine** 500 micrograms; **nicotinamide** 10mg; **pyridoxine hydrochloride** 2.5mg

Obsolete formulation. See HEPACON-B FORTE.

HEPACON-B FORTE
Consolidated
[POM] Injection

Liver extract *(equivalent to vitamin B_{12}* 15 micrograms)
Folic acid 2.5mg
Thiamine pyrophosphate 50mg

Liver extract for injection is considered obsolete as a source of vitamin B_{12}, and should no longer be used. Hydroxocobalamin is the agent of choice [M28 p.1646].

HEPACON LIVER EXTRACT
Consolidated
[POM] Injection

Liver extract *(equivalent to vitamin B_{12}* 100 and 1000 micrograms per 2ml ampoule).

Similar to HEPACON-B FORTE.

HEPACON-PLEX
Consolidated
[POM] Injection (per ml)

B vitamins: thiamine hydrochloride 50mg; **riboflavine** 1mg; **nicotinamide** 75mg; **pyridoxine hydrochloride** 2.5mg; calcium pantothenate 5mg; **cyanocobalamin** 4 micrograms

Hydroxocobalamin, rather than cyanocobalamin, should be used to prevent or treat vitamin B_{12} deficiency states: it is better absorbed and utilised in the body [M28 p.1645]. Calcium pantothenate has no accepted therapeutic uses in human medicine [M28 p.1650].

HEWLETTS ANTISEPTIC CREAM
Astra
Cream for minor infections, abrasions etc

Boric acid 2.5%
Hydrous wool fat 4%
Zinc oxide 8%

Unlikely to be necessary or useful. Boric acid has weak antiseptic properties but has been superseded by safer, more effective agents [M28 p.337]. Use of preparations containing borax or boric acid should be avoided in infants.

HEXOPAL
Winthrop
Tablets, tablets forte, suspension

Inositol nictotinate 500mg, 750mg (tablets) 1g/5ml (suspension)
Peripheral vasodilator: intended to improve blood flow in skin and muscle, and used mainly to treat circulation disorders in legs.

Lacks evidence of effectiveness. Inositol nicotinate is hydrolysed to nicotinic acid (ie reacts with water to form nicotinic acid) and there is reported to be 'no basis for the use of nicotinic acid in peripheral vascular diseases' [Coffman J. D. *New Engl. J. Med.*, 1979; 300, 713: cited in M28 p.1649]. See PERIPHERAL VASODILATORS. NHS expenditure on this product is over £6 million a year.

HIBITANE
ICI
Lozenges

Chlorhexidine hydrochloride 5mg
Antimicrobial/disinfectant.
Benzocaine 2mg
Local anaesthetic: intended to relieve sore throat.

There is no good evidence that this preparation is of any real value. The dose of benzocaine may be too low to be effective (cf. MEROCAINE).

HIPREX
Carnegie
Tablets

Hexamine hippurate 1g
Antiseptic used to prevent or suppress urinary tract infections.

The UK Joint Formulary Committee recommends hexamine no longer be used – though other authorities suggest it is of some value. The Committee considers treatment is relatively ineffective and inconvenient; side effects are fre-

quent. These include nausea, stomach upsets and pain when urinating. They are partly caused by agents (often ammonium chloride) taken concurrently to acidify the urine: hexamine works only in a strongly acid medium [BNF No.6 1983 p.206].
NHS expenditure on hexamine preparations is about £¼ million a year. Similar products: G500; MANDELAMINE.

HIRUDOID
Luitpold-Werk
Cream; gel

Heparinoid 0.3%
Intended to improve circulation, reduce inflammation in bruises, strains etc.

There is no convincing evidence of value [DTB 1976, 14, 67].

HISTALIX
Wallace Mfg
Syrup (per 5ml)

Ammonium chloride 135mg
Diphenhydramine hydrochloride 14mg
Menthol 1.1mg
Sodium citrate 57mg

Irrational combination, same as BENYLIN EXPECTORANT.

HISTRYL
SK & F
Slow-release capsules

Diphenylpyraline hydrochloride 2.5mg (paediatric) and 5mg
Antihistamine: used to relieve symptoms of allergy, eg in hay fever or urticaria (nettle rash).

The action of slow-release antihistamines may be uneven and unpredictable, and they are also more expensive than standard formulations. This product appears to have no significant advantage over other antihistamines. It costs about twice as much as slow-release chlorpheniramine: if this were prescribed instead of HISTRYL, the NHS could save about £100,000 a year.

HYALASE
CP Pharmaceuticals
Injection (1500 units)

Hyaluronidase *(bovine)*
Enzyme intended to enhance the diffusion and absorption of local anaesthetics and other drugs administered with it.

Hyaluridonase has been found useful in eye surgery [AMADE 1983, p.503] but its value in other applications is doubtful. Local anaesthetics administered with this enzyme may be too rapidly absorbed, and may then cause local irritation and sensitisation. Because of this, 'its value is seriously questioned and it is now seldom used' [AMADE 1980, p.1050].

HYDERGINE
Sandoz
[POM] Tablets

Co-dergocrine mesylate 1.5mg; 4.5mg
Peripheral vasodilator: mainly promoted to improve mental function in the elderly.

Though widely used, its value has not been clearly established. It has 'not been shown clinically to be of much benefit in senile dementia' (BNF No.6, 1983; p.90). See PERIPHERAL VASODILATORS.
NHS expenditure on this product is about £¾ million a year.

HYDROCORTISONE AND NEOMYCIN CREAM
[POM] Cream

Hydrocortisone 0.5%
Corticosteroid to reduce inflammation.
Neomycin sulphate 0.5%
Anti-infective agent.

Only likely to be of value where an area of eczema or dermatitis is infected. See CORTICOSTEROID + ANTI-INFECTIVE SKIN PREPARATIONS.

HYDRODERM
MSD
[POM] Ointment

Hydrocortisone 1%
Corticosteroid to reduce inflammation.
Neomycin sulphate 0.5%
Bacitracin zinc 1,000 units/gram
Anti-infective agents.

Only likely to be of value where an area of eczema or dermatitis is infected. See CORTICOSTEROID + ANTI-INFECTIVE SKIN PREPARATIONS.
NHS expenditure on this product is about £100,000 a year.

HYGROTON
Geigy
[POM] Tablets

Chlorthalidone 50mg; 100mg
See HYGROTON-K.

HYGROTON-K
Geigy
[POM] Slow-release tablets

Chlorthalidone 25mg
Diuretic: helps to control high blood pressure; removes excessive fluid from body tissues by increasing output of urine.
Potassium 6.7mmol
Supplement intended to replace potassium which the body loses through diuresis.

Many people do not need a potassium supplement with a diuretic. If a supplement is needed it is best taken separately, and preferably in solution not tablet form. The required dose may be higher than the amount in this preparation. See POTASSIUM SUPPLEMENTS. Chlorthalidone has no clear advantage over thiazide diuretics, such as bendrofluazide [DTB 1975; 13, 102; M28 p.592], but it costs much more. If bendrofluazide (or bendrofluazide + potassium) were prescribed instead of HYGROTON and HYGROTON-K products, the NHS could save about £1 million a year.

HYPERCAL
Carlton
[POM] Tablets

Rauwolfia alkaloids 2mg

Less suitable for prescribing. See HYPERCAL-B; RESERPINE.

HYPERCAL-B
Carlton
[POM] Tablets

Rauwolfia alkaloids 2mg
Antihypertensive: used to control high blood pressure.
Amylobarbitone 15mg
Barbiturate sedative.

BARBITURATES (see entry) do not significantly contribute to the lowering of blood pressure, and their use as sedatives is obsolete. They are addictive and may cause other unpleasant side effects [DTB 1980, 18, 10]. If a sedative is needed it should be separately prescribed. The possibility of serious side effects (mainly depression) limits the usefulness of rauwolfia. See RESERPINE.

HYPON
Calmic
Tablets

Aspirin 325mg
Analgesic/antipyretic (for lowering of temperature)/anti-inflammatory.
Codeine phosphate 5mg
Narcotic analgesic for mild to moderate pain.
Caffeine 10mg
Weak stimulant.

The dose of codeine is less than effective, and the caffeine is not needed at all. This combination is much more expensive – but probably no more effective – than aspirin 325mg alone. See ASPIRIN AND CODEINE.
NHS expenditure on this product is estimated at £100,000 a year.

IBERET 500
Abbott
Slow-release tablets

Dried ferrous sulphate 325mg (105mg **iron**)
B vitamins: thiamine mononitrate 6mg; **riboflavine** 6mg; **nicotinamide** 30mg; **pyridoxine hydrochloride** 5mg; **calcium pantothenate** 10mg
Vitamin C: ascorbic acid 500mg
(as sodium salt).

VITAMINS (see entry) should not be added to iron preparations: independent authorities say that there is 'no justification' for it, and consider that the use of such combinations should be 'strongly discouraged'. Vitamin C increases absorption of iron – but to no avail (see VITAMINS). See also IRON SUPPLEMENTS.

IBEROL
Abbott
Slow-release tablets

Dried ferrous sulphate 325mg (105mg **iron**)
B vitamins: thiamine mononitrate 3mg; **riboflavine** 3mg; **nicotinamide** 15mg; **pyridoxine hydrochloride** 1.5mg; **liver fraction** 100mg
Vitamin C: ascorbic acid 75mg
(as sodium salt).

Undesirable combination. See IBERET 500.

ILONIUM
Ilon
Ointment for minor skin infections etc

Colophony 15.6%
Pine resin extract used as protectant.

Phenol 0.1%
Thymol 0.03%
Antiseptics.
Turpentine oil 8%
Venice turpentine 8.1%
Essential oils with counter-irritant action.

Less suitable for prescribing because it is very old-fashioned and has been superseded by more effective compounds [AMADE p.1022]. Phenol and thymol are seldom used as antiseptics or disinfectants [AMADE p.1386].

IMBRILON

Berk
[POM] Capsules

Indomethacin 25mg, 50mg
suppositories
Indomethacin 100mg

See INDOCID.

INDERAL

ICI
[POM] Tablets

Propranolol hydrochloride 10mg, 40mg, 80mg, 160mg
Beta-blocker: controls over-stimulation of the heart and regularises the heartbeat. Used mainly to treat high blood pressure, angina and other heart disorders.

This is an effective and widely prescribed drug, strongly promoted by brand name. If the identical medicine were prescribed by generic name, propranolol hydrochloride, the NHS could save at least £2½ million a year.

INDERAL LA

ICI
[POM] Sustained-release tablets

Propranolol hydrochloride 160mg

See INDERAL. This is an effective and widely prescribed drug, strongly promoted by brand name. It offers the convenience and the theoretical advantages of a once-daily dosage, but otherwise has the same effect on the body as propranolol taken at half the dose, twice a day. If propranolol (80mg × 2) were prescribed instead of INDERAL LA, the NHS would save about £4 million a year.

INDERETIC

ICI
[POM] Capsules

Propranolol hydrochloride 80mg
Beta-blocker.
Bendrofluazide 2.5mg
Diuretic

Used to control high blood pressure. See BETA-BLOCKER + DIURETIC PREPARATIONS.

INDEREX

ICI
[POM] Capsules

Propranolol hydrochloride 160mg, for sustained release
Beta-blocker.
Bendrofluazide 5mg
Diuretic.

Used to control high blood pressure. See BETA-BLOCKER + DIURETIC PREPARATIONS.

INDOCID

Morson
[POM] Capsules; suppositories; mixture (per 5ml)

Indomethacin 25mg (all formulations other than suppositories)
Indomethacin 50mg (capsules only)
Indomethacin 100mg (suppositories only)
Non-steroidal anti-inflammatory drug (NSAID) *used mainly to treat pain and inflammation in rheumatic and related disorders.*

Indomethacin is widely prescribed (around 5 million prescriptions a year) and is effective; though its value is limited by frequent side effects, especially stomach ulceration, headache and dizziness. Between 1964–1972, the Committee on Safety of Medicines received over 1,250 reports of adverse reactions, including 50 deaths (from blood disorders and stomach bleeding). For this reason, the UK Joint Formulary Committee has recommended that doctors prescribe indomethacin only after other NSAIDs have been tried and found ineffective (BNF No.6, 1983, p.296). There are around 20 alternatives. See NSAIDs. This product has been strongly promoted by brand name. If the identical medicine (indomethacin) were prescribed by generic name, the NHS would save £4–£5 million a year.
Other brands of indomethacin include ARTRACIN (DDSA); IMBRILON (Berk); INDOFLEX (Unimed); INDOLAR (Lagap); and MOBILAN (Galen).

INDOCID R
Morson
[POM] Slow-release capsules

Indomethacin 75mg

See INDOCID.

INDOFLEX
Unimed
[POM] Capsules

Indomethacin 25mg

See INDOCID.

INDOLAR
Lagap
[POM] Capsules

Indomethacin 25mg, 50mg

See INDOCID.

INDOLAR SR
Lagap
[POM] Sustained-release capsules

Indomethacin 75mg

See INDOCID.

INTAL COMPOUND
Fisons
[POM] Cartridges for use with insufflator

Sodium cromoglycate 20mg
Preventative treatment for asthma and certain other allergic conditions.
Isoprenaline sulphate 100 micrograms
Bronchodilator: used to relieve wheezing and other breathing difficulties in asthma, bronchitis etc.

Sodium cromoglycate on its own can effectively prevent asthma attacks; nothing is gained by using it with isoprenaline. Isoprenaline is added to counteract throat irritation and breathing problems that may occur when sodium cromoglycate is taken alone in powder form. However, if such problems arise, isoprenaline should be taken separately, shortly before sodium cromoglycate is taken on its own.
Because isoprenaline gives immediate symptomatic relief, users may take this product only to treat symptoms of asthma – rather than take it regularly as a preventative measure [DTB, 1971, 9, 82].
NHS expenditure on this product is about £5 million a year.

INTRALGIN
Riker
Gel

Benzocaine 2%
Salicylamide 5% *in an alcoholic basis*
Intended to relieve pain in muscles, joints etc. when rubbed into skin.

A 5%–20% concentration of benzocaine is required for effective local anaesthetic action. There is no convincing evidence of the effectiveness of salicylamide [FR 44 234 4/12/79 p.69845]. Methyl Salicylate Ointment BP or Methyl Salicylate Liniment BP are effective and cheaper alternatives.

IPECACUANHA AND MORPHINE MIXTURE BP
Main ingredients (per 10ml)

Ipecacuanha tincture 0.2ml
Chloroform and morphine tincture 0.4ml

Irrational combination: includes ingredients intended both to stimulate the cough reflex (ipecacuanha), and to suppress it (chloroform and morphine). The value of ipecacuanha is doubtful. See entry for EXPECTORANTS AND MUCOLYTICS.

IROFOL C
Abbott
[POM] Slow-release tablets

Dried ferrous sulphate 325mg (105mg **iron**)
Folic acid 350 micrograms
Ascorbic acid 500mg
Vitamin C as sodium salt.

Undesirable combination. See IBERET 500.

IRONORM
Wallace Mfg
[POM] Capsules

Dried ferrous sulphate 195mg (59mg **iron**)
Folic acid 1.7mg
B vitamins: thiamine hydrochloride 1mg; **riboflavine** 2mg; **nicotinamide** 10mg; **cyanocobalamin** 5 micrograms; **liver fraction II** 130mg
Vitamin C: ascorbic acid 15mg

Cyanocobalamin is not reliably absorbed by mouth; the other vitamins can be expected to add to the cost rather than the benefit. VITAMINS (see entry) should not be added to iron preparations. See IRON SUPPLEMENTS. This product costs several times more than iron and folic acid alone.

IRONORM

Wallace Mfg
Tonic with iron (per 5ml)

Ferric ammonium citrate 250mg (50mg **iron**)
Calcium glycerophosphate 10.75mg
Manganese glycerophosphate 1mg
Potassium glycerophosphate 1.75mg
Sodium glycerophosphate 21.25mg
B vitamins: thiamine hydrochloride 500 micrograms; **riboflavine** 250 micrograms; **nicotinamide** 3.75mg; **pyridoxine hydrochloride** 125 micrograms; **cyanocobalamin** 2.5 micrograms; **calcium pantothenate** 125 micrograms; **proteolysed liver extract** *equivalent to* 2g *fresh liver*

Ferrous salts are preferred to ferric salts, which are less well absorbed. Glycerophosphates have been advocated in the past as tonics, appetite stimulants etc, but are of no value. See also IRONORM capsules.

IRON SUPPLEMENTS

Iron supplements are used to prevent or treat deficiency states (anaemias). Iron is often given to pregnant women, and in the last trimester of pregnancy is often prescribed with folic acid (a B vitamin) because of possible deficiency in both. However, there is no evidence to suggest that such treatment is necessary. A review of 17 studies on the effect of iron and/or vitamins on healthy pregnant women in industrialised countries reported that iron supplements had no significant effect on the health of either mother or child [Starfield B.; Hemminki E.: *Brit. J. Obstet. & Gynaec.*, 1978, 85, 404–9].

Women do need more iron in pregnancy, but can usually get all they need without iron supplements: they absorb much more iron from their food, and can also draw on large reserves stored in the liver and in bone marrow. A susceptible minority – perhaps 5 per cent of women – will benefit from iron supplements [Weitz, 1982, p.240]. For most women they are unnecessary and may be positively undesirable: about 10 per cent of users suffer unpleasant side effects, including stomach pain, constipation and nausea. (Side effects can be minimised by lowering the dose, or taking the supplement with or after meals.)

If iron is needed, ferrous sulphate is the drug of choice. It does what is required at least as well as other forms of iron, and is cheap. People who cannot tolerate ferrous sulphate are unlikely to benefit from other iron salts [AMADE p.794].

Slow-release iron preparations, and iron in combination with succinic acid or vitamin C are not recommended: see page 22. Iron + vitamin combinations are generally undesirable: see VITAMINS. Over half of all NHS prescriptions for iron are for products rated 'less suitable for prescribing' in the *British National Formulary*; and less suitable products in the BNF outnumber suitable ones by about 2:1.

ISO-AUTOHALER

Riker
[POM] Breath-actuated metered aerosol

Isoprenaline sulphate 80 micrograms per dose
Bronchodilator: relieves breathing difficulties in asthma, bronchitis etc.

Isoprenaline acts less selectively than some other agents: it does improve airflow, but may also over-stimulate the heart. Unwanted effects – which include erratic heartbeat, headache and nervousness – are quite common. There are generally better alternatives to isoprenaline. See BRONCHODILATORS.

ISO-BROVON

Various preparations

See BROVON.

JUVEL

Bencard
Multivitamin tablets; syrup

Broadly similar to ABIDEC. See VITAMINS.

KARVOL

Crookes Products
Inhalation capsules

Menthol 35.9mg (with **cinnamon oil, pine oil, terpineol, thymol** and **chlorbutol**)
Nasal decongestant: used to relieve symptoms of bronchitis, sinusitis and related conditions.

Inhalations of this kind (eg Menthol and Benzoin Inhalation; Menthol and Eucalyptus Inhalation) may be comforting, but there is no convincing evidence of their effectiveness.
NHS expenditure on this product is estimated at £100,000 a year.

K-CONTIN CONTINUS

Napp
Slow-release tablets

Potassium chloride 600mg (8mmol each of potassium and chloride ions)

Slow-release POTASSIUM SUPPLEMENTS (see entry) may irritate or cause ulcers in the gut; there are preferable alternatives.

KEFADOL
Lilly
[POM] Powder for injection

Cephamandole 500mg, 1g

Cheaper and more effective alternatives available. See CEPHALOSPORIN ANTIBIOTICS.

KEFLIN
Lilly
[POM] Powder for injection

Cephalothin 1g

More effective alternatives available. See CEPHALOSPORIN ANTIBIOTICS.

KEST
Berk
Tablets

Phenolphthalein 50mg
Laxative.
Magnesium sulphate 300mg
Short-acting laxative.

PHENOLPHTHALEIN (see entry) is considered less satisfactory than other laxatives. The dose of magnesium sulphate is very low. The combination of short- and long-acting ingredients is unwarranted.

KOLANTICON
Merrell
Gel (per 5ml)

Dicyclomine hydrochloride 2.5mg
Antispasmodic: intended to relieve abdominal spasms and ulcer-like pain.
Dried aluminium hydroxide 200mg
Light magnesium oxide 100mg
Antacids: neutralise excess stomach acid.
Dimethicone 20mg
Anti-foaming agent: to relieve flatulence.

Antispasmodic drugs like dicyclomine have not been shown to better the results of antacids given alone, and can produce unpleasant side effects, such as dry mouth, blurred vision, and retention of urine [DTB 1980, 18, 19]. The dose of dicyclomine is low: the recommended dose is half the amount usually given (30–80mg/day). The value of dimethicone is uncertain. See ASILONE.
NHS expenditure on this product is over £½ million a year.

KOLANTYL
Merrell
Gel

Similar to KOLANTICON, but without dimethicone.
NHS expenditure on this product is about £¼ million a year.

LABITON
LAB
Elixir (per 10ml)

Alcohol 2.78ml
Thiamine hydrochloride 750 micrograms
Vitamin B_1
Caffeine 7mg
Kola nut dried extract 6.05mg
Source of insignificant amount of caffeine.
Aminobenzoic acid 4mg
Glycerophosphoric acid (20%) 0.02ml
Caramel 10mg
Syrup 3mg

The Data Sheet (1983/4) explains: 'The kola nut contains complex catecholcaffeinates which give immediate central stimulation, increase muscular performance and reduce fatiguability. Vitamin B_1 is included to make up deficiency resulting from recent illness or anorexia. Labiton is indicated for use as a tonic for fatigue in convalescence after infections such as influenza and after operations.'
The only significant ingredient in this concoction is alcohol (28 per cent). The smallest bottle of this product (200ml = between ¼ and ⅓ pint) contains the equivalent of over five pub measures of whisky. Though the 'recommended dosage' is 20–40ml/day, abuse seems inevitable. Ironically, alcoholism is one of the main causes of vitamin B deficiency in the UK.
This product should be avoided, especially by patients taking sedatives and tranquillisers, during or soon after hepatitis, and by road users and operators of machinery.
An estimated 100,000 NHS prescriptions are written each year for alcohol-based tonics. This product has the highest alcohol content and is the most prescribed.

LABOPHYLLIN
LAB
Tablets

Theophylline 100mg
Bronchodilator: relieves breathing difficulties in asthma, bronchitis etc.

Lysine 74mg
Amino acid.

There is no obvious reason for the addition of lysine; the manufacturer claims no advantage for it in the Data Sheet (1983/4). Standard (rapid-release) oral preparations of theophylline are considered less suitable for prescribing than the newer slow-release preparations, because of the relatively high frequency of side effects – eg headache, nausea, stomach irritation and over-stimulation [BNF No.6, 1983, p.104].

LANCE B + C
Kirby-Warrick
Tablets

Vitamins B + C

The same as, but cheaper than OROVITE.

LASIKAL
Hoechst
[POM] Tablets

Frusemide 20mg (see LASIX); with slow-release **potassium** (10mmol)

Many people do not need a potassium supplement with a diuretic. If a supplement is needed it is best taken separately, and preferably in solution not tablet form. The required dose may be higher than the amount in this preparation. See POTASSIUM SUPPLEMENTS.
This product is strongly promoted by brand name. If frusemide + potassium were prescribed instead, the NHS could save around £½ million a year.

LASIX
Hoechst
[POM] Tablets

Frusemide 20mg, 40mg, 500mg
Diuretic: helps to control high blood pressure; removes excessive fluid from body tissues by increasing output of urine.

An effective and widely prescribed drug, strongly promoted by brand name. It is also relatively very expensive.
If doctors prescribed the identical medicine under its generic name (frusemide BP), the NHS would save at least £6 million a year.

LASIX + K
Hoechst
[POM] Tablets

Frusemide 40mg; *with slow-release potassium tablets* (20mmol) *supplied separately in calendar pack to help patients remember to take the tablets.*

See comment on LASIKAL. If prescriptions were written instead for frusemide + potassium, the NHS could save over £½ million a year.

LASONIL
Bayer
Ointment (per gram)

Heparinoid 50 units
Hyaluronidase 150 units
Intended to improve circulation, reduce inflammation, in bruises, strains etc; also recommended for haemorrhoids.

There is no convincing evidence of the value of this product [BNF No.6, 1983, p.364; DTB 1976, 14, 67].
NHS expenditure on this product is estimated at over £100,000 a year.

LEDERMYCIN
Lederle
[POM] Capsules and syrup (per 10ml)

Demeclocycline hydrochloride 150mg (drops: 60mg/ml; tablets: 300mg)
Bacteriostatic antibiotic: used in the treatment of bronchitis and other infections.

Demeclocycline has essentially the same actions and uses as tetracycline but is active in the body for longer, so therapeutic blood levels can be maintained with longer intervals between doses. The advantage is convenience for users, and perhaps also less irritation to the stomach (no claim for this in the Data Sheet [1983/4]). However, demeclocycline is believed to cause sensitivity reactions to light, particularly sunlight.
It seems unlikely that any net advantage is often worth the extra cost, since LEDERMYCIN costs up to 15 times more than unbranded versions of tetracycline.
LEDERMYCIN syrup and drops are for children, but should be avoided if possible [BNF No.6 1983 p.192]. See TETRACYCLINE MIXTURE.

LEDERPLEX
Lederle
Elixir (per 5ml)

B vitamins: thiamine hydrochloride 2mg; **riboflavine** 2mg; **nicotinamide** 10mg; **pyridoxine hydrochloride** 200 micrograms; **pantothenic acid** 2mg; **choline** 20mg; **inositol** 10mg; **cyanocobalamin** 5 micrograms; **soluble liver fraction** 470mg

There is no convincing evidence of the value of choline, inositol, pantothenic acid, or cyanocobalamin (by mouth). They add to cost – over five times more than good alternatives, such as Compound Vitamin B Tablets (Strong).

LEO K
Leo
Tablets formulated in slow-release wax core

Potassium chloride 600mg (8mmol *each of potassium and chloride ions*)

Slow-release POTASSIUM SUPPLEMENTS (see entry) may irritate or cause ulcers in the gut: there are preferable alternatives.

LEXOTAN
Roche
[POM] Tablets

Bromazepam 1.5mg, 3mg

Bromazepam has actions, uses and unwanted effects similar to diazepam and other BENZODIAZEPINE TRANQUILLISERS (see entry), but costs about fifty times more [DTB 1983, 21, 64].

LIBRAXIN
Sauter
[POM] Tablets

Clidinium bromide 2.5mg
Antispasmodic: intended to relieve abdominal spasms and ulcer-like pain by reducing contractions of the stomach and intestine.
Chlordiazepoxide 5mg
Benzodiazepine tranquilliser for treatment of anxiety.

Tranquillisers are rarely indicated in ulcer therapy, and their long-term use may cause dependence. If needed, a tranquilliser should be separately prescribed. See BENZODIAZEPINE TRANQUILLISERS.
NHS expenditure on this product is estimated at £¾ million a year.

LIBRIUM
Sauter
[POM] Tablets, capsules

Chlordiazepoxide 5mg, 10mg (tablets; capsules); 25mg (tablets only)
Benzodiazepine tranquilliser: for treatment of anxiety.

An effective drug, though widely misused. See entry for BENZODIAZEPINE TRANQUILLISERS. This product has been strongly promoted by brand name. If the same medicine were prescribed under its generic name (chlordiazepoxide), the NHS could save perhaps £¾ million a year.
(Another brand of chlordiazepoxide: TROPIUM [DDSA].)

LIMBITROL 5
Sauter
[POM] Capsules

Amitriptyline 12.5mg *(as hydrochloride)*
Tricyclic antidepressant: mainly used to treat depressive illness.
Chlordiazepoxide 5mg
Benzodiazepine tranquilliser: for treatment of anxiety and tension.

Most illness involving both depression and anxiety is controlled with an antidepressant drug on its own. Anti-anxiety drugs may occasionally help, and may be useful at the start of treatment, as it can take several weeks before antidepressants become fully effective. However, these two drugs are rarely indicated for routine use, and the fixed ratio combination is undesirable.
If the same ingredients were prescribed separately and by generic name, users would pay two prescription charges – but the NHS would save about £½ million a year. A crazy anomaly.

LIMBITROL 10
Sauter
[POM] Capsules

Contains double the dosages in LIMBITROL 5.

LINCOCIN
Upjohn
[POM] Capsules; syrup (per 10ml)

Lincomycin hydrochloride 500mg
Antibiotic: for use in moderately severe infections against susceptible penicillin- or erythromycin-resistant organisms; or in patients who cannot tolerate other antibacterial agents.

Lincomycin may cause diarrhoea or sometimes fatal colitis, and some authorities consider its use should be reserved for a few, very specific treatments in hospitalised patients only [AMADE 1980, p.1261]. If diarrhoea or colitis develop, treatment should be stopped immediately. Lincomycin is thought to be less potent, less well absorbed and more toxic than a closely related drug, clindamycin (Dalacin C) – and therefore 'has become obsolete' [AMADE 1983 p.1663].

LINCTIFED EXPECTORANT

Wellcome
Syrup (per 5ml)

Codeine phosphate 7.5mg
Cough suppressant.
Guaiphenesin 100mg
Expectorant: intended to help removal of phlegm from the airways.
Pseudoephedrine hydrochloride 20mg
Nasal, bronchial decongestant.
Triprolidine hydrochloride 1.25mg
Antihistamine: used to suppress symptoms of allergy eg to dry up nasal secretions in hay fever.

It is irrational to combine an antihistamine (which dries up secretions in the airways) with an expectorant (which is intended to liquefy and loosen secretions); and to combine ingredients which both stimulate and suppress the cough reflex. The effectiveness of guaiphenesin is doubtful. See entry for EXPECTORANTS AND MUCOLYTICS. The UK Joint Formulary Committee considers that 'there is no scientific basis' for prescribing mixtures of this kind, and says that their use is 'to be deprecated' [BNF No.6, 1983, p.120).
NHS expenditure on this product is estimated at £1 million a year.

LINCTIFED EXPECTORANT PAEDIATRIC

Wellcome
Syrup (per 5ml)

Codeine phosphate 3mg
Guaiphenesin 50mg
Pseudoephedrine hydrochloride 12mg
Triprolidine hydrochloride 600 micrograms

Irrational combination. See LINCTIFED EXPECTORANT.
NHS expenditure on this product is estimated at £200,000 a year.

LIPOFLAVONOID

Lewis
Capsules

B vitamins: thiamine hydrochloride 330 micrograms; **riboflavine** 330 micrograms; **nicotinamide** 3.33mg; **pyridoxine hydrochloride** 330 micrograms; **choline bitartrate** 233mg; **inositol** 111mg; **hydroxocobalamin** 1.66 micrograms; **lemon bioflavonoid complex** 100mg; **methionine** 28mg; **dexpanthenol** 330 micrograms
Vitamin C: ascorbic acid 100mg

Choline, inositol, methionine, dexpanthenol and bioflavonoids are considered of little or no value. The amounts of the main B vitamins are lower than would be found in an average helping of a vitamin-fortified cereal. This product costs about five times more than Compound Vitamin B Tablets – which would provide three times the amount of the three main B vitamins.
NHS expenditure on LIPOFLAVONOID and LIPOTRIAD (see below) is over £300,000 a year.

LIPOTRIAD

Lewis

Essentially similar to LIPOFLAVONOID.

LIQUID PARAFFIN AND PHENOLPHTHALEIN MIXTURE BP

Phenolphthalein 30mg
Laxative.
Liquid paraffin 10ml
Laxative, lubricant.

PHENOLPHTHALEIN (see entry) is considered less satisfactory than many other laxatives. Prolonged use of liquid paraffin may be harmful and should be avoided [M28 p.1063].

LOBAK

Winthrop
[POM] Tablets

Paracetamol 450mg
Analgesic; antipyretic: used to reduce temperature.
Chlormezanone 100mg
Tranquilliser: for treatment of anxiety; muscle spasm.

Chlormezanone is similar to MEPROBAMATE (see entry), and considered less effective as a muscle relaxant than diazepam and other BEN-

ZODIAZEPINE TRANQUILLISERS (see entry), though it costs 3–5 times more. The fixed-ratio combination is undesirable, and increases costs. If diazepam 5mg and paracetamol 500mg were separately prescribed instead of this product, the NHS could save about £1 million a year.

LOCABIOTAL

Servier
[POM] Metered aerosol (per nasal inhalation)

Fusafungine 125 micrograms
Topical antibiotic.

Significant infections would normally be treated systemically: this preparation is unlikely to be of real benefit.
NHS expenditure on this and other products like it is over £1½ million a year.

LOCAN

Duncan Flockhart
Cream; ointment

Amethocaine 0.8%
Amylocaine 1%
Cinchocaine 0.4%
Local anaesthetics: intended to relieve pain, itching etc.

Local anaesthetic ointments and creams are not very effective in relieving painful or itchy conditions and may cause sensitivity reactions: cinchocaine in particular. This product is specifically recommended for the treatment of ano-rectal pain and itching, but a US expert panel has found that there is insufficient evidence of the effectiveness of either cinchocaine or amethocaine for such conditions [FR 45 103 27/5/80 p.35616].

LOCOID C

Brocades
[POM] Cream; ointment

Hydrocortisone butyrate 0.1%
Corticosteroid to reduce inflammation.
Chlorquinaldol 3%
Anti-infective agent.

Only likely to be of value where an area of eczema or dermatitis is infected. See CORTICOSTEROID + ANTI-INFECTIVE SKIN PREPARATIONS.
NHS expenditure on this product is about £200,000 a year.

LOESTRIN 20

Parke Davis
[POM] Oral contraceptive

Norethisterone acetate 1mg
Ethinyloestradiol 20 micrograms
Hormones.

Rated 'less suitable for prescribing' in the BNF because the dosage of the oestrogen component (ethinyloestradiol) may be too low to be fully effective. Theoretically, effective concentrations of oestrogen may not be achieved in large women, and the risk of failure may be greater if pills are missed. In addition, certain drugs may increase the metabolism (and therefore reduce blood levels) of the oestrogen. There have been reports of pregnancies and breakthrough bleeding when oral contraceptives have been taken with barbiturates, anti-convulsants, and the anti-tuberculosis drug, rifampicin [AMADE 1983, p.969, 978]. See ORAL CONTRACEPTIVES.

LOMOTIL

Gold Cross
[POM] Liquid for children (per 5ml)

Diphenoxylate hydrochloride 2.5mg
Antidiarrhoeal: opiate constipating agent.
Atropine sulphate 25 micrograms
A sub-therapeutic dosage. At higher dosages, atropine produces unpleasant side effects – intended to discourage abuse of diphenoxylate, which may be addicting.

Drug treatment for acute diarrhoea is best avoided. Diarrhoea is a natural defence mechanism (like coughing or sneezing) which helps the body get rid of irritants or toxins. Drinking fluids aids this process and speeds recovery, but potent chemical plugs do not. LOMOTIL is particularly unsuitable for young children, because it may be toxic at a dose only slightly higher than the therapeutic dose.
This product is over-used: an estimated 100,000 NHS prescriptions for it are written each year (at a cost of about £¼ million). In Australia, the authorities have withdrawn it, and its use for young children has been restricted elsewhere.

LOPRESOR

Geigy
[POM] Tablets

Metoprolol tartrate 50mg, 100mg
Beta-blocker: controls over-stimulation of the heart and regularises the heartbeat. Used mainly

for high blood pressure, angina and heart disorders.

This is an effective and widely prescribed drug, strongly promoted by brand name. Selected users (eg with a history of wheezing) would benefit from metoprolol, which is more selective for the heart than the close equivalent, propranolol. But as a general rule 'propranolol remains the drug of choice since it is cheap and its long-term risks are clearly understood' [DTB 1980, 18, 64].
It costs the NHS about £3/4 million a year because this brand is prescribed instead of propranolol.

LOPRESOR SR
Geigy
[POM] Slow-release tablets

Metoprolol tartrate 200mg

See LOPRESOR.

LOPRESORETIC
Geigy
[POM] Tablets

Metoprolol hydrochloride 100mg
Beta-blocker.
Chlorthalidone 12.5mg
Diuretic.

Used to control high blood pressure. See BETA-BLOCKER + DIURETIC PREPARATIONS.

LOTUSSIN
Searle
Linctus (per 5ml)

Dextromethorphan hydrobromide 6.25mg
Cough suppressant.
Diphenhydramine hydrochloride 5mg
Antihistamine, cough suppressant and sedative.
Ephedrine hydrochloride 7.5mg
Bronchial, nasal decongestant.
Guaiphenesin 50mg

Irrational combination. See LINCTIFED EXPECTORANT.
NHS expenditure on this product is about £1/4 million a year.

LUMINAL
Winthrop
[POM] Tablets

Phenobarbitone 15mg, 30mg, 60mg

This product is primarily an anti-convulsant, though it is also recommended as a general sedative and hypnotic [Data Sheet 1983/4]. The Committee on Review of Medicines has said that barbiturates should be used only for 'severe intractable insomnia' and not as daytime sedatives or anti-anxiety agents at all [DTB, 1980, 18, 9]. For these uses, BARBITURATES (see entry) have been superseded by BENZODIAZEPINE TRANQUILLISERS (see entry) and other safer agents.

LURSELLE
Merrell
[POM] Tablets

Probucol 250mg
Used to lower blood levels of lipids (fatty substances, like cholesterol).

This drug is used to prevent/treat atherosclerosis ('hardening of the arteries'; ie the thickening of artery walls due to deposits of fat-like substances, which can seriously impair blood flow to the heart). It has not been clearly established that drug-induced lowering of blood fat levels has benefits in the treatment of atherosclerosis or coronary heart disease [PDR 1983; p.1355]. However, this drug may help carefully selected users, if alternative measures fail: restrictions on diet, alcohol intake and smoking should normally be tried first.

MAALOX PLUS
Rorer
Antacid tablets, mixture

See similar product ASILONE.

MAGNESIUM CARBONATE, COMPOUND
Antacid powder, tablets

Considered less suitable for prescribing because they contain CALCIUM CARBONATE (see entry), and SODIUM BICARBONATE (see entry).

MAGNESIUM TRISILICATE AND BELLADONNA MIXTURE BPC

Lacks evidence of effectiveness. See comparable product ALUDROX SA.

MANDELAMINE
Warner
Enteric-coated tablets

Hexamine mandelate 250mg, 500mg
Urinary tract antiseptic.

Outmoded; considered less suitable for prescribing as it frequently causes side effects. See HIPREX.

MARPLAN
Roche
[POM] Tablets

Isocarboxazid 10mg
Anti-depressant: one of the monoamineoxidase inhibitor (MAOI) *class of drugs.*

In the US, this drug is indicated only for patients who cannot use or benefit from other ('tricyclic') anti-depressant drugs or from electroconvulsive therapy (ECT). MARPLAN is rated 'probably effective' by the US Food and Drug Administration, since 'it has not been established that isocarboxazid is as effective as other monoamine-oxidase inhibitors or the tricyclic compounds . . .' [AMADE p.264]. However the UK Joint Formulary Committee considers isocarboxazid a drug of choice, if an MAOI is to be used at all [BNF No.6 1983 p.147]. Life-threatening reactions to this and other MAOI anti-depressant drugs can occur if taken with certain foods, drink and other drugs: a throbbing headache warns of a rise in blood pressure. This should be explained to users, who should also get written instructions on a treatment card.

MARVELON
Organon
[POM] Oral contraceptive

Desogestrel 150 micrograms
Ethinyloestradiol 30 micrograms
Hormones.

A lower-strength pill may be safer. See ORAL CONTRACEPTIVES.

MAXITROL
Alcon
[POM] Eye drops; ointment

Dexamethasone 0.1%
Corticosteroid.
Neomycin 0.35% as sulphate
Polymyxin B sulphate 6000 units (per ml in drops; per gram in ointment)
Hypromellose 0.5% per ml
Lubricant.

Corticosteroid/antibiotic combinations have serious limitations. See BETNESOL-N.

MAXOLON
Beecham
[POM] Tablets; syrup; paediatric liquid

Metoclopramide hydrochloride tablets: 10mg; syrup and paediatric liquid: 1mg/ml
Metoclopramide speeds the emptying of the stomach's contents into the gut, and also closes off the sphincter (valve) between the gullet and stomach. It is mainly prescribed for digestive disorders and to control nausea and vomiting.

Metoclopramide is a useful anti-emetic drug, though the dosage has to be very carefully controlled if it is to be effective. Many paediatricians are not in favour of giving it to children. MAXOLON is strongly promoted and widely prescribed by brand name.
If the identical drug were prescribed by generic name (metoclopramide), the NHS could save about £2 million per year.

MEDIHALER-DUO
Riker
[POM] Metered aerosol (per inhalation)

Isoprenaline sulphate 160 micrograms
Bronchodilator.
Phenylephrine bitartrate 240 micrograms
Nasal decongestant.

Less suitable product. See DUO-AUTOHALER.

MEDIHALER-EPI
Riker
[POM] Metered aerosol (per inhalation)

Adrenaline acid tartrate 280 micrograms

Considered less effective than other BRONCHODILATORS. See ADRENALINE.

MEDIHALER-ISO; MEDIHALER-ISO FORTE
Riker
[POM] Metered aerosol

Isoprenaline sulphate 80 micrograms; 400 micrograms per dose.

See ISO-AUTOHALER.

MEDILAVE
Martindale
Antiseptic mouthwash, gargle

Cetylpyridinium chloride 0.025%

See MEROCAINE.

MEDISED
Martindale
Paediatric suspension (per 5ml), and tablets

Paediatric suspension
Paracetamol 120mg
Analgesic; antipyretic: reduces temperature.

Promethazine hydrochloride 2.5mg
Phenothiazine tranquilliser/antihistamine: sedative and hypnotic.

Tablets
Paracetamol 500mg
Promethazine hydrochloride 10mg

Undesirable combination: if needed, the ingredients should be separately prescribed in doses adjusted to the needs of the individual patient.

MEDOCODENE
Medo
Analgesic tablets

Paracetamol 500mg
Codeine phosphate 8mg

The dose of codeine may be less than effective. This product is much more expensive – but not much more effective – than paracetamol 500mg alone. See CODEINE AND PARACETAMOL.

MEDOMIN
Geigy
[POM] Tablets

Heptabarbitone 200mg

The Data Sheet [1983/4] for this product does not emphasise the Committee on Review of Medicines' recommendation that barbiturates should be used as hypnotics only for 'severe intractable insomnia' [DTB, 1980, 18, 9]. BENZODIAZEPINE TRANQUILLISERS (see entry) have superseded barbiturates as hypnotics, because they are safer.

MEDRONE
Upjohn
[POM] Acne lotion

Colloidal sulphur 5%
Antiseptic, and keratolytic: promotes sloughing or peeling of scaly, callused skin.
Methylprednisolone acetate 0.25%
Corticosteroid: reduces inflammation.
Aluminium chlorhydroxide complex 10%
Astringent.

Topical corticosteroids should be avoided if possible, especially for treatment on the face: they may complicate treatment and cause unpleasant side effects, and may alter the appearance of skin, making it thin and shiny. The UK Joint Formulary Committee says: 'Topical corticosteroids should not be used in acne' [BNF No.6 1983, p.348]. Aluminium chlorhydroxide complex lacks evidence of effectiveness [OTC-PDW 178]; and the value of sulphur is uncertain. See RESORCINOL AND SULPHUR PASTE.

MENTHOL AND BENZOIN INHALATION

Effectiveness questionable. See similar product KARVOL.

MENTHOL AND EUCALYPTUS INHALATION

Effectiveness questionable. See similar product KARVOL.

MEPRATE
DDSA
[POM] Tablets

Meprobamate 400mg
Tranquilliser.

There are safer, more effective alternatives. See MEPROBAMATE.

MEPROBAMATE
[POM] Tablets

Meprobamate 400mg
Tranquilliser: for treatment of anxiety, particularly with muscle spasm.

Meprobamate is considered less effective than diazepam and other benzodiazepine tranquillisers. It tends to induce dependence and is hazardous in overdose [AMADE p.207; BNF 1983, No.6 p.128; M28 p.1546].
Meprobamate is still extensively used: an estimated ¼ million NHS prescriptions (costing about £¼ million) are written each year for products such as EQUANIL; MEPRATE; MILTOWN; TENAVOID.

MERALEN
Merrell
[POM] Capsules

Flufenamic acid 100mg

Similar to mefenamic acid. See PONSTAN; NSAIDS.

MEROCAINE
Merrell
Lozenges

Cetylpyridinium chloride 1.4mg
Antimicrobial: checks the growth of bacteria.
Benzocaine 10mg
Local anaesthetic: to relieve sore throat.

The US Food and Drug Administration has reportedly found that cetylpyridinium lacks evidence of safety and effectiveness [OTC-PDW p.56]. There is no good evidence that this preparation is of any real value, but the NHS spends about £1½ million a year on products of this kind.

MEROCET

Merrell
Antiseptic gargle

Cetylpyridinium chloride 0.05%

See MEROCAINE.

MEROCETS

Merrell
Antiseptic throat lozenge

Cetylpyridinium chloride 0.066%

See MEROCAINE.

METATONE

Parke Davis
Elixir (per 5ml)

Thiamine hydrochloride 500 micrograms
Calcium glycerophosphate 45.6mg
Manganese glycerophosphate 5.7mg
Potassium glycerophosphate 45.6mg
Sodium glycerophosphate 22.8mg

Thiamine (vitamin B_1) is the only ingredient of recognised value, but the amount present in this concoction is insignificant. Glycerophosphates have been advocated in the past as tonics, appetite stimulants etc, but there is no evidence to support their value [M28 p.712].
Over one million NHS prescriptions for tonics are written each year: about one-third of them are for this product.

MICROGYNON 30

Schering
[POM] Oral contraceptive

Levonorgestrel 150 micrograms
Ethinyloestradiol 30 micrograms
Hormones.

A lower-strength pill may be safer. See ORAL CONTRACEPTIVES.

MIDRID

Carnrick
[POM] Capsules

Isometheptene mucate 65mg
Sympathomimetic: claimed to relieve head pain in migraine attacks by constricting cerebral and cranial arteries.
Dichloralphenazone 100mg
Sedative.
Paracetamol 325mg
Analgesic; antipyretic (reduces temperature).

There is 'a paucity of data' about the actions and effectiveness of isometheptene [AMADE p.164], and use of this drug is not thought justified on the available evidence [DTB, 1972, 10, 64]. Evidence from controlled trials suggests that this combination is no more effective than isometheptene alone, and that the combination is only slightly better than paracetamol or placebo. A sedative might benefit some patients with migraine, but should be separately prescribed.
NHS expenditure on this product is estimated at £100,000 a year.

MIGRALEVE

International Laboratories
Pink tablets; yellow tablets

Pink tablets
Paracetamol 500mg
Codeine phosphate 8mg
Analgesics: for relief of headache.
Buclizine hydrochloride 6.25mg
Antihistamine: intended to prevent nausea and vomiting.
Docusate sodium 10mg
Laxative: intended to counteract the constipating effect of codeine.

Yellow tablets
Paracetamol 500mg
Codeine phosphate 8mg
Docusate sodium 20mg

This product is recommended for the prevention and treatment of migraine attacks. Pink tablets (2 at night) are meant to be taken 'during periods of impending attack' and/or (2 tablets immediately) at the onset of attack; yellow tablets (2 tablets every 3/4 hours) 'to relieve residual symptoms' are to be taken if symptoms persist. Very confusing.
Buclizine is an effective anti-emetic, but usually at much higher doses (25–50mg, three times daily). The analgesic combination may be no more effective than paracetamol alone. See CODEINE AND PARACETAMOL. The combination of ingredients is undesirable.
NHS expenditure on this product is over £½ million a year.

MIGRAVESS

Miles
[POM] Effervescent tablets for treatment of acute migraine attack

Metoclopramide 5mg
Anti-emetic. See MAXOLON
Aspirin 325mg
Analgesic.

This product was originally (1982) classified as 'less suitable for prescribing': it has since been upgraded, though the Joint Formulary Committee suggested it is safer if the two ingredients are taken separately [BNF, 1983, No.5, p.159]. If separately prescribed by generic name, the user would pay two prescription charges, but the NHS would save about £¼ million a year.

MIGRAVESS FORTE

Miles
Effervescent tablets

Metoclopramide 5mg
Aspirin 450mg

See MIGRAVESS.

MIGRIL

Wellcome
[POM] Tablets

Ergotamine tartrate 2mg
Vasoconstrictor: helps to relieve head pain in migraine attacks by constricting cranial arteries (but for reasons not well understood).
Cyclizine hydrochloride 50mg
Antihistamine: intended to allay nausea and vomiting in migraine attack (which ergotamine may exacerbate).
Caffeine hydrate 100mg
Intended to increase absorption of ergotamine in the stomach.

This combination has been classified as 'possibly effective' by the US Food and Drug Administration, and is considered 'less suitable for prescribing' by the UK Joint Formulary Committee. 'The value of ergotamine is limited by difficulties in absorption and by its side effects. . . . Ergotamine treatment should *not* be repeated at intervals of less than 4 days and it should never be prescribed prophylactically' [BNF No.6 1983 p.165]. There is controversy about the value of caffeine, and the fixed-ratio combination prevents adjustment of the dosage of the two main ingredients. NHS expenditure on this product is about £1½ million a year.

MILLOPHYLINE

Martindale
Suppositories for children, and other formulations

Etamiphylline camsylate 200mg
Bronchodilator: relieves breathing difficulties in asthma, bronchitis etc.

See BRONCHODILATORS. Etamiphylline is considered of doubtful efficacy and less suitable for prescribing, particularly the suppositories. The slow-release oral preparations of (the related drugs) theophylline and aminophylline are preferred [BNF No.6, 1983, p.104; DTB, 1979, 17, 92]. Rectal absorption of theophylline and related drugs tends to be erratic, and suppositories may cause local irritation as well. See ETOPHYLATE.

MILONORM

Wallace
[POM] Tablets

Meprobamate 400mg

See MEPROBAMATE.

MILTOWN WITHDRAWN

Pharmax
[POM] Tablets

Meprobamate 400mg
Tranquilliser.

There are safer, more effective alternatives. See MEPROBAMATE.

MINAMINO

Consolidated
Elixir/syrup (per 5ml)

B vitamins: thiamine hydrochloride 15mg; **riboflavine** 2mg; **pyridoxine hydrochloride** 1.75mg; **nicotinamide** 20mg; **cyanocobalamin** 5 micrograms
Amino acids
Extracts of liver, spleen and gastric mucosa
Nutrients.
Iron citrate, manganese sulphate and copper sulphate
Mineral supplements.

An inappropriate and unwarranted combination of ingredients: of dubious value.

MINILYN
Organon
[POM] Oral contraceptive

Lynoestrenol 2.5mg
Ethinyloestradiol 50 micrograms
Hormones.

A lower-strength pill may be safer. See ORAL CONTRACEPTIVES.

MOBILAN
Galen
Capsules

Indomethacin 25mg, 50mg

See INDOCID.

MODUCREN
Morson
[POM] Tablets

Timolol maleate 10mg
Beta-blocker: controls over-stimulation of the heart and irregular heartbeat. Used here with diuretics, mainly to control high blood pressure.
Amiloride hydrochloride 2.5mg
Hydrochlorothiazide 25mg
Diuretics: remove excessive fluid from body tissues and increase the output of urine – which also lowers blood pressure.

There is no real advantage to this combination of ingredients [DTB, 1981, 19, 59]. It is considered 'less suitable for prescribing' (BNF No.6, 1983; p.80).
NHS expenditure on this product is about £1 million a year.

MOGADON
Roche
[POM] Tablets, capsules

Nitrazepam 5mg
Benzodiazepine tranquilliser for treatment of insomnia.

An effective drug, though over-prescribed. See entry for BENZODIAZEPINE TRANQUILLISERS. It accumulates, especially in the elderly.
This product has been strongly promoted by brand name. If the identical medicine were prescribed under its generic name (nitrazepam), the NHS could save at least £3 million a year.
Other brands of nitrazepam include NITRADOS (Berk); NOCTASED (Unimed); REMNOS (DDSA); SOMNITE (Norgine); SUREM (Galen); UNISOMNIA (Unigreg).

MOLCER
Wallace Mfg
Ear drops to soften ear wax, before removal

Dioctyl sodium sulphosuccinate (docusate sodium) 5%

Unnecessary product. See identical preparation WAXSOL.

MONPHYTOL
LAB
Paint for nail infections

Boric acid 2%
Weak antiseptic.
Methyl undecenoate 5%
Propyl undecenoate 2%
Antifungal agents.
Salicylic acid 31%
Keratolytic: helps sloughing and peeling of scaly and callused skin.
Chlorbutol 3%
Antibacterial; antifungal; preservative.

Less suitable for prescribing: the combination has no advantage over simpler preparations, and boric acid has been superseded by safer and more effective agents [M28 p.337].

MOTIPRESS
Squibb
[POM] Tablets

Fluphenazine hydrochloride 1.5mg
Phenothiazine tranquilliser: used to treat psychotic illness, confusion and agitation.
Nortriptyline 30mg *(as hydrochloride)*
Tricyclic antidepressant: mainly used to treat depressive illness.

Most illness involving both depression and anxiety is controlled with an antidepressant drug on its own. Anti-anxiety drugs may occasionally help, and may be useful at the start of treatment, as it can take several weeks before antidepressants become fully effective. However, these two drugs are rarely indicated for routine use, and the fixed-ratio combination is undesirable.
NHS expenditure on this product is about £½ million a year.

MOTIVAL
Squibb
[POM] Tablets

Contains one-third of the amount of each of the ingredients in MOTIPRESS.
NHS expenditure on this product is about £1 million a year.

MOVELAT

Luitpold-Werk
[POM] Counter-irritant cream, gel

Corticosteroids 0.02% *(as adrenocortical extract)*
Heparinoid 0.2%
Salicylic acid 2%
Intended to relieve pain in muscles, joints etc. when rubbed into skin.

The concentration of corticosteroids (anti-inflammatory agents) seems too low to be effective [FR 44 234 4/12/79 p.69823]. The UK Joint Formulary Committee considers this product less suitable for prescribing: Methyl Salicylate Ointment BP or Methyl Salicylate Liniment BP are effective and much cheaper alternatives. If these were prescribed instead of this product, the NHS could save about £½ million a year.

MUCAINE

Wyeth
[POM] Antacid mixture (per 5ml)

Aluminium hydroxide mixture 4.75ml
Magnesium hydroxide 100mg
Antacids: neutralise excess stomach acid.
Oxethazaine 10mg
Surface anaesthetic, intended to relieve discomfort in the gullet.

British and US authorities have condemned the use of oxethazaine in this product: its effectiveness is doubtful and it could cause sensitivity reactions.
NHS expenditure on this product is over £½ million per year.

MUCODYNE

Berk
[POM] Capsules; syrup

Capsules
Carbocisteine 375mg

Syrup *(per 5ml)*
Carbocisteine 125mg, 250mg
Mucolytic: reduces viscosity of phlegm, to help expectoration.

There is no convincing evidence of the value of carbocisteine and it 'does not seem worth using' [DTB, 1975, 13, 12]. It may help some patients but, on the available evidence (1983), is not recommended for routine use. See entry for EXPECTORANTS AND MUCOLYTICS.
NHS expenditure on this product is estimated at £3½ million a year.

MUCOLEX

Warner
[POM] Tablets

Carbocisteine 375mg

Syrup *(per 5ml)*
Carbocisteine 250mg

Mucolytic of questionable value. See MUCODYNE.

MULTIVITE

Duncan Flockhart
Multivitamin pellets

Vitamin A 2500 units
B vitamins: thiamine hydrochloride 500 micrograms
Vitamin C: ascorbic acid 12.5mg
Vitamin D 250 units

Vitamins Capsules BPC contain slightly higher amounts of vitamins B and C, plus riboflavine 500 micrograms, and are a little cheaper. See VITAMINS.
NHS expenditure on this product is about £¼ million a year.

MURIPSIN

Norgine
Tablets

Glutamic acid hydrochloride 500mg
Acidifying agent: intended to help digestion by increasing the acidity of the stomach contents to 'normal' levels.
Pepsin 35mg
Digestive enzyme: *intended as a supplement when pepsin levels in the stomach are abnormally low.*

This treatment is considered obsolete. Acidification of stomach contents serves 'no useful clinical or physiological purpose . . .' [Medical Letter 1972, 14, 56]. The supplementary intake of pepsin is not considered of value [M28 p.654].

MYCARDOL

Winthrop
Tablets

Pentaerythritol tetranitrate 30mg
Coronary vasodilator: intended to improve circulation by relaxing and opening blood vessels around the heart. Used for the prevention of angina (heart pain caused by lack of oxygen in heart muscle).

The value of long-acting nitrates is uncertain: variation in dosage response is wide but poorly understood so individualisation of therapy is imperative for each patient. The US Food and Drug Administration has classified this drug as 'possibly effective' – though acknowledges it 'is widely regarded as useful' in preventing attacks of angina [PDR, 1983, p.1533].

MYOLGIN

Cox-Continental
Dispersible tablets

Aspirin 200mg
Paracetamol 200mg
Codeine phosphate 5mg
Caffeine citrate 15mg

The dose of codeine is less than effective; and caffeine is unnecessary. This product is much more expensive – but unlikely to be more effective – than, say, paracetamol 500mg on its own. See ASPIRIN AND CODEINE.

MYSTECLIN

Squibb
[POM] Capsules, tablets

Tetracycline hydrochloride 250mg
Bacteriostatic antibiotic: used in the treatment of a variety of infections.
Nystatin 250,000 units
Antifungal antibiotic: active against thrush (Candida) and other yeast-related fungi.

The US National Research Council has stated that 'in its informed judgement MYSTECLIN is ineffective as a fixed combination' [PDR 1983 p.1943]. The American Medical Association's evaluation concludes: 'Because proof of efficacy is lacking, no dosage recommendation is made' [AMADE 1983 p.1681]. MYSTECLIN combines an effective dose of an antibacterial with what is intended as a deterrent (prophylactic) dose of an otherwise effective antifungal. The theory is that a broad-spectrum antibacterial like tetracycline will not stop at suppression of harmful bacteria, but will also suppress the useful bacteria which normally prevent the proliferation ('overgrowth') of intestinal fungi. This rationale is considered weak, first, because overgrowth of intestinal fungi does not occur frequently; second, because there is no hard evidence that routine administration of prophylactic doses of an antifungal reduces overgrowth; and third, because if an antifungal is needed, the dose for most users should be higher than the amount in this preparation. NHS expenditure on this product is about £¾ million a year.

MYSTECLIN SYRUP

Squibb
[POM] Syrup (per 5ml)

Tetracycline 125mg
Amphotericin 25mg

See MYSTECLIN. See also TETRACYCLINE MIXTURE.

NAPSALGESIC

Dista
[POM] Tablets

Dextropropoxyphene napsylate 50mg
Aspirin 500mg

A potentially dangerous combination. See DISTALGESIC.

NATIROSE NATIVELLE

Lewis
[POM] Tablets

Glyceryl trinitrate 750 micrograms
Coronary vasodilator: improves circulation by relaxing and opening blood vessels around the heart. Used to treat and prevent angina (heart pains caused by lack of oxygen in heart muscle).
Ethylmorphine hydrochloride 3mg
Narcotic analgesic: intended to relieve pain from angina.
Hyoscyamine hydrobromide 50 micrograms
A sub-therapeutic dose. At higher dosages, hyoscyamine has unpleasant side effects, intended to discourage abuse of ethylmorphine, which may be addictive.

The combination of ingredients is most undesirable. If an analgesic is needed (*not* for the prevention of angina attacks) it should be prescribed separately and the dosage adjusted to the individual patient's needs.

NATRILIX

Servier
[POM] Tablets

Indapamide 2.5mg
Antihypertensive: reduces and controls high blood pressure.

Indapamide is related to the thiazide diuretics – drugs used to reduce high blood pressure and to remove excessive fluid from body tissues (oedema). Unlike other thiazides, this drug is claimed to reduce high blood pressure without a significant diuretic effect. The therapeutic value of this novel action has not been established – but it seems doubtful if it is often worth the extra cost.

Indapamide can cost up to 30–40 times more than other thiazides: if these were prescribed instead of indapamide, the NHS would save about £2 million a year.

NAVIDREX-K
Ciba
[POM] Tablets

Cyclopenthiazide 250 micrograms
Diuretic: helps to control high blood pressure; removes excessive fluid from body tissues by increasing output of urine.
Potassium 8.1mmol *(in a slow-release wax core)*
Supplement intended to replace potassium which the body loses through diuresis.

Many people do not need a potassium supplement with a diuretic. If a supplement is needed it is best taken separately – and preferably in solution not tablet form. The required dose may be higher than the amount in this preparation. See POTASSIUM SUPPLEMENTS.
NHS expenditure on this product is over £4 million a year.

NEMBUTAL
Abbott
[POM] Capsules

Pentobarbitone sodium 100mg
For severe intractable insomnia.

See BARBITURATES.

NEO-CORTEF
Upjohn
[POM] Ointment; lotion

Hydrocortisone acetate 1%
Corticosteroid to reduce inflammation.
Neomycin sulphate 0.5%
Anti-infective agent.

[POM] Ointment
Hydrocortisone acetate 2.5%
Neomycin sulphate 0.5%

Only likely to be of value where an area of eczema or dermatitis is infected. See CORTICOSTEROID + ANTI-INFECTIVE SKIN PREPARATIONS.

NEO-MEDRONE
Upjohn
[POM] Acne lotion

Colloidal sulphur 5%
Methylprednisolone acetate 0.25%
Neomycin sulphate 0.25%
Antibacterial antibiotic.
Aluminium chlorhydroxide complex 10%

Corticosteroids should not be used in acne. See MEDRONE. Topical antibiotic treatment is of questionable value, and sensitisation to neomycin is not uncommon [AMADE 1983, p.1699]. See notes on CORTICOSTEROID + ANTI-INFECTIVE SKIN PREPARATIONS. Sulphur is discussed under RESORCINOL AND SULPHUR PASTE.

NEO-MEDRONE
Upjohn
[POM] Cream

Methylprednisolone acetate 0.25%
Corticosteroid to reduce inflammation.
Neomycin sulphate 0.5%
Anti-infective.

Only likely to be of value where an area of eczema or dermatitis is infected. See CORTICOSTEROID + ANTI-INFECTIVE SKIN PREPARATIONS.

NEO-NACLEX-K
Duncan Flockhart
[POM] Tablets

Bendrofluazide 2.5mg
Diuretic: helps to control high blood pressure; removes excessive fluid from body tissues by increasing output of urine.
Potassium 8.4mmol *(slow-release)*
Supplement intended to replace potassium which the body loses through diuresis.

Many people do not need a potassium supplement with a diuretic. If a supplement is needed it is best taken separately – and preferably in solution not tablet form. The required dose may be higher than the amount in this preparation. See POTASSIUM SUPPLEMENTS.
NHS expenditure on this product is estimated at £1 million a year.

NEO-SULPHAZON WITHDRAWN
Wallace Mfg
[POM] Mixture (per 5ml)

Phthalylsulphathalazole 500mg
Sulphonamide antibacterial.
Pectin 62.5mg
Binding agent.
Kaolin 750mg
Adsorbent.

Drug treatment for acute diarrhoea is best avoided. Diarrhoea is a natural defence mechanism (like coughing or sneezing) which helps the body get rid of irritants or toxins. Drinking fluids aids this process and speeds recovery, but anti-infective drugs do not, and there is evidence they may even prolong illness. The US Food and Drug Administration has found that both pectin and kaolin lack evidence of effectiveness as antidiarrhoeal ingredients [FR 40 76 21/3/75 p.12928].

NESTOSYL

Bengue
Ointment for internal/external use

Zinc oxide 10%
Protectant with mild astringent action, intended to relieve discomfort of haemorrhoids and related ano-rectal disorders.
Resorcinol 2%
Skin preparation with antiseptic, itch-relieving and other actions.
Benzocaine 2%
Butyl aminobenzoate 2%
Local anaesthetics.
Hexachlorophane 0.1%
Antiseptic.

A US expert panel has concluded that resorcinol is neither effective nor safe and 'has no legitimate internal use' [FR 45 103 27/5/80 p.35668]. It is rapidly absorbed into the body through mucous membranes and can interfere with the functioning of the thyroid gland.
Use of antiseptics inside the anus or rectum makes little sense, because of the overwhelming numbers of unresponsive organisms in the bowel. Antiseptics used externally are not helpful in haemorrhoidal states.
The safety and effectiveness of local anaesthetics used internally is doubtful [FR 45 103 27/5/80 p.35607].

NETHAPRIN DOSPAN

Merrell
[POM] Sustained-release tablets

Bufylline 180mg
Etaphedrine hydrochloride 50mg
Bronchodilators: relieve breathing difficulties in asthma, bronchitis etc.
Phenylephrine hydrochloride 25mg
Nasal decongestant.
Doxylamine succinate 25mg
Antihistamine: used to suppress symptoms of allergy.

The effectiveness of bufylline (a theophylline analogue) depends on careful adjustment of dose: its use in fixed-ratio combination products is undesirable (see: AMESEC). Etaphedrine is related to EPHEDRINE (see entry) and may also cause unwanted effects. A decongestant may be temporarily useful if asthma is complicated by a cold, but routine use is undesirable. Antihistamines are ineffective in the treatment of asthma [M28 p.1295]. Oral administration of phenylephrine seldom produces nasal decongestion: a nasal spray is much more likely to work (but only for short-term use) [AMADE p.552].

NETHAPRIN EXPECTORANT

Merrell
[POM] Syrup (per 5ml)

Bufylline 60mg
Bronchodilator: relieves breathing difficulties in asthma, bronchitis etc.
Doxylamine succinate 6mg
Antihistamine.
Etaphedrine hydrochloride 20mg
Bronchial, nasal decongestant.
Guaiphenesin 100mg
Expectorant: intended to help removal of phlegm from the airways.

It is irrational to combine an antihistamine (which dries up secretions in the airways) with an expectorant (intended to liquefy and loosen secretions). The effectiveness of guaiphenesin is doubtful: see entry for EXPECTORANTS AND MUCOLYTICS. See also NETHAPRIN DOSPAN. NHS expenditure on this product is about £¼ million a year.

NEURODYNE

Rorer
Capsules

Paracetamol 500mg
Codeine phosphate 8mg
For relief of mild to moderate pain.

The dose of codeine may be less than effective. This product is much more expensive – but not much more effective – than paracetamol 500mg alone. See CODEINE AND PARACETAMOL.

NEUROPHOSPHATES

SK & F
[POM] Liquid (per 10ml)

Glycerophosphates of calcium 179.3mg
Sodium 171.4mg
Strychnine alkaloid *(in acid solution)* 1.1mg

Glycerophosphates have been advocated as tonics, but have no value. Strychnine increases production of saliva and stomach acid – a traditional 'remedy' for loss of appetite.
Over one million NHS prescriptions a year are written for tonics of this kind.

NEUTRADONNA
Nicholas
Powder; tablets

See comparable product ALUDROX SA.

NEZCAAM
Rybar
Syrup (per 5ml)

Phenylpropanolamine hydrochloride 7.5mg
Nasal decongestant.
Guaiphenesin 30mg
Expectorant.

This product was formerly called CAM DECONGESTANT. The combination of ingredients is undesirable, and the value of guaiphenesin doubtful (see EXPECTORANTS). This product is intended for children aged 2 and over. Some authorities consider this acceptable [FR 41 176; 9/9/76, p.38401]; others say that phenylpropanolamine is 'not recommended for children under 8 years' [AMADE, 1983, p.556].

NILSTIM
De Witt
Tablets

Cellulose *(microcrystalline)* 220mg
Methylcellulose '2500' 400mg
Bulk-forming agent: intended to help users eat less by making the stomach feel full.

A daily dose of at least 20 tablets might significantly help to reduce food intake, but there is little evidence to suggest that this product would be effective at the recommended dose (two tablets before meals or when hungry). Only about one person in eight in a Consumers' Association survey found bulk-forming agents at all helpful in suppressing appetite: an apple eaten before meals was recommended as more effective [*Which?* April 1983, p.144].

NITRADOS
Berk

Nitrazepam
Benzodiazepine tranquilliser.

See MOGADON.

NOBRIUM
Roche
[POM] Capsules

Medazepam 5mg, 10mg

Medazepam has actions and uses similar to diazepam and other BENZODIAZEPINE TRANQUILLISERS (see entry). In the body, medazepam is extensively converted to desmethyl diazepam: therefore the similarities between these drugs are much more striking than any differences – though medazepam may cause a little less drowsiness. Medazepam (NOBRIUM) costs about 2–3 times more than diazepam, and it seems doubtful if its possible advantages are often worth this extra cost.
If diazepam were prescribed instead of medazepam, the NHS could save an estimated £100,000 each year.

NOCTAMID
Schering
[POM] Tablets

Lormetazepam 500 micrograms, 1mg

See BENZODIAZEPINE TRANQUILLISERS.

NOLUDAR
Roche
[POM] Capsules

Methyprylone 200mg

This drug is related to the BARBITURATES (see entry) and has some comparable unwanted effects. In the treatment of anxiety and insomnia, it has no significant advantage over BENZODIAZEPINE TRANQUILLISERS (see entry), but is less safe.

NORADRAN
Norma
Syrup (per 5ml)

Diphenhydramine hydrochloride 5mg
Antihistamine, cough suppressant, sedative.
Guaiphenesin 25mg
Ephedrine hydrochloride 7.5mg
Decongestant.
Diprophylline 50mg
Bronchodilator.

Irrational combination. See NETHAPRIN EXPECTORANT.

NORFLEX
Riker
[POM] Sustained-release tablets

Orphenadrine citrate 100mg
Antispasmodic.

Diazepam (see VALIUM) is considered the drug of first choice for painful muscle spasm: it is at least as effective and may be safer [M28 p.307], and costs around five times less. The clinical efficacy of orphenadrine as a muscle relaxant is '*not* well established' [BNF No.6, 1983, p.308].

NORGESIC

Riker
[POM] Tablets

Paracetamol 450mg
Orphenadrine citrate 35mg

Orphenadrine is not a drug of first choice. See NORFLEX. The fixed-ratio combination is undesirable.

NORGOTIN

Norgine
Ear drops

Amethocaine hydrochloride 1%
Local anaesthetic.
Chlorhexidine acetate 0.1%
Antiseptic.
Ephedrine hydrochloride 1%

Effectiveness doubtful. See AURALGICIN.

NORLESTRIN

Parke Davis
[POM] Oral contraceptive

Norethisterone acetate 2.5mg
Ethinyloestradiol 50 micrograms
Hormones.

A lower-strength pill may be safer. See ORAL CONTRACEPTIVES.

NORMISON

Wyeth
[POM] Capsules

Temazepam 10mg, 20mg

See BENZODIAZEPINE TRANQUILLISERS.

NSAIDs

NSAIDs are Non-Steroidal Anti-Inflammatory Drugs. As their name implies, these drugs act differently from (cortico)steroid drugs (eg cortisone, prednisolone) which reduce inflammation by acting on the body's own hormones. The NSAIDs act like high-dose aspirin (3g–4g/day). They reduce inflammation, pain and fever, and are widely used to treat rheumatism, arthritis and related diseases.

In general, there is little to choose between different NSAIDs. None is clearly superior to aspirin and 'overall they seem remarkably similar in efficacy and, with a few exceptions, also in toxicity' [DTB 1981, 19, 53]. The main exceptions are phenylbutazone and related drugs (see BUTAZOLIDIN), but side effects are a problem with all NSAIDs (see INDOCID). Choice between products is further complicated by inadequate research data and/or unwarranted promotional claims (see FLOSINT and SURGAM; see also pp.38–40). Though different NSAIDs have been compared in hundreds of trials, the results have often been conflicting and misleading: 'Sometimes the advantage in efficacy or toxicity claimed is simply a consequence of the dosages chosen for comparison' (DTB 1981, 19, 53].

In spite of their general similarity, individual response to different NSAIDs varies considerably. Unfortunately, individual response cannot usually be predicted, so some trial and error is inevitable. People who cannot tolerate aspirin have often found naproxen (Naprosyn) or ibuprofen (Brufen, and other cheaper brands) good alternatives – but there are many other drugs to choose from.

In fact, in 1983 there were over 20 different NSAIDs available in the UK. It has been suggested that 'in a country where economic constraints are not a major problem' between 10–15 NSAIDs would be sufficient [Dukes M. N. G.; Lunde I., 1981]. There is no need for more 'me-too' products (ones closely resembling the prototype), which offer no significant advantages and cost more.

NU-K

Consolidated
[POM] Slow-release capsules containing granules

Potassium chloride 600mg (8mmol *each of potassium and chloride ions*).

Slow-release POTASSIUM SUPPLEMENTS (see entry) may irritate or cause ulcers in the gut. There are preferable alternatives.

NULACIN

Bencard
Antacid tablets

Calcium carbonate 130mg
Heavy magnesium carbonate 30mg
Heavy magnesium oxide 130mg
Magnesium trisilicate 230mg
Antacids: neutralise excess stomach acid.
Milk solids, dextrins, maltose
Included in order to improve taste.

If used for long periods, calcium salts are more likely to upset body chemistry than magnesium and/or aluminium salts. See CALCIUM CARBONATE.

NUPERCAINAL
Ciba
Local anaesthetic ointment

Cinchocaine hydrochloride 1.1%

These ointments are not usually very effective in relieving painful or itchy conditions. Cinchocaine is more likely to irritate than other local anaesthetics. See ANETHAINE, LOCAN.

NYSTADERMAL
Squibb
[POM] Cream

Triamcinolone acetonide 0.1%
Corticosteroid to reduce inflammation.
Nystatin 100,000 units/gram
Antifungal agent.

Only likely to be of value where an area of eczema or dermatitis is infected. See CORTICOSTEROID + ANTI-INFECTIVE SKIN PREPARATIONS.

NYSTAFORM-HC
Miles
[POM] Cream

Hydrocortisone 0.5%
Corticosteroid to reduce inflammation.
Nystatin 100,000 units/gram
Anti-infective agent.
Chlorhexidine hydrochloride 1%
Disinfectant.

[POM] Ointment
Hydrocortisone 1%
Nystatin 100,000 units/gram
Chlorhexidine acetate 1%

Only likely to be of value where an area of eczema or dermatitis is infected. See CORTICOSTEROID + ANTI-INFECTIVE SKIN PREPARATIONS.
NHS expenditure on these two preparations is around £1 million a year.

ONADOX-118
Duncan Flockhart
[POM] Dispersible tablets

Aspirin 300mg
Dihydrocodeine tartrate 10mg

See DIHYDROCODEINE AND PARACETAMOL.

OPIATE SQUILL LINCTUS AND PASTILLES
In equal volumes (per 5ml):

Camphorated opium tincture *(equivalent to 0.8mg of anhydrous morphine)*
Squill oxymel
Tolu syrup
(One pastille = 2ml of linctus).

Irrational combination: includes ingredients intended both to stimulate the cough reflex (squill) and to suppress it (opium). The safety of squill is questionable [FR 41 176 9/9/76 p.38358] and its value doubtful. See entry for EXPECTORANTS AND MUCOLYTICS. Also known as GEE'S LINCTUS.

OPIATE SQUILL LINCTUS PAEDIATRIC BP

Similar to OPIATE SQUILL LINCTUS but about one-fifth of the adult dose.

OPILON
Warner
[POM] Tablets

Thymoxamine 40mg *as hydrochloride*
Peripheral vasodilator: intended to improve blood flow in skin and muscle, and used mainly to treat circulation disorders in legs, and Raynaud's syndrome.

See PERIPHERAL VASODILATORS. Thymoxamine is poorly absorbed from the gut and its value in the treatment of peripheral vascular disease is not well established.
NHS expenditure on this product is about £2½ million a year.

OPOBYL
Bengue
[POM] Pills

Aloes 20mg
Podophyllin 2mg
Euonymus 2mg
Bile salts 50mg
Boldo extract 10mg
Laxatives.
Desiccated liver 50mg
Nutrient.

Both aloes and podophyllin have 'been superseded by less toxic purgatives' [M28 pp.1362–6]. Their laxative effect may be violent, and both are associated with unpleasant side effects, particularly in large doses. In spite of the low dosage here, neither drug should be used in pregnancy: the Data Sheet for the product makes no reference to this. Evidence for the safety and effectiveness of bile salts as laxatives is weak [FR 40 56 21/3/75 p.12918].

OPTIMINE
Kirby-Warrick
Tables and syrup (per 10ml)

Azatadine maleate 1mg
Antihistamine: used to relieve symptoms of allergy, eg in hay fever or urticaria (nettle rash).

US prescribing information states that OPTIMINE tablets are not intended for use in children under 12 years of age [PDR 1983 p.1816]. The official UK Data Sheet (1983/4) suggests dosages for children aged 6–12 years old. Azatadine acts for longer than most antihistamines, and needs be taken only twice a day. Otherwise, it seems to have no significant advantage over other antihistamines, though it costs much more. If chlorpheniramine were prescribed instead of this product, the NHS would save about £¼ million a year.

ORALCER
Vitabiotics
Lozenges

Clioquinol 35mg
Anti-infective agent: intended as treatment for sore throat and mouth ulcers.
Ascorbic acid 6mg
Vitamin C.

Clioquinol was implicated in one of the greatest ever epidemics, in Japan, of drug-induced disease. When taken in large doses for long periods of time it has been found to cause severe and sometimes irreversible damage to the nervous system, and there is therefore the possibility it will do some harm at any therapeutic dosage. The amount of vitamin C in this preparation is negligible.

ORAL CONTRACEPTIVES

All of the oral contraceptives listed combine an oestrogen (ethinyloestradiol) with a progestogen component (ethynodiol, desogestrel, levonorgestrel, lynoestrenol, norethisterone or norgestrel). This combination of ingredients is rational: at the right dosage, both of these hormones prevent conception – but give better and safer contraceptive protection than either ingredient on its own.

Individual users should aim to use a pill with the lowest oestrogen and progestogen components compatible with effective contraception and good control of the menstrual cycle. Usually this can be achieved with a pill with an oestrogen component of between 30 and 50 micrograms. With the lower oestrogen preparations (30–35 micrograms), the margin of safety is reduced, so it is more important to take pills regularly without missing a dose. One of the listed products (LOESTRIN 20) has an oestrogen content of 20 micrograms: the BNF rates it 'less suitable for prescribing' because this dosage may be too low to be fully effective.

With one exception (LOESTRIN 20) the oral contraceptive products listed have a relatively high 'progestogen potency': these are often used to control bleeding between periods. Two studies published in late 1983* have suggested that combination oral contraceptives with a higher 'progestogen potency' may be associated with an increased risk of breast cancer. The relationship between higher progestogen potency pills and this (relatively small but apparently significant) increased risk is not clearly established. However, these studies did prompt the Committee on Safety of Medicines to 'recommend that women should be prescribed a product with the lowest suitable content of both oestrogen and progestogen' (letter to doctors, ref. MF/580/212, dated 20 October 1983).

Brands with a relatively high 'progestogen potency' are: ANOVLAR 21; CONOVA 30; EUGYNON 30; EUGYNON 50; GYNOVLAR 21; MARVELON; MICROGYNON 30; MINILIN; NORLESTRIN; OVRAN; OVRAN 30; OVRANETTE; OVULEN 50.

*Pike M. C. et al., p.926; and Vessey M. P. et al., p.930 in *The Lancet*, October 1983.

ORGANIDIN
WBP
Elixir (per 5ml)

Iodinated glycerol 60mg

The safety of iodide expectorants is questionable [FR 41 176 9/9/76 p.38357] and their value doubtful. See EXPECTORANTS AND MUCOLYTICS.

OROVITE
Bencard
Tablets; elixir (per 12.5ml)

B vitamins: thiamine hydrochloride 50mg; **riboflavine** 5mg; **nicotinamide** 200mg; **pyridoxine hydrochloride** 5mg
Vitamin C: ascorbic acid 100mg

See VITAMINS. Clear vitamin deficiency is normally treated by injection of rather larger amounts of vitamins B and C. For the routine prevention of deficiency states, this product is less suitable for prescribing because it provides far higher doses of vitamins than the body either needs or can utilise. (Vitamins B and C are rapidly excreted, rather than stored in the body.) It costs nearly twice as much as an identical product (LANCE B + C), and at least three times more than unbranded vitamin preparations which supply daily needs in full. If appropriate amounts of Compound Vitamin B Tablets (Strong) and Ascorbic Acid Tablets BP were prescribed instead of this product, the NHS could save about £¾ million a year.

OROVITE 7

Bencard
Multivitamin granules in sachets

Vitamin A 2500 units
B vitamins: thiamine mononitrate 1.4mg; **riboflavine sodium phosphate** 1.7mg; **nicotinamide** 18mg; **pyridoxine hydrochloride** 2mg
Vitamin C: ascorbic acid 60mg
Vitamin D: ergocalciferol 100 units (per 5g sachet)

Broadly similar to ABIDEC and therapeutically equivalent to two Vitamins Capsules BPC. See VITAMINS.
If Vitamins Capsules BPC were prescribed instead of this product, the NHS would save about £1 million a year.

ORTHOXICOL

Upjohn
Syrup (per 5ml)

Codeine phosphate 10.95mg
Cough suppressant.
Methoxyphenamine hydrochloride 16.9mg
Bronchodilator.
Sodium citrate 325mg
Expectorant and buffer.

Undesirable combination. See notes on methoxyphenamine in the next entry.

ORTHOXINE HYDROCHLORIDE

Upjohn
Tablets

Methoxyphenamine hydrochloride 100mg
Bronchodilator: relieves breathing difficulties in asthma, bronchitis etc.

The US Food and Drug Administration has reportedly 'reclassified this drug as lacking substantial evidence of effectiveness for its labelled indications' [PDW 1981, p.141]. There are better alternatives. See BRONCHODILATORS.

OSPOLOT

Bayer
[POM] Tablets

Sulthiame 50mg, 200mg

Suspension
Sulthiame 50mg per 5ml

Although said to be rarely used and 'less suitable for prescribing', because it is a relatively weak anti-epileptic which readily causes unwanted drug interactions [BNF 1983 No.6, p.163], NHS expenditure on this product nevertheless exceeds £100,000 a year.

OSSOPAN

Labaz
Tablets

Hydroxyapatite compound 200mg
(calcium 43mg and phosphorus 20mg)

Powder
Hydroxyapatite compound 820mg/g
(*calcium* 176mg *and phosphorus* 82mg)
Supplement used to prevent and treat calcium deficiency states.

A relatively expensive source of calcium, considered less suitable for prescribing.

OTOPRED

Loveridge
[POM] Ear drops

Prednisolone 0.25%
Corticosteroid: to reduce inflammation.
Chloramphenicol 1%
Antibiotic.

See remarks about corticosteroid + antibiotic combinations under SOFRADEX. Chloramphenicol ear drops have been found to cause an unacceptably high incidence (10%) of hypersensitivity reactions: the corticosteroid would mask the allergic response, which would worsen the patient's condition.

OTOSEPTIL

Napp
[POM] Ear drops

Neomycin 0.067%
Tyrothricin 0.1%
Antibiotics.

Hydrocortisone 0.1%
Corticosteroid: to reduce inflammation.
Ethylene oxidepolyoxypropylene glycol condensate 1%
Solvent, penetrating agent.

See OTOSPORIN.

OTOSPORIN

Calmic
[POM] Ear drops

Hydrocortisone 1%
Corticosteroid: reduces inflammation.
Neomycin sulphate 0.439%
Polymyxin B sulphate 0.119%
Antibacterial antibiotics.

The combination of antibiotics is reasonable, though sensitivity reactions may occur with either ingredient, and the corticosteroid would then complicate treatment by masking the allergic response. See remarks about corticosteroid + antibiotic combination under SOFRADEX. This combination is considered less suitable for prescribing as it is unlikely to give any great advantage over simpler and much cheaper preparations. NHS expenditure on this product exceeds £1¼ million a year.

OTOTRIPS

Consolidated
[POM] Ear drops

Bacitracin 9%
Polymyxin B sulphate 0.194%
Antibiotics.
Trypsin 25,000 USP units/3ml
Enzyme intended to relieve inflammation.
Gelatin 0.5%
Sodium chloride 0.9%
Solvents/penetrating agents.

Trypsin is of doubtful value [BNF No.6, 1983, p.309–310]. The combination of antibiotics offers no great advantage over simpler, cheaper products.

OTRIVINE-ANTISTIN

Ciba
Nose drops; spray

Xylometazoline hydrochloride 0.05%
Sympathomimetic: nasal decongestant.
Antazoline sulphate 0.5%
Antihistamine: suppresses symptoms of allergy.

Antihistamines are not effective when locally applied, and sympathomimetic nasal decongestants are less suitable for treatment of allergic conditions. See HAYPHRYN.

OVRAN

Wyeth
[POM] Oral contraceptive

Levonorgestrel 250 micrograms
Ethinyloestradiol 50 micrograms
Hormones.

A lower-strength pill may be safer. See ORAL CONTRACEPTIVES.

OVRAN 30

Wyeth
[POM] Oral contraceptive

Levonorgestrel 250 micrograms
Ethinyloestradiol 30 micrograms
Hormones.

A lower-strength pill may be safer. See ORAL CONTRACEPTIVES.

OVRANETTE

Wyeth
[POM] Oral contraceptive

Levonorgestrel 150 micrograms
Ethinyloestradiol 30 micrograms
Hormones.

A lower-strength pill may be safer. See ORAL CONTRACEPTIVES.

OVULEN 50

Gold Cross
[POM] Oral contraceptive

Ethynodiol diacetate 1mg
Ethinyloestradiol 50 micrograms
Hormones.

A lower-strength pill may be safer. See ORAL CONTRACEPTIVES.

OXYTETRACYCLINE MIXTURE

[POM] Paediatric syrup (per 5ml)

Oxytetracycline hydrochloride 125mg (as calcium salt).

Tetracyclines are not for children under 12. See TETRACYCLINE MIXTURE.

PAEDO-SED

Pharmax
[POM] Paediatric syrup (per 5ml)

Paracetamol 100mg
Analgesic; antipyretic: lowers temperature.

Dichloralphenazone 200mg
Hypnotic: induces sleep.

Undesirable combination: if needed the ingredients should be separately prescribed, in doses adjusted for the individual patient.

PANADEINE CO
Winthrop
Tablets

Paracetamol 500mg
Codeine phosphate 8mg

The dose of codeine may be less than effective. This product is much more expensive – but not much more effective – than paracetamol 500mg alone. See CODEINE AND PARACETAMOL.
If paracetamol 500mg were prescribed instead of this combination, the NHS could save an estimated £1 million a year.

PANADOL
Winthrop
Tablets, effervescent tablets

Paracetamol 500mg

Elixir *(per 5ml)*
Paracetamol 120mg
For relief of mild to moderate pain.

Effective but expensive: about twice the cost of unbranded versions. If paracetamol BP were prescribed instead of this product, the NHS could save at least £½ million a year.

PANASORB
Winthrop
Tablets

Paracetamol 500mg in sorbitol basis.

Effective but expensive: it costs around five times more than paracetamol BP.

PARABAL WITHDRAWN
Sinclair
[POM] Tablets

Phenobarbitone 10mg *(as phenobarbitone sodium dihydroxyaluminiumaminoacetate claimed to be therapeutically equivalent to phenobarbitone 60mg)*
Anticonvulsant: depresses epileptic activity in the brain.

This odd formulation of phenobarbitone claims no therapeutic advantage over traditional versions, but costs over five times more. See BARBITURATES.

PARACODOL
Fisons
Effervescent tablets

Paracetamol 500mg
Codeine phosphate 8mg

The dose of codeine may be less than effective. This product is much more expensive – but not much more effective – than paracetamol 500mg alone. See CODEINE AND PARACETAMOL.
If paracetamol 500mg were prescribed instead of this combination, the NHS could save an estimated £¾ million a year.

PARADEINE
Scotia
Tablets

Paracetamol 500mg
Analgesic; antipyretic: reduces temperature.
Codeine phosphate 10mg
Narcotic analgesic.
Phenolphthalein 2.5mg
Laxative.

Undesirable combination: if needed, the ingredients should be separately prescribed at appropriate doses. PHENOLPHTHALEIN (see entry) is not a drug of choice, though the amount in this preparation is well below the usual laxative dose (50–200mg). The dose of codeine may be less than effective. See ASPIRIN AND CODEINE.

PARADIONE
Abbott
[POM] Capsules

Paramethadione 300mg
Anti-epileptic.

Less safe and effective than alternative treatments, and reported to be rarely used [BNF No.6, 1983, p.169]. Should be used under strict medical supervision, and only when other less toxic drugs have been found ineffective.

PARAGESIC
Sandoz
Effervescent tablets

Pseudoephedrine hydrochloride 20mg
Sympathomimetic: nasal decongestant.
Paracetamol 500mg
Analgesic/antipyretic: relieves mild to moderate pain; reduces fever/temperature.
Caffeine 10mg
Mild stimulant.

Because of the relatively high paracetamol content, the maximum recommended dose for this product is eight tablets per day. Even at this maximum dose, the decongestant action would be less than effective: the effective adult dose of pseudoephedrine is probably 180mg–240mg a day [M28 p.27; AMADE p.557].

PARAHYPON
Calmic
Tablets

Paracetamol 500mg
Codeine phosphate 5mg
Caffeine 10mg

The dose of codeine is less than effective, and caffeine is unlikely to have any significant effect. This product is much more expensive – but not more effective – than paracetamol 500mg alone. See CODEINE AND PARACETAMOL.
If paracetamol 500mg were prescribed instead of this product, the NHS could save an estimated £1½ million a year.

PARAKE
Galen
Tablets

Paracetamol 500mg
Codeine phosphate 8mg

The dose of codeine may be less than effective. See CODEINE AND PARACETAMOL.

PARALGIN
Norton
Tablets

Paracetamol 450mg
Codeine phosphate 6mg
Caffeine 20mg

The dose of codeine is probably less than effective, and caffeine is unlikely to have any significant effect. See CODEINE AND PARACETAMOL.

PARAMAX
Beecham
[POM] Tablets, sachets (per unit)

Metoclopramide hydrochloride 5mg
Anti-emetic. See MAXOLON
Paracetamol 500mg *(analgesic; antipyretic: lowers temperature).*

This product was originally (1982) classified as 'less suitable for prescribing': although it has since been upgraded, the Joint Formulary Committee has suggested that it is safer if the two ingredients are taken separately [BNF 1983, No.5, p.159]. If separately prescribed by generic name, the user would pay two prescription charges, though the NHS would save about £½ million a year.

PARAMOL
Duncan Flockhart
[POM] Tablets

Dihydrocodeine tartrate 10mg
Paracetamol 500mg

Considered less suitable for prescribing. See DIHYDROCODEINE AND PARACETAMOL.
NHS expenditure on this product is estimated at £2½ million a year.

PARA-SELTZER
Sandoz
Effervescent tablets

Paracetamol 500mg
Caffeine 20mg

This combination is about five times more expensive than paracetamol 500mg alone, but is no more effective. There is more caffeine in half a cup of tea.

PARAZOLIDIN
Geigy
[POM] Tablets

Phenylbutazone 50mg
Analgesic and anti-inflammatory agent.
Paracetamol 500mg
Analgesic; antipyretic: lowers temperature.

Hazardous. See BUTAZOLIDIN.

PARDALE
Martindale
Tablets

Paracetamol 400mg
Codeine phosphate 9mg
Caffeine hydrate 10mg

The dose of codeine may be less than effective, and the caffeine contributes little or nothing. This product costs about five times more – but is not much more effective – than paracetamol 400mg alone. See CODEINE AND PARACETAMOL.

PARNATE

SK & F
[POM] Tablets

Tranylcypromine sulphate 10mg
Anti-depressant: one of the monoamine-oxidase inhibitor (MAOI) class of drugs.

In the US, this drug is indicated only for patients who cannot use or benefit from other ('tricyclic') anti-depressant drugs or from electroconvulsive therapy (ECT). PARNATE is rated 'probably effective' by the US Food and Drug Administration. It is the most hazardous of the MAOI antidepressant drugs [BNF No.6 1983 p.147]: it should be used only by hospitalised or closely supervised patients and, in the US, is contraindicated for use by patients over 60 years old [PDR, 1983, p.1807]. Life-threatening reactions to this and other MAOI antidepressant drugs can occur if taken with certain foods, drink and other drugs: a throbbing headache warns of a rise in blood pressure. This should be explained to users, who should also get written instructions on a treatment card.

PAROVEN

Zyma
Capsules

Oxerutins 250mg
A 'vitamin P' derivative claimed to strengthen small blood vessels; and used to treat leg cramps and other peripheral circulation disorders.

Widely prescribed, but 'not generally regarded as effective' [BNF No.6, 1983; p.90]. Promotion of comparable products is restricted in the US because of lack of proven efficacy.
NHS expenditure on this product is around £1½ million a year.

PARSTELIN

SK & F
[POM] Tablets

Tranylcypromine sulphate 10mg
MAOI *antidepressant.*
Trifluoperazine hydrochloride 1mg
Phenothiazine tranquilliser.

Tranylcypromine is a particularly hazardous antidepressant (see PARNATE), and the combination of ingredients is undesirable (see LIMBITROL 5).
NHS expenditure on this product is about £¼ million a year.

PAVACOL D

WBP
Mixture (per 5ml)

Pholcodine 5mg
Cough suppressant.
Papaverine hydrochloride 1mg
Muscle relaxant.

Pholcodine is effective, but the use of papaverine is not justified [M28 p.1059; AMADE p.678; PDW p.28].
NHS expenditure on this product is estimated at £100,000 a year.

PAXIDAL

Wallace Mfg
[POM] Tablets

Paracetamol 325mg
Analgesic; antipyretic: lowers temperature.
Meprobamate 135mg
Tranquilliser: for treatment of anxiety, and of muscle spasm.
Caffeine 65mg
Mild stimulant.

Undesirable combination. MEPROBAMATE (see entry) is less suitable for prescribing. Caffeine contributes little or nothing at all.

PENBRITIN

Beecham
[POM] Various formulations

Capsules: 250mg, 500mg

Syrup and syrup forte *(per 5ml):* 125mg, 250mg

Paediatric tablets and suspension *(per 1.25ml):* 125mg

Ampicillin (as trihydrate)
Antibacterial antibiotic: semi-synthetic penicillin, widely used to treat respiratory, urinary tract and other infections.

An effective drug, strongly promoted by brand name. If the identical medicine were prescribed by generic name (ampicillin), the NHS could save about £2½ million each year.

PENTOXYLON

Riker
[POM] Tablets

Alseroxylon 1mg
Antihypertensive: reserpine-related rauwolfia derivative, used to control high blood pressure.
Pentaerythritol tetranitrate 10mg
Coronary vasodilator: intended to improve circulation by relaxing and opening blood vessels around the heart. Used for the prevention of angina (heart pains caused by lack of oxygen in heart muscle).

The possibility of serious side-effects (mainly depression) limits the usefulness of alseroxylon. See RESERPINE. The value of long-acting nitrates is uncertain. The US Food and Drug Administration has classified pentaerythritol tetranitrate only as 'possibly effective', while acknowledging that it 'is widely regarded as useful' in preventing attacks of angina [PDR 1983 p.1533]. The combination of ingredients is most undesirable: it is 'imperative' that dosage of long-acting nitrates is individualised [M28 p.1621].

PERIPHERAL VASODILATORS

Peripheral vasodilator drugs (PVDs) are meant to improve blood circulation in the legs and other limbs. They are used to treat a variety of numbing or painful conditions which immobilise and handicap mainly elderly people. Some PVDs are marketed as 'cerebral vasodilators'. by improving blood flow in the brain, they are meant to improve mental function, especially in senile states.

PVDs can improve circulation by dilating *healthy* blood vessels, but the evidence suggests that they do not work when most needed – when blood vessels in the extremities are diseased. If blood vessels are diseased, PVDs may actually do more harm than good: by improving circulation in healthy blood vessels, they may divert blood from diseased to non-diseased areas – a so-called 'steal effect' [AMADE pp.674–676].

The US Food and Drug Administration, the American Medical Association, the UK Joint Formulary Committee and other independent authorities have concluded that PVDs are unlikely to be of much use in treating peripheral vascular disorders or senile dementia; and 'the clinical literature overwhelmingly indicates that they are not useful for these indications' [Avorn J. et al., 1982]. The AMA's assessments of drugs like CYCLOSPASMOL, DUVADILAN and RONICOL conclude by saying: 'because the place of this agent in the treatment of peripheral vascular disease has not been established, no dosage is suggested'.

Nevertheless, these drugs are widely prescribed, partly because of vigorous sales promotion and lack of information, and possibly because there appears to be no satisfactory drug alternative. Doctors are usually unable to supervise the kinds of treatment that may be most effective. These include such things as proper exercise and good rest; stopping smoking; and avoiding exposure to either trauma or cold.

PERITRATE

Warner
Tablets

Pentaerythritol tetranitrate 10mg
Coronary vasodilator: intended to improve circulation by relaxing and opening blood vessels around the heart. Used for the prevention of angina (heart pains caused by lack of oxygen in heart muscle).

The value of long-acting nitrates is uncertain: variation in dosage response is wide but poorly understood so individualisation of therapy is imperative for each patient [M28 p.1621]. The US Food and Drug Administration has classified pentaerythritol tetranitrate only as 'possibly effective' – though acknowledges that it 'is widely regarded as useful' in preventing attacks of angina [PDR 1983 p.1533].

PERITRATE SA

Warner
Slow-release tablets

Pentaerythritol tetranitrate 80mg
See PERITRATE.

PERNIVIT

Duncan Flockhart
Tablets

Nicotinic acid 25mg
(Vitamin B7)
Acetomenaphthone 7mg
(Vitamin K)
Peripheral vasodilator: intended to improve blood flow in skin and muscle. Mainly used for the prevention and treatment of chilblains.

Lacks evidence of effectiveness. The rationale for the use of vitamin K is lost in the mists of time.

PERNOMOL
LAB
Paint for chilblains

Camphor 10%
Chlorbutol 2%
Phenol 0.95%
Soap spirit 34%
Tannic acid 2.2%

Of no real value: chilblains generally do not respond to drug treatment. Warmth and body movement are more likely to prevent and cure them.

PERSANTIN
Boehringer Ingelheim
[POM] Tablets

Dipyridamole 25mg, 100mg
Anti-platelet drug; see below.

Dipyridamole has been widely used as a coronary vasodilator, mainly to help prevent attacks of angina by relaxing blood vessels around the heart. Dipyridamole is used to treat angina in the UK, though it is not *formally* recommended for such use here, as it is elsewhere. However, the value of this drug in the treatment of angina is doubtful. The US Food and Drug Administration has rated it 'possibly effective', while the American Medical Association has concluded: 'Double-blind studies have demonstrated that this agent does not significantly decrease the incidence or severity of anginal attacks' [AMADE p.667].
NHS expenditure on this product is estimated at over £3 million a year.

PETROLAGAR No.2
Wyeth
Mixture (per 5ml)

Phenolphthalein 0.35%
Laxative.
Liquid paraffin 7%
Light liquid paraffin 18%
Lubricants, stool softeners.

PHENOLPHTHALEIN (see entry) is considered less satisfactory than other laxatives. Prolonged use of liquid paraffin may be harmful and should be avoided [M28 p.1063].

PHANODORM
Winthrop
[POM] Tablets

Cyclobarbitone calcium 200mg
For severe intractable insomnia.
See BARBITURATES.

PHARMIDONE
Farmitalia Carlo Erba
Tablets

Codeine phosphate 10mg
Narcotic analgesic.
Paracetamol 400mg
Analgesic; antipyretic: lowers temperature.
Diphenhydramine hydrochloride 5mg
Antihistamine + sedative: see below.
Caffeine 50mg
Mild stimulant.

Highly undesirable fixed-ratio combination product, recommended for the treatment of headache, migraine, muscle and nerve pain. It could be expected to be about as effective as paracetamol 500mg, which costs around ten times less. The dose of codeine may be less than effective: a combination of paracetamol 400mg plus codeine 10mg has not been shown to be more effective than paracetamol 400mg alone (see CODEINE AND PARACETAMOL). Diphenhydramine (at less than one-quarter the usual adult dose) is intended simply to 'contribute to a feeling of well-being in the patient' [Data Sheet 1980/1]: its sedative action may impair driving skills etc. Caffeine is meant to counteract the sedative effect, but there is no evidence that it does [AMADE p.575].
NHS expenditure on this product and on the identical product, PROPAIN, is estimated at over £100,000 a year.

PHAZYME
Stafford-Miller
Tablets

Dimethicone with silica 40mg (in enteric-coated inner layer)
Anti-foaming agent: intended to relieve flatulence.
See notes on dimethicone in entry for ASILONE.

PHENERGAN COMPOUND EXPECTORANT
May & Baker
Linctus (per 5ml)

Promethazine hydrochloride 5mg
Antihistamine.
Ipecacuanha liquid extract 0.01ml
Potassium guiacolsulphonate 45mg
Citric acid 65mg
Expectorants.

It is irrational to combine an antihistamine (which dries up secretions in the airways) with expectorants (intended to liquefy and loosen them). The safety of ipecacuanha liquid extract is questionable [FR 41 176 9/9/76 p.38356] and its value doubtful. The antihistamine is used for its sedative effect: it has no place in the treatment of the common cold.

PHENERGAN CREAM

May & Baker
Cream

Promethazine 2%
To relieve allergic and itchy skin conditions.
Dibromopropamidine isethionate 0.15%
Anti-infective.

Antihistamine creams are relatively ineffective and may cause skin reactions: antihistamines are more effective by mouth. The manufacturer recommends this cream for the treatment of burns, but warns against its use for more than three or four days. Other authorities suggest that systemic treatment with antihistamines is preferable: promethazine cream 'is not recommended since it may delay healing and produce skin sensitisation' [M28 p.1296].

PHENOBARBITONE SPANSULE

SK & F
[POM] Slow-release capsules

Phenobarbitone 60mg, 100mg

This product is primarily an anti-convulsant, though it is also identified as a sedative [Data Sheet 1983/4]. The Committee on Review of Medicines has said barbiturates should not be used as daytime sedatives or anti-anxiety agents [DTB, 1980, 18, 9]. For these uses, BARBITURATES have been superseded by BENZODIAZEPINE TRANQUILLISERS (see entries for both) and other safer agents.

PHENOLPHTHALEIN

Tablets

Phenolphthalein 125mg
Laxative.

Phenolphthalein is considered less satisfactory than many other preparations because its laxative action is unpredictable and sometimes violent. Because it is slowly excreted and tends to be recycled in the body, the laxative effect of a single dose may last for several days. Allergic reactions have been reported [M28 p.1366].
Simple constipation responds best to simple changes in diet, such as more fibre, more fruit – but 5 million NHS prescriptions for laxatives (costing over £7 million) are written each year. Millions of other over-the-counter laxatives are sold.

PHENSEDYL

May & Baker
Linctus (per 5ml)

Codeine phosphate 9mg
Ephedrine hydrochloride 7.2mg
Promethazine hydrochloride 3.6mg
Antihistamine.

Undesirable combination. See ACTIFED COMPOUND LINCTUS.
NHS expenditure on this product is about £1½ million a year.

PHOLCOLIX

Parke Davis
Syrup (per 5ml)

Pholcodine 5mg
Cough suppressant.
Phenylpropanolamine hydrochloride 12.5mg
Nasal, bronchial decongestant.
Paracetamol 150mg
Analgesic/antipyretic: relieves mild to moderate pain; reduces fever/high temperature.

Undesirable combination: these ingredients cannot be expected to be effective unless the doses of each are individualised.
NHS expenditure on this product is about £¾ million a year.

PHOLCOMED

Medo
Linctus (per 5ml)

Pholcodine 5mg
Cough suppressant.
Papaverine hydrochloride 1.25mg
Muscle relaxant.

Pholocomed Diabetic:
As for Pholcomed Linctus, but sugar-free

Pastilles
Pholcodine 4mg
Papaverine hydrochloride 1.25mg

Pholocodine is effective, but the use of papaverine is not justified [M28 p.1059; AMADE p.678; PDW p.28].
NHS expenditure on this product is estimated at £100,000 a year.

PHOLCOMED EXPECTORANT
Medo
Syrup (per 5ml)

Guaiphenesin 62.5mg
Expectorant.
Methylephedrine hydrochloride 0.625mg
Bronchial, nasal decongestant.

Undesirable combination. The effectiveness of guaiphenesin is doubtful. See EXPECTORANTS AND MUCOLYTICS. Unwanted effects limit the usefulness of methylephedrine, which has actions similar to EPHEDRINE (see entry).

PHOLCOMED FORTE
Medo
Linctus (per 5ml)

Pholcodine 19mg
Papaverine hydrochloride 5mg
(Also available in sugar-free formulation: Pholcomed Forte Diabetic.)

See PHOLCOMED.

PHOLTEX
Riker
Mixture, formulated for slow-release (per 5ml)

Pholcodine 15mg
Cough suppressant.
Phenyltoloxamine 10mg
Antihistamine.

Undesirable combination: there is no scientific basis for prescribing it [BNF No.6, 1983, p.120]. NHS expenditure on this product is estimated at £300,000 a year.

PHORTINEA
Philip Harris
Paint (4-nitrophenol 2%) for fungal skin infections

This compound 'is reported to have anti-fungal activity' [M28 p.1734] but is not well established. Considered less suitable for prescribing.

PHYLDROX
Carlton
[POM] Tablets; enteric-coated tablets (ones designed to dissolve in the small intestine rather than the stomach)

Theophylline 128mg
Ephedrine hydrochloride 12mg
Phenobarbitone 4mg

Undesirable combination of doubtful efficacy and safety. See similar product FRANOL.

PHYTEX
Pharmax
Paint for nail infections

Borotannic complex 9%
Antiseptic.
Salicylic acid 1%
Keratolytic: helps sloughing and peeling of scaly and callused skin.
Methyl salicylate 0.7%
Glacial acetic acid 2%
Benzyl hydroxybenzoate 0.35%

Outmoded and relatively expensive preparation.

PLEX-HORMONE
Consolidated
[POM] Tablets

Methyltestosterone 5mg
Male sex hormone used in treatment of arrested sexual development.
Deoxycortone acetate 500 micrograms
Corticosteroid used to treat adrenal insufficiency.
Ethinyloestradiol 2 micrograms
Synthetic female sex hormone.
Tocopherol acetate 5mg
Vitamin E.

Undesirable combination. Methyltestosterone and deoxycortone are normally injected, and both are relatively inactive by mouth. There is no convincing evidence of the value of vitamin E.

POLYALK
Galen
Antacid tablets; mixture

See similar product ASILONE.

POLYCROL, POLYCROL FORTE
Nicholas
Antacid tablets; mixture

See similar product ASILONE.

POLYVITE
Medo
Multivitamin capsules

Broadly similar to ABIDEC. See VITAMINS.

PONDOCILLIN
Burgess
[POM] Tablets, suspension

See similar product AMOXIL.

PONSTAN

Parke Davis
[POM] Capsules 250mg, paediatric suspension (per 25ml), tablets forte 500mg

Mefenamic acid 250mg
Non-steroidal anti-inflammatory drug (NSAID) *with relatively mild anti-inflammatory action: used for mild to moderate pain.*

Some authorities suggest that PONSTAN may be 'less effective than aspirin' [Parish, 1983, p.184]. The American Medical Association has said: 'Evidence supporting the use of mefenamic acid is limited. Few welldesigned, double-blind clinical trials have been done and the results of comparative studies have not shown mefenamic acid to be more effective than aspirin and other mild analgesics. Since its use has been associated with a number of serious adverse reactions, other mild analgesics are preferred' [AMADE, p.96]. Uncertainty about the efficacy of this drug is complicated also by variation in the recommendations for use. In the UK, the recommended dose for PONSTAN is double the dose recommended in the US. In the US, the manufacturer says in addition that treatment 'for periods exceeding one week is not recommended.' . . . 'The margin of safety is reduced at higher dosages and for longer administration' [PDR, 1983, pp.1535–6]. US prescribing information also says this drug should not be given to children aged under 14, 'because safe and effective use in this age group has not been established'. In the UK Data Sheet 1983/4 dosage schedules are suggested for infants under one year old.

All of this underlines warnings (given in the UK Data Sheet) to stop taking PONSTAN if it causes diarrhoea, rash or other symptoms of intolerance. People who take this drug for prolonged periods should be seen regularly by their doctor, and have periodic blood counts as well.

There are about one million prescriptions a year for this drug, but the number of long-term users is not known. If soluble aspirin were prescribed instead of PONSTAN, the NHS would save about £2½ million a year.

POTABA

Glenwood
Capsules, tablets

Potassium aminobenzoate 500mg
B vitamin intended as treatment for fibrosis (excessive formation of fibrous/scar tissue in muscle and skin).

Powder in sachet
Potassium aminobenzoate 3g

In 1977, the US Food and Drug Administration proposed withdrawal of this drug [PDW p. 162]. It has been rated 'possibly effective' in the US. The UK Joint Formulary Committee considers it of doubtful value.

POTABA + 6

Glenwood

As POTABA, plus pyridoxine vitamin B_6 1mg.

POTASSIUM SUPPLEMENTS

Potassium is an essential body element. Potassium supplements are mainly prescribed for people taking diuretics – drugs which reduce blood pressure and remove excessive fluid from body tissues, by increasing the output of urine. Though diuretics do promote potassium excretion, most patients probably do not need a supplement – and many who do can compensate for potassium depletion by adjusting their diet. A normal diet provides 60–100mmol (2.3–3.9g) of potassium a day, mainly from vegetables, meat and milk. Potassium-rich foods include fruit (dried fruit and juices too), tomatoes, beans (haricot and butter) and potatoes. Four ounces (100g) of potato, for example, provides about 500g of potassium. If possible, potassium intake should be increased by adjusting the diet – not least because potassium supplements tend to irritate and cause ulcers in the gut. (Too much potassium in the body can have a serious effect on the heart.) If potassium supplements are needed, it is always better to take them separately rather than in a diuretic + potassium fixed-ratio combination. The 'average' amount of potassium in these combinations is inevitably either more or less than some people need – and they have never been convincingly shown to be of benefit in preventing a fall in body potassium levels [Parish p.170]. The safest way of taking a supplement is in a liquid – usually prepared by dissolving an effervescent tablet in water. Neither uncoated nor enteric-coated tablets (ones designed to dissolve in the small intestine) should be used. Slow-release preparations of potassium salts appear to be safer than enteric-coated tablets, but tend to irritate the gut. Recent research [McMahon F. G. et al., 1982] strongly suggests that slow-release potassium supplements cause much more damage to the lining of the stomach and gut than has previously been suspected or reported. Micro-encapsulated formulations of

potassium salts appear safer than the widely-used wax-matrix preparations.
Potassium supplements are clearly misused and overprescribed. In the early 1980s, there were an estimated 3 million prescriptions a year for supplements – and well over 10 million prescriptions a year for diuretic + potassium fixed-ratio combination products as well.

PRAXILENE
Lipha
Capsules

Naftidrofuryl oxalate 100mg
Peripheral vasodilator: mainly promoted to improve mental function in the elderly.

See PERIPHERAL VASODILATORS. Though widely used, PRAXILENE has 'not been shown clinically to be of much benefit in senile dementia' [BNF No.6, 1983; p.90].
NHS expenditure on this product is about £5 million a year.

PREDSOL-N
Glaxo
[POM] Eye drops

Prednisolone sodium phosphate 0.5%
Corticosteroid.
Neomycin sulphate 0.5%
Antibiotic.

Combinations of corticosteroids and antibiotics have serious limitations. See SOFRADEX.

PREFIL
Norgine
Granules

Sterculia 55%
Guar gum 5%
Bulk-forming agents, intended to help users eat less by making the stomach feel full.

A daily dose of at least 10g a day might significantly help to reduce food intake, but there is little evidence to suggest that this product would be effective at the recommended dose (two 5ml spoonfuls before meals, or less). Only about one person in eight in a Consumers' Association survey found bulk-forming agents at all helpful in suppressing appetite: an apple eaten before meals was recommended as more effective [*Which?* April 1983, p.144].

PREGNAVITE FORTE
Bencard
Tablets
WITHDRAWN

Dried ferrous sulphate 84mg (25.2mg **iron**)
Vitamin A 1333 units
B vitamins: thiamine hydrochloride 500 micrograms; **riboflavine** 500 micrograms; **nicotinamide** 5mg; **pyridoxine hydrochloride** 330 micrograms
Vitamin C: ascorbic acid 13.3mg
Vitamin D 133 units
Calcium phosphate 160mg

VITAMINS (see entry) should not be added to iron preparations. See IRON SUPPLEMENTS. This product costs about five times more than equally effective iron preparations.

PREGNAVITE FORTE F
Bencard
[POM] Tablets

As PREGNAVITE FORTE, but with folic acid 360 micrograms.

PRESSURISED BROVON
PRESSURISED ISO-BROVON
PRESSURISED ISO-BROVON PLUS
Napp

See BROVON.

PRESTIM
Leo
[POM] Tablets

Timolol maleate 10mg
Beta-blocker.
Bendrofluazide 2.5mg
Diuretic.

Used to control high blood pressure. See BETA-BLOCKER + DIURETIC PREPARATIONS.

PRIMALAN
S & N Pharmaceuticals
[POM] Tablets

Mequitazine 5mg
Antihistamine: used to treat symptoms of allergy, eg in hay fever or urticaria (nettle rash).

This is an effective drug, but it appears to have no significant advantage over other, well-established antihistamines which are cheaper. It costs about five times as much as chlorpheniramine.

PRISCOL
WITHDRAWN

Ciba
[POM] Tablets

Tolazoline hydrochloride 25mg
Peripheral vasodilator: intended to improve blood flow in skin and muscle, and used mainly to treat circulation disorders in the legs.

The US Food and Drug Administration has classified this drug only as 'possibly effective' for its labelled indications. See PERIPHERAL VASODILATORS.

PRO-ACTIDIL
Wellcome
Slow-release tablets

Triprolidine hydrochloride 10mg
Antihistamine: used to treat symptoms of allergy, eg in hay fever or urticaria (nettle rash).

The action of slow-release antihistamines may be uneven and unpredictable, and they are also more expensive than standard formulations. This product appears to have no significant advantage over other antihistamines, and is much more expensive. If slow-release chlorpheniramine 12mg (as Piriton Spandets) were prescribed instead of this product, the NHS could save at least £¼ million a year.

PRO-BANTHINE WITH DARTALAN
Searle
[POM] Tablets
WITHDRAWN

Propantheline bromide 15mg
Antispasmodic: intended to relieve abdominal spasms and ulcer-like pain by reducing contractions of the stomach and intestine.
Thiopropazate hydrochloride 3mg
Phenothiazine tranquilliser.

The combination of ingredients is undesirable: effective drug use requires doses to be carefully adjusted to individual needs. Phenothiazine tranquillisers are mainly used to treat psychotic illness: their use in ulcer therapy is unnecessary.

PROCTOSEDYL
Cassenne
[POM] Ointment

Hydrocortisone 0.5%
Corticosteroid: to reduce swelling and inflammation associated with haemorrhoids and related disorders.
Framycetin sulphate 1%
Antibacterial antibiotic.
Cinchocaine hydrochloride 0.5%
Local anaesthetic.
Aesculin 1%
Extract of horse chestnut seeds: see below.

Suppositories
Hydrocortisone 5mg
Framycetin sulphate 10mg
Cinchocaine hydrochloride 5mg
Aesculin 10mg

Antibiotics are likely to be ineffective in rectal preparations, because of the overwhelming numbers of bacteria in the bowel area. Sensitisation and sensitivity reactions to framycetin are not uncommon, but the anti-inflammatory action of hydrocortisone could disguise the evidence of this. Aesculin has been used to treat various blood circulation problems, but is said to be 'of doubtful value' [M28 p.1675]. The safety and effectiveness of local anaesthetics used internally is doubtful [FR 45 103 27/5/80 p.35607]. Cinchocaine is more likely to cause sensitivity reactions than other local anaesthetics.
NHS expenditure on this product is estimated at over £1 million a year.

PROPADERM-A
Allen & Hanburys
[POM] Ointment

Beclomethasone dipropionate 0.025%
Corticosteroid to reduce inflammation.
Chlortetracycline hydrochloride 3%
Anti-infective.

Only likely to be of value where an area of eczema or dermatitis is infected. See CORTICOSTEROID + ANTI-INFECTIVE SKIN PREPARATIONS.
NHS expenditure on this product is over £100,000 a year.

PROPADERM-C
Allen & Hanburys
[POM] Cream and ointment

Beclomethasone dipropionate 0.025%
Corticosteroid to reduce inflammation.
Clioquinol 3%
Anti-infective agent.

Only likely to be of value where an area of eczema or dermatitis is infected. See CORTICOSTEROID + ANTI-INFECTIVE SKIN PREPARATIONS.

PROPAIN
Luitpold-Werk

Highly undesirable fixed-ratio combination product. See identical product PHARMIDONE.

P.R. SPRAY
Crookes Products
Cooling aerosol spray

Dichlorodifluoromethane 15%
Trichlorofluoromethane 85%
For pain relief.

Considered less suitable for prescribing: Methyl Salicylate Ointment BP or Methyl Salicylate Liniment BP are effective and much cheaper alternatives.

PYOREX
Bengue
Toothpaste

Acetarsol 0.45%
Anti-infective.
Aminacrine hydrochloride 0.006%
Antiseptic.
Sodium ricinoleate 0.76%
Surface-active agent: to improve contact between toothpaste and gum-tooth surfaces.

Lacks convincing evidence of value in treating gingivitis and similar disorders; and considered less suitable for prescribing. Acetarsol is a derivative of arsenic now replaced by less toxic drugs [M28 p.973].

QUESTRAN
Bristol-Myers
[POM] Powder (per sachet)

Cholestyramine 4g
Used to lower blood levels of lipids (fatty substances, like cholesterol).

This drug is used to prevent/treat atherosclerosis ('hardening of the arteries', ie the thickening of artery walls due to deposits of fat-like substances, which can seriously impair blood flow to the heart). It has not been clearly established that drug-induced lowering of blood fat levels has benefits in the treatment of atherosclerosis or coronary heart disease [PDR 1982; p.1192]. However, this drug may help carefully selected users if alternative measures fail: restrictions on diet, alcohol intake and smoking should normally be tried first.
NHS expenditure on this drug exceeds £1 million a year.

QUINODERM WITH HYDROCORTISONE
Quinoderm
[POM] Cream

Benzoyl peroxide 10%
Keratolytic: promotes sloughing or peeling of scaly, callused skin. Also thought to be active against bacteria which aggravate acne.
Hydrocortisone 1%
Corticosteroid: reduces inflammation.
Potassium hydroxyquinoline sulphate 0.5%
Antibacterial, antifungal.

Topical corticosteroids should be avoided if possible, especially for treatment on the face: see notes on CORTICOSTEROID + ANTI-INFECTIVE SKIN PREPARATIONS. Corticosteroids may complicate treatment and cause unpleasant side effects, and may alter the appearance of skin, making it thin and shiny. The UK Joint Formulary Committee says: 'Topical corticosteroids should not be used in acne' [BNF No.6 1983, p.348].

RABRO
Sinclair
Tablets

Deglycyrrhizinised liquorice extract 400mg
Treatment of peptic ulcer.
Calcium carbonate 500mg
Magnesium oxide 100mg
Antacids: neutralise excess stomach acid.
Frangula 25mg
Laxative.

Deglycyrrhizinised liquorice 'is of doubtful efficacy' [BNF No.6 1983; p.45]. Frangula has an unpredictable, sometimes violent laxative effect. A US expert panel has concluded that there is insufficient evidence to establish either an effective or safe dose for it [FR 40 56 21/3/75; p.12918]. If taken for long periods, CALCIUM CARBONATE (see entry) is more likely to upset body chemistry.

RAUDIXIN
Squibb
[POM] Tablets

Rauwolfia serpentina 50mg

Less suitable for prescribing. See RAUTRAX; RESERPINE.

RAUTRAX
Squibb
[POM] Tablets

Rauwolfia serpentina 50mg
Antihypertensive: used to control high blood pressure.
Hydroflumethiazide 50mg
Diuretic: augments the antihypertensive effect.

Potassium 8.4mmol
Supplement: intended to replace potassium the body loses through diuresis.

The possibility of serious side-effects (mainly depression) limits the value of rauwolfia. See RESERPINE.
The fixed-ratio combination is undesirable. Many people do not need a potassium supplement with a diuretic. If a supplement is needed, it is best taken separately – and preferably in solution not tablet form. The required dose may be higher than the amount in this preparation. See POTASSIUM SUPPLEMENTS.
NHS expenditure on this relatively expensive brand is about £200,000 a year.

RAUWILOID
Riker
[POM] Tablets

Alseroxylon 2mg

Less suitable for prescribing. See RAUWILOID + VERILOID; RESERPINE.

RAUWILOID + VERILOID
Riker
[POM] Tablets

Alseroxylon 1mg
Antihypertensive: rauwolfia derivative used to control high blood pressure.
Alkavervir 3mg
Antihypertensive: a derivative of veratrum (green hellebore) used to control high blood pressure.

Alkavervir has toxic effects at doses close to the therapeutic dose. Adverse effects include nausea, vomiting, dizziness, sweating, abnormal heart rhythms and shallow breathing (respiratory depression). It is 'no longer recommended for routine use' [M28 p.136]; 'should no longer be used' [BNF No.6, 1983, p.85]. The possibility of serious side-effects (mainly depression) limits the usefulness of alseroxylon. See RESERPINE.

RBC
Rybar
Cream

Antazoline hydrochloride 1.8%
Antihistamine: to relieve allergic and itchy skin conditions.
Calamine 8%
Mild astringent: allays itching.
Camphor 0.1%
Counter-irritant.
Cetrimide 0.5%
Antiseptic.

Antihistamine creams are relatively ineffective, and may cause skin reactions: antihistamines are more effective by mouth.

REACTIVAN
E. Merck
[POM] Tablets

Fencamfamin hydrochloride 10mg
B vitamins: thiamine phosphate 10mg; **pyridoxine phosphate** 20mg; **cyanocobalamin** 10 micrograms
Vitamin C: ascorbic acid 100mg

Fencamfamin is intended as treatment for debility and fatigue, but its value is doubtful [BNF No.6, 1983, p.149]. Vitamins add to cost rather than therapeutic benefit.
NHS expenditure on this product is over £100,000 a year.

REMIDERM
Squibb
[POM] Cream and ointment

Triamcinolone acetonide 0.025%
Corticosteroid to reduce inflammation.
Halquinol 0.75%
Anti-infective.

[POM] Pressurised aerosol spray (per 3-second spray)
Triamcinolone acetonide 0.1mg
Halquinol 0.62mg

Only likely to be of value where an area of eczema or dermatitis is infected. See CORTICOSTEROID + ANTI-INFECTIVE SKIN PREPARATIONS.
NHS expenditure on this product is about £100,000 a year.

REMNOS
DDSA
Tablets

Nitrazepam 5mg, 10mg

See BENZODIAZEPINE TRANQUILLISERS.

RESERPINE
[POM] Tablets

Reserpine 100 micrograms, 250 micrograms
Antihypertensive: used to control and reduce high blood pressure.

Reserpine is one of several derivatives of rauwolfia, a tropical shrub. These drugs reduce high

blood pressure, but may also cause or contribute to serious (and occasionally suicidal) depression, which can arise long after treatment starts. These drugs should not normally be used by anyone at risk from depression, or with a history of depressive illness. Other side effects include dry mouth, nasal congestion, and fluid retention. Reserpine and related drugs are therefore usually taken with a diuretic – a drug which also helps to lower blood pressure and which removes excessive fluid from body tissues by increasing the output of urine.
The UK Joint Formulary Committee has modified its views on reserpine and other rauwolfia derivatives, though it has consistently said that they are 'less suitable for prescribing'. Up to 1982, the Committee warned that such products were 'generally ineffective by mouth and cause an unacceptably high incidence of depression'. Since 1983, the Committee has retracted that warning, instead noting that: 'Rauwolfia and reserpine are not much used in Britain but if their dose is kept low and tablets are taken at night, blood pressure control can be achieved in mild hypertensives with few side effects.' [BNF No.6, 1983, p.82].
In fact, about a quarter of a million prescriptions for such products are written each year. Moreover, prescribing information given to doctors in the official Data Sheets for rauwolfia/reserpine products generally recommends medication during the day, and does not specifically say that the dosage should be kept low. Reserpine has also been used as an anti-psychotic drug, but is now considered obsolete: tranquillisers (such as chlorpromazine) are more effective, and less likely to cause depression [AMADE, p.215].

RESORCINOL AND SULPHUR PASTE/LOTION/OINTMENT

Resorcinol 5%
Keratolytic: promotes sloughing or peeling of scaly, callused skin. Also relieves itching and has mild antiseptic action.
Sulphur 5%
Keratolytic; antiseptic.
Zinc oxide 40%
Protectant and mild astringent.
Emulsifying ointment 50%
Inert greasy base.

Resorcinol is best avoided: with prolonged application, enough may be absorbed into the body to interfere with the functioning of the thyroid gland. The value of sulphur is questionable: some authorities think it encourages growth of blackheads, and recommend avoiding it [AMADE p.1368]. Smothering the skin with oily or greasy preparations tends to aggravate acne rather than help treat it [BNF No.6 1983 p.348].

RHINAMID

Bengue
[POM] Nasal drops

Sulphanilamide 0.4%
Bacteriostatic antibiotic: for treatment of nasal infections.
Butacaine sulphate 0.026%
Local anaesthetic.
Ephedrine hydrochloride 1%
Sympathomimetic: reduces nasal congestion and inflammation.

Significant infections would normally be treated systemically: treatments applied to the affected areas are unlikely to be of real benefit. The combination of ingredients is undesirable: the dose of the anti-infective would tend to be governed by the user's need for a decongestant – just as the need for anti-infective treatment could lead to excessive use of the decongestant. Sympathomimetic decongestant sprays are suitable only for short-term use: if used for more than a few days, they tend to cause 'rebound congestion', involving recurrence or deterioration of the original discomfort.

RINUREL

Warner
Tablets

Phenyltoloxamine citrate 22mg
Antihistamine.
Phenylpropanolamine hydrochloride 25mg
Decongestant.
Paracetamol 300mg
Analgesic; antipyretic: reduces temperature.

Linctus *(per 5ml)*
Pholcodine 5mg
Cough suppressant.
Phenyltoloxamine citrate 11mg
Phenylpropanolamine hydrochloride 12.5mg
Paracetamol 150mg

Undesirable combinations. Antihistamines have no place in treating common cold symptoms. It is doubtful whether sympathomimetics (used here to reduce nasal congestion and inflammation) add to the effectiveness of antihistamines in the treatment of allergy. Analgesics should be separately prescribed.
NHS expenditure on these products, and on RINUREL SA, is about £½ million a year.

RINUREL SA WITHDRAWN
Warner
[POM] Slow-release tablets

Phenyltoloxamine citrate 66mg
Phenylpropanolamine hydrochloride 100mg
Paracetamol 600mg

The action of slow-release preparations can be uneven and unpredictable, and they tend to be more expensive than standard formulations. See RINUREL.

ROBAXIN
Robins
[POM] Tablets

Methocarbamol 750mg
Skeletal muscle relaxant.

Diazepam is considered the drug of first choice in treating painful muscle spasm, and it is about ten times cheaper. The UK Joint Formulary Committee considers that the clinical efficacy of methocarbamol as a muscle relaxant is '*not* well established'.

ROBAXISAL FORTE
Robins
[POM] Tablets

Aspirin 325mg
Analgesic/antipyretic/anti-inflammatory agent.
Methocarbamol 400mg
Skeletal muscle relaxant.

Undesirable combination. Methocarbamol is not the drug of first choice. See: ROBAXIN.

ROBINUL
Robins
[POM] Tablets

Glycopyrronium bromide 2mg
Antispasmodic: intended to relieve abdominal spasms and ulcer-like pain by reducing contractions of the stomach and intestine.

This product has no clear advantage over many other atropine-like antispasmodic drugs, but costs much more than most.

ROBITUSSIN
Robins
Liquid (per 5ml)

Guaiphenesin 100mg

See ROBITUSSIN AC.

ROBITUSSIN AC
Robins
Elixir (per 5ml)

Codeine phosphate 10mg
Cough suppressant.
Guaiphenesin 100mg
Expectorant: intended to help removal of phlegm.
Pheniramine maleate 7.5mg
Antihistamine: used to control symptoms of allergy, eg to dry up nasal secretions in hay fever.

It is irrational to combine an antihistamine (which dries secretions in the airways) with an expectorant (meant to liquefy and loosen these secretions), and to combine ingredients which both stimulate and suppress the coughing reflex. The effectiveness of guaiphenesin is doubtful. See EXPECTORANTS AND MUCOLYTICS. The UK Joint Formulary Committee considers that 'there is no scientific basis' for prescribing mixtures of this kind, and says their use is 'to be deprecated' [BNF No.6, 1983, p.120].

ROHYPNOL
Sauter
[POM] Tablets

Flunitrazepam 1mg
Tranquilliser marketed for insomnia.

See BENZODIAZEPINE TRANQUILLISERS. Fifteen or so different benzodiazepines were already on the market before this product was introduced in 1982. It is said to have 'nothing to offer over those [benzodiazepines] already available' [DTB, 1983, 21, 64]. It is over three times the cost of nitrazepam (MOGADON).

RONDOMYCIN
Pfizer
[POM] Capsules

Methacycline hydrochloride 150mg
Bacteriostatic antibiotic: used in the treatment of a variety of infections.

The uses, antibacterial activity, and effectiveness of methacycline are essentially the same as other tetracyclines, though it is cleared from the body relatively slowly, and absorption is decreased in the presence of food [AMADE p.1677–8]. The official Data Sheet [1983/4] says RONDOMYCIN is well absorbed and suggests that poor absorption has a positive advantage: 'RONDOMYCIN has the property of maintaining therapeutic blood levels for at least 24 hours following interruption of several days' continuous administration.' RONDOMYCIN costs around ten times more than unbranded versions of tetracycline.

RONICOL; RONICOL TIMESPAN

Roche
Tablets

Nicotinyl alcohol 25mg
Slow-release tablets
Nicotinyl alcohol 150mg
Peripheral vasodilator: intended to improve blood flow in skin and muscle, and used mainly to treat circulation disorders in legs.

Nicotinyl alcohol lacks evidence of effectiveness: its benefits, if any, appear marginal. A US expert panel has classified this drug only as 'possibly effective' for its stated indications [PDR p.1685], and the AMA concurs.
NHS expenditure on this product is about £¼ million a year.

RONYL

Lipha
[POM] Tablets

Pemoline 20mg

The effectiveness of pemoline in counteracting lethargy and fatigue is doubtful; its actions have been studied but its effectiveness not demonstrated [AMADE p.291]. The Data Sheet [1983/4] recommends this product for (among other things) 'fatigue arising post-operatively'. But US prescribing information for pemoline states that 'significant clinical benefit may not be evident until the third or fourth week of drug administration' [PDR, 1982 p.510]. Any benefit might therefore be too little and come too late.

ROTER

Roterpharma
Antacid tablets

Bismuth subnitrate 300mg
Magnesium carbonate 400mg
Sodium bicarbonate 200mg
Antacids: neutralise excess stomach acid.
Frangula 25mg
Laxative.

Bismuth salts have been largely superseded by more effective antacids. Their use has been restricted in some countries (eg France, Switzerland, Australia) because they may be seriously toxic if over-used. Frangula has an unpredictable, sometimes violent laxative effect: a US expert panel has concluded that there is not enough evidence to establish either a safe or effective dose for it [FR 40 56 21/3/75; p.12918]. SODIUM BICARBONATE should not be taken regularly, and some people should not take it at all.
NHS expenditure on this product is about £100,000 a year.

ROTERSEPT

Roterpharma WITHDRAWN
Aerosol

Chlorhexidine gluconate 0.2%

Skin disinfectant rated less suitable for prescribing [BNF No.6, 1983, p.360].

RUBELIX

Pharmax
Elixir (per 5ml)

Pholcodine 4mg
Cough suppressant
Ephedrine hydrochloride 6mg
Decongestant.

Undesirable combination. See EPHEDRINE. Similar (and cheaper) product FALCODYL.

RYBARVIN INHALANT

Rybar
Spray solution

Adrenaline 0.4%
Atropine methonitrate 0.1%
Papaverine hydrochloride 0.08%
Benzocaine 0.08%

Less suitable preparation. See ADRENALINE AND ATROPINE.

SAFAPRYN

Pfizer
Enteric-coated tablets

Aspirin 300mg
Paracetamol 250mg

This combination would relieve pain about as well as aspirin 500mg or paracetamol 500mg, but costs several times more. Enteric-coated tablets are designed to dissolve in the small intestine, rather than in the stomach – and may irritate the stomach less. They tend to give an unpredictable response [FR 42 131 8/7/77 p.35376] but may be useful in the long-term treatment of conditions such as rheumatoid arthritis. They are not appropriate for the prompt relief of pain. NHS expenditure on this product is over £300,000 a year.

SAFAPRYN-CO

Pfizer

SAFAPRYN *(see previous entry)* + **codeine phosphate** 8mg

See ASPIRIN, PARACETAMOL AND CODEINE. NHS expenditure on this product is over £100,000 a year.

SALICYLIC ACID AND SULPHUR OINTMENT

Thick, greasy preparations should not be used to treat acne [BNF No.6 1983 p.348]. The value of sulphur is uncertain. See RESORCINOL AND SULPHUR PASTE.

SALZONE

Wallace Mfg
Elixir for children (per 5ml)

Paracetamol 120mg
Relieves pain; lowers temperature.

Effective but expensive. It costs about three times more than the identical drug: Paracetamol Elixir, Paediatric.

SANCOS CO

Sandoz
Syrup (per 5ml)

Pholcodine 5mg
Cough suppressant.
Chlorpheniramine maleate 2mg
Antihistamine.
Pseudoephedrine hydrochloride 20mg
Decongestant.
Glycerol 600mg
Demulcent: soothing liquid.

Undesirable combination. See ACTIFED COMPOUND LINCTUS.

SECADERM SALVE

Rorer
Ointment for boils, chilblains

Colophony 26%
Protectant.
Phenol 2.4%
Antiseptic.
Melaleuca oil 5.6%
Terebene 5.25%
Turpentine oil 6%
Essential oils.

Of no real value. See ILONIUM.

SECADREX

May & Baker
[POM] Tablets

Acebutolol 200mg
Beta-blocker.
Hydrochlorothiazide 12.5mg
Diuretic.

Used to control high blood pressure. See BETA-BLOCKER + DIURETIC PREPARATIONS.

SECONAL SODIUM

Lilly
[POM] Capsules

Quinalbarbitone sodium 50mg, 100mg

The manufacturers recommend this product as 'a valuable hypnotic for the patient whose chief difficulty is that of getting off to sleep, but who sleeps fairly well thereafter' [Data Sheet 1983/4]. The Committee on Review of Medicines has said that barbiturates should be used only for 'severe intractable insomnia' [DTB, 1980, 18, 9]. As hypnotics, BARBITURATES have been superseded by BENZODIAZEPINE TRANQUILLISERS (see entries for both) and other safer agents.

SECTRAL

May & Baker
[POM] Capsules, tablets

Acebutolol 100mg, 200mg *(*capsules*)* or 400mg *(*tablets*)*
Beta-blocker: controls over-stimulation of the heart and regularises the heartbeat. Used mainly to treat high blood pressure, angina and heart disorders.

This is an effective and widely prescribed drug, strongly promoted by brand name. For selected users, acebutolol would offer a significant advantage over the close equivalent, propranolol hydrochloride, but as a general rule 'propranolol remains the drug of choice since it is cheap and its long-term risks are clearly understood' [DTB 1980, 18, 64].
If propranolol were prescribed instead of this product, the NHS would save over £2½ million a year.

SEDONAN
Napp
Ear drops

Phenazone 5%
Chlorbutol 1%

Of doubtful effectiveness. See AUDAX.

SEOMINAL
Winthrop
[POM] Tablets

Reserpine 200 micrograms
Antihypertensive: used to control high blood pressure.
Phenobarbitone 10mg
Barbiturate sedative.
Theobromine 325mg
Xanthine derivative: intended to enhance the effect of the barbiturate.

The possibility of serious side effects (mainly depression) limits the usefulness of RESERPINE (see entry).
There is no justification for the use of BARBITURATES in the treatment of hypertension [BNF No.6 1983 p.85], and their use as sedatives is obsolete. They may cause dependence and addiction, among other unpleasant side effects (see entry). If a sedative is needed it should be prescribed separately [DTB 1980, 18, 10]. The combination of theobromine and phenobarbitone 'has no advantage over phenobarbitone alone' [M28 p.349].

SEPTEX No. 2
Norton
[POM] Cream

Boric acid 5.15%
Weak antiseptic.
Sulphathiazole 4.94%
Sulphonamide antibiotic.
Zinc oxide 7.4%
Protectant with mild astringent action.

Boric acid has been superseded by safer and more effective antiseptics [M28 p.337]. Sulphonamides are ineffective in the treatment of minor skin infections: pus and other wound debris are thought to render them inactive [AMADE p.1724].

SERC
Duphar
[POM] Tablets

Betahistine hydrochloride 8mg
Vasodilator, histamine analogue.

This product is specifically recommended for treatment of the symptoms of Ménière's disease: vertigo, dizziness, nausea, ringing and other noises in the ear (tinnitus), and progressive nerve deafness. (These symptoms can occur in many inner ear disorders: the condition is called Ménière's disease when the underlying cause is not found.) The value of different drug treatments in controlling these symptoms is hard to assess, partly because sufferers may be symptom-free for months between attacks. But there is no convincing evidence that this product is more effective than many other drugs in the treatment of Ménière's disease: a 60–80% 'success rate' has been reported, regardless of the treatment used [DTB, 1981, 19, 17].
SERC (8–16mg three times daily) is relatively very expensive. It costs 2–5 times more than other well-established treatments (cinnarizine 15–30mg, or prochlorperazine 5mg, both three times daily). If these were prescribed instead of SERC, the NHS could save around £2 million a year.

SERENID D
Wyeth
[POM] Tablets

Oxazepam 10mg, 15mg

Oxazepam has actions and uses similar to diazepam and other BENZODIAZEPINE TRANQUILLISERS (see entry), but is more rapidly excreted from the body. It could therefore be expected to cause less drowsiness in treating anxiety, though drowsiness is reported as being the most common unwanted effect.
Oxazepam (SERENID-D) is about three times as expensive as diazepam, and it seems doubtful if its advantages would often be worth this extra cost. If diazepam were prescribed instead of oxazepam (SERENID-D and SERENID-FORTE), the NHS could save about £¾ million a year.

SERENID-FORTE
Wyeth
[POM] Capsules

Oxazepam 30mg

See SERENID-D.

SERPASIL
Ciba
[POM] Tablets

Reserpine 100 micrograms, 250 micrograms

Less suitable for prescribing. See SERPASIL-ESIDREX K; RESERPINE.

SERPASIL-ESIDREX
Ciba
[POM] Tablets

Reserpine 150 micrograms
Hydrochlorothiazide 10mg

Less suitable for prescribing. See SERPASIL-ESIDREX K; RESERPINE.

SERPASIL-ESIDREX K
Ciba
[POM] Tablets

WITHDRAWN

Reserpine 150 micrograms
Antihypertensive: used to control high blood pressure.
Hydrochlorothiazide 10mg
Diuretic: augments the antihypertensive effect of reserpine.
Potassium 8.1mmol
Supplement: intended to replace potassium the body loses through diuresis.

The possibility of serious side effects (mainly depression) limits the value of RESERPINE (see entry). The fixed-ratio combination is undesirable. Many people do not need a potassium supplement with a diuretic. If a supplement is needed, it is best taken separately, and preferably in solution not tablet form. The required dosage may be higher than the amount in this preparation. See POTASSIUM SUPPLEMENTS.

SIDROS
Arun Products
Tablets

Ferrous gluconate 300mg (35mg **iron**)
Ascorbic acid 30mg
Vitamin C.

Ascorbic acid improves absorption of iron only at much higher doses (7mg:1mg iron). See IRON SUPPLEMENTS. See also p.22. This product costs the NHS about four times more than simple, equally effective iron preparations.

SILBE INHALANT
Berk
[POM] Spray

WITHDRAWN

Adrenaline acid tartrate 1%
Atropine methonitrate 0.125%
Papaverine hydrochloride 0.95%
Hyoscine hydrobromide 0.05%

Less suitable preparation. See ADRENALINE AND ATROPINE.

SILBEPHYLLINE
Berk
Suppositories and tablets

Diprophylline 400mg (suppositories), 200mg (tablets)
Bronchodilator: relieves breathing difficulties in asthma, bronchitis etc.

Diprophylline is considered of doubtful efficacy and less suitable for prescribing than slow-release preparations of (the related drugs) theophylline and aminophylline [BNF No.6, 1983, p.104]. Rectal absorption of aminophylline and related drugs tends to be erratic – and suppositories may cause local irritation as well. Oral preparations are usually preferred [AMADE p.591; DTB, 1979, 17, 92). See BRONCHODILATORS.

SILDERM
Lederle
[POM] Cream

Triamcinolone acetonide 0.1%
Corticosteroid to reduce inflammation.
Neomycin 0.35%
Undecylenic acid 2.5%
Anti-infective agents.

Only likely to be of value where an area of eczema or dermatitis is infected. See CORTICOSTEROID + ANTI-INFECTIVE SKIN PREPARATIONS.

SILOXYL
Martindale
Antacid tablets; mixture

See similar product ASILONE.

SIMETHICONE

See ASILONE.

SKEFRON
SK & F
Cooling aerosol spray, intended for pain relief

Identical to P. R. SPRAY.

SLOW-FE
Ciba
Slow-release tablet

Dried ferrous sulphate 160mg (50mg **iron**)

See Chapter One: Slow-release preparations (p.23–4); and IRON SUPPLEMENTS. This product costs about three times more than standard formulations of iron which may be more effective.

SLOW-FE FOLIC

Ciba

[POM] Slow-release tablet

Dried ferrous sulphate 160mg (50mg **iron**)
Folic acid 400 micrograms

See SLOW-FE.

SLOW-K

Ciba

Tablets formulated in slow-release wax core

Potassium chloride 600mg (8mmol *each of potassium and chloride ions*)

Slow-release POTASSIUM SUPPLEMENTS (see entry) may irritate or cause ulcers in the gut. There are preferable alternatives.
NHS expenditure on this product is estimated at £1¼ million a year.

SLOW-TRASICOR

Ciba

[POM] Sustained-release tablets

Oxprenolol hydrochloride 160mg
Beta-blocker: controls over-stimulation of the heart and regularises the heartbeat. Used mainly to treat high blood pressure, angina and heart disorders.

This is a widely prescribed drug, strongly promoted by brand name. It offers the convenience and the theoretical advantages of a once-daily dosage but, in practice, may not be as effective as oxprenolol taken at half the dosage, twice a day. Some evidence suggests that the effect of SLOW-TRASICOR on blood pressure does not last a full 24 hours [DTB 1980, 18, 63]. If oxprenolol (80mg × 2) were prescribed instead of SLOW-TRASICOR, the NHS could save about £3 million a year. There may be exceptions but, as a general rule, oxprenolol offers no real advantage over the close equivalent, propranolol hydrochloride: for most purposes, 'propranolol remains the drug of choice since it is cheap and its long-term risks are clearly understood' [DTB 1980, 18, 64].
If propranolol (80mg × 2) were prescribed instead of SLOW-TRASICOR (160mg), the NHS would save about £6 million a year.

SODIUM AMYTAL

Lilly

[POM] Tablets; capsules

Amylobarbitone sodium 60mg, 200mg

The manufacturers recommend this product 'as a routine hypnotic' and 'of value as a daytime sedative in the neurotic patient' [Data Sheet 1983/4]. The Committee on Review of Medicines has said that barbiturates should be used only for 'severe intractable insomnia', and not as daytime sedatives or anti-anxiety agents [DTB, 1980, 18, 9]. For these purposes, BARBITURATES (see entry for both) have been superseded by BENZODIAZEPINE TRANQUILLISERS and other safer agents.

SODIUM BICARBONATE BP

Compound tablets

This is an effective antacid: it acts fast, but not for long. It should not be taken regularly because it is likely to upset body chemistry. Sodium bicarbonate raises blood sodium levels which tends to cause water retention: it should not be used by people with fluid retention problems (oedema) or with impaired heart or kidney function, or by people on a low-sodium diet.

SOFRADEX

Roussel

[POM] Eye/ear drops; ointment

Dexamethasone 0.05%
Corticosteroid: used to reduce inflammation.
Framycetin sulphate 0.5%
Gramicidin 0.005%
Antibacterial antibiotics.

Corticosteroid + antibiotic combinations are widely prescribed but should normally be avoided. They are not suitable for routine treatment of eye disorders and should be used only under close specialist supervision. Corticosteroids may seriously aggravate some eye infections which are difficult to diagnose, and may cause serious side effects (steroid glaucoma) in susceptible individuals. Corticosteroids also reduce the body's resistance to infection, and may worsen the patient's condition if the antibiotic does not work (eg the dosage of the antibiotic may be too low, or the infection may be caused by non-susceptible organisms, including fungi and viruses). In addition, if the patient is hypersensitive to the antibiotic, the corticosteroid may mask the allergic response. This is a potentially serious drawback with combinations of neomycin (or framycetin) as both readily produce sensitisation.
About one million NHS prescriptions – including many for this product – are written each year for corticosteroid and antibiotic combinations for eye disorders alone. NHS expenditure on this product is estimated at about £½ million a year.

SOFRAMYCIN
Roussel
[POM] Nasal spray

Framycetin sulphate 1.25%
Gramicidin 0.005%
Antibacterial antibiotics.
Phenylephrine hydrochloride 0.25%
Sympathomimetic: nasal decongestant.

Significant infections would normally be treated systemically. This preparation is unlikely to be of real benefit, and the combination of ingredients is undesirable. See BIOMYDRIN.

SOLARCAINE
Plough
Cream; lotion; spray

Cream
Benzocaine 1%
Local anaesthetic.
Triclosan 0.2%
Antiseptic.

Lotion
Benzocaine 0.5%
Triclosan 0.2%

Spray
Benzocaine 5%
Triclosan 0.1%
Intended for minor skin infections, wounds etc.

Minor skin infections generally need no treatment. A 5–20% concentration of benzocaine is required for an effective local anaesthetic action.

SOLIS
Galen

See VALIUM.

SOLIWAX
Martindale
Ear capsules/drops to soften ear wax, before removal

Dioctyl sodium sulphosuccinate (docusate sodium) 5% in oil.

This product is not needed. There are many simple, effective and cheaper alternatives, eg sodium bicarbonate ear drops, baby oil, arachis oil, almond oil etc.

SOLPADEINE
Winthrop
Effervescent tablets

Paracetamol 500mg
Codeine phosphate 8mg
Caffeine 30mg

The dose of codeine may be less than effective, and caffeine is unlikely to have any significant effect. This product costs nearly ten times more than paracetamol 500mg, but is not much more effective. See CODEINE AND PARACETAMOL.
If paracetamol 500mg were prescribed instead of this product, the NHS could save an estimated £2½ million a year.

SOMNITE
Norgine
[POM] Tablets

Nitrazepam 5mg

Suspension
Nitrazepam 2.5mg/5ml

See MOGADON; BENZODIAZEPINE TRANQUILLISERS.

SONERYL
May & Baker
[POM] Tablets

Butobarbitone 100mg
Barbiturate: for severe intractable insomnia.

See BARBITURATES.

SOTAZIDE
Bristol-Myers
[POM] Tablets

Sotalol hydrochloride 160mg
Beta-blocker.
Hydrochlorothiazide 25mg
Diuretic.

Used to control high blood pressure. See BETA-BLOCKER + DIURETIC PREPARATIONS.

SPARINE
Wyeth
[POM] Tablets; suspension; injection

Promazine hydrochloride (tablets: 25mg, 50mg, 100mg; suspension *(per 5ml)* and injection (per ml): 50mg)
Phenothiazine tranquilliser: used to control symptoms of psychotic illness.

The Joint Formulary Committee suggests that promazine 'may be of value in elderly patients with minor psychiatric problems' [BNF No.6, 1983, p.134]. The American Medical Association considers it obsolete 'because it has extremely weak anti-psychotic activity and the incidence of agranulocytosis is greater than with other phenothiazines' [AMADE p.215]. (Agranulocytosis: a serious, potentially fatal blood disorder, which reduces the body's resistance to infection.)

STELABID
SK & F
[POM] Tablets

Isopropamide 5mg *(as iodide)*
Antispasmodic: intended to relieve abdominal spasms and ulcer-like pain by reducing contractions of the stomach and intestine.
Trifluoperazine hydrochloride 1mg
Phenothiazine tranquilliser.

Tablets Forte
Isopropamide iodide 7.5mg
Trifluoperazine hydrochloride 2mg

The combination of ingredients is undesirable: effective drug use requires doses to be carefully adjusted to individual needs. Phenothiazine tranquillisers are mainly used to treat psychotic illness: their use in ulcer therapy is unnecessary and not recommended [BNF No.6 1983 p.44]. The US version of this product is rated less-than-effective ('possibly effective') by the US Food and Drug Administration [PDR 1983 p.1892].

STEROXIN-HYDROCORTISONE
Geigy
[POM] Cream

Hydrocortisone 1%
Corticosteroid to reduce inflammation.
Chlorquinaldol 3%
Anti-infective agent.

Only likely to be of value where an area of eczema or dermatitis is infected. See CORTICOSTEROID + ANTI-INFECTIVE SKIN PREPARATIONS.

STREPSILS
Crookes Products
Lozenges

Amylmetacresol 0.6mg
2,4-dichlorbenzyl alcohol 1.2mg
Antimicrobials.

There is no good evidence that this preparation is of any real value. The NHS spends about £1½ million a year on products of this kind.

STREPTOTRIAD
May & Baker
[POM] Tablets

Sulphadiazine 100mg
Sulphadimidine 100mg
Sulphathiazole 100mg
Bacteriostatic antibacterials.
Streptomycin 65mg
Bactericidal antibiotic.

This combination is recommended [Data Sheet 1983/4] for the prevention and treatment of non-specific ('travellers'') diarrhoea. These diarrhoeas may not be caused by bacteria but, even if they are, treatment with an antibacterial agent should be avoided. Antibacterials may prolong diarrhoeal states; and there is no convincing evidence they prevent them [BNF No.6, 1983, p.48]. The manufacturer claims that the combination of sulphonamides, which are more and less well absorbed in the gut, reduces the incidence of side effects and, notably, crystalluria (crystals in the urine). This rationale is now considered 'obsolete', because of the introduction of single-entity agents (eg sulphafurazole) which are more soluble in urine (AMADE p. 1732].

STROMBA
Sterling Research
[POM] Tablets

Stanozolol 5mg
Anabolic steroid: stimulates growth of body tissues.

This product has been recommended as an aid in the treatment of debilitating diseases and for convalescence from serious illness or injury, but the evidence of its effectiveness is inadequate. In the official Data Sheet [1983/4] there are references also to 6–8 week courses of treatment for young children. No specific recommendation is made for treatment of delayed development in children, though in West Germany, it reportedly is [IOCU, 1983]. Such treatment is not justifiable: the evidence suggests that the possible benefits of treatment are slight, but there is a serious risk of irreversible disturbances of growth and sexual development, particularly in younger children. [AMADE p.920; DTB, 1979, 17, 54].

SUDAFED
Calmic
Tablets; syrup (per 10ml)

Pseudoephedrine hydrochloride 60mg
Decongestant.

A rational drug, though considered 'o' doubtful value' and less suitable for prescribing [BNF No.6, 1983, p.123]. Nasal decongestant sprays tend to be more effective than oral preparations for short-term use.
NHS expenditure on this product is about £1 million per year.

SUDAFED CO
Calmic
Tablets

Pseudoephedrine hydrochloride 60mg
Paracetamol 500mg
Analgesic; antipyretic: lowers temperature.

Undesirable combination. See SUDAFED.

SUDAFED EXPECTORANT
Calmic
Syrup (per 5ml)

Guaiphenesin 100mg
Expectorant.
Pseudoephedrine hydrochloride 30mg
Bronchial, nasal decongestant.

Undesirable combination. Guaiphenesin is of doubtful value. See EXPECTORANTS AND MUCOLYTICS. NHS expenditure on this product is about £100,000 a year.

SULFAPRED
Wallace
[POM] Eye drops

Prednisolone sodium phosphate 0.5%
Corticosteroid.
Sulphacetamide sodium 10%
Antibiotic.

Combinations of corticosteroids and antibiotics have serious limitations. See SOFRADEX.

SULPHATRIAD
May & Baker
[POM] Tablets; mixture (per 5ml)

Sulphadiazine 185mg
Sulphathiazole 185mg
Sulphamerazine 130mg

Undesirable combination of sulphonamide anti-infective agents. See STREPTOTRIAD.

SULPHUR OINTMENT

Greasy preparations, and possibly also sulphur, should be avoided in the treatment of acne. See RESORCINOL AND SULPHUR PASTE.

SURBEX T
Abbott

Vitamins B + C

Similar to, but cheaper than OROVITE.

SUREM
Galen
[POM] Capsules

Nitrazepam 5mg

See MOGADON; BENZODIAZEPINE TRANQUILLISERS.

SURGAM 200; SURGAM 300
Cassenne
[POM] Tablets

Tiaprofenic acid 200mg; 300mg
Non-steroidal anti-inflammatory drug (NSAID) *used mainly to treat pain and inflammation in rheumatic and related disorders.*

SURGAM was launched in 1982 with extravagant and unjustified claims for 'gastric protection'. These claims were dropped in 1983, but some patients might have been endangered in the meantime [DTB 1983, 21, 50]. SURGAM is effective, but no more so than chemically related and well-established alternatives such as ibuprofen or naproxen. See NSAIDS. It is 2–4 times more expensive than these.

SUSTAMYCIN
MCP
[POM] Slow-release capsules

Tetracycline hydrochloride 250mg
Bacteriostatic antibiotic: for bronchitis and other infections.

This formulation of tetracycline is taken twice rather than 3–4 times a day. For a few selected patients this could be an advantage. For most, the advantage does not seem worth the extra cost: treatment with SUSTAMYCIN is 3–4 times more expensive than with tetracycline. If tetracycline were prescribed instead, the NHS could save about £½ million a year.

SYLOPAL
Norton
Antacid mixture

See similar product ASILONE.

SYNALAR C
ICI
[POM] Cream and ointment

Fluocinolone acetonide 0.025%
Corticosteroid to reduce inflammation.
Clioquinol 3%
Anti-infective agent.

Only likely to be of value where an area of eczema or dermatitis is infected. See CORTICOSTEROID + ANTI-INFECTIVE SKIN PREPARATIONS.

SYNALAR N
ICI
[POM] Cream, ointment and lotion

Fluocinolone acetonide 0.025%
Corticosteroid to reduce inflammation.
Neomycin sulphate 0.5%
Anti-infective agent.

Only likely to be of value where an area of eczema or dermatitis is infected. See CORTICOSTEROID + ANTI-INFECTIVE SKIN PREPARATIONS.

SYNDOL
Merrell
[POM] Tablets

Codeine phosphate 10mg
Narcotic analgesic: relieves mild to moderate pain.
Paracetamol 450mg
Analgesic; antipyretic: lowers temperature.
Doxylamine succinate 5mg
Antihistamine: used here for its sedative effect.
Caffeine 30mg
Mild stimulant.

Highly undesirable fixed-ratio combination product, recommended for the treatment of 'tension headache'. It could be expected to be about as effective as paracetamol 500mg, which costs around ten times less. The dose of codeine may be less than effective: a combination of paracetamol 400mg plus codeine 10mg has not been shown to be more effective than paracetamol 400mg alone (see CODEINE AND PARACETAMOL). Doxylamine (at about one-quarter the usual adult dose) is probably just meant to make users feel good (see PHARMIDONE): its sedative action may impair driving and other skills. Caffeine is meant to counteract the sedative effect, but there is no evidence it does [AMADE p.575]. If paracetamol were prescribed instead of this product, the NHS could save around £1 million a year.

SYRTUSSAR
Armour
Syrup (per 5ml)

Dextromethorphan hydrobromide 10mg
Cough suppressant.
Pheniramine maleate 7.5mg
Antihistamine.

Undesirable combination: dextromethorphan alone is effective in suppressing cough.

TACITIN WITHDRAWN
Ciba
[POM] Tablets

Benzoctamine hydrochloride 10mg

BENZODIAZEPINE TRANQUILLISERS (see entry) are considered more effective in the treatment of anxiety [BNF 1983, No.6, p.129]. Diazepam also costs about half as much.

TALPEN
Beecham

See similar product AMOXIL.

TANCOLIN
Ashe
Linctus for children (per 5ml)

Dextromethorphan hydrobromide 2.62mg
Cough suppressant.
Theophylline 15mg
Bronchodilator
Glycerol 655mg
Demulcent: soothing liquid.
Sodium citrate 99.56mg
Citric acid 45.85mg
Expectorants.
Ascorbic acid 12.35mg
Vitamin C.

Undesirable combination. Dextromethorphan alone is effective in suppressing cough; theophylline, if needed, should be prescribed separately. See AMESEC. The contribution of vitamin C is negligible. See VITAMINS.

TANDACOTE
Geigy
[POM] Enteric-coated tablets

Oxyphenbutazone 100mg

Hazardous. See TANDERIL.

TANDALGESIC

Geigy
[POM] Tablets

Oxyphenbutazone 50mg
Paracetamol 500mg

Hazardous. See TANDERIL.

TANDERIL

Geigy
[POM] Tablets

Oxyphenbutazone 100mg

Suppositories
Oxyphenbutazone 250mg

Non-steroidal anti-inflammatory drug (NSAID) used to treat pain and inflammation in rheumatic and related conditions. Serious and not uncommon side effects drastically limit the usefulness of this otherwise effective drug. It can aggravate high blood pressure and give rise to leg swelling by causing salt and water retention. It can irritate and severely ulcerate the stomach; and may cause serious and sometimes fatal abnormalities of the blood cells. In the UK alone, at least 440 people are known to have died from using this and related drugs. Oxyphenbutazone and related drugs should therefore only be used if alternative treatments have failed; and treatment should normally be limited to short courses (not exceeding one week). In the US, though not in the UK, this drug is contra-indicated for children under 14 ('since controlled clinical trials in patients of this age group have not been conducted'). Chronic use by people over 60 is especially inadvisable 'because of the exceedingly high risk of severe fatal toxic reactions in this age group' [PDR, 1983, p.969].
This product and identical or closely related agents (BUTACOTE, BUTAZOLIDIN, BUTAZOLIDIN ALKA, BUTAZONE, TANDALGESIC and TANDACOTE) are nevertheless still widely prescribed: around one and a quarter million prescriptions in 1981. (Prescribing these products by brand name costs the NHS over £1 million a year.) There are at least 20 alternative NSAIDs: it should rarely if ever be necessary to prescribe this product at all.

TANDERIL-CHLORAMPHENICOL

Zyma
[POM] Eye ointment

Oxyphenbutazone 10%
Used to reduce inflammation.
Chloramphenicol 1%
Antibacterial antibiotic.

Non-steroidal anti-inflammatory drugs (NSAIDs) are not well established for the treatment of eye inflammation, though they avoid some of the complications found with corticosteroid drugs (see SOFRADEX). Chloramphenicol may cause less sensitisation than other antibiotics used to treat eye infections, though it can produce serious disorders after prolonged use. The combination of ingredients is considered less suitable for prescribing [BNF No.6, 1983 p.316].

TAUMASTHMAN

Wallace Mfg
[POM] Tablets

Theophylline 100mg
Bronchodilator: relieves breathing difficulties in asthma, bronchitis etc.
Ephedrine hydrochloride 10mg
Bronchodilator.
Atropine sulphate 300 micrograms
Antispasmodic: used to control coughing spasms.
Phenazone 100mg
Analgesic: relieves mild to moderate pain.
Caffeine 50mg
Mild stimulant.

The effectiveness of theophylline depends on careful adjustment of dose: its use in fixed-ratio combination products is undesirable (see AMESEC). Careful adjustment of the dose of both atropine and EPHEDRINE (see entry) is also necessary, if either is to be effective. The analgesic is totally out of place, and phenazone is outmoded. And there is more caffeine in a cup of tea.

TEDRAL

Warner
[POM] Tablets

Theophylline 120mg
Ephedrine hydrochloride 24mg

[POM] Elixir for children *(per 5ml)*
Theophylline 30mg
Ephedrine hydrochloride 6mg

TEDRAL SA

Warner
[POM] Slow-release tablets

Theophylline 180mg
Ephedrine hydrochloride 48mg

Undesirable fixed-ratio combination products. See similar product AMESEC.

TEDRAL EXPECTORANT

Warner
[POM] Elixir (per 5ml)

Guaiphenesin 50mg
Expectorant.
Diprophylline 100mg
Theophylline-related bronchodilator.
Ephedrine hydrochloride 10mg
Bronchial, nasal decongestant.

Guaiphenesin is of doubtful value. See EXPECTORANTS AND MUCOLYTICS. Diprophylline, if needed, should be separately prescribed. See AMESEC.

TENAVOID

Burgess
[POM] Tablets

Meprobamate 200mg
Tranquilliser: for treatment of anxiety, muscle spasm.
Bendrofluazide 3mg
Diuretic: removes excessive fluid from body tissues by increasing the output of urine.

Undesirable combination, prescribed for premenstrual tension. MEPROBAMATE (see entry) is considered less effective, less safe than BENZODIAZEPINE TRANQUILLISERS (see entry).

TENORET 50

Stuart
[POM] Tablets

Atenolol 50mg
Beta-blocker.
Chlorthalidone 12.5mg
Diuretic.

Used to control high blood pressure. See BETA-BLOCKER + DIURETIC PREPARATIONS.

TENORETIC

Stuart
[POM] Tablets

Atenolol 100mg
Beta-blocker.
Chlorthalidone 25mg
Diuretic.

Used to control high blood pressure. See BETA-BLOCKER + DIURETIC PREPARATIONS. See also notes on relative advantages of atenolol and propanolol: TENORMIN.

If propranolol and bendrofluazide were prescribed instead of this product, the NHS could save about £3½ million a year.

TENORMIN

Stuart
[POM] Tablets

Atenolol 100mg
Beta-blocker: controls over-stimulation of the heart and regularises the heartbeat. Used mainly to treat high blood pressure, angina and heart disorders.

This is an effective and widely prescribed drug, strongly promoted by brand name. Selected users (eg with a history of wheezing) would benefit from atenolol, which is more selective for the heart than the close equivalent, propranolol. But as a general rule 'propranolol remains the drug of choice since it is cheap and its long-term risks are clearly understood' [DTB 1980, 18, 64]. It costs the NHS about £10 million a year because this product is widely prescribed instead of propranolol.

TENORMIN LS

Stuart
[POM] Tablets

Atenolol 50mg

See notes on TENORMIN.

TENSIUM

DDSA
[POM] Tablets

Diazepam 2mg, 5mg, 10mg

See VALIUM.

TERCODA

Sinclair
Elixir (per 5ml)

Codeine phosphate 8mg
Cough suppressant.
Terpin hydrate 8mg
Expectorant.
Menthol 4mg
Cineole 0.02ml
Peppermint oil 0.01ml
Pumilio pine oil 0.02ml
Aromatic oils.

The combination of a cough suppressant and an expectorant (intended to stimulate the cough reflex) is irrational. Similar product COPHOLCO.

TERPALIN
Norton
Elixir (per 5ml)

Codeine phosphate 13mg
Terpin hydrate 6.5mg
Menthol 1.5mg
Cineole 0.002ml

Irrational combination. Similar products TERCODA; COPHOLCO.

TERPOIN
Hough, Hoseason
[POM] Elixir (per 5ml)

Codeine phosphate 15mg
Terpin hydrate 9.15mg
Guaiphenesin 50mg
Menthol 18.3mg
Cineole 4.15mg

Irrational combination. Similar products TERCODA; COPHOLCO.
NHS expenditure on this product is about £100,000 a year.

TERRA-BRON
Pfizer
[POM] Syrup (per 5ml)

Oxytetracycline hydrochloride 250mg *(as calcium salt)*
Bacteriostatic antibiotic: used here for bronchitis and respiratory tract infections.
Ephedrine hydrochloride 7.5mg
Bronchodilator.
Ipecacuanha liquid extract 0.03ml
Expectorant.

Undesirable combination: if such ingredients are needed, the dose of each should be individualised. EPHEDRINE (see entry) often causes unwanted effects, even at the optimal dose. The safety of ipecacuanha liquid extract is questionable [FR 41 176 9/9/76 p.38358] and its value doubtful. See EXPECTORANTS AND MUCOLYTICS.

TERRA-CORTRIL
Pfizer
[POM] Ointment

Hydrocortisone 1%
Corticosteroid to reduce inflammation.
Oxytetracycline hydrochloride 3%
Anti-infective agent.

[POM] Pressurised aerosol
Hydrocortisone 0.17%
Oxytetracycline hydrochloride 0.5%

Only likely to be of value where an area of eczema or dermatitis is infected. See CORTICOSTEROID + ANTI-INFECTIVE SKIN PREPARATIONS.
NHS expenditure on this product is about £400,000 a year.

TERRA-CORTRIL NYSTATIN
Pfizer
[POM] Cream

Hydrocortisone 1%
Corticosteroid to reduce inflammation.
Oxytetracycline *as calcium salt* 3%
Nystatin 100,000 units/gram
Anti-infective agents.

Only likely to be of value where an area of eczema or dermatitis is infected. See CORTICOSTEROID + ANTI-INFECTIVE SKIN PREPARATIONS.
NHS expenditure on this product is about £100,000 a year.

TETRABID
Organon
[POM] Slow-release capsules

Tetracycline hydrochloride 250mg
Bacteriostatic antibiotic: for bronchitis and other infections.

This formulation of tetracycline is taken twice rather than 3–4 times a day. The manufacturer also claims a reduced incidence of side effects (eg stomach upsets) because of the slow-release formulation. For a few selected patients, this product could offer advantages, but for most the advantage does not seem worth the extra cost: treatment with TETRABID is 3–4 times more expensive than with conventional formulations of tetracycline.
If tetracycline were prescribed instead of this product, the NHS could save about £½ million a year.

TETRACHEL WITHDRAWN
Berk
[POM] Paediatric syrup (per 5ml)

Tetracycline hydrochloride 125mg

Tetracyclines are not for children. See TETRACYCLINE MIXTURE.

TETRACYCLINE MIXTURE BPC
[POM] Paediatric syrup (per 5ml)

Tetracycline hydrochloride 125mg
Bacteriostatic antibiotic: used to treat a variety of infections.

Tetracyclines are contra-indicated for use in children under 12 (and pregnant women and nursing mothers) because they can retard growth of bones and permanently stain growing teeth an unsightly yellow/brown. Demeclocycline (LEDERMYCIN) may be the worst offender [M28 p.1153]. Many companies make and recommend tetracycline products for children, though Data Sheets warn of the hazard and suggest that physicians should use tetracyclines in children under 8 only if they consider it essential. There were about 100,000 prescriptions for tetracycline mixtures in 1981: it seems very unlikely they were all justifiable.

TETRALYSAL
Farmitalia Carlo Erba
[POM] Capsules

Lymecycline hydrochloride 204mg, equivalent to 150mg of tetracycline base.

Lymecycline is much more soluble than tetracycline, but the manufacturer claims no therapeutic advantage for it [Data Sheet 1983/4]. It costs up to five times more than unbranded versions of tetracycline.

TETREX
Bristol-Myers
[POM] Capsules

Tetracycline hydrochloride 250mg as phosphate complex
Bacteriostatic antibiotic: for bronchitis and other infections.

The manufacturer claims that this formulation improves the absorption of tetracycline. The theory is that calcium ions in the stomach (which may inhibit absorption of tetracycline) combine with the phosphate component in TETREX, leaving more tetracycline to be absorbed. The American Medical Association considers that 'there is no definitive evidence that it is any more effective than other oral forms when administered in comparable doses' [AMADE p.1675]. The AMA does suggest that this formulation reduces stomach upsets – which can trouble about 10% of tetracycline users – but no claim is made for this in the UK Data Sheet (1983/4.)
NHS expenditure on this product is estimated at £100,000 a year. It costs about six times more than conventional formulations of tetracycline.

THEAN
Lagap
Tablets

Proxyphylline 300mg
Bronchodilator: relieves breathing difficulties in asthma, bronchitis etc.

Proxyphylline is considered less suitable for prescribing than slow-release preparations of (the related drugs) theophylline and aminophylline [BNF No.6, 1983, p.104]. See BRONCHODILATORS.

THEOSOL
Martindale
Suppositories

Theophylline 300mg
Bronchodilator: relieves breathing difficulties in asthma, bronchitis etc.

Rectal absorption of theophylline (and related drugs) tends to be erratic, and suppositories may irritate as well. Most reported cases of theophylline and aminophylline toxicity in children have been associated with the use of aminophylline suppositories [FR 41 176 9/9/76 p.38373]. Oral preparations are generally preferred [AMADE p.591].

THIAVER
Riker
[POM] Tablets

Alkavervir 4mg
Antihypertensive: a derivative of veratrum (green hellebore) used to control high blood pressure.
Epithiazide 4mg
Diuretic: augments the antihypertensive effect of alkavervir.

Alkavervir has toxic effects at doses close to the therapeutic dose. Adverse effects include nausea, vomiting, dizziness, sweating, abnormal heart rhythms and shallow breathing (respiratory depression). It is 'no longer recommended for routine use' [M28 136] and 'should no longer be used' [BNF No.6, 1983, p.85]. The fixed-ratio combination is undesirable.

TIGLYSSIN
Duncan Flockhart
[POM] Tablets

Tigloidine hydrobromide 250mg
Anticholinergic: used in the treatment of muscle spasm in spasticity.

Has been superseded by more effective drugs (eg diazepam, baclofen, dantrolene) which are also cheaper.

TIMODINE
Reckitt & Colman
[POM] Cream

Hydrocortisone 0.5%
Corticosteroid to reduce inflammation.
Nystatin 100,000 units/gram
Anti-infective agent.
Dimethicone '350' 10%
Water repellant.
Benzalkonium chloride solution 0.2%
Disinfectant.

Only likely to be of value where an area of eczema or dermatitis is infected. See CORTICOSTEROID + ANTI-INFECTIVE SKIN PREPARATIONS. NHS expenditure on this product is over £1 million a year.

TINSET
Janssen
[POM] Tablets

Oxatomide 30mg
Antihistamine: used to treat symptoms of allergy, eg in hay fever or urticaria (nettle rash).

Oxatomide produces fewer side effects than conventional antihistamines such as chlorpheniramine, but it costs about eight times more [DTB, 1983, 21, 36]. People who find conventional antihistamines unacceptable (eg too sedating), would be likely to benefit more from a non-sedating antihistamine (astemizole or terfenadine) than from this drug. See ANTIHISTAMINES.

TITRALAC
Riker
Antacid tablets

Calcium carbonate 420mg
Antacid: neutralises excess stomach acid.
Glycine 180mg
Intended to enhance antacid effect.

There is no convincing evidence of the value of glycine [FR 47 2 5/1/82 p.458]. See also CALCIUM CARBONATE.

TIXYLIX
May & Baker
Linctus (per 5ml)

Pholcodine 1.5mg *as citrate*
Cough suppressant.
Promethazine hydrochloride 1.5mg
Antihistamine.
Phenylpropanolamine hydrochloride 5mg
Decongestant.

Undesirable combination: pholcodine alone is effective in suppressing cough.
NHS expenditure on this product is over £100,000 a year.

TOFRANIL
Geigy
[POM] Tablets and syrup

Tablets
Imipramine hydrochloride 10mg, 25mg

Syrup *(per 5ml)*
Imipramine hydrochloride 25mg

An effective tricyclic antidepressant drug, strongly promoted by brand name.
If the identical medicine were prescribed by generic name (imipramine), the NHS could save around £½ million each year.

TOLERZIDE
Bristol-Myers
[POM] Tablets

Sotalol hydrochloride 80mg
Beta-blocker.
Hydrochlorothiazide 12.5mg
Diuretic.

Used to control high blood pressure. See BETA-BLOCKER + DIURETIC PREPARATIONS.

TONIVITAN
Medo
Multivitamin capsules

Broadly similar to ABIDEC. See VITAMINS.

TONIVITAN B
Medo
Vitamin B complex tonic syrup

Likely to have the therapeutic impact of a bowl of cornflakes. Broadly similar to METATONE.

TONIVITAN A & D
Medo
Syrup (per 5ml)

Ferric ammonium citrate 150mg (22mg **iron**)
Calcium glycerophosphate 25mg
Manganese glycerophosphate 400 micrograms
Vitamin A 700 units
Vitamin D_2 (Ergocalciferol) 70 units
Copper sulphate 400 micrograms

Ferrous salts are preferred to ferric salts, which are less well absorbed. Glycerophosphates have been advocated in the past as brain foods, appetite stimulants etc, but are of no value. VITAMINS (see entry) add to cost rather than benefit. See IRON SUPPLEMENTS.

TOPAL
Concept
Antacid mixture

See similar product GAVISCON.

TOTOLIN
Galen
Syrup (per 20ml)

Phenylpropanolamine hydrochloride 30mg
Decongestant.
Guaiphenesin 120mg
Expectorant.

Undesirable combination. Guaiphenesin is of doubtful value. See EXPECTORANTS AND MUCOLYTICS. Nasal decongestant sprays tend to be more effective than oral preparations for short-term use.

TRANCOPAL
Winthrop
[POM] Tablets

Chlormezanone 200mg

Chlormezanone is a minor tranquilliser similar to MEPROBAMATE (see entry). It is less well established than diazepam, nitrazepam and other BENZODIAZEPINE TRANQUILLISERS (see entry) and may be less effective – and it costs much more. Since 1983, TRANCOPAL has been promoted for insomnia, but it costs about five times more than nitrazepam [DTB 1983, 21, 32]. See also LOBAK; TRANCOPRIN.
NHS expenditure on this product is over £100,000 a year.

TRANCOPRIN
Sterling Research
[POM] Tablets

Aspirin 300mg
Chlormezanone 100mg

Undesirable combination, including a less suitable ingredient. See also LOBAK.

TRANSVASIN
Reckitt & Colman
Counter-irritant cream

Benzocaine 2%
Ethyl nicotinate 2%
Hexyl nicotinate 2%
Tetrahydrofurfuryl salicylate 14%
Intended to relieve pain in muscles, joints etc when rubbed into skin.

A 5–20% concentration of benzocaine is required for effective local anaesthetic action. Methyl Salicylate Ointment BP or Methyl Salicylate Liniment BP are effective and cheaper alternatives.
If these were prescribed instead of this product, the NHS could save an estimated £100,000 a year.

TRANXENE
Boehringer Ingelheim
[POM] Capsules

Clorazepate dipotassium 7.5mg; 15mg

Clorazepate has actions and uses similar to diazepam and other BENZODIAZEPINE TRANQUILLISERS (see entry). In the body, clorazepate is converted to desmethyldiazepam, the main metabolite of diazepam: therefore the similarities between these drugs are much more striking than any differences – though clorazepate may be less sedating. The real value of this potential advantage is probably small, since clorazepate is usually taken as a sedative in a single dosage at night. See table (pp.50–3).
Clorazepate (TRANXENE) is about ten times more expensive than diazepam, and it seems doubtful if its advantages are often worth this extra cost. If diazepam were prescribed instead of TRANXENE, the NHS would save an estimated £2½ million each year.

TRASICOR
Ciba
[POM] Tablets

Oxprenolol hydrochloride 20mg, 40mg, 80mg, 160mg
Beta-blocker: controls over-stimulation of the heart and regularises the heartbeat. Used mainly to treat high blood pressure, angina and heart disorders.

This is an effective and widely prescribed drug, strongly promoted by brand name. There may be exceptions but, as a general rule, oxprenolol offers no real advantage over the close equiva-

lent, propranolol: for most purposes 'propranolol remains the drug of choice since it is cheap and its long-term risks are clearly understood' [DTB 1980, 18, 64].
If propranolol were prescribed instead of this product, the NHS could save about £3½ million a year.

TRASIDREX
Ciba
[POM] Tablets

Oxprenolol hydrochloride 160mg *for sustained release*
Beta-blocker.
Cyclopenthiazide 250 micrograms
Diuretic.

Used to control high blood pressure. See notes on slow-release mechanism of SLOW-TRASICOR. This combination has no clear advantage over other combinations of BETA-BLOCKER + DIURETIC (see entry) but is much more expensive.
If propranolol (80mg × 2) and bendrofluazide (2.5mg) were prescribed instead of this product, the NHS would save about £3½ million a year.

TRI-ADCORTYL
Squibb
[POM] Cream and ointment

Triamcinolone acetonide 0.1%
Corticosteroid to reduce inflammation.
Gramicidin 0.025%
Neomycin 0.25%
Nystatin 100,000 units/gram
Anti-infective agents.

Only likely to be of value where an area of eczema or dermatitis is infected. See CORTICOSTEROID + ANTI-INFECTIVE SKIN PREPARATIONS. NHS expenditure on this product is about £¾ million a year.

TRI-ADCORTYL OTIC
Squibb
[POM] Ear ointment

Triamcinolone acetonide 0.1%
Corticosteroid.
Neomycin 0.25% *as sulphate*
Gramicidin 0.025%
Antibacterial antibiotics.
Nystatin 3.33%
Antifungal antibiotic.

Less suitable for prescribing. See OTOSPORIN.

TRIDIONE
Abbott
[POM] Capsules

Troxidone 300mg
Anti-epileptic.

Less safe and effective than alternative treatments, and reported to be rarely used [BNF No.6, 1983, p.169]. Should be used under strict medical supervision, and only when less toxic drugs have been found ineffective.

TRIMOVATE
Glaxo
[POM] Cream

Clobetasone butyrate 0.05%
Corticosteroid to reduce inflammation.
Oxytetracycline 3% *as calcium salt.*
Nystatin 100,000 units/gram
Anti-infective agents.

[POM] Ointment
Clobetasone butyrate 0.05%
Chlortetracycline hydrochloride 3%
Nystatin 100,000 units/gram.

Only likely to be of value where an area of eczema or dermatitis is infected. See CORTICOSTEROID + ANTI-INFECTIVE SKIN PREPARATIONS. NHS expenditure on this product is over £½ million a year.

TRIOCOS
Dorsey
Syrup (per 5ml)

Pholcodine 5mg
Cough suppressant.
Chlorpheniramine maleate 2mg
Antihistamine.
Pseudoephedrine hydrochloride 20mg
Decongestant.
Glycerol 600mg
Demulcent: soothing liquid.
Menthol 80 micrograms

Undesirable combination. See ACTIFED COMPOUND LINCTUS.

TRIOGESIC
Dorsey
Tablets; elixir (per 20ml)

Phenylpropanolamine hydrochloride 12.5mg (elixir 12mg)
Paracetamol 500mg
Analgesic; antipyretic: reduces temperature.

Undesirable combination. Nasal decongestant sprays tend to be more effective than oral preparations for short-term use.
NHS expenditure on this product is about £¼ million a year.

TRIOMINIC
Dorsey
Tablets; syrup (per 20ml)

Mepyramine maleate 25mg
Pheniramine maleate 25mg
Antihistamines.
Phenylpropanolamine hydrochloride 50mg
Decongestant.

Undesirable combination. It is doubtful whether sympathomimetics (used here to reduce nasal congestion and inflammation) add to the effectiveness of antihistamines in the treatment of allergy. No advantage is gained by combining two antihistamines with similar actions.
NHS expenditure on this product is about £¼ million a year.

TRIOTUSSIC
Dorsey
Mixture (per 5ml)

Noscapine 20mg
Cough suppressant.
Terpin hydrate 90mg
Expectorant.
Mepyramine maleate 6.25mg
Pheniramine maleate 6.25mg
Antihistamines.
Paracetamol 160mg
Analgesic; antipyretic: reduces temperature.
Phenylpropanolamine hydrochloride 12.5mg
Nasal decongestant.

Irrational combination, similar to DIMOTANE WITH CODEINE.

TRIPTAFEN
Allen & Hanburys
[POM] Tablets

Amitriptyline hydrochloride 25mg
Tricyclic antidepressant: mainly used to treat depressive illness.
Perphenazine 2mg
Phenothiazine tranquilliser: used to treat psychotic illness, confusion and agitation.

Most illness involving both depression and anxiety is controlled with an antidepressant drug on its own. Anti-anxiety drugs may occasionally help, and may be useful at the start of treatment, as it can take several weeks for antidepressants to become fully effective. However, these two drugs are rarely indicated for routine use. The fixed-ratio combination is undesirable, because the dose of each component should be individualised for the patient.
NHS expenditure on the three TRIPTAFEN products (see also below) is about £1 million a year.

TRIPTAFEN-FORTE
Allen & Hanburys
[POM] Tablets

WITHDRAWN

Amitriptyline hydrochloride 25mg
Perphenazine 4mg

TRIPTAFEN-M
Allen & Hanburys
[POM] Tablets

Amitriptyline hydrochloride 10mg
Perphenazine 2mg

Undesirable combinations. See TRIPTAFEN.

TROPIUM
DDSA
[POM] Capsules and tablets

Chlordiazepoxide 5mg and 10mg (both formulations), 25mg (tablets)

See LIBRIUM.

TRYPTIZOL
Morson
[POM] Tablets and syrup

Amitriptyline hydrochloride 10mg, 25mg, 50mg (tablets), 10mg/5ml (syrup).

An effective tricyclic antidepressant drug, strongly promoted by brand name.
If the identical medicine were prescribed by generic name, the NHS could save about £½ million a year.

TRYPURE

Novo

[POM] Topical wound-cleansing agent

Of doubtful value. See VARIDASE TOPICAL.

TUINAL

Lilly

[POM] Capsules

Amylobarbitone sodium 50mg
Quinalbarbitone sodium 50mg

The manufacturers say that this product is 'indicated whenever prompt and moderately sustained hypnosis is required' [Data Sheet 1983/4], though the CRM has said barbiturates should be used only for 'severe intractable insomnia' [DTB, 1980, 18, 9]. BARBITURATES (see entry) have been superseded as hypnotics by BENZODIAZEPINE TRANQUILLISERS (see entry) and other safer agents.

TUSSIFANS

Norton

Syrup (per 5ml)

Belladonna liquid extract 0.007ml
Antispasmodic: to control coughing spasms. Anticholinergic: dries bronchial secretions.
Ipecacuanha liquid extract 0.013ml
Squill syrup 0.3ml
Potassium citrate 250mg
Expectorants: intended to help removal of phlegm from airways.
Tolu syrup 0.4ml
Soothing liquid; flavouring.

It is irrational to combine agents which dry up bronchial secretions (belladonna) with other ingredients intended to liquefy and loosen them (ipecacuanha, squill). The safety of both ipecacuanha liquid extract and squill is questionable [FR 41 176 9/9/76 p.38356] and their value doubtful. See EXPECTORANTS AND MUCOLYTICS.

TYROSOLVEN

Warner-Lambert Health Care

Lozenges

Cetylpyridinium chloride 1mg
Antimicrobial.
Tyrothrycin 1mg
Topical antibiotic.
Benzocaine 10mg
Local anaesthetic: intended to relieve sore throat.

The commonest cause of a sore throat is a viral infection – which does not respond to antibiotic treatment. In some states in the USA (eg California) antibiotics have been banned from products of this kind [Rubinstein, 1977, p.18]. Cetylpyridinium lacks evidence of safety and effectiveness [OTC-PDW p.56].

TYROZETS

MSD

Antiseptic throat lozenges

Tyrothricin 1mg
Benzocaine 5mg

See TYROSOLVEN.

ULTRALANUM

Schering

[POM] Ointment

Fluocortolone 0.25%
Fluocortolone hexanoate 0.25%
Corticosteroids to reduce inflammation.
Clemizole hexachlorophane 2.5%
Disinfectant.

Only likely to be of value where an area of eczema or dermatitis is infected. See CORTICOSTEROID + ANTI-INFECTIVE SKIN PREPARATIONS. NHS expenditure on this product is over £100,000 a year.

UNIFLOR

Aplin & Barrett

Tablets

Lactobacillus acidophilus
Harmless bacteria intended to inhibit the growth of disease-causing bacteria, by making the contents of the gut more acid.

There is no good evidence that such preparations are effective [M28 p.786]. A US expert panel has reported: 'In the past 60 years well over 200 papers have been reported on the use of lactobacillus . . . in the treatment of diarrhea. Despite the proliferation of studies the very few controlled studies more often show lack of effectiveness than any antidiarrheal effect' [FR 40 56 21/3/75 p.12931].

UNIFLU PLUS GREGOVITE C

Unigreg

Composite pack of pairs of tablets

Codeine phosphate 10mg
Cough suppressant; analgesic.
Diphenhydramine hydrochloride 15mg
Antihistamine: used to suppress symptoms of allergy, and also to suppress cough.
Phenylephrine hydrochloride 10mg
Nasal decongestant.

UNIGESIC

Paracetamol 500mg
Analgesic/antipyretic: relieves mild to moderate pain; reduces fever/high temperature.
Caffeine 30mg
Mild stimulant.
Ascorbic acid 300mg
Vitamin C.

Undesirable combination. Phenylephrine is seldom effective taken by mouth [AMADE p.556]: nasal decongestant sprays tend to be more effective than oral preparations for short-term use. Codeine alone is an effective and preferable treatment for cough. Diphenhydramine does suppress cough but also has a marked sedative effect, and may interfere with expectoration because of its drying effect on bronchial secretions. It is also likely to impair driving and other skills. There is no evidence of the value of caffeine in counteracting drowsiness caused by ANTIHISTAMINES. The value of VITAMIN C in treating cold symptoms is questionable.

UNIGESIC
Unimed
Tablets

Paracetamol 500mg
Caffeine 30mg

This combination costs about five times more than paracetamol 500mg alone. There is no evidence that caffeine adds to effectiveness [AMADE p.575]; and there is anyway more caffeine in half a cup of tea.

UNIROID
Unigreg
[POM] Treatment for haemorrhoids etc.

Ointment and suppositories

Ointment
Hydrocortisone 0.5%
Reduces inflammation.
Neomycin sulphate 0.5%
Polymyxin B sulphate 6250 units/gram
Antibacterial antibiotics.
Cinchocaine hydrochloride 0.5%
Local anaesthetic.

Suppositories
Hydrocortisone 5mg
Neomycin sulphate 10mg
Polymyxin B sulphate 12500 units
Cinchocaine hydrochloride 5mg

Undesirable preparations. See similar product PROCTOSEDYL.

UNISOMNIA
Unigreg
[POM] Tablets

Nitrazepam 5mg

See MOGADON; BENZODIAZEPINE TRANQUILLISERS.

UROMIDE
Consolidated
[POM] Tablets

Sulphaurea 500mg
Sulphonamide antibacterial: used here to treat urinary tract infections.
Phenazopyridine hydrochloride 50mg
Intended to reduce urinary tract pain.

The combination is undesirable, because treatment with phenazopyridine should be stopped when pain is controlled, though anti-infective treatment may need to be prolonged. The effectiveness of phenazopyridine as a pain-killer is questionable [PDW 1981 p.57], and the recommended dosage is low. (The recommended dosage of phenazopyridine with this product is a usual 300mg/day to a maximum of 500mg/day. The suggested dosage with some other preparations is 600mg/day.)
The Data Sheet (1983/4) for this product omits warnings: eg this product should not be taken by people with serious kidney or liver problems. In the UK, this product is recommended for use by infants: in the US, comparable products are recommended only for adults [PDR, 1983, p.1720].

VALIUM
Roche
[POM] Various formulations

Diazepam 2mg (syrup per 5ml; tablets, capsules)
Diazepam 5mg (tablets, capsules, suppositories)
Diazepam 10mg (tablets, suppositories)
Benzodiazepine tranquilliser: for treatment of anxiety or insomnia.

An effective drug, though widely misused. See BENZODIAZEPINE TRANQUILLISERS. This product has been strongly promoted by brand name. If the identical medicine were prescribed under its generic name (diazepam), the NHS could save about £3 million a year. Other brands of diazepam include ALUPRAM (Steinhard); ATENSINE (Berk); EVACALM (Unimed); SOLIS (Galen); TENSIUM (DDSA); and VALRELEASE (Roche).

VALLEDRINE WITHDRAWN
May & Baker
[POM] Linctus (per 5ml)

Pholcodine 4mg *as citrate*
Cough suppressant.
Ephedrine hydrochloride 7.5mg
Bronchial, nasal decongestant.
Trimeprazine tartrate 2.5mg
Phenothiazine tranquilliser.

Undesirable combination. See VALLEX.

VALLEX WITHDRAWN
May & Baker
[POM] Linctus (per 5ml)

Ipecacuanha liquid extract 0.015ml
Guaiphenesin 25mg
Citric acid 65mg
Sodium citrate 200mg
Expectorants: intended help removal of phlegm from airways.
Trimeprazine tartrate 2.5mg
Phenothiazine tranquilliser: sedative.
Phenylpropanolamine hydrochloride 10mg
Nasal decongestant.
Menthol 1.2mg
Aromatic oil.

Trimeprazine has antihistaminic actions, and tends to dry bronchial secretions: it is irrational to combine it with expectorants (intended to liquefy and loosen secretions). The safety of ipecacuanha liquid extract is questionable [FR 41 176 9/9/76 p.38358] and its value doubtful. See EXPECTORANTS AND MUCOLYTICS. A sedative, if needed, should be separately prescribed. Nasal decongestant sprays tend to be more effective than oral preparations. The UK Joint Formulary Committee considers that 'there is no scientific basis' for prescribing such mixtures, and says their use is 'to be deprecated' [BNF No.6, 1983, p.120].

VALRELEASE
Roche
[POM] Slow-release capsules

Diazepam 10mg
Benzodiazepine tranquilliser.

Conventional formulations of diazepam are rapidly absorbed and quickly take effect. The point of this slow-release formulation is to give a less abrupt onset of action and to prolong the drug's effect. In practice, there may be no real gain: if the user takes 10–15mg of conventional diazepam at night, the rapid sedation helps sleep, and the anxiolytic (anxiety-reducing) effect of diazepam persists throughout the next day. See BENZODIAZEPINE TRANQUILLISERS.
This product costs many times more than conventional formulations of diazepam, and 'there is no evidence to indicate it has a place in therapeutics' [DTB, 1982, 20, 68].

VARIDASE
Lederle
[POM] Tablets

Streptokinase 10,000 units
Streptodornase 2,500 units
Enzymes used as wound-cleansing agent, intended to dissolve and help remove dead tissue and other wound debris.

Oral streptokinase-streptodornase is considered of doubtful value by the UK Joint Formulary Committee, though the powder prepared for topical use (VARIDASE TOPICAL) may be more effective [BNF No.6 1983 p.363].

VEGANIN
Warner-Lambeth Health Care
Tablets

Aspirin 250mg
Paracetamol 250mg
Codeine phosphate 6.8mg

The dose of codeine is probably less than effective (see ASPIRIN, PARACETAMOL AND CODEINE). This product is about five times as expensive as paracetamol 500mg, but there is no reason to think it would be much more effective.

VERACOLATE
Warner
Tablets

Cascara extract 65mg
Phenolphthalein 32mg
Bile salts 70mg
Laxatives.
Capsicum oleoresin 3mg
Gut irritant: may produce a sensation of heat.

A US expert panel has found that 'there is no medical or scientific rationale' for combination laxative products which include capsicum [FR 40 56 21/3/75 p.12915]. The laxative action of both cascara and PHENOLPHTHALEIN (see entry) is unpredictable: neither is a laxative of choice. Evidence for the safety and effectiveness of bile salts as laxatives is weak [FR 40 56 21/3/75 p.12918].

VERDIVITON
Squibb
Alcohol-based (17 per cent) liquid tonic

Recommended as vitamin B supplement for adults and children. See VIRVINA.

VERILOID
Riker
[POM] Tablets

Alkavervir 2mg
Anti-hypertensive: a derivative of veratrum (green hellebore) used to control high blood pressure.

Alkavervir has toxic effects at doses close to the therapeutic dose. Adverse effects include nausea, vomiting, dizziness, sweating, abnormal heart rhythms, and shallow breathing (respiratory depression). It is 'no longer recommended for routine use' [M28 p.136] and 'should no longer be used' [BNF No.6, 1983, p.85].

VIBRAMYCIN
Pfizer
[POM] Paediatric syrup (per 5ml)

Doxycycline hydrochloride 50mg

Tetracyclines are not for children under 12. See TETRACYCLINE MIXTURE.

VIBROCIL
Zyma
[POM] Nasal drops; gel; spray

Neomycin sulphate 0.35%
Antibacterial antibiotic: for treatment of nasal infections.
Phenylephrine hydrochloride 0.25%
Sympathomimetic: reduces nasal congestion and inflammation.
Dimethindene maleate 0.025%
Antihistamine: to control symptoms of allergy, eg in hay fever.

Antibiotics have no place in the treatment of allergy or the common cold (for which this product is recommended). ANTIHISTAMINES are of no value in the treatment of common cold symptoms, and are ineffective when locally applied. See BIOMYDRIN.

VI-DAYLIN
Abbott
Multivitamin syrup

Broadly similar to ABIDEC. See VITAMINS.

VIGRANON B
Wallace Mfg
Syrup (per 5ml)

B vitamins: thiamine hydrochloride 5mg; **riboflavine** 2mg; **nicotinamide** 20mg; **pyridoxine hydrochloride** 2mg; **panthenol** 3mg

Essentially the same as Compound Vitamin B Tablets Strong – but much more expensive.

VILLESCON
Boehringer Ingelheim
[POM] Tablets; liquid (per 20ml)

Both formulations
Prolintane hydrochloride 10mg
Sympathomimetic: claimed to stimulate appetite and to produce 'an increased feeling of well-being in debilitated patients'.

Tablets
B vitamins: thiamine hydrochloride 5mg; **riboflavine** 3mg; **nicotinamide** 15mg; **pyridoxine hydrochloride** 1.5mg
Vitamin C: ascorbic acid 50mg

Liquid *(per 20ml)*
B vitamins: thiamine hydrochloride 6.68mg; **riboflavine sodium phosphate** 5.44mg; **nicotinamide** 20mg; **pyridoxine hydrochloride** 2mg

Prolintane is of doubtful value (BNF No.6, 1983, p.149).
NHS expenditure on this product is about £¼ million a year.

VIOFORM-HYDROCORTISONE
Ciba
[POM] Cream and ointment

Hydrocortisone 1%
Corticosteroid to reduce inflammation.
Clioquinol 3%
Anti-infective agent.

Only likely to be of value where an area of eczema or dermatitis is infected. See CORTICOSTEROID + ANTI-INFECTIVE SKIN PREPARATIONS.
NHS expenditure on this product is over £100,000 a year.

VIRVINA WITHDRAWN
MSD
Elixir (per 5ml)

Alcohol 0.85ml
B vitamins: thiamine hydrochloride 0.676mg;

riboflavine 0.338mg; **nicotinamide** 5mg; **pyridoxine hydrochloride** 0.017mg; **Glycerophosphates of calcium** (21.5mg); **manganese** (2.5mg); **potassium** (4mg); **sodium** (43.5mg)

The official Data Sheet [1983/4] recommends this product for the prevention or treatment of vitamin deficiency, and suggests use by children aged 6 or over. It contains 17% alcohol and has about the same quantity of B vitamins as a large helping of a fortified cereal. Glycerophosphates (see METATONE) are useless. Similar product LABITON.

VISCLAIR

Sinclair
Tablets

Methylcysteine hydrochloride 100mg
Mucolytic: reduces viscosity of phlegm and intended to help expectoration.

There is no convincing evidence of the value of such products [DTB, 1975, 13, 12]. See EXPECTORANTS AND MUCOLYTICS.

VISKALDIX

Sandoz
[POM]Tablets

Pindolol 10mg
Beta-blocker.
Clopamide 5mg
Diuretic.

Used to control high blood pressure. See BETA-BLOCKER + DIURETIC PREPARATIONS. This combination of ingredients has no clear advantage over other beta-blocker + diuretic preparations, but is much more expensive.
If propranolol and bendrofluazide were prescribed instead of this product, the NHS would save an estimated £¾ million a year.

VITA-E

Bioglan
Vitamin E tablets and capsules

See EPHYNAL.

VITAMINS

Vitamins are essential accessories to the main ingredients of the diet: protein, carbohydrate and fat. Mild deficiency states contribute to poor health, but are very difficult to diagnose, and therefore easily imagined or overlooked. Prolonged and drastic vitamin deficiency causes serious ill-health, but in Britain this is very rare. Most vitamins are not made by the body and are taken in as food. A good mixed diet provides enough of all the vitamins, plenty for good health. Too much vitamin A or D is harmful (these vitamins are fat-soluble and accumulate in the body) and too much of the others is useless, at best. Excess of the water-soluble vitamins (including B & C) is excreted unused.
The vitamin preparations listed in this report are generally not intended for therapeutic use – ie would not be used to treat clear deficiency states, or to prevent them when patients are clearly at risk. Most of the products listed here are dietary supplements, intended for routine use. These may be used to correct poor nutrition or digestion, or to meet extra demand (eg in pregnancy, during lactation, or after some serious illnesses), but are mostly used as placebos, both as dietary insurance, and for general peace of mind. 'Vitamins have taken the place of prayer' [Thomas L., 1980, p.38].
The preparations listed are all rated in the *British National Formulary* as 'less suitable for prescribing'. They include products with unnecessary and ineffective ingredients; products with inappropriate dosages; and unnecessarily elaborate and expensive preparations. Many products contain ingredients of no proven value, such as biotin, choline, pantothenic acid, methionine, lecithin, bioflavonoids, and inositol. (Biotin, for example, is made in the body, by bacteria in the gut; deficiency can be produced only by eating large quantities of raw egg white, which contains an inactivating protein, avidin.) Other products contain either negligible or excessive amounts of particular vitamins: for example, several contain much more than 5mg of thiamine (vitamin B_1), the maximum individual dose the body can absorb – but other 'supplements' contain well under 1mg.
Some preparations – and notably iron supplements – include vitamins as a little (or not so little) extra on the side. The American Medical Association, among others, says the use of such combinations should be strongly discouraged: 'Avoidance of mixtures not only is better therapy, but may be an absolute necessity when the preferred routes of administration for two therapeutic agents are different. . . . Mixtures are an added expense when a completely adequate and less expensive regimen is available' [AMADE pp.807–8]. For example, iron + vitamin B_{12} combinations are irrational, because iron should be taken by mouth – but vitamin B_{12} is useless unless injected. Iron in combination with large

amounts of vitamin C is also undesirable, because it increases the likelihood of gastro-intestinal side effects.
Extravagant claims have and always will be made for vitamins. And in the meantime, UNICEF estimates that 100,000 children a year go blind, just for want of vitamin A.

VITAVEL
Bencard
Multivitamin syrup

Broadly similar to ABIDEC. See VITAMINS.

VOLITAL
LAB
[POM] Tablets

Pemoline 20mg

The effectiveness of pemoline in counteracting lethargy and fatigue is doubtful; its actions have been studied but its effectiveness not demonstrated [AMADE p.291]. The Data Sheet [1983/4] recommends this product for (among other things) 'fatigue arising post-operatively'. But US prescribing information for pemoline states that 'significant clinical benefit may not be evident until the third or fourth week of drug administration' [PDR 1982, p.510]. Any benefit might therefore be too little and come too late.

WALLACHOL
Wallace Mfg
Tablets; liquid with B vitamins

Similar to LIPOFLAVONOID (capsules); LIPOTRIAD (elixir).

WAXSOL
Norgine
Ear drops to soften ear wax, before removal

Dioctyl sodium sulphosuccinate (docusate sodium) 5%

This product is not needed. There are many simple, effective and cheaper alternatives, eg sodium bicarbonate ear drops, baby oil, arachis oil, almond oil etc.

XANAX
Upjohn
[POM] Tablets

Alprazolam 250 micrograms, 500 micrograms
For anxiety, and anxiety associated with depression.

See BENZODIAZEPINE TRANQUILLISERS.

Alprazolam may prove useful in treating anxiety associated with depression, but cannot yet be recommended for this 'because its dependence liability has yet to be assessed'. For treating anxiety alone, 'alprazolam is unremarkable': its effects are similar to those of diazepam, though it costs about 25 times more [DTB, 1983, 21, 64].

XERUMENEX
Napp
Ear drops

Triethanolamine polypeptide oleate condensate 10%
Organic solvent for the removal of ear wax.
Chlorbutol 5%
Antibacterial and antifungal; preservative.
Propylene glycol
Solvent.

This solvent has not been shown to be more effective than other preparations, and 'must be used with extreme care since it may cause severe contact dermatitis in some patients' [AMADE p.547]. Agents which soften ear wax (eg glycerol, sodium bicarbonate ear drops, warm baby oil) are cheap, effective and relatively safe.

XYLOCAINE
Astra
Local anaesthetic ointment

Lignocaine 5%

These ointments are not usually very effective in relieving painful or itchy conditions, and occasionally cause sensitivity reactions. This preparation is recommended for the treatment of ano-rectal pain and itching, but there is inadequate evidence of the effectiveness of lignocaine for such conditions [FR 45 103 27/5/80 p.35619]. See also ANETHAINE.

ZACTIPAR WITHDRAWN
Wyeth
[POM] Tablets

Ethoheptazine citrate 75mg
Narcotic analgesic.
Paracetamol 400mg
Analgesic; antipyretic: lowers temperature.
For mild to moderate pain.

Ethoheptazine has been rated as 'lacking substantial evidence of effectiveness' by the US Food and Drug Administration. There is no convincing evidence that this combination is more effective than an appropriate dosage of paracetamol alone [PDW p.192].

ZACTIRIN
Wyeth
[POM] Tablets

Ethoheptazine citrate 75mg
Aspirin 325mg

Lacks evidence of effectiveness. See ZACTIPAR.

ZYLORIC
Calmic
[POM] Tablets

Allopurinol 100mg, 300mg
Enzyme inhibitor, reduces the formation of uric acid; widely used for prevention of gout.

An effective drug, strongly promoted by brand name.
If the identical medicine were prescribed by its generic name (allopurinol), the NHS could save an estimated minimum of £3 million a year.